Frontispiece. Map of principal Black homesteader communities in the Great
Plains, with location of several unaffiliated homesteaders. Map by Katie Nieland.

The First Migrants

How Black Homesteaders' Quest for Land and
Freedom Heralded America's Great Migration

RICHARD EDWARDS *and* JACOB K. FRIEFELD

Preface by ANGELA BATES

University of Nebraska Press   Lincoln

The University of Nebraska Press is part of a land-grant institution with campuses and programs on the past, present, and future homelands of the Pawnee, Ponca, Otoe-Missouria, Omaha, Dakota, Lakota, Kaw, Cheyenne, and Arapaho Peoples, as well as those of the relocated Ho-Chunk, Sac and Fox, and Iowa Peoples.

Royalties from this book go to support the Nicodemus Historical Society and the Great Plains Black History Museum (Omaha). No endorsement of the book's content by those organizations is implied.

Library of Congress Cataloging-in-Publication Data
Names: Edwards, Richard, 1944–, author. | Friefeld, Jacob K., author. | University of Nebraska. The Homesteading Project, issuing body.
Title: The first migrants: how black homesteaders' quest for land and freedom heralded America's Great Migration / Richard Edwards and Jacob K Friefeld.
Other titles: How black homesteaders' quest for land and freedom heralded America's Great Migration
Description: Lincoln: University of Nebraska Press, 2023. | "The Homesteading Project, University of Nebraska."—Title page. | Includes bibliographical references and index.
Identifiers: LCCN 2022043594
ISBN 9781496236494 (pdf)
ISBN 9781496230843 (hardcover)
ISBN 9781496236487 (epub)
Subjects: LCSH: African American farmers—Great Plains—History. | African Americans—Migrations. | Agricultural colonies—Great Plains—History. | African Americans—Land tenure—Great Plains—History. | African American pioneers—Great Plains—History. | Frontier and pioneer life—Great Plains. | Great Plains—History. | BISAC: HISTORY / African American & Black | SOCIAL SCIENCE / Ethnic Studies / American / African American & Black Studies
Classification: LCC E185.925.E283 2023 | DDC 978/.020896073—dc23/eng/20221109
LC record available at https://lccn.loc.gov/2022043594

Contents

Illustrations

Preface

ANGELA BATES

Over 160 years ago, the U.S. government emancipated enslaved African Americans but made little attempt to make land available to them. That changed during Reconstruction, when homestead land became available to all who dared venture west. African Americans, who found it hard to adjust to life as free men or women in the Jim Crow South, found they could join scores of others homesteading in the West by paying only a small filing fee. All over the state of Kansas, immigrant towns rose from the prairie, as speculators and developers created them with a pencil sketch. They then promoted their creations through their own newspapers.

Nicodemus, Kansas, was one such town developed to attract newly emancipated African Americans. Developers working with a white speculator and railroad agent named W. R. Hill, targeted African Americans in central Kentucky to settle their new creation. After five black men, four of whom were ministers, joined this town company partnership, the group traveled back to Kentucky to promote Nicodemus to area church congregations. Soon afterward, settlers left for Kansas in three large groups, joined by a few smaller clusters and other individuals who trickled in. At that time Nicodemus was one of many all-Black towns that dotted the West. Now it is the oldest and only remaining all-Black town established during Reconstruction west of the Mississippi.

I am a descendant of those first settlers and the great-granddaughter of the first woman to give birth to the first baby born at Nicodemus, in October 1877. I grew up in Pasadena, California, but traveled every year with family to Nicodemus's annual Emancipation Celebration. This annual trek "back home," as we always called it, fostered in me a desire to keep the oral histories and stories of Nicodemus alive, if only in my mind. I began documenting, recording through letters and a diary my own experiences of our annual treks back home. I recognized the value of the stories and history I was collecting. While living in Denver in the late 1980s I established the Nicodemus Historical Society, with the mission to officially collect, preserve, and interpret our history at Nicodemus. My parents, both from Nicodemus, had retired and bought my mother's childhood dream farm. I visited them often and saw the importance of saving these family stories. I moved to Nicodemus in 1989 and never left. I have worked tirelessly collecting, preserving, and interpreting Nicodemus settlers' epic histories. Since securing the National Historic Site designation for Nicodemus, I have worked with various institutions and individual scholars who continue to uncover its history and tell its story.

When I met Rick Edwards, at the time the director of the Center for Great Plains Studies at the University of Nebraska, I was asked to work on a team to identify and document African American homesteads in the West. I gladly accepted and pulled out one of my earliest research projects, begun after I arrived in Nicodemus in the late eighties. It was a large map of the Nicodemus Township within Graham County that identified all the original settlers on their homestead sections. It was precisely the kind of research the center wanted to create and save.

When we completed the project I was pleased to know there was a concerted effort to record the previously undocumented settling of the Great Plains and the West by African Americans. Their stories have been absent in the annals of western history. Their history is rich and diverse, and it speaks of the tenacity, strength, and determination of people whose lives were altered by the institution of slavery. These people had a vision that was emboldened by their determination and fortitude to make it a reality. Their lives are written in the soils of the Great Plains and the West. The winds that sweep its prairies no longer silence their voices. Their stories speak of shattered dreams and the effects of Jim Crow, including their vanquished hope to secure the railroad through Nicodemus. They fought in organized towns such as Nicodemus, or in groups of settlements, or as individuals holding onto their claims as though it were their last hope of survival in a harsh and unfriendly land among people determined to keep them in their place. They experienced real freedom, land ownership, and self-determination, if only for a short while for many. Those who stuck it out and have descendants to tell their stories or leave evidence of their existence attest to their role in settling the West and furthering the nation's goal of achieving Manifest Destiny. To this end I praise the work of Rick Edwards and his colleagues who recorded these stories. They add African American settlers' voices to those already recorded, who shared the struggles and accomplishments of pioneering the West. Homesteaders were the brave who dared to plow resistant virgin sod. Their efforts broke deep roots to give fertile soil new life, producing rich crops for a new people experiencing freedom in this great land called America.

This work tells these unique stories. As a descendant of Nicodemus's first settlers, I am honored to be a part of this still unfolding story. Ad Astra Per Aspera: To the stars through difficulties.

Acknowledgments

We began this book at the Center for Great Plains Studies with support received from the Homestead National Historic Park. The book is based on five years of our own original research, but our work would not have been possible without the scholars and authors who came before us. They are listed in the notes at the back of this volume, but some individuals' contributions are so foundational to our project that they deserve special commendation and thanks: Angela Bates, Robert Brunswig, Todd Guenther, Kenneth Hamilton, Charlotte Hinger, Deanda Johnson, George Junne Jr., Timothy Nelson, and Nell Irvin Painter.

We want to thank all the descendants of Black homesteaders who generously assisted us. They agreed to be interviewed, shared memories and photographs, and in other ways helped make this book possible. We especially thank Ashley Adams, Catherine Meehan Blount, Wayne Brown, Elizabeth Burden, Delbert DeWitty, Terri Gentry, Joyceann Gray, Cecil Leo McGruder, Jeanettee Parton, and Denise Scales.

Many other individuals read the manuscript, provided archival help, and assisted us with images. We are grateful for their help. We particularly thank Peter Longo, Ann Weisgarber, Katie Nieland, Adam Edwards Mayhew, John Holland, and Jay Crowley.

We appreciate the liberal assistance we received during difficult pandemic times from staff members at a number of museums and archives, especially Mary-Jo Miller at History Nebraska; Kate Johnson at University of Northern Colorado Special Collections; Teri Barnett at the Abraham Lincoln Presidential Library and Museum; John LeMay at the Historical Society of Southeast New Mexico; Elizabeth Villa at New Mexico State University Archives; Judy Rada at the Saline County Historical Society, Nathaniel C. Ball at the Benjamin L. Hooks Institute at the University of Memphis; Deborah Dandridge at Spencer Library of the University of Kansas; Miranda Todd at the Greeley History Museum; and staffs at the Kansas Historical Society, the Nicodemus Historical Society, the South Dakota State Historical Society, the Great Plains Black History Museum, the Perkins Library at Hastings College, the National Historic Trails Interpretive Center, and the Schomburg Center of the New York Public Library.

We owe thanks for institutional and personal support to Mark Engler, former superintendent, Homestead National Historical Park, National Park Service; Eric Ewing, Great Plains Black History Museum; Margaret Jacobs, Center for Great Plains Studies, University of Nebraska; and Bridget Barry, University of Nebraska Press. We also are deeply grateful to our colleague and friend Mikal Brotnov Eckstrom, who contributed so much to our book.

We remain solely responsible for the content of this book.

Note on Terminology

We use the terms "Black" and "African American" interchangeably to refer to Americans of African descent. Black homesteaders and other contemporaries referred to their communities as "colonies," and we use the terms "colonies" and "communities" interchangeably. We include as "homesteaders" all individuals who filed claims under the Homestead Act of 1862 or its various amending or companion statutes based on the homestead principle.

Royalties from this book go to support the Nicodemus Historical Society and the Great Plains Black History Museum (Omaha). No endorsement of the book's content by those organizations is implied.

The First Migrants

1

Land!

Well, we never owned a home of our own, so when we talked
of moving into our own house it was a happy thought.

—ELVIRA WILLIAMS, Nicodemus homesteader

In September 1877, 308 Black people left the verdant hills around Lexington, Kentucky, on a perilous journey they hoped would bring them to their Promised Land. They were led by Rev. Simon Roundtree, a formerly enslaved man, and a white developer named W. R. Hill. The following spring another large group left Kentucky, led by the freedman Rev. Daniel Hickman. Their Canaan was called Kansas.

The first group gathered at the station near nightfall, men, women, and children carrying their household goods and leading a few cows and horses. They crowded together, jostling each other as they boarded the train. Agents for competing railroads badgered them to buy tickets to travel on their lines. The Cincinnati Southern, a new line running north which had only started carrying passengers the previous summer, offered a fare of $9.50 for travel all the way to Ellis, Kansas. The Short-Line, with tracks running west to Louisville, cut its price to $7.75, crushing its competitors. Meanwhile, the travelers, growing tired and with crying babies, sat waiting for hours. Finally, around midnight, the special Short-Line train started moving, departing Lexington for Louisville. Other migrants joined the train when it stopped at Midway, Kentucky. Twenty people at Sadieville, north of Lexington, started their own journey to Ellis by boarding a northbound Cincinnati Southern train.

The travelers shivered and tried to sleep, crowded into the noisy, unheated cars. At Louisville they climbed down, unloaded their goods, and changed to the Louisville and Indianapolis line. On they went, changing trains several more times, unloading and loading their goods and livestock until finally they reached Ellis. At the Ellis stop, they descended for the last time. Exhausted as they were, they still had miles to go.

The Lexington folks, like Black people across the South, had celebrated the new world that opened to them after 1865. Their hopes soared with the Great Emancipation and the promises of Reconstruction. It was a time of jubilee! But by the mid-1870s, those promises had turned to ash, producing anguish and horror. Black people wanted land—needed land—and after generations working the tobacco, rice, corn, and cotton fields, they surely deserved land. But southern whites denied it to them. They subjected Black people to unremitting violence, intimidation, swindle, and murder. Blacks began to seek relief elsewhere.

Some Black people migrated west. They were looking for freedom, opportunity, and land. W. R. Hill, the white town developer who accompanied Reverend Roundtree to Kentucky to recruit settlers, assured the settlers that Blacks lived as equals to whites in western Kansas. And word was out that the federal government would give them free land under the Homestead Act. The migrants came, trusting that officials would at least keep *that* promise.

Newspapers took little notice of their leaving—in truth, Black people rarely appeared in Kentucky papers, except for church announcements and arrests. The *Louisville Courier-Journal* did run a story when the first group left called "Bound for Kansas." It reported, "The Kansas emigration fever has been raging among the colored people around Lexington for some time." If the migrants prospered, the paper declared, hundreds of their friends in northern Kentucky would be eager to join them. The departure of Reverend Hickman's

1. Rev. Daniel Hickman, leader of a second group of Kentucky migrants to Nicodemus. From *Promised Land on the Solomon: Black Settlement at Nicodemus, Kansas*, fig. 3–3. U.S. Department of the Interior, National Park Service, 1986.

group the next spring confirmed its prediction. The *Courier-Journal* worried, though, that the migrants were poor and lacked money to build houses for the oncoming winter. The *Kentucky Advocate*, out of Danville, was more hopeful, saying of the migrant party, "[It] is made up of those who work at home, and we have not the least doubt they will succeed in Kansas or anywhere else they may go."[1]

The Kentuckians descended at Ellis, the depot nearest their destination. They had trouble finding shelter, this sudden influx of Black people overwhelming the tiny white town. And there was a further problem. Hill had assured them when they bought their train tickets that the cost of freighting their goods and livestock had been included. Now, in Ellis, the railroad agent informed the migrants this was not true, and the freight office would not release their belongings until they paid the bill in full. The confusion created a nasty standoff between the migrants and the agent, but eventually they paid, further draining their diminishing savings. It also provided the first clue that Hill was not as trustworthy as he had first appeared.

The most discouraging news, however, was that Ellis, where they left the train, was thirty-seven miles from their destination, their Promised Land at Nicodemus. They were already exhausted from the difficult train trip and discouraged by the dispute over the freight bill. Now, they learned, to reach their new home they had to trek two days across the prairie. A few had brought wagons; most had not. Those with money sought to hire the few drays available in Ellis. Even so, the wagons were filled to overflowing with their possessions, and most families had to walk.

They set off across the prairie. There were no roads, so they followed deer trails and buffalo wallows. They guided themselves by compass and the few terrain features they could spot in the seemingly endless grassland. They mounted the large limestone bluffs north of Ellis and descended into the Saline River Valley and forded the river. Their eyes ached from searching for signs of human habitation, but they could find none. There was no settlement anywhere in sight, from Ellis to Nicodemus; not even a cowboy came in view, although between the Saline and Solomon Rivers the migrants could spot herds of cattle grazing in the distance. The prairie's vastness overwhelmed them, making them feel insignificant and helpless. There were no trees, and it was hard to keep their bearings. The unfamiliar surroundings disoriented and alarmed them. Never far away was the gnawing dread that they were lost.

As they moved deeper and deeper into this remote, forbidding country, their rising anxiety and fear became constant companions. They suffered from fatigue and the worries of travel and from the utter strangeness of the place, so unlike the lush bluegrass and towering forests they knew in Kentucky. Some began to regret their rash decision to leave behind everything they knew—everything familiar—and risk their lives in such an alien place.

At least the travelers were buoyed by the thought of what awaited them. As the Townsite Company's promotional poster boasted, Nicodemus was "The Largest Colored Colony in America." Back in Kentucky, Hill had told them that the South Solomon Valley was a sparsely settled region teeming with game and wild horses. The horses could easily be caught and tamed to do the farm work. The valley had limestone to build their homes and abundant firewood for cooking and heating, and they might even discover coal. The valley offered excellent water in the river and in its numerous springs. W. H. Smith, a Black man who was president of the company, had happily lived in the Solomon Valley for the last three years.

So Nicodemus would be a fine sight when it finally came into view. The handbills promised that the colony would already have erected houses and opened many branches of mercantile business. It would have constructed a church edifice and other public buildings. It would even have its own post office. Oh, the relief they would feel when finally they arrived at this marvelous place!

The migrants had been stirred by such visions to give the new country a try, despite their fears of wild animals, hostile Indians, and unknown and possibly dangerous whites. And sweetest to the ears of these former slaves was Hill's promise that, because of the Homestead Act, they would own their own farms. They knew they would have to work hard, but that was no obstacle. They had worked hard all their lives, and now at last they would be tilling their own fields and living in their own homes, reaping the rewards of their own labors. Nor were they expecting fancy houses like the ones lining Lexington's finer streets. Elvira Williams, who traveled in the second group with her husband, Thorton, and their small children, was thrilled with the possibilities: "Well, we never owned a home of our own, so when we talked of moving into our own house it was a happy thought."[2]

They were also bucked up by the warm welcome they knew must await them once they reached Nicodemus. The company had already escorted its first thirty clients to their new homes the previous July. So Nicodemus was up and running, its residents surely preparing a joyous welcome, perhaps even a celebratory feast. What a comfort that would be at the end of a long, tiring, stressful trip.

Finally they drew near their destination. But there was as yet no "town" of Nicodemus; so far it was only a townsite and a dream. No real houses, no buildings, no church. They saw rolling hills covered by endless grasses that stretched to the horizon. Everything was low; there was nothing that reached toward the sky at all. They were especially distressed to find no trees under which they could shelter and be comforted. The promised "abundant timber" to warm their houses was a lie. They were shocked to see how bare the prairie was. They had arrived too late to plant crops that year. Sixty migrants found the prospects so discouraging that they simply refused to stay, and the next day they turned around and started the long trip back to Lexington.[3]

More than two hundred migrants stayed and began to dig in for the coming winter—literally digging holes in the ground to create the dugouts they would live in. They had little food, and for fuel they used sunflowers, willows, and dried buffalo droppings. Many had exhausted their savings just to transport themselves and their goods from Kentucky, but even those who still had money had no place to spend it. There were no branches of mercantile business, no stores closer than Ellis at which to replenish their supplies. It was September, and already in the evenings Nicodemus's first residents could feel the chill of the oncoming hard winter.

Two hundred miles to the northeast of Nicodemus, Henry Burden had just proved up on his homestead in Saline County, Nebraska. Burden was born into slavery about 1842 near Petersburg, Virginia. In 1864 or 1865, his owner took him, perhaps along with other young, enslaved men, to help build fortifications for General Lee's army, which the Union troops encircling Richmond pressed hard.

One evening, Burden escaped to the federal lines. He soon enlisted in the U.S. Army, signing up with a recruiter for Racine, Wisconsin. After the war, Burden moved north, first to Wisconsin and then, in 1868, to Nebraska. He worked for two years at an upscale hotel in Lincoln and saved what money he could.

But Henry Burden's ambitions soared far beyond hotel work. He wanted his own land—to build his future on land he *owned*. So in 1870 he set out by himself for Saline County, about sixty miles southwest of Lincoln, where he could find unclaimed prairie available for homesteading. He filed on an eighty-acre tract just south of the little village of Pleasant Hill. He was the only Black person for miles and miles around.

Moses Speese, like Henry Burden, wanted to own the fields he worked. Speese found himself emancipated but smothered under an ever-growing debt owed to his North Carolina landlord. The landlord told him what to plant and when to plant it, set the prices of the goods he was required to buy at the landlord's store, and kept the books and counted up the interest he claimed Speese owed. Despite his hard work, Speese kept falling further and further behind. His debt tied him to the landlord's fields nearly as tightly as when he had been enslaved. In 1871 or 1872, this "free" man decided to escape.

With the help of a friendly neighbor, Speese hid under a load of hay, and the neighbor took him to a railroad depot beyond the county line. Speese caught a northbound train and rode it to New Castle, Indiana. For the next two years, he took any job available, saving his money. When he had enough, he arranged with the neighbor to hide his wife and two children, again under a load of hay, and they too escaped. Gathering themselves in New Castle, they soon moved on to their real destination: Nebraska. They had heard about the government giving farms to settlers. They filed a homestead claim near Westerville, Nebraska, beginning the process to own their own land.

This book recounts the largely unknown story of Black people like Thorton and Elvira Williams, Henry Burden, Moses Speese, and others who moved from the South to the Great Plains to homestead. The map shows the expansive swathe of the country to which they headed.

They migrated between 1877 and 1920 to own land and, they hoped, to find freedom. They constituted the opening wave of the massive movement of Black people out of the South known as the Great Migration. Compared to the huge numbers of migrants who later moved into northern cities, the homesteaders going west were few. Yet they were the first signs, like the early light before the coming dawn, of that later movement of people seeking freedom.

They fled conditions in the South that similarly oppressed the later migrants, and their goal—to find a place of security and freedom where they could rise by their own toil—was the same as those in the Great Migration. So too their courage in leaving behind all that was familiar to journey to a new place with its unknown risks and dangers, to live among people whom they did not know, foreshadowed the bravery and resolution of those later migrants. They constituted the vanguard of the Great Migration, as if sent out in advance of the main body to explore the unknown terrain that lay ahead. Homesteading in the west did not prove to be the answer for those in the Great Migration, but as we will see, the homesteaders did demonstrate one extremely valuable lesson: Black southerners could leave the region and, using their talents, ingenuity, pluck, and fortitude, make successful lives for themselves elsewhere.

Some of the migrants stopped first in Illinois or Wisconsin, or even Canada, before they arrived in the Great Plains. Once in the region, they established and prospered in many communities, which they called "colonies" (we will use the terms *community* and *colony* interchangeably). Nicodemus was the most famous, but there were others, and we focus on the most important of them—Nicodemus;

2. The Great Plains, extending from Mexico to Edmonton and Kansas City to Denver. By permission of the Center for Great Plains Studies.

DeWitty, Nebraska; Dearfield, Colorado; Empire, Wyoming; Sully County, South Dakota; and Blackdom, New Mexico. (There were still more, including Bliss, Nebraska; The Dry, Colorado; Hodgeman and Logan Counties, Kansas; Las Cruces, New Mexico; and dozens of others.) We also follow the experiences of individuals like Henry Burden and Moses Speese who homesteaded by themselves, unaffiliated with any larger Black community.

These colonies have conventionally been misidentified as *towns*, but they were in fact rural neighborhoods of concentrated Black homesteading. Only Nicodemus developed a larger town center, and then only for a short time; the other colonies did not. When a historian asked Roosevelt Boyer Sr., son of Blackdom, New Mexico, founder Frank Boyer, if it was the founder's dream to have a Black town, he replied, "He said if they had a negro colony they be better off."[4] Most people in the homesteader communities lived on their farms, and the lifeblood of these communities, the essence which determined their success or failure, coursed through the countryside.

Homesteaders came to "town"—typically a tiny crossroads with just two or three buildings—only to attend church or school, get their mail, and perhaps buy a few items at the general store. And they came to enjoy the big communal celebrations on the Fourth of July and Emancipation Day, come to see their neighbors and kinfolk. But the reason they had disrupted their lives and undertaken the risky and dangerous journey to a new and alien place, the reason they endured hardship, danger, disappointment, and struggle, was not to live in town but to achieve their ultimate goal: *to own land.*

Their troubles were many. Like white homesteaders, they struggled to create successful farms in the harsh climate of the region. They suffered from unpredictable crop prices that were manipulated by the giant milling companies and from exorbitant freight costs that were fixed in far-off corporate offices. They had to build supportive communities from scratch to provide themselves with the cultural and civic benefits of longer-settled societies.

But Black homesteaders also differed from their white neighbors because of their traumatic experience in the South and the enduring racism in some Great Plains communities. In surrounding towns, hotels and restaurants refused them entry, and banks and insurance companies limited or denied them mortgages. Having been prohibited even minimal literacy when enslaved, Black homesteaders brought a very different understanding of the link between education and freedom. And as we will see, they came to think of the "success" of their communities in their own unusual and revealing way.

Despite these obstacles, Black homesteaders succeeded. They were few in comparison with the multitudes of white settlers, but they created homes, farms, self-governing communities, and places all their own. Most, about 70 percent of them, homesteaded as part of organized colonies. The remaining 30 percent filed claims independent of a larger Black community. But wherever they settled, they set about using the skills and deep knowledge of farming they had developed as a largely agricultural people in the South, both during slavery and afterward.

They found in the Great Plains an opportunity to start over, to claim land they could own themselves and on which they could build new futures. Andrew Wall, the distinguished historian who led New Mexico State University's Black Studies program for over two decades, said the West served as an escape valve, drawing Black people from the horrors of the South. "It was a haven, it was the Promised Land . . . It was like the legacy of the children of Israel, leaving an oppressed bondage and going to find freedom to establish their own property in their own land."[5]

Land was at the center of their hopes. Wherever they moved from, African Americans arrived in the Great Plains seeking land. Owning land in their eyes affirmed that they were now free and fully equal citizens. Blackdom descendant Rodney Bowe said his ancestors came to Blackdom to homestead so they could own their own land and have a legacy to pass on to their children. "And also to get away from the Jim Crow South. This was an opportunity to really experience freedom." Freedman James Suggs, when leaving Mississippi to homestead in Kansas, said simply: "When the car of freedom comes along, I'm getting on board."[6]

Knowing the story of Black homesteaders changes our understanding of our past, and their history disrupts and enriches the conventional story of who settled the Great Plains. It also adds a new opening act to the enormous drama of the Great Migration, that great leap of faith starting in 1915 that brought millions of Black people to the North. The homesteaders' achievements add a new and largely unrecognized dimension to African Americans' long struggle for full equality.

Black people came to the Great Plains to claim land, and for them, owning land was intrinsically linked to freedom. Their experience in the South taught them that, in Nell Irvin Painter's phrase, "farming one's own land on one's own account meant being one's own master." The postwar defeat of southern land reform and the tethers of sharecropping and debt peonage meant that many Black people found themselves dominated by white landowners and unable to leave the South. And so they found the prospect of homesteading alluring; as Blackdom resident Roosevelt Boyer Sr. observed, "Negroes talked that kind of thing back South, in Georgia, where [my father] was from."[7]

The Black migrants consciously identified their journey out of the South with the Jews' exodus from Egypt, a connection that gave them strength and hope. The Jews too had been held in bondage stretching back to generations unknown, and their exodus brought them into a bewildering and menacing new land in which they created new farms, new cities, and new lives. Black migrants framed their journey as likewise fulfilling the Covenant, providing them the freedom and prosperity they were promised. They believed they were migrating to their Promised Land.

Names like Moses and Abraham sprinkle their family trees. They referred to their intended new home as their "promised land" or Canaan. One large group of migrants was called and called themselves "Exodusters," that is, people of the Exodus, although other Black migrants including the Lexington folks carefully distinguished themselves from the destitute and mostly illiterate Exodusters. An early recruiting poster for Nicodemus appealed for migrants by saying, "We invite our colored friends of the Nation to come and join with us in this beautiful Promise[d] Land."[8]

Organizers of the first and most famous colony named it Nicodemus. Other colonists gave their communities similarly evocative and audacious names—Dearfield, Blackdom, Empire, Bliss, even Audacious. As one white reporter who visited Nicodemus in 1881 wrote, "White folks would have called their place by one of the romantic names which stud the map of the United States, Smithville, Centreville, Jonesborough; but these colored people wanted something high-sounding and biblical, and so hit on Nicodemus." Nicodemus evoked something of the jubilation of people coming out of bondage who proposed to do great things in a new country.[9]

Black homesteaders believed they were about high purpose. Understandably, most of them turned first to the urgent tasks of feeding and sheltering their own families. But they and especially their leaders saw their enterprise in a larger sweep, contributing to something bigger than their own self-betterment. They were exploring and living new opportunities that could show the way for Black people still trapped in the South.

White opinion agreed that the experiment of Black people settling on public lands had much broader implications. The *Chicago Tri-*

THE NEGRO EXODUS.

A Visit to the Nicodemus Colony, in Graham County, Kansas.

How They Have Managed to Get Along in Their Effort to Secure Homes.

They Had Very Hard Times for Awhile, but Are Now in a Self-Supporting Condition.

What Must Be Done with the Lower-Mississippi Negroes Now Crowding into Kansas.

3. Headline in *Chicago Tribune*, April 25, 1879. Newspapers.com.

bune, in 1879, under the headline "The Negro Exodus," discussed Nicodemus. "The country has not got through with the negro question yet," it said. It noted that emancipation, the federal Freedman's Bureau set up to assist Black people, and the Fifteenth Amendment, which guaranteed them the right to vote, were not enough. Reconstruction had failed. "The negroes have been bulldozed [terrorized by nightriders] and abused, deprived of civil and political rights, cheated, whipped, and shot," the *Tribune* reported. "And now they are coming North en masse, under such conditions and circumstances as to impose upon the Christianity and philanthropy of the country the duty of PROMPT AND LIBERAL ACTION IN THEIR BEHALF."[10]

The *Atchison Daily Champion* in 1881 picked up on the theme of finding a new future for Black people. It argued that if Nicodemus succeeded, Black people everywhere would benefit; but if it failed, "it would darken the whole future of the colored race in this country." For the *Champion*, the logic was simple: "If the late slave could make of himself a successful colonist and occupant of the public lands, he might defy the Bourbon politician and the bulldozer of the South, and when life there became unprofitable or unbearable, could depart thence with the assurance of doing well elsewhere, and leave his besotted persecutor to literally 'hoe his own row.'"[11]

And it wasn't just Nicodemus. In 1903, when organizers announced the founding of Blackdom, a new African American homesteader colony in New Mexico, papers across the country carried the story. In 1907, when Black homesteaders in Nebraska founded the DeWitty colony, the *Omaha Daily Bee* reported the event in a long page-one article under the headline, "Colony of Colored People— Success is Predicted." The *Bee* quoted Burlington Railroad land agent D. Clem Deaver, who consulted with the migrants: "My judgment is this colony of colored people in Nebraska is the pioneer step of a movement which will work a tremendous transformation in the social status of the colored race. It will be watched, I believe, with more than ordinary interest all over the country."[12] The nation was watching Nicodemus, Blackdom, DeWitty, and the other communities to see whether Black people could make the public domain their new promised land.

To succeed in this new land, Black migrants had much to learn, and learn quickly. Most southern field workers had previously tended cotton, but cotton wouldn't grow in the Great Plains' arid environment. They didn't try to grow cotton, but old habits were hard to lose. Lillian Westfield Collins, who grew up in Blackdom, remembered, "They depended on rainfall for their moisture and they aren't used to having to irrigate . . . That was the thing they just couldn't seem to understand, that they wouldn't get enough moisture to raise their crops." In some years they were successful with corn, beans, squash and a sorghum they called "Kaffir corn."[13] But wresting livelihoods from the unfamiliar conditions of prairie farming meant abandoning many farming techniques they had used in their prior, more humid locations and learning new ones.

Black migrants found farming on the plains required new techniques that were costly in both labor and money. First they had to break the tough prairie sod to prepare fields. Until the big steam-driven tractors appeared in the 1900s, breaking was a task as likely to break backs as sod. Then, typically, they planted a first crop of Kaffir corn, which grew tolerably well in the overturned sod. Only later could they diversify to include corn, potatoes, wheat, flax, and other crops.

They had to rely on hard labor, trial and error, and quick learning, because they suffered dire consequences when they made wrong decisions. Crutcher Eubank arrived at his Blackdom homestead during winter, and he immediately started planting sorghum in the sandy loam. But the "Kaffir" variety of sorghum needs to be sown when the ground is warm. Eubank harvested very little during that first year, and it took him years to dig out of the financial hole his costly mistake had put him in.

The semiarid conditions of the Great Plains required planting crops that needed to be farmed on a more extensive scale, in turn requiring bigger machinery, as well as more fencing and more draft animals to power the plows, planters, discs, hay balers, and harvesters. Oscar Micheaux, homesteading in South Dakota, regularly hitched as many as eight or ten horses to work his fields. Many homesteaders were poor, so accumulating the funds to purchase such machinery and draft animals took years, even when, as typically happened, farmers shared them.

The first few years usually proved to be the most challenging. Homesteaders were still preparing fields, digging wells, and erecting fences, and typically they didn't harvest much that could be sold for cash money. Sometimes migrants arrived too late in the year and missed the growing season, as did the Lexington arrivals at Nicodemus, putting their very survival in jeopardy. They faced disaster when drought dried up their laboriously planted fields, as in the 1890s in Nicodemus, from 1907 to 1910 in Blackdom, and with distressing frequency elsewhere. They could lose everything when clouds of grasshoppers descended to eat up their crops. Robert Anderson, a Black Nebraska homesteader, spent years working his first claim. Then the locusts came and drove him to simply abandon it and walk away.

Most Black homesteaders sought to earn their livelihoods as farmers, but by necessity they, like their white counterparts, supplemented their often-meager farm earnings by working at nearby ranches or in town jobs. DeWitty residents often found employment on the neighboring Hanna, Lee, and Faulhaber ranches. Some Dearfield, Colorado, homesteaders worked in Greeley, and a number of Blackdom residents kept their jobs in Roswell even as they attempted to homestead. A few homesteaders became entrepreneurs, land agents, and even lawmakers. But for most, their goal remained owning land and building successful farms.

The Black movement to own land through homesteading differed from a parallel effort to establish all-Black towns. Benjamin "Pap" Singleton and other activists urged the establishment of Black towns, creating communities like Langston and Boley, Oklahoma. These distinct movements were separated by geography: Black homesteaders mostly filed their claims in the upper Great Plains, whereas the all-Black town builders focused their efforts farther south, in Missouri, Arkansas, and especially Texas. Only in Oklahoma did homesteaders and town builders overlap. The homesteading movement was broader in scope than Black town building and lasted over a longer period. Most importantly, their motivations were entirely different: homesteaders sought land to farm and saw land ownership as the key to freedom, whereas town builders envisioned building up Black businesses, commerce, and political power as the path to full citizenship. As noted, none of the homesteading settlements, except Nicodemus during the 1880s, can accurately be described as a "town." They were instead rural neighborhoods of concentrated Black homesteading.

Despite the many perils and setbacks, Black homesteaders persisted and prospered. The *Kentucky Advocate* was right that these industrious, hard-working people with grit would succeed in Kansas and elsewhere. They recovered from the shock of dislocation and the anxieties of prairie farming, and they reaffirmed their hopes that *land* would lead to their becoming fully free and equal citizens.[14]

Black homesteaders showed the way out of the South in advance of the Great Migration. From the end of Reconstruction in 1877 to when southern migrants started going north in large numbers in 1915—that is, for nearly forty years—they were first. They took the momentous step of moving away from what was known and seeking a new life in an alien and forbidding place. They experienced the enduring loss of all that was familiar and dear, the kin ties and Black neighbors and shared customs they clung to, even as they felt relief at leaving behind the perpetual Jim Crow humiliations and violence that haunted them. They demonstrated they could make new lives in strange surroundings amid people they did not know.

The first Nicodemus settlers from Topeka and Kentucky were followed in the months and years after by hundreds more from Kentucky, Tennessee, and Mississippi. Thousands more arrived in the Great Plains from all points in the South and from temporary stopping-points elsewhere, and they settled throughout the Great Plains states, forming colonies and taking up farms.

Today, a few historic buildings remain at Nicodemus, two buildings at Dearfield, and a foundation at DeWitty, but only roadside markers remain at the Blackdom, Empire, and Sully County colonies.

Nothing marks the fields where Henry Burden or Moses Speese, unaffiliated with any colony, homesteaded. To understand the Black homesteaders' lives and accomplishments, we must perform an act of imagination, a conscious recreation in our minds of the world they made. When we do so, we see that the homesteaders risked their lives for big stakes. And what they achieved was equally big.

2

Push and Pull

Tell my people to go west. There is no justice for them here.
—Last words of THOMAS MOSS before he was lynched,
Memphis, March 9, 1892

Most Black homesteaders were pushed from the South by their bitter experiences, and they were pulled to the Great Plains by the opportunity to own land. Some Southern migrants moved directly to the Great Plains, like the Kentuckians coming to Nicodemus and the Exodusters who fled Louisiana, Mississippi, and east Texas for Kansas. Others made intermediate stops. Moses Speese escaped North Carolina and stopped in Indiana before moving on to Nebraska. Norvel Blair was born into slavery in Tennessee. After emancipation he resided for some years in Illinois, then he moved his large family to Sully County, South Dakota. William P. Walker, descendant of slaves, traveled from the Black community of North Buxton, Ontario, to join the early homesteaders at DeWitty, Nebraska.

Regardless of their departure points, all Black migrants shared—either as personal experience or close family memory—the torment of slavery and postwar Southern violence. This personal and collective ordeal necessarily shaped their ambitions, anxieties, and dreams. Norvel Blair, Moses Speese, Henry Burden, and others whom we will meet later started life enslaved. Younger homesteaders, including Charles Speese, Betty Blair, and William P. Walker, had parents who had been enslaved and uncles, aunts, grandparents, and neighbors who had endured slavery and post-Reconstruction violence and terrorism. The memories of those horrible times endured.

In 1908 the white journalist and muckraker Ray Stannard Baker published a pioneering study of American race relations called *Following the Color Line*. He asked Black people, "What is your chief cause of complaint?" He found that "in the South the first answer nearly always referred to the Jim Crow cars or the Jim Crow railroad stations; after that, the complaint was of political disfranchisement, the difficulty of getting justice in the courts, the lack of good school facilities, and in some localities, of the danger of actual physical violence."[1] The homesteaders' agenda, as we will see, grew directly out of these grievances. They wanted to create places of their own where they could escape the evils and humiliations of discrimination, of the denial of their right to vote, of courts deaf to their appeals, of poor schools run by uncaring or malevolent whites, and of the ever-present danger of being assaulted or killed. The key to creating a place free from these evils, they believed, was owning land.

One of the bitterest memories of the postwar years was the destruction of freedpeople's hopes to own land in the South. Congress created the Freedman's Bureau—officially the Bureau of Refugees, Freedmen, and Abandoned Lands—to assist Black people construct their lives as free people. Newly emancipated, they believed they would own the fields they and their ancestors had worked for so long. There was much talk of "forty acres and a mule" and other land redistribution plans. General William Sherman, in his Special Field Orders No. 15, issued in Savannah on January 16, 1865, promised that "each family [of freedpeople] shall have a plot of not more than forty acres of tillable ground."

Freedman's Bureau officials focused on the roughly one million acres of plantation lands confiscated from former Confederate officers. Freedpeople lived on these lands. But in 1866 President Andrew Johnson pardoned the Confederates for their treason and ordered the Freedmen's Bureau to return the officers' plantations. His order left the bureau with little land on which to settle Black people. Although here and there Black individuals or small groups of Black people managed to gain ownership of small parcels, whites retained ownership of the overwhelming majority of southern acreage, especially the most fertile lands.

Congress in 1866 passed the Southern Homestead Act to open to homesteaders 46 million acres of public land in Florida, Alabama, Louisiana, Mississippi, and Arkansas, states in which the federal government owned land. Homesteading in these states had already been legal under the 1862 act, but the Southern Homestead Act added especially favorable terms that applied only in the named states, including a reduced filing fee and limiting claims to eighty acres so that the available land would accommodate more families. As Kansas senator Samuel Pomeroy, chairman of the Senate Public Lands Committee, declared when introducing the measure, "It need not be disguised that [the bill] is aimed particularly for the benefit of the colored man, those who have not been able hitherto to acquire homesteads on the public domain in these States."[2]

The Southern Homestead Act, however, failed to deliver land to the masses of southern Black people. It failed because the freedpeople were so poor that they could not move to the regions open to homesteading and invest the resources needed to establish viable farms. It failed because little good land was available to homestead, the South's best land still being owned by the white planters. The public land left for homesteading was harder to farm—many had poor soils and were forested, raising the cost of starting a farm and extending the time before homesteaders could harvest a crop.

But mostly the Southern Homestead Act failed because southern whites were determined to prevent widespread Black landholding. Black people who tried to homestead in the South were regularly harassed, turned away, swindled, threatened, deprived of critical information, and killed by hostile whites. Local officials and even some Army officers charged with implementing the Freedmen's Bureau's programs conspired to get Black laborers back on to white-owned fields. Historian Nell Irvin Painter points out that "Southern white determination that Blacks must not own farmland at any cost matched the freedpeople's desire to own it."[3] And we might add that southern whites' willingness to use violence completely overwhelmed Blacks' ability to defend themselves.

Even before federal troops were withdrawn from the region in 1877, white supremacist groups like the night riders, the White League, and the Ku Klux Klan terrorized individual Black farming families and brutalized or killed freedpeople. Whites unleashed a wave of unremitting and inescapable violence throughout the South. The violence was entirely one-sided. In Mississippi, where white violence against Blacks was pervasive, a reporter fifty years later could uncover no cases where freedmen responded with violence against whites to avenge wrongs they suffered under slavery.[4]

One example of white violence, from which there are unfortunately thousands to choose, occurred in 1871 in Meridian, Mississippi, a rapidly growing railroad town. An appointed white Republican mayor, William Sturgis, governed with the assistance of a council of Black leaders. Local race relations were tense. Sturgis called a meeting of Black residents to discuss the situation. During the meeting, Sturgis discovered that his store had been set on fire, and the meeting broke up. The next day local whites persuaded a lawyer who had not attended the meeting to swear in court that the Black leaders' speeches had been "incendiary"—it's not clear if the irony was intended—and officials brought several Black men to trial the following Sunday.

At trial Warren Tyler, one of the Black men, interrupted James Brantley, a white witness, declaring that he intended to bring three Black witnesses to impeach Brantley's testimony. Brantley then lunged at Tyler to strike him with his walking stick. White men sitting at the back of the courtroom drew their pistols and started firing, filling the air with smoke. When they stopped, they discovered they had mistakenly killed Judge Bramlette and mortally wounded another man.[5] The riot was now on.

White men ran to get their guns; Black men in mortal terror sought to hide. The whites discovered Warren Tyler concealed in a shack and shot him to death. The feverish mob killed an unknown number of Black people, but observers estimated that between twenty-five and thirty people died. Mayor Sturgis fled the city and, after negotiation, agreed to leave Mississippi within twenty-four hours. The violence ended Republican rule in the region.[6]

The "Meridian riot" became a model for southern whites elsewhere, so that any minor conflict could trigger violence. After each resulting riot, Black resistance to white domination in the surrounding area collapsed. John Kemp was president of a Black political club in Louisiana and spent his spare time teaching freedpeople about their constitutional rights. He was killed by night riders, a victim of the massive campaign to murder Black leaders and suppress freedpeople's organized political action.[7]

Only a few Black people were willing to stake out homesteads on the South's public lands in the face of such implacable violence and hostility. Even fewer succeeded in gaining title to their claims. Congress recognized the failure of the Southern Homestead Act, and members were anyway being pressed to open the South's pristine yellow-pine forests to logging by northern lumber companies. Congress repealed the Southern Homestead Act on July 4, 1876. It was a bitter and ironic memorial to the Glorious Fourth's centennial.

Freedpeople had such great hunger for land that despite these obstacles, they nonetheless managed to acquire some land by purchasing it. They scraped together money using their soldier's bonuses, artisans' savings, money pooled through cooperatives, and other sources. They slowly increased their southern holdings to 12 million acres during the last three decades of the nineteenth century. But the average Black farmer found it difficult to buy land in the South. As W. E. B. Du Bois observed in 1907, "The land which has been bought has been bought by the exceptional men or by the men who have had unusual opportunity . . . who have been helped by members of their own families in the North or in the cities." In 1900 7.2 million Black people lived in the South, making up 37 percent of the region's population; their 12 million acres constituted only 2.4 percent of the South's land. The hoped-for forty acres, with an average Black family size of 4.3 persons, would have resulted in 9.3 acres per person. Actual Black holdings amounted to a miniscule 1.7 acres per person.[8]

A U.S. Senate Select Committee documented the violence inflicted on African Americans across the South, although that was not their intention. In 1878 Democrats had regained the upper hand in the chamber, their first majority since southerners walked out of Congress seventeen years earlier at the start of the Civil War. Senators heard from southern planters alarmed at the prospect of losing their field workers as the Exodusters fled to Kansas. Democrats established the committee "to investigate the causes of the removal of the Negroes from the Southern States to the Northern States." Democratic Senator Daniel Voorhees chaired the committee, which heard lengthy testimony from freedpeople, officials, and others. In 1880 it issued its conclusions, known as the "Voorhees Report."

Voorhees and Democratic members of the committee found no discrimination of any kind against Blacks in the South. They arrived at their conclusion despite witnesses' dramatic and convincing evidence to the contrary. They found no unfair treatment in the court systems, in voting, in tenant-landlord relations, or otherwise. "On the whole," they concluded, "the condition of the colored people of the South is not only as good as could have been reasonably expected, but is better."

A minority report, however, written by the two Republican members of the committee, told a different story. They recognized that thousands of Black people fled the South because by the spring of 1879 they could no longer endure its worsening hardships and injustices. Some migrants even feared they would be re-enslaved. They fled, panic-stricken, from their homes. The Republicans said the refugees "sought protection among strangers in a strange land. Homeless, penniless, and in rags, these poor people . . . [threw] themselves upon the charity of Kansas."[9]

The minority pointed to testimony like that of Robert H. Knox, a prominent Black leader in Montgomery. In 1872 Knox addressed a convention of African Americans, saying he had initially counseled Black people to stay in the South. His advice had been, "Let us trust in God, the President, and Congress to give us what is most needed here, personal security to the laboring masses, the suppression of violence, disorder, and kukluxism." But Knox became convinced that Black people in the South would never be safe, secure, and free. So, reluctantly, he changed his advice, telling his fellow Black citizens to leave the South and seek security and freedom elsewhere, "where there may be enjoyed in peace and happiness by your own fireside the earnings of your daily toil."[10]

The evils of the South and hope for freedom in the West were never more powerfully, or tragically, linked than by Thomas Moss. Moss, along with two other Black men, Calvin McDowell and Will Stewart, ran the cooperative People's Grocery in the Curve, a mixed-race neighborhood of Memphis. The store's increasing success irritated, then enraged a white grocer, William Barrett, whose rival store had largely monopolized grocery sales in the Curve before People's Grocery opened. Barrett threatened and harassed the Black grocers.

4. A delivery cart in front of Peoples Grocery, thought to be in
Memphis. Wikimedia Commons, http://historic-memphis.com
/biographies/peoples-grocery/peoples-grocery.html.

On March 2, 1892, Black and white children playing marbles
on the street got into a dispute, which then escalated into a fight
between Black and white adults. Barrett and Stewart faced off, and
while accounts vary, Barrett may have been slightly injured. He
swore out a warrant against Stewart. Accompanied by a policeman,
he showed up the next day at People's Grocery, intending to have
Stewart arrested. But that day only McDowell was in the store, and
even after a struggle he refused to say where Stewart was. Barrett, infuriated, vowed to return with greater force. The Black men
appealed for police protection, but they were denied on the grounds
that their store was a mile beyond city limits. They armed themselves
for the coming attack.[11]

Barrett persuaded the sheriff to deputize him, and he returned to
People's Grocery with ten other deputies. They broke in through the

back door. The Black men inside, not realizing the intruders were now lawmen, fired shots. Three of the white men were wounded. The sheriff soon came and arrested all three Black men and put them in jail.

Tennessee law prescribed execution for a Black man who killed a white man, but it left the punishment uncertain if the white man was only injured. City residents were tense as they waited to hear whether the most severely wounded deputy would live or die. After three days, the hospital announced he would survive. But before the Black men could be brought to trial for assault, seventy-five white men in masks descended on the jail. They hauled off Moss, McDowell, and Stewart, taking them to a rail yard. There, they shot and killed them. No one was ever charged for the murders.

These killings might not have gained wider notoriety—after all, there had already been at least fourteen lynchings in Memphis between 1868 and 1892—but for the fact that Moss's close friend was a young teacher and journalist named Ida B. Wells. Wells was horrified at her friend's murder. She was editor and part owner of *Free Speech*, a local Black weekly. Wells began publishing scathing editorials protesting southern lynchings. As she wrote, "Thus, with the aid of the city and county authorities and the daily papers, that white grocer had indeed put an end to his rival Negro grocer as well as to his business."[12]

In one editorial Wells scandalized Memphis white society by suggesting some white women would willingly have sex with Black men. Whites labeled any such unthinkable liaisons rape, which then in their minds justified lynching the Black man. Wells wrote, "Nobody in this section of the country believes the old thread bare lie that Negro men rape white women. If Southern white men are not careful, they will overreach themselves and public sentiment will be very damaging to the moral reputation of their women." White supremacists in the city went bonkers.

A mob trashed and burned the office of *Free Speech* and threatened Wells's life. She fled north for safety. The *Memphis Commercial*, voice of the whites' venom and rage, called Wells a "black wench" and "Black harlot" and declared she would soon "gather in a goodly store of shekels" in the North, and "if she doesn't come off with a white husband we shall be surprised." Wells went on to publish pamphlets proving that many alleged Black rapes were in fact consensual interracial relationships. The killing of Moss and the others launched Wells on a lifelong anti-lynching campaign, leading to one of the most brave and illustrious careers in American journalism.[13]

Thomas Moss was married with a young daughter, to whom Wells was godmother. He owned his home. He delivered mail during the day as well as managing the People's Grocery. He was energetic and entrepreneurial, a young man quick to follow up on new opportunities.

Moss may have read G. W. Jones's articles about Kansas in the *Memphis Watchman*, a Black newspaper. Jones was a Black lawyer and traveling correspondent for the paper, and in 1887, five years before the lynchings, he toured Kansas to report back on the state's treatment of Black people and opportunities opening for them. Arriving in Nicodemus, Jones met nearly a hundred Black people who owned their own farms, which they valued at anywhere from one to five thousand dollars each.

Jones praised the business prospects available to Black people in Graham County. One profile would have particularly piqued Moss's interest. Jones told the story of Foster Williams, a Black man who migrated from Memphis. Williams's grocery business in Nicodemus was so profitable that he was now building a second store. In another profile, Jones described how Z. T. Fletcher took Jones to Millbrook, where in a further surprise, a white man hired him to argue his lawsuit. Jones was astonished at the easy and respectful interaction between Blacks and whites and the many opportunities for Black people.[14]

But Thomas Moss was not given the chance to explore these opportunities for himself. The enraged mob murdered McDowell and Stewart and then turned to Moss. Before he was shot and killed, Moss uttered these last words: "Tell my people to go west. There is no justice for them here."[15]

Black migrants like Reverend Hickman, Henry Burden, and Norvel Blair were also pulled to the Great Plains by the government's offer of free land. They came to homestead.

The U.S. government had accumulated immense western lands, especially after President Thomas Jefferson bought the Louisiana Purchase in 1803 and Congress annexed Mexican lands in 1848. In the years prior to 1860, the land-rich but tax-revenue-poor federal government sold land to finance its operations, and it paid war veterans' bounties for their service in the form of warrants redeemable in land.

The system became increasingly infected with corruption and favoritism, as land agents, speculators, political insiders, investment companies, and land aggregators learned to manipulate government land sales for their own benefit. Many returning veterans did not want to leave their homes in Ohio or Virginia and relocate onto raw land in the west, so they sold their warrants to speculators at deep discount. William Scully, the Brown-Ives-Goddard group, Ira Davenport, and other big investors bought up the warrants and used them to amass tens of thousands of acres. Public anger at the speculators' greed boiled over.

How the government should dispose of its vast public domain sparked sectional conflict and class tensions. Southern states eyed the West for expansion of its slave system. They achieved a major victory in 1854 when Congress passed the Kansas-Nebraska Act. This law transferred to the voters of each new state carved from western territories the power to decide whether it would enter the Union as a slave or a free state. Proslavery and abolitionist settlers poured into Kansas ahead of the vote, raiding each other's settlements and murdering families in what came to be known as "Bleeding Kansas." And poor whites, hungry for land, began entering the vast Nebraska Territory to squat or "pre-empt" land. Squatting was illegal, but the squatters could not be held back, so Congress responded to its reality by periodically passing new laws, each more accommodating to the squatters' rights.

Advocates believed that homesteading was the solution to this chaos and to the threat of slavery's expansion. They proposed that the government grant land to "actual settlers," not sell it directly or indirectly to rich investors. They hoped to create a yeomanry of small landowners on the public domain, land going neither to slave owners nor to rich speculators. Many groups had favored passage of a homestead law, including northern Whigs, the Liberty Party, Free Soilers, northern Democrats disaffected by southern Democrats' growing insistence that they support slavery, a few lonely southern pro-homesteaders like Andrew Johnson, and "western" interests generally.

During the 1840s and 1850s, however, homesteading advocates saw their proposals all go down to defeat. Southern congressmen and senators, with few dissenters, vehemently opposed the "free land" idea, believing it would strengthen the North and end their dreams of expanding slavery. In early 1860, homesteading advocates finally succeeded in getting both houses of Congress to approve a homestead bill, but President James Buchanan, a Pennsylvanian who sympathized with the South, vetoed it.[16]

The Republican Party emerged in the late 1850s, attracting followers mainly on the basis of its opposition to extending slavery into the territories. The principal alternative plan for western lands was homesteading. The new party gathered in the diverse homestead advocates, and in 1860 it promised in plank thirteen of its party platform to enact a homestead law. Republicans swept the 1860 congressional elections in the North, and Abraham Lincoln was elected president.

Republicans had also pledged in their platform not to interfere with each state's right to control its own "domestic institutions" (that is, slavery), and Lincoln promised to adhere to this policy. But slave-state leaders didn't believe the party's pledges and denounced Lincoln's election as an attack on the South. Eleven southern states seceded. When southern congressmen and senators, the most unyielding foes of homesteading, withdrew from Congress in 1861, they left the Republicans an open field. Homestead advocates wasted little time.

Congress passed the Homestead Act—"An Act to secure Homesteads to actual Settlers on the Public Domain"—and on May 20, 1862, President Lincoln signed it into law. It said that any person who was the head of a family, was twenty-one years old, and was either a U.S. citizen or had declared his or her intention to become a citizen, could claim 160 acres of public land. The "entryman" or claimant had to pay fourteen dollars in filing fees, build a dwelling, cultivate at least ten acres, and reside on the land for five years. The residency requirement was intended to ensure that only "actual settlers," and not speculators, would get the land. When the entryman had completed the five years, he or she could "prove up," documenting to the General Land Office (GLO) in Washington that all the law's requirements had been met. The GLO then sent out a patent, the government's name for the land title, to the claimant, as it did to Reverend Hickman. This completed the transfer of land from the public domain to the homesteader.[17] The homesteader now owned his or her "free" land.

The land on offer to homesteaders had not been empty. The government spent several decades wresting it from Native Americans

The United States of America,

TO ALL TO WHOM THESE PRESENTS SHALL COME, GREETING:

Homestead Certificate No. 8816
Application 15623

Whereas there has been deposited in the GENERAL LAND OFFICE of the United States a CERTIFICATE of the Register of the Land Office at *Kirwin. Kansas.* whereby it appears that, pursuant to the Act of Congress approved 20th May, 1862, "To secure Homesteads to actual settlers on the public domain," and the acts supplemental thereto, the claim of *Daniel Hickman* has been established and duly consummated in conformity to law for the *north west quarter of section six in township eight south, of range twenty two west of the Sixth Principal Meridian in Kansas, containing one hundred and fifty six acres and seventy seven hundredths of an acre*

according to the Official Plat of the Survey of the said Land returned to the GENERAL LAND OFFICE by the SURVEYOR GENERAL.

Now know ye, That there is therefore granted by the UNITED STATES unto the said *Daniel Hickman* the tract of Land above described: TO HAVE AND TO HOLD the said tract of Land, with the appurtenances thereof, unto the said *Daniel Hickman* and to his heirs and assigns forever.

In testimony whereof I, *Grover Cleveland* President of the United States of America, have caused these letters to be made Patent, and the Seal of the General Land Office to be hereunto affixed.

Given under my hand, at the City of Washington, the *fourteenth* day of *June*, in the year of Our Lord one thousand eight hundred and *eighty seven*, and of the Independence of the United States the one hundred and *eleventh*.

[L.S.]

By the President: *Grover Cleveland*

By *M. McKean* Sec'y

Robt W. Ross Recorder of the General Land Office

5. Rev. Daniel Hickman's patent, granting him title to his homestead. General Land Office.

through military conquest, suspect treaties, permitting the distribution of alcohol and other destabilizing trade goods, appointing corrupt agents and murderous officers, and other policies that pressured Indians to give up legal claims to their land.

The pressure of white intrusion came in many forms. Hundreds of thousands of migrants on their way to the goldfields in California, farms in Oregon and Utah, and mining camps in Colorado and Nevada killed the game or drove it away while passing through the Great Plains. Commercial hunters exterminated an estimated eight to ten million buffalo in little more than a decade, between 1871 and 1883. They destroyed the western Kansas buffalo herds in just four years, between 1871 and 1874, those of western Texas in fewer than five years, from 1875 to 1879, and those of eastern Montana in about four years from 1880 to 1883. The hunters took only the hides, for which there was a lucrative market to make machinery drive belts for eastern and European factories. This industrial slaughter left millions of pounds of meat to rot in the killing fields.[18] The intrusion of white trappers, hunters, miners, railroad builders, forty-niners, Mormons, and others, along with the extirpation of the buffalo, weakened Indian nations throughout the region.

Whites bound for the West Coast unintentionally spread diseases previously unknown among Indians, who had little or no immunity. In the winter of 1831–32, smallpox killed five to six thousand Pawnee along the Platte River, cutting the nation's population in half. In 1837 a great smallpox epidemic in North Dakota killed 90 percent of the Mandan. Wars among tribal nations, especially the expansion of the Lakota empire, disrupted annual buffalo hunts and placed additional stress on Native societies. After victory in one battle during the winter of 1837–38, Pawnee warriors returned to their village with twenty captive Oglala women and children. Unfortunately, the captives had smallpox, and children in the Pawnee villages, who were already suffering from influenza and whooping cough, contracted the disease. Many children died. The government began removing the weakened tribes to Indian Territory (Oklahoma) or confining them to reservations.[19]

In most locations where Black people homesteaded, Native populations had already been removed or confined to reservations long before the homesteaders arrived. In Nebraska, for example, the government dispossessed and transferred to the public domain thirty million of the state's forty-nine million acres before the Homestead Act of 1862 was even passed; only Nebraska's northwest corner remained legally in limbo. In Kansas, the government had dispossessed Indians of thirty-five million of Kansas's fifty-three million acres as early as 1850.

In other places, especially the Dakotas and Oklahoma, events were more compressed, and homesteading proceeded concurrently with dispossession. In 1876, Chiefs Crazy Horse and Sitting Bull led their Lakota, Arapaho, and Northern Cheyenne warriors to victory at Little Bighorn in eastern Montana. Just eight years later but four hundred miles to the east, Black homesteader Norvel Blair and his family filed claims in central South Dakota. President Theodore Roosevelt opened the Rosebud Indian Reservation in South Dakota to homesteading in 1904, and 107,000 aspiring claimants—more than forty times the number of available homesteads—responded. They flooded into tiny Gregory to enter the GLO lottery, hoping to win the right to claim a homestead. Here, homesteaders—mostly whites—sometimes intermingled with the remaining Indian populations and became part of the process (legal or otherwise) of extinguishing Indian land claims.[20]

Starting in the late 1860s, would-be homesteaders began pouring into Nebraska and Kansas. Nebraska's non-Indian population ballooned in just thirty years from 28,841 in 1860 to 1,062,656 in 1890. Kansas grew from 107,206 in 1860 to 1,428,108 in 1890.

Homesteaders drove most of this this growth. Horse-drawn wagons and crowded trains passed through every day, offloading streams of families seeking land.

They soon filled up the eastern and central portions of the states, pushing later arrivals farther west. Toward the end of the century, people intending to homestead needed to go to eastern Dakota Territory and the eastern plains of Colorado to find suitable and available land. Still later arrivals, those homesteading between 1900 and 1920, shifted to the western edge of the Great Plains, creating a homesteading boom in central and western North and South Dakota, eastern Montana, eastern New Mexico, and newly opened Oklahoma. More claims were proved up between 1901 and 1920 than during any other period. By 1920, homesteading was mostly over.

Homesteading was the primary way in which non-Indigenous people settled the nine Great Plains states. Migrants came to take up the offer of free land, even if some of them, after arriving in the region, wound up buying land on credit from railroads or speculators rather than homesteading. Whether measured by the number of people involved or the amount of land transferred, homesteading was the chief cause of this mass movement. In some states, the government transferred more public land via the Homestead Act than by any other means.

About 957,000 persons entered homestead claims in the Great Plains states and successfully proved them up. They gained ownership of 180,475,000 acres. Among them were approximately 3,500 Black claimants, who with family members numbered nearer 20,000 persons. They filed claims and gained ownership of roughly 650,000 acres. In the South, Black people during this period managed to become owners of approximately 1.7 acres per person. In the Great Plains, Black homesteaders became owners of approximately 32.5 acres per person.[21]

Homesteading and its history, photographs, and literature continue to be at the core of the region's culture. Farming and ranching families pass the legacy down the generations, proudly pointing out that they are the fourth- (or fifth- or sixth-) generation descendants of homesteading ancestors. The history of homesteading is kept alive by the wildly popular, if often misleading, *Little House on the Prairie* books and the long-running TV show. However propagated, homesteading is foundational to the region's identity. Black people are usually missing from this constructed past, although they participated fully in Great Plains homesteading.

The Homestead Act of 1862 is often lauded as the first major piece of national legislation that did not restrict its benefits to white people. When the act took effect on January 1, 1863, however, people of African descent were not eligible to participate. The act did not contain a clause specifically excluding Blacks, but it did contain that clause about citizenship. And the Supreme Court's 1857 *Dred Scott* decision had ruled that African Americans were not U.S. citizens and never could be. Thus, the Homestead Act's citizenship requirement—"a citizen of the United States, or who shall have filed his declaration of intention to become such"—effectively excluded Black people.

Congress likely did not intend to exclude Black people when it passed the Homestead Act, though the evidence is indirect. At the surface level, *Dred Scott* was the law of the land and congressmen and senators would have known the citizenship requirement would exclude Blacks. During the debate on the act, they engaged in no discussion of race or the possibility, pro or con, of African Americans gaining homesteads, or at least none entered the public record. Congressmen did voice the hope that the Act would attract many European immigrants. And it seems clear that when congressmen thought about how homesteading would populate the West, most assumed that white people would be the ones filing the claims.

The lack of debate on race during passage of the Homestead Act is striking. In addition to four million enslaved persons who, it was widely anticipated, would soon be emancipated, the number of free Blacks in northern cities was rapidly growing. Some free Black people were *state* (but not U.S.) citizens, and they voted in most New England states. Members of Congress, who dealt nearly every day with bills and petitions relating to Black people, must have asked themselves how the homesteading law would affect them.

The 37th Congress—now minus its southerners—was deeply opposed to laws excluding Black people. Abolitionist Radical Republicans dominated both houses of Congress.[22] Expecting the West to be settled by whites was entirely different from *prohibiting* Black people from homesteading there. The Radicals' strong antipathy to racial exclusion laws was expressed in multiple ways, including passing bills for confiscation of Rebel property (that is, enslaved people), for abolishing slavery in the District of Columbia, for arranging for schooling of the district's Black children, for changing the rules of (effectively gutting) the Fugitive Slave law, and for enrolling Black men in the army and navy. The Radicals pushed and prodded Lincoln toward emancipation and other revolutionary measures which he seemed slow to adopt.

Illustrating the thirty-seventh Congress's sentiment was their proposal to "remove all disqualification of color in carrying the mails." The southern-dominated Congress had inserted the clause restricting postal business to whites back in 1825. The bill to remove the color bar easily passed in the Senate and won a "large majority" of support in the House Committee on the Post Office and Post Roads. It failed only when Congressman Schuyler Colfax pointed out that the bill not only removed the ban against Black people but also Native Americans and Chinese.[23]

The Republicans were also busy directly undercutting the *Dred Scott* decision. They were outraged at the court's decision, now widely hated as a vestige of the old, disgraced, and seceded southern planter autocracy. Congress remedied the decision's damage by passing the Civil Rights Act of 1866, which clearly established that African Americans were U.S. citizens. They ratified the Fourteenth Amendment to the Constitution to embed that principle in constitutional law. Within four years of passing the Homestead Act, Congress, over President Johnson's veto, had definitively overturned *Dred Scott*. The four-year gap, though lamentable, did not prove very costly, because the war years were uncongenial to homesteading anyway—fewer than 1 percent of all proved-up claims were filed during the period when Black people were excluded.

Whatever it intended in 1862, by 1866 Congress made it clear that Black Americans were eligible to homestead. Unlike their mostly unsuccessful attempts to homestead in the South, Black claimants in the Great Plains, so far as we can determine, were treated fairly by the GLO and local land agents. And they found a remarkable degree of acceptance, not without exceptions, among their white neighbors.

The two great legacies of the thirty-seventh Congress—emancipation and the Homestead Act—thus came together in Black homesteading. Black migrants left behind kin and friends and everything that was familiar to move to a region they did not know, with strange weather and different growing conditions and different soils. And they moved among white people whose attitudes and behavior were unfamiliar and possibly malicious. The risks they took to build new lives must have felt enormous and very scary.

None suffered those risks and experienced those fears more acutely than the first Black homesteaders who built Nicodemus.

3

A New Start at Nicodemus

It was such an unusual place . . . There was nothing to arrest the
sight and my eyes ached from looking so far and seeing nothing.

—ELVIRA WILLIAMS, Nicodemus homesteader

Driving from either the east or west on U.S. 24 in northwest Kansas,
visitors are given little notice of Nicodemus until they're nearly on
top of it. This part of the Sunflower state is sparsely populated. Thick
grasses cover the rolling hills, interrupted here and there by yellow
limestone outcroppings. In spring and early summer, the prairie is
a soothing green. Finally one sees Nicodemus, a small collection of
low buildings just off the highway punctuated by a tall blue water
tower with "Nicodemus" running down its length. Brown signs
with the National Park Service shield announce the location as a
National Historic Site, making it one of NPS's most hallowed places.
The town itself is tiny, low, and windblown. Its population, almost
entirely elderly, fluctuates but was recently pegged at twenty-two. But
on its shoulders Nicodemus carries an immense weight of history.

This small, rather dilapidated village became a National Historic
Site because Angela Bates, a descendant of Nicodemus homesteaders, spent many years working to preserve its story. Bates and her
parents left Nicodemus when she was five years old, and she grew up
in Pasadena, California. After graduating from college, she pursued
successful careers in government and education.

Bates returned in 1989 determined to recover and preserve the
community's past. Descendant Veryl Switzer had started this work

decades earlier, when in 1976 he succeeded in placing Nicodemus's central district on the National Registry of Historic Places. Now Bates dreamed bigger. She founded the Nicodemus Historical Society and tirelessly engaged descendants and a growing circle of supporters in her vision. She proposed seeking National Historic Site designation for Nicodemus, an implausibly audacious idea, because the National Park Service has awarded that designation to fewer than a hundred sites nationwide. Congress rewarded her gumption by approving the designation in 1996. She and others developed a guided tour of the Ellis Trail followed by the original homesteaders, and they created other programs to engage schoolchildren and grow the community's visibility and outreach.

Bates and her team succeeded, because the history of Nicodemus is so important to our national narrative. Nicodemus is the oldest and most long-lived Black homesteader community in America. It is unique and indeed a site of national historic significance.

"I being raised a slave, I have no Record of my age," wrote early Nicodemus resident Zachary Taylor Fletcher. "My first Master was a Batchler and he Died when I was a Baby and willed all of his Slaves to his Sister Mary who had married a Man by the name of Antny Robb and She died in a few years and we was all Diveed out with her children."[1] Fletcher, like most who came to Nicodemus, carried deep memories of being enslaved and of the bitterly broken hopes of Reconstruction. But rather than being defeated and dispirited, Fletcher arrived brimming with entrepreneurial energy and grit.

He joined W. R. Hill, the white land developer, and six Black investors, several of them ministers, who formed the Nicodemus Townsite Company. W. H. Smith served as president, Simon P. Roundtree was secretary, and Fletcher became the company's corresponding secretary. How they chose the name Nicodemus remains a mystery. The Bible records Nicodemus as a Pharisee who became a secret follower

6. First page of Z. T. Fletcher's letter to the federal pension commissioner, November 12, 1918. National Archives and Records Administration.

of Jesus and brought embalming spices to prepare his body for burial after his crucifixion. More likely, organizers named the town for a later Nicodemus, an African prince who, the story goes, was captured, enslaved, and brought to America. Tradition honors this Nicodemus as the first slave in America to buy his freedom. Whatever its origin, the name is striking, with bold biblical and historical echoes.

In a combination characteristic of the time, Smith and the others intended to establish an all-Black community which would both uplift the race and profit the investors. The new settlement would be a refuge and opportunity for the South's oppressed and increasingly restless Black population, especially those from the upper South. And the investors would make a nice profit by selling "memberships" in the form of town lots, five dollars for a residential lot and seventy-five for a commercial lot. Historian Clayton Fraser saw the venture as unbalanced toward the latter goal, designed principally to make money for the company's directors.[2] Probably true of Hill, maybe less likely for his Black collaborators. In any event, none saw a conflict between doing good and making money.

One obstacle to making money was that most southern freedmen were very poor. The challenge for the Nicodemus promoters was to identify and recruit Black people who were financially able to move to Nicodemus and buy town lots. Black promoters in Tennessee had studied this question, and they found that migration and resettlement in Kansas would cost each family between $200 and $1,000. Almost no potential migrants would have as much as $1,000 and very few would have even $200 in ready savings. Other homesteader communities besides Nicodemus, especially Sully County, South Dakota, would also struggle with finding potential settlers with "means." And how to deal with migrants *without* means, especially the destitute Exodusters who arrived in Nicodemus in 1879 and 1880, would bedevil the new colonists.[3]

Smith, Roundtree, and Fletcher escorted the first group of thirty individuals from Topeka to Nicodemus in July 1877, and Reverend Roundtree and Hill led the group of 308 Kentuckians that fall. Reverend Hickman led a third group, from Scott County, Kentucky, numbering about 150 persons, who arrived in spring 1878. A fourth group included twenty-five Kentuckians and Tennesseans who arrived in May 1878. Reverend Goodwin led a fifth and final group of about fifty Mississippians who arrived in February 1879.[4] But beyond these organized migrations, many individuals and family groups filtered into Nicodemus, attracted by its growing reputation as "The Largest Colored Colony in America."

The new arrivals were not impressed with what they saw. When Reverend Hickman's group arrived at Ellis in April 1878, they had trouble finding shelter. The Hickmans stayed the first night at a farmhouse, then managed to erect a canopy for the next night. It was their first time sleeping under a tent. Many of the group's children had contracted measles during the trip, and several died. The migrants were quarantined in Ellis for two weeks.[5]

The group was joined by John Niles, coming from Leavenworth, where he had been soliciting food and other supplies for the colony's hungry residents. With him came two men he had met in Leavenworth, Abram Hall and E. P. McCabe. A delegation from the colony, including Henry Smith, Grant Harris, Charles Page, and John DePrad, arrived. They drove three wagons and teams, borrowed from the Bow Creek settlement. The men quickly loaded the wagons with the supplies Niles had gathered and perhaps migrants' household goods, and off they set for Nicodemus.

It was hard going. Hall was a newspaperman from Chicago who had intended to follow his reporter's nose to the emerging Black settlement in Hodgman County, Kansas, though he knew nothing about it yet. But a chance encounter with Niles caused him to change direction. He was resting up and awaiting the arrival of his Chicago friend McCabe when he heard that Niles was soliciting aid for desperate Black farmers in Graham County. Niles persuaded Hall to join the Nicodemus colony instead of going to Hodgeman. Now Hall, McCabe, and Niles joined Reverend Hickman's group progressing toward Nicodemus.

As they walked along, Hall, who had dropped a bit behind the wagons, noticed something peculiar. The men ahead were picking up sundried droppings left by the large cattle herds they could see off in the distance. The men chucked the patties into the feed box at the end of the nearest wagon. Neither Hall nor McCabe could figure out why they were doing it.

They hiked all day long, and when they arrived at the first night's camp at Happy Hollow, they were both exhausted and hungry. McCabe told everyone how famished he was. Some in the party got busy preparing the evening's meal, for which they lit a big blaze using the day's collection of cow chips. McCabe now realized the consequence of not seeing any wood along the way, and he was appalled. Despite being ravenous, he completely lost his appetite. Seeing cow chips so near his food turned off his delicate "city" stomach, and while the rest of the party gorged themselves, he starved in silence. Only later did he become an adept cow-chip cook himself.

At night, wolves howling, coyotes yipping, and perhaps even bears prowling nearby frightened them. The men built bonfires and sat around, firing guns to keep the wild animals from coming near. Nicodemus lay on the eastern edge of Graham County, then a still-unorganized region without law enforcement or courts. One hundred thirty miles to the south, Assistant Marshall Wyatt Earp that year was pursuing bank robbers and stopping cowboys from shooting up Dodge City.[6] The dark night around the campers seemed filled with dangers.

They set out early the next morning, and they soon crossed the Rooks County line into Graham County, still eight miles from Nicodemus. They discovered a bluff offering a lookout. As Hall remembered, "as Moses had to climb Mount Sinai to view the promised land," so Hall, McCabe, and Niles clambered up the steep grade to view Nicodemus. They disturbed two rattlesnakes sunning themselves, which they killed with stones and their boots. At the top, the three men who more than anyone else would shape the colony's early history could see the whole panorama of the grassland open out before them. Niles instructed them to look north, where just beyond a fringe of trees, they saw some black spots. That was Nicodemus. Hall said, "I confess to feeling disappointed. I had never seen a 'Dug-lur' nor a 'Sod-up' and I had not the least conception of how either of them looked. . . . We saw the dugouts of the colony looming up across the gleaming river like anthills in the distance."[7] His first look at Nicodemus's present dispirited him, but he would soon become euphoric about its future.

Finally, as the party neared their destination, the men at the front shouted, "There is Nicodemus!" Willianna Hickman was lying sick in the wagon, and so she was overjoyed to finally arrive. She strained her eyes to see the glorious sight, but she could see nothing. After some moments, her husband pointed out wisps of smoke arising from the ground. "That is Nicodemus," he said. The colony's families lived in dugouts, with little visible above ground. Willianna recalled, "The scenery was not at all inviting, and I began to cry."[8]

Willianna Hickman's distress upon seeing Nicodemus was compounded as her family traveled fourteen miles farther west to their own homestead. Again there was no road, so they navigated by compass across the prairie. Night fell, with its terrible, lonely darkness, lighted only by the brilliant Milky Way. She and the children fell asleep in the wagon bed. Willianna's brother Austin and a friend had gone ahead of them to set up the new homestead. When her husband Daniel thought they were near, he started blowing his horn. Willianna, awakened, rose up. After a time, they heard the sound of horns in the distance answering Daniel's calls, and then they heard gun shots. They drove toward the gunfire, and relieved, they spotted the fire Austin had built to direct them home. Bleak as Willianna had found Nicodemus, she would live her life in an even more isolated place.[9]

The first group of Kentucky migrants arrived on September 17, which would later be celebrated as Founders Day. At that time of year, the desiccated prairie appears especially forbidding. The newcomers must have looked with deep concern at this open and unpromising landscape, so different from the humid, thickly wooded lands most of them had known. Clouds bring just twenty-one inches of precipitation to this part of Kansas during an average year, although the area is moderately well watered by streams, including the South Fork of the Solomon River near Nicodemus. However, creeks and rivers tend to dwindle to trickles by late summer, and many dry up entirely.

There was nothing at Nicodemus to make a shadow. One migrant remembered, "I did not think anyone could live in a place like that. There was nothing to be seen, not a tree, not a house, not a drop of water, except away down to the river. . . . Oh Lord, it was the barest place I ever seed. I thought I could not stay. I walked away." Sixty migrants in the first group were so desolated by sight of their new home that they turned around and returned to Kentucky.[10]

Others, hot and tired after their long trek from Ellis, became furious with Hill's deception when they saw where they were to live. They threatened to hang him. Hill hid in a friend's dugout, but his pursuers followed him. The friend's wife was a large woman, and she covered Hill, a small man, with her shawl as he hid behind her back. The couple helped Hill escape through their back door. He went next to the home of Reuben Lawlis, who hid Hill under a load of hay and drove him to Stockton, twenty miles away. Hill stayed in Stockton until he judged it safe to return to Nicodemus.

Unlike the sixty who returned home, most migrants stayed. Elvira Williams came with her husband, Thorton, and seven small children in the spring of 1878. They had very few household goods and little money. They had always lived in the woods in Kentucky, and when she saw their homestead, she was disappointed, discouraged, and troubled. "It was such an unusual place. I wondered if we could live there. There was nothing to arrest the sight and my eyes ached from looking so far and seeing nothing." After two days on the homestead, she was so dejected she broke down crying. "I wanted to stop crying but just couldn't." Thorton said, "Now, Vira, don't take on so, there's no sense in that, we have got to try to stay here. We can't move away, and if we work as hard here as we did in Kentucky, we ought to be able to make a living for the children and besides we will have a home of our own, same as the rich people in Kentucky had."[11]

This land surely tested the newcomers' deep belief that owning land would bring them freedom. They brought with them memories of what they had experienced back "home," and they wanted to build a community beyond the close scrutiny of white authority that was free of the South's pervasive white violence. They believed in their bones that owning land was the surest path to their larger goal. But could they succeed in such a harsh and unwelcoming place?

Nicodemus was becoming nationally known as an interesting, perhaps crucial, trial of whether Black people could prosper if they left the South. Abram Hall's articles in the *Chicago Conservator* and other newspapers, including some written pseudonymously, raised Nicodemus's national profile. White reporters and editors were printing stories about the colony, too. People *knew* about Nicodemus.

The settlement raised the question that national Black leaders debated and would continue to debate in coming decades: Should African Americans stay in the South, despite all the violence and oppression, or should they leave, escaping southern brutality and possibly raising Black political influence in other states?

Frederick Douglass urged Black people to remain in the South. He argued his point in an article reprinted in 1879 in the *Colored Citizen*, Kansas's most prominent Black newspaper, well known in Nicodemus. "There is in my judgment no part of the U.S. where an industrious and intelligent colored man can serve his race more wisely and efficiently than upon the soil where he was born and reared and is known." One can almost hear his powerful voice rising as he thundered, "Shall we, who have born so many hardships and outrages and seen so many changes in our favor now throw up the sponge, abandon our vantage ground of possession . . . and go among strangers in pursuit of homes in a cold and uncongenial climate, rather than remain on the soil of our birth?" He told a Baltimore audience, "I am opposed to this exodus."[12]

On the other side were people like Benjamin "Pap" Singleton, the chief instigator of the Exoduster migration, and Robert Knox, who in 1872 reluctantly advised, "It is time, then, I repeat, to desert [Alabama] and seek homes elsewhere."[13] In the next generation, Booker T. Washington and W. E. B. Du Bois would famously continue this debate.

Nicodemus was a commitment to leave the South. Its residents had voted with their feet and so had already taken sides in the debate. Now that choice, and indeed their whole proposition that owning land would bring freedom, would be validated or not by whether their colony succeeded.

Black homesteaders rarely stated exactly what in their view reaching success would look like or what they meant by "freedom." Here we sorely miss transcripts of the lengthy and much-admired oratory that held pride of place in the communities' big Fourth of July and Emancipation Day celebrations. But the homesteaders nonetheless had a fairly simple (that is to say *fundamental*) understanding of freedom. Lulu Craig was a child during the early settlement of Nicodemus and lived in homesteader communities most of her long life. Her granddaughter, Alice McDonald, recalled about her Grandmother Craig, "She always said [to] 'stay in a position where you ask no quarter and you give none' and I think that was an old war term, to 'ask no quarter and give none' and Grandmother Craig always said stay in a position in your life where you ask no quarter and give none. That meant that you could be your own man."[14]

Migrants hoped that in their new promised land they would be safe in their own homes, they would be free to exercise their constitutional right to vote, and they would be able to establish good schools and have access to education. Led by E. P. McCabe, Abram Hall, and John Niles, the Nicodemus homesteaders insisted that

All Colored People

THAT WANT TO

GO TO KANSAS,

On September 5th, 1877,

Can do so for $5.00

IMMIGRATION.

WHEREAS, We, the colored people of Lexington, Ky,. knowing that there is an abundance of choice lands now belonging to the Government, have assembled ourselves together for the purpose of locating on said lands. Therefore,

BE IT RESOLVED, That we do now organize ourselves into a Colony, as follows:— Any person wishing to become a member of this Colony can do so by paying the sum of one dollar ($1.00), and this money is to be paid by the first of September, 1877, in instalments of twenty-five cents at a time, or otherwise as may be desired.

RESOLVED, That this Colony has agreed to consolidate itself with the Nicodemus Towns, Solomon Valley, Graham County, Kansas, and can only do so by entering the vacant lands now in their midst, which costs $5.00.

RESOLVED, That this Colony shall consist of seven officers—President, Vice-President, Secretary, Treasurer, and three Trustees. President—M. M. Bell; Vice-President —Isaac Talbott; Secretary—W. J. Niles; Treasurer—Daniel Clarke; Trustees—Jerry Lee, William Jones, and Abner Webster.

RESOLVED, That this Colony shall have from one to two hundred militia, more or less, as the case may require, to keep peace and order, and any member failing to pay in his dues, as aforesaid, or failing to comply with the above rules in any particular, will not be recognized or protected by the Colony.

7. Recruiting poster for Nicodemus, pledging "From one to two hundred militia." Permission of Kansas State Historical Society.

instead of waiting for these constitutional protections to be given to them, they would actively reach out and take them.

To have peace and to ask no quarter and give none, Black homesteaders first needed safety and security. Civic peace and being safe in one's home, freedoms that white citizens regularly enjoyed, were viciously and cruelly denied Black people in the South. A Nicodemus Town Company poster used to recruit new residents to the Solomon Valley directly addressed this concern. Organizers promised, "this colony shall have from one and two hundred militia, more or less, as the case may require, to keep peace and order, and any member failing to pay in his dues, as aforesaid, or failing to comply with the above rules [listed on poster] in any particular, will not be recognized or protected by the Colony."

This promise seemingly offered each member of the colony protection from other colony members who might not "comply with the above rules." But it was surely *understood* quite differently, as offering protection against marauding and violent whites—the kind whom Hill's listeners unfortunately knew too well. A Black militia hearkened back to the "colored" regiments in the Union Army and to the celebrated Buffalo Soldiers. Indeed, just ten years earlier, in August 1867, and not too distant from where Nicodemus would be established, Buffalo Soldiers fought one of their first engagements. Company F of the tenth Cavalry clashed with Cheyenne warriors in the "Battle of the Saline River." The migrants must have been highly comforted in thinking they would have such a force as protectors in a Kansas society they did not yet know. (There is no evidence that the militia was ever formed or needed.)

The poster betrayed the dual motives of the Nicodemus founders. It claimed that people joining the colony could only get land "by entering [filing on] the vacant lands now in their midst, which costs $5.00." But this was not true: the five dollars purchased a town membership, entitling the buyer to a town lot. Virtually all settlers spurned town lots because they came to own farmland, which the government was giving away almost free, and so they filed instead on homesteads outside of town.

The homesteaders discovered that transforming the alien plains landscape into working farms was a mountainous task. Everything was different from what they had known "at home." The seasons were different, how to break the tough carpet of prairie sod was unknown, the best crops to plant and when to plant them had to be learned. The lack of trees was continually distressing. In 1878 a prairie fire, an unknown phenomenon in Kentucky, killed Henry Blackman and Peter Jackson and destroyed some of the community's precious food supplies. The homesteaders were threatened by snakes, cyclones, and deep snows, as well as the familiar dangers of injury, illness, and childbirth.

They found that the promised "many wild horses easily tamed," if ever sighted, could not be caught on foot or with bony plow horses. Even the night seemed different: when the sun went down, it was dark, and without wood for bonfires, they found it hard to do chores or socialize together in the evenings as they had traditionally done.

Lack of "means" plagued the newcomers. Some Kentucky migrants arrived with money in their pockets because they had been skilled stone masons, blacksmiths, carpenters, and horse handlers at home. Many others, though, had little money, having spent their savings just to get to Nicodemus. One report, probably referring to Hill, suggested "they have been the prey of several sharpers who have defrauded them of considerable money."[15] Smith's and Hill's feeble or irresponsible planning, which failed to anticipate the colonists' limited savings and their need for cash *after* they arrived, caused many of the migrants' problems.

Those with money had to travel the thirty-seven miles to Ellis over prairie trails to find shops carrying the shovels and winter coats and flour they needed. "That was the darkest period that I have experienced since I crossed the Mississippi," Jenny Fletcher recalled. Her husband, Z. T. Fletcher, had gone to Topeka to work, and he sent her some money. But she had no place to buy anything when the weather turned cold and snow drifts blocked travel. No traders wanting to sell supplies showed up. The settlers went without bread for more than a month. Finally, a man with some rye to sell passed through, on his way from Ellis to Bow Creek. "We boiled the rye and ate it without seasoning, not even salting it, as we had no salt."[16]

As 1877 drew to a close, the colony was in danger of running out of food. Winter settled deep snow over the prairie, making foraging trips to Ellis impossible. Lulu Craig recorded their delight when, just before Christmas, two men traveling through Nicodemus from Bow Creek brought a few wild turkeys, which the colonists purchased. During the deep winter months, the settlers shared their supplies and shared the hunger, but they somehow survived. Their deprivation lasted well into the spring until their gardens started producing. The *Hays City Sentinel* in early April described them as "people in the most impoverished state of indigency."[17]

There were two possible solutions to their poverty. The first was that they could work at off-farm jobs, as most homesteaders both Black and white did, to support themselves until their homesteads yielded crops to sell. Unfortunately, Graham County was so sparsely settled there were few ranches or farms nearby to provide employment. And Nicodemus was so remote from the populated areas of eastern Kansas that people couldn't travel to jobs and still return at night or even on weekends to work the farm.

Some men found work elsewhere in the county doing the dangerous job of digging wells. Others found employment on the railroads or in cities far to the east of Nicodemus, and some traveled to eastern Colorado seeking work. Z. T. Fletcher, the Town Company secretary, left Jenny even during the perilous wintertime so he could work

8. Z. T. Fletcher and Frances "Jenny" Fletcher, early Nicodemus residents. Library of Congress, Prints and Photographs Division, HABS KS-49–25.

in Topeka. The men would work some days or weeks at the job, returning for a brief visit with their families, then travel back for more weeks of work. When the snows were too deep, making travel dangerous, the men's absences could stretch into months. Letters were slow to arrive. Some Nicodemus women found employment as cooks or cleaners in Ellis homes.[18]

The second solution was aid. Hungry homesteaders received help from several sources. That first winter, they received some food contributed by local whites. A white man, "Uncle Johnny Furrow," made multiple trips, traveling ninety miles east to Beloit, where he stocked up with a load of provisions and then distributed them to the neediest Nicodemians. Salina churches sent reverends W. A. Simkins and J. H. Lockwood to assess the condition of the colony, its need for aid, and whether it deserved help. They reported that people were mainly living on bread and water. They called for their congregations to donate food and for farmers to bring in a few chickens each. "We will send them to the colony and let them raise all the chickens they can."[19]

A food donation that perhaps saved the colony came from an unanticipated source—Osage Indians, and possibly Potawatomie as well. The Indians were returning from their annual buffalo hunt in the mountains, traveling back to eastern Kansas. They found the colonists shockingly hungry, and they generously offered them food. The "hostile Indians" the migrants had feared when leaving Kentucky turned out to be big-hearted neighbors. The Indians may have given the Nicodemus folks half of their hard-earned harvest of buffalo meat.[20]

The homesteaders also received supplies from more distant donors. In March 1878, community leaders organized a formal system to solicit food and other goods and to distribute them. They petitioned Governor George T. Anthony for state relief, but he refused. They sent agents to seek private donations in the populous eastern part of Kansas and in other states. Reverend Roundtree appealed for support at the Michigan State Fair, and in response, Michiganders sent money and several rail carloads of commodities to Nicodemus. Rev. James Suggs, who had visited Nicodemus, preached about their plight at his church in Princeton, Illinois, and in Chicago. He succeeded in raising $140.82 and clothing supplies for the colonists.

Homesteader and hustler John Niles was particularly effective in collecting donations in eastern Kansas, though not without controversy. He tended to exaggerate his credentials, and others were suspicious that he pocketed some of the proceeds. But he and other solicitors raised enough donations for Nicodemus to set up a storehouse for charity goods in a sod commissary, later replaced by a stone-front half-dugout.[21]

Reverends Simkins and Lockwood, the Salina pastors, reported that the colonists had good ground that was well located, but unfortunately "there [was] but one little pony team in the entire colony" and what they needed most were teams to break the prairie sod and get some fields under cultivation. The pastors appealed for $300 in contributions to purchase two oxen teams to loan them for the summer. The *Saline County Journal* complimented the pastors' plan to loan the oxen, because both the pastors and the *Journal* editors worried that gifting the oxen might encourage dependency. Come fall, the pastors would decide "in the best interests of the colony" what to do with the oxen.[22]

Most early residents built half-dugouts or sod houses to live in. With no forests nearby and residents lacking money to purchase lumber, sod was the most readily available building material. The builders started by digging out a three- or four-foot depression in the ground. Cutting through the masses of tangled prairie roots was tough work, because while buffalo grass only sent roots down three feet, needlegrass could extend its roots to sixteen feet. What made it worse for Nicodemus settlers was that the grub hoes and mattocks they had brought from Kentucky were poor excavating tools, and they lacked shovels and picks.

Once they completed the dig, they cut sod into usable strips, tough labor in the best of circumstances, and built up the side walls to three or four feet above ground. They covered the structure with cottonwood or hackberry boughs cut at a riverbank. They made a roof by layering sod, dirt, and other material over the boughs.

The first settlers constructed their dugouts close to the townsite because they liked the increased sense of security and sociability that clustering together afforded them. But Abram Hall soon pointed out that they needed to disperse out onto their homesteads, or else claim jumpers would come along and file on "their" land. They would be left landless after their long migration to own land. They reluctantly headed out to construct second dugouts.

Reverends Simkins and Lockwood were impressed with the people, whom they found in better shape than the pastors feared. They

9. Half-dugout, half-soddy, a typical house in western Kansas during early
settlement. *Promised Land on the Solomon: Black Settlement at Nicodemus,
Kansas*, fig 3–3. U.S. Department of the Interior, National Park Service, 1986.

praised the colonists' industry and skill in constructing their cabins
and half-dugouts. "They have indeed done a great deal of hard work
since they sat down upon on the raw prairie . . . They have had to
do most of the work in getting material for their homes with their
hands and backs, 'toting' it together on their backs."[23]

Little by little, the colonists succeeded. Vera Williams recalled
that first summer her husband, Thorton, spaded up a big garden
in which they planted beans, squash, and a few rows of corn. They
raised enough beans and squash for the winter. Thorton continued
to enlarge the garden each year, and Elvira and the children cared
for it when he was away at work. "In a few seasons [Thorton] had a
field to farm instead of a garden."[24]

Until they could dig wells, they carried water from the Solomon
River or a nearby creek, when it had water. They sweated hauling
heavy jugs or barrels for what seemed excruciatingly long distances.

They relied on buffalo chips and scrub wood for fuel. A few collected buffalo bones, left scattered on the prairie where industrial hunters had slaughtered the bison. They sold the bones for six dollars a ton to processors who turned them into fertilizer.

Residents eventually established peaceful relations with surrounding whites, though at the start they had to work through some scary incidents. The first involved cattle ranchers and their cowboys, who disliked any "dirt-busters." Their plows upended the grass the ranchers needed for grazing, and their fencing closed off the open range. Several times the cowboys intentionally ran their herds over Black farmers' fields, destroying their crops (they similarly harassed white homesteaders). In 1878 Mrs. A. L. Stanley, a colonist, complained in a letter to Governor Anthony that cowboys had made six raids that summer. One time some cowboys got irritated that Nicodemus people were watering their cows in the South Solomon River, and they drove off the Nicodemus cows. But the Nicodemus men managed to capture one of the cowboys. They held him hostage until the cowboys returned their cows. After the Black folks, joined by some nearby white homesteaders, defended themselves a few times, the cowboys left them alone.[25]

Another incident involved the killing of John Landis, a white man whom the migrants hired to conduct the surveys required in their homestead filings. Residents chose Landis because he seemed to be the only surveyor willing to take the job. Soon after completing the surveys, Landis was ambushed and shot in the back near his own home up in Norton County. Oral tradition in Nicodemus fingers his killers, Dr. William Cummings Jr. and Henry Gandy, as racists angry about the Black settlement who shot Landis as payback for helping the settlers. Without doubt, his killers were race haters: Doc Cummings had been a Confederate bushwhacker during the war.

More likely, however, Cummings and Gandy killed Landis as part of their long-running and frequently violent political fights in Norton

County, a wild area only partially settled. They were Democratic vigilante "Regulators," while Landis was a lower-tier but pugnacious Republican. Landis enjoyed the scorn of his enemies as much as the praise of his friends. For ten years he had been in continual conflict—legal and extralegal, including several shoot-outs—with the Confederates now turned Democrats.

Landis often served as a delegate to the bitter Norton County Republican Party conventions. At the July 18, 1878, convention, delegates refused to elect Landis to represent them at the First Congressional District convention. Instead, they selected a long-time Landis enemy. Landis believed he had been cheated by Democrats who infiltrated the Republican convention, and he and his supporters noisily walked out. Delegates Doc Cummings and Henry Gandy were both heard to say that that was the last convention John Landis would ever attend. Next day, Cummings and Gandy burned Landis's wheat field and haystack and shot five bullets into his house. On September 19, they shot Landis from the cover of some willow trees while Landis helped a new (white) emigrant survey his claim. The motivation of his killers remains lost to history, but circumstances suggest Cummings and Gandy murdered Landis in their political dispute.[26]

A third incident occurred on July 3, 1879. William Sheppard, a white man from Smith County, was hauling beer and liquor to Nicodemus to sell at the community's popular Fourth of July celebration. As he passed through Stockton, three young Black men from Nicodemus, including Erasmus Kirtley, asked if they could ride back home on his wagon. Sheppard told them to climb aboard. About halfway to Nicodemus, Sheppard said they would have to pay him twenty-five cents each for the ride. The men said they had no money and emptied their pockets to prove it.

Sheppard, who was drunk and now angry, pulled out his pistol and shot Kirtley in both legs. The other men quickly overpowered Sheppard and forced him to take Kirtley home, where he was attended by a doctor and survived. Sheppard was taken to Stockton and fined. The *Kirwin Chief*, among other white newspapers, called the attack a "brutal outrage" and wished Kirtley a swift recovery. The larger white community apparently agreed. Nicodemus historian Charlotte Hinger thought this episode, as ugly as it was, nonetheless gave confidence to the African American community that in Kansas, justice was possible.[27]

Despite these incidents, for the most part Nicodemus residents had established congenial relationships with the white community by the spring of 1878. The harassment and assaults ended when it became clear to all that the Black colonists intended to stay and could defend themselves.[28]

Hill and other Nicodemus Town Company officials may have assumed their new town residents would stick to their homesteading chores and let the officials run the colony. After all, many of the newcomers were illiterate and nearly all were from the South, where they had learned to keep their heads bowed. But the officials soon discovered how wrong they were—perhaps the realization hit them when Hill had to cower behind the skirts of his friend's wife to escape being hanged. The migrants hadn't come all this way to again be told by others how to run their own affairs.

Rather soon after reaching Nicodemus, the migrants established a community government. Town Company President W. H. Smith and Secretary Simon Roundtree installed themselves as its leaders. But not long into their tenure, residents replaced them with John Niles as President and Edward McCabe as Secretary. Abram Hall joined the leadership team informally in charge of communications. He sent numerous letters to surrounding towns' newspapers to advocate for the colony. These three ambitious and capable men quickly demonstrated that Nicodemus residents and their leaders would govern their own community.

Colony leaders faced a major crisis when Exodusters began arriving in Nicodemus in large numbers. The federal government had

10. Mississippi migrants on a riverbank, waiting for a boat to Kansas. Library of Congress, Prints and Photographs Division, lc-usz62–26365.

withdrawn its troops from the South in 1877, and African Americans suffered the consequences. Black people in Mississippi, Louisiana, and east Texas endured especially brutal and vicious repression. In 1878 and 1879 "Pap" Singleton and other Black leaders urged African Americans to flee Mississippi and nearby areas, setting off what became known as the "Kansas Fever Exodus." Fleeing Blacks overloaded riverboats and trains from that region in their frenzy to get out and get to Kansas.

Ten to fifteen thousand Exodusters arrived in Kansas in 1878 and 1879. Most arrived destitute, illiterate, and without knowledge of where to go or how they could earn a living in Kansas. The Exodusters' needs swamped local aid societies. The *Leavenworth Times*, claiming to express the worry of many Kansans, assured readers that while the publication did not care that the Exodusters were

Black, it was concerned that they "are destitute and helpless, and immediately upon their arrival here would become a charge upon the public." Stockton, twenty miles east of Nicodemus, complained that "Our city is filled with colored refugees, utterly destitute. Large numbers have died and many are now sick."

Aid groups tried to step in to help the Exodusters. In Topeka, the small Black community formed the Kansas Colored State Immigration Bureau to relieve the Exodusters' suffering. The Kansas Freedmen's Relief Association, newly established, soon joined the relief effort as well. At a meeting at the Topeka Opera House, new governor John St. John waxed poetic about Kansas's abolitionist past, boasting that the Exodusters came to Kansas because of its "history devoted to liberty." He suggested that aiding the Exodusters was the final act of the Civil War. The Exodusters, who had received only abuse and discouragement on their passage through Natchez and Memphis, must have welcomed the governor's words. Unfortunately, actual aid and not just words was harder to come by.[29]

Exodusters began arriving in Nicodemus, and the community gave them food, clothing, and other aid. But the colony's slender resources were soon overtaxed. The Exodusters' presence brought to the surface deeper philosophical differences growing among community leaders. Dependence on charity ran contrary to the Nicodemus dream of an autonomous, self-supporting Black community. The homesteaders had joined an intentional colony to own land and become self-sustaining—not to be charity wards. Company investors Hill, Smith, and Roundtree had specifically targeted Kentuckians who possessed some resources and could therefore afford town memberships, but the migrants discovered that they needed money to survive and for the colony to succeed. The Exodusters were much poorer even than the Kentucky migrants—some literally had nothing. While many Nicodemus residents must have felt great sympathy for the Exodusters, they also realized that Nicodemus itself survived on such a thin margin that the influx of penniless migrants might sink their colony.

Exodusters presenting themselves for help and the community's own continuing dependence on aid brought these internal tensions to a boil. E. P. McCabe, representing Nicodemus, lobbied Governor St. John for greater action to help the Exodusters, but the governor turned him down.

Community members called a mass meeting in April 1879 to consider what to do. Abram Hall argued that they should not give the new Black immigrants any further aid, fearing it would breed an unhealthy dependence. W. B. Townsend, a Black leader from Leavenworth, rebuked Hall for his attitude toward the Exodusters, insisting they were people in need of aid and that Hall made his drastic recommendations only to further his political future. Hall accused Reverends Roundtree and Silas Lee of keeping for themselves some of the aid donated by outsiders. The colony seemed about to break apart.

In the end, residents decided to reject further charity and the dependence it bred. They voted to dissolve their community government, and they declared themselves now to be "citizens of Graham County in common with all others." They disbanded the organization they had set up to solicit and distribute outside aid. Nicodemus would now live on the fruits of its own labors.[30]

By 1880 the homesteaders' fortunes began looking up. The residents had survived the difficult migration and the first terrible winters. They had built shelters. Residents had filed on their homestead claims and were establishing successful farms. They now had sixteen teams of livestock to power the plowing and other heavy farm work. The community gained experience with wells and found workers able to dig them, so more families could afford them. Though most families still did not have a well, those homesteaders who dug them were pleased that they usually found water at manageable depths, and even the deeper wells only reached forty-five to sixty feet. Having a well, even sharing one, relieved families of the tedious and exhausting job of hauling water from a stream.

Most of the migrants filed homestead claims. Roundtree entered a homestead claim outside town in 1879. He worked and lived on his land for the required five years and proved up in 1885. Charles Williams, Rev. Silas M. Lee, and Jonas Moore also received patents that year. William Kirtley received his patent a year later. Z. T. Fletcher filed on 160 acres under the Timber Culture Act, an 1873 law that complemented the Homestead Act. Almost every family, except those few who could make a living in town, settled on homestead land. Most claimed the full quarter section allowed by law. Some also purchased or leased additional land.

The colony's farmers expanded their fields and learned how to make them produce growing yields. Most people were still poor— they certainly could have used more farm equipment and livestock— and their fields were worryingly vulnerable to prairie fire, drought, hail, locusts, and crop failure. But they now cultivated on average an impressive twelve acres per homestead, mostly planting corn and wheat along with smaller amounts of millet and sorghum. Their increasing yields supplied crop surpluses to sell. Every family also had a large vegetable garden. If they carefully watered the rich prairie soil, they produced enough beans and squash and peas for the winter. Most kept chickens, a hog or two, and a cow as well.

The township population stabilized at around three hundred. Abram Hall, in a letter to Kansas's leading Black newspaper, the *Colored Citizen*, declared that "every week brings its quota of newcomers, who come to stay. . . . [They] have come out to Kansas to make a home, and get their children a start toward that glorious future for *our race* which has already cast up shadows on the horizon of the future."[31]

The migrants grew accustomed to their new surroundings. Willianna Hickman recalled that over time she became reconciled to her isolated prairie home. "We improved the farm and lived their [*sic*] nearly twenty years, making visits to Nicodemus to attend church, entertainments, and other celebrations." Her three daughters became beloved schoolteachers in Nicodemus. Elvira Williams remembered how, when her boys grew old enough to leave home and work, each of them sent money home. That allowed Thorton to stay at home, and they could carry on. "I got used to the prairie life after awhile and became satisfied. The little sod house was home. I was happy."[32]

Residents could now foresee how their community would grow and prosper.

4

Nicodemus Flourishes

The young folks then enjoyed themselves dancing,
swinging, eating ice cream drinking lemonade &c.
—*Western Cyclone* (Nicodemus), July 8, 1886

The 1880s were Nicodemus's golden years, as both the town and the countryside prospered. Z. T. Fletcher, corresponding secretary for the Nicodemus Town Company, opened his general store. "Generally out of everything store," the complaint went at first, but soon he filled his shelves more reliably. He opened it in a dugout, and then moved it to a sod structure. Jenny Fletcher, Nicodemus's first postmistress and Z. T.'s wife, ran the post office out of the store as well. The town's first hotel failed, but two other entrepreneurs stepped up to open Myers House and Union House. Their owners attached fancy names to sod structures that were, in truth, simply enlarged houses with a couple of guest rooms. Two white merchants, William Green and C. H. Newth, each built two-story commercial properties, using locally quarried and dressed limestone. Their lead was followed by others putting up frame-and-stone structures. And Nicodemus's leaders, E. P. McCabe, John Niles, and Abram Hall, extended their activities into Graham County politics.

The new buildings ushered in a more mature phase in the town's built environment, just as its leaders' growing prominence signaled the community's coming of age politically. The town began presenting a new, more permanent appearance as it emerged from the dugouts. Residents constructed a frame schoolhouse and opened

Graham County's first public school. By 1879, they had built the nucleus of the town, including thirty-five dwellings, the general store, post office, hotel, real estate office, two livery stables, and two churches. For a time the influx of recruits made Nicodemus the most populous town in the northwest quadrant of Kansas. It became a convenient stopping point for travelers heading west. The presence of Green and Newth, followed by other white businessmen who opened other lines of commerce, changed the composition of the town's leading citizens: for the next few years it would be harmoniously biracial.[1]

Black homesteaders developed their farms in the surrounding countryside. They began to amass the livestock, farm machinery, fencing, storage bins, and other equipment needed on successful farms. Many now drew water from wells to irrigate vegetable gardens and fruit trees. They raised chickens and milch cows and sold eggs, milk, cream, and butter in town. They marketed their wheat at decent prices, prices that declined slightly over the next decade but, in this era of general deflation, less than the prices of goods they purchased. More limiting was the difficulty farmers had in transporting their crops to market because they had a long trip to the nearest railroad.[2]

In the countryside as in town, the population was biracial. Black people were the great majority, but twenty-five whites filed for homesteads near Nicodemus, surrounded by Black farmers. Whites resided on their claims for at least five years, long enough to prove up, and many stayed longer. Newspapers and personal accounts record no serious disputes between Black farmers and their white neighbors. Nicodemus farmers also endured no further conflicts with white cowboys.

Increasing rural prosperity attracted more farmers to Nicodemus. William Belleau wrote his master's thesis on Nicodemus in 1943, when there were still a few residents who remembered the early days. He created an annual time series of the Black population

11. Edward P. McCabe,
Nicodemus leader
and Kansas politician.
Permission of Kansas
State Historical Society.

of Nicodemus Township. His numbers, while somewhat higher than the decennial censuses (which chronically undercounted Black populations), are broadly consistent with the official figures. The Black population stabilized at about three hundred people, some years higher and some lower, for the next three decades. The rural population remained stable deep into the twentieth century.[3]

McCabe, Hall, and Niles, ambitious and capable political leaders, pushed their way to the top, giving direction and eloquent voices to Nicodemus governance. They worked alongside other educated and influential residents like Rev. Simon Roundtree, Thomas Johnson and his son Henry Johnson, Rev. Silas Lee and his son Willis Lee, John DePrad, George Washington Jones, and the couple seemingly at the center of town life, Zachary and Jenny Fletcher. Jenny was the daughter of Nicodemus Town Company president, W. H. Smith.

This was a talented and tenacious group of leaders for such a small community. McCabe was born in Troy, New York, and educated in the Newport, Rhode Island, public schools. He lived for a time in Chicago, where he met Hall. He arrived in Nicodemus in 1878 and in the same year obtained appointment as a notary public for then-unorganized Graham County. A notary public had the power to certify deeds, contracts, and other official papers and may have acted informally as a justice of the peace. Before his appointment, Nicodemus residents trekked to Stockton in Rooks County to have their deeds and contracts notarized, and so McCabe's new position came as a great convenience for them. And McCabe benefited, too, launching him on his political career. Governor St. John appointed him as the interim Graham County clerk, the county's chief administrator, to serve until an election could be held. McCabe appointed John Niles as his deputy county clerk.

Graham County, before and after it was officially organized, was a hotbed of intense, nasty politics. Millbrook, Roscoe, Hill City, Gettysburg, and Nicodemus all had their homegrown candidates for lucrative county jobs. They competed for county contracts, and they fought for the ultimate prize, becoming the county seat. Each town's newspaper charged candidates from rival towns with fraud, corruption, and malfeasance, apparently often with good justification.

McCabe's interim appointment expired at the next election. Despite being widely recognized as having done a good job, he did not run for the regular term. The next two county clerks, John DePrad from Nicodemus and L. P. Boyd from Gettysburg Township on the other side of the county, each served but a few months in office before outrage at their malfeasance ousted them. Boyd, a white man, was seen as particularly incompetent, venal, and lazy. McCabe, running on the good reputation he earned as an interim, won the 1881 election by a convincing majority, despite most county voters being white.

McCabe then audaciously sought the Republican Party nomination to become state auditor in the 1882 election. State auditor was the fourth-highest government officer in Kansas. The auditor wielded great authority and patronage, and the job carried a handsome salary of $2,000 per year. In arguing for McCabe, the *Millbrook Herald*, a white Graham County paper, labeled him "one of the most brilliant and talented colored men in the state." It noted, "There are more than 30,000 colored Republicans in Kansas, and the party ought to recognize them and accede to their demand [to nominate McCabe]." He won the nomination at the state party convention. In the campaign, Democrats and some Republicans opposing McCabe used anti-Black slurs and lies against him, but the party establishment stumped for "the whole ticket."[4]

McCabe won 79,148 votes to the Democratic candidate's 60,505 votes. McCabe's election was even more surprising because his political sponsor at the top of the ticket, Governor John St. John, was defeated. St. John tried to win a third two-year term, bucking strong Kansas tradition, and lost to Democrat George Washington Glick. (Some St. John allies accused McCabe of "treachery," because even Graham County, previously a St. John stronghold, voted for Glick.) So despite Republicans losing the governorship, McCabe won his office. Kansans and especially western Kansans showed they were open to Black leaders. McCabe ran for re-election in 1884, a presidential year, and won again—this time garnering 150,811 votes to the Democrats' 96,169.[5]

The Democrats were not pleased. The *Wichita Beacon*, a Democratic newspaper, sought to stir up discord in the Republican Party by putting out a story that Republican bosses, when nominating McCabe in 1882, had expected and wanted him to lose: "He was put up to be knocked down." That way, the *Beacon* said, they could conciliate Black voters without having to actually give a Black man a high position. The *Beacon* said the scheme fell apart because McCabe "is a clever and courteous gentleman, and a good officer as far as we know, and if he was white skinned, we would not esteem him any higher." Because he was so appealing, the *Beacon* claimed, the Republicans were stuck and had to nominate him again in 1884.[6] This was rich coming from a newspaper that in the same article praised the growing amity between the races in the South—"amity" which caused thousands of Black people to flee in terror—and cheered the end of Reconstruction when "the intolerant and infamous federal political-chattelism [in the South was] wiped out." Whether the story about McCabe had any truth nonetheless is hard to tell.

Abram Hall Jr., a freeborn Chicagoan and homesteader, came from a distinguished family. His father was well educated, an African Methodist Episcopal (AME) minister who with his wife occupied a prominent place in Chicago's Black society. Hall Jr. grew up in this privilege. He was educated in the public schools and spent one year in medical school. He may have also had some legal training. He was perhaps the best-educated person in Graham County. His true love, however, was journalism, and he developed an engaging, sophisticated style of writing.

Governor St. John appointed Hall in 1879 to be the census taker for as-yet-unorganized Graham County. Before the county could be officially established, it had to contain fifteen hundred certified residents. The governor appointed Hall to conduct a special census, separate from the federal decennial census. Census taker was a politically sensitive and quite lucrative job, paying three dollars per day plus six cents per mile in travel costs, and Hall's appointment came despite objections from other towns' candidates. He traveled all over the county doing the enumeration. He approached white farmers on isolated farms, men with unknown attitudes toward an unfamiliar Black man coming to gather information about them. Hall showed great courage in carrying out his task, evidently without incident.

Finished with census work, Hall made himself in effect the communications director for Nicodemus. Just two months after his arrival, Hall sent a letter published in the *Stockton News*:

As we are too young on this side of the [county] line to afford a paper of our own, and as there will now and then occur something which might adorn a column and prove interesting to your many readers, I submit the following unconsidered trifles:

A wedding occurred in the settlement, on the 3rd Inst. It was the initial movement in a connubial way among us, and enshrouded somewhat in romance. The high contracting parties were a Miss Mary Robb and Mr. Henry Johnson. Rev. Silas Lee of Ellis, Kan., tied the knot. . . .

Sheriff Shaw and deputy Kent, visited our Sabbath School last Sunday, while halting here for dinner. They were making an official call we believe, on a party of riotous herders in the western part of our county. . . .

Crops are looking very fair and the colonists are hopeful. . . .

The people of Nicodemus intend to celebrate on the 4th of July. The programme is arranged as follows: Salute in the morning parade of Co. A 1st Regt. Rag Muffins, at high meridian reading of the Declaration of Independence . . . followed by a festival at the church at night.

—A. T. HALL JR.[7]

His letter contained anything but "unconsidered trifles," as author Charlotte Hinger brilliantly decoded. It was in fact a very clever piece of propaganda. Hall carefully chose his news bits to reassure the white readers of the *Stockton News* that Nicodemus was no threat to them and should be considered a valuable addition to prairie settlement. Hall reported the wedding and mentioned Pastor Lee to plant in readers' minds a view of Black colonists as stable family members who valued religion. He mentioned Sheriff Hall's and deputy Kent's visit and further dropped in mention of the Sabbath School to reinforce the image of Nicodemus as a law-abiding, peaceful, Christian-based community.

Hall provided a crop report to assuage concerns that the colonists could not support themselves and so might become a drain on public charity. He announced the Fourth of July celebration and mentioned (Black) troops and a public reading of the Declaration of Independence to show that the colonists shared the *News'* readers' patriotism, also subtly reminding them of the crucial role Black soldiers played in winning the Civil War. And finally, he connected celebrating the Fourth with a festival in the church, that is, he linked patriotism and Christianity, a surefire pleaser for white prairie audiences.

Hall accomplished all this using a form that small-town readers would find familiar and not threatening: the gossipy town column. But he had a deadly serious purpose, framing readers' views of the new Black settlement as a peaceful, self-sufficient ally, and he made no stuffy, theoretical pronouncements. Instead, he followed the writer's oldest rule, "Show, don't tell!" Unconsidered trifles, indeed.

Hall wrote a continuing flood of letters and columns for the *Colored Citizen*, the *Stockton News*, the *Atchison Daily Champion*, the *Hays City Sentinel*, the *Roscoe Tribune*, and even the *Chicago Conservator*, a national Black newspaper he had worked for before arriving in Nicodemus. His articles were thoughtful and cogent, tailored to appeal to and persuade a particular audience—Black people in the *Colored Citizen* or the *Chicago Conservator*, white western Kansans in the *Stockton News* or the *Hays City Sentinel*. He sprinkled his writings with classical allusions and down-to-earth examples, and his facility with words made his writings sparkle.

If McCabe was the shrewd politician and competent administrator and Hall the eloquent writer, John Niles was the commanding orator. He brought a dominating presence as soon as he entered a room. "Mr. Niles is a big, brown man, with a large head, two rows of very white teeth, and an everlasting flow of conversation."[8] He was born enslaved, with a Black mother and white father. He killed a man in Tennessee, for which he served time in prison and was

15. Recruiting poster for Nicodemus, June 28, 1877. Permission of Kansas State Historical Society, kansasmemory.org.

16. America Bates and her four daughters, at Nicodemus, ca. 1888.
Permission of Nicodemus Historical Society Collection, Kenneth
Spencer Research Library, University of Kansas Libraries.

17. The Bates family on its homestead near Nicodemus, ca. 1880.
Permission of Nicodemus Historical Society Collection, Kenneth
Spencer Research Library, University of Kansas Libraries.

To the Colored Citizens of the United States.

NICODEMUS, GRAHAM CO., KAN., July 2d. 1877.

We, the Nicodemus Town Company of Graham County, Kan., are now in possession of our lands and the Town Site of Nicodemus, which is beautifully located on the N. W. quarter of Section 1, Town 8, Range 21, in Graham Co., Kansas, in the great Solomon Valley, 240 miles west of Topeka, and we are proud to say it is the finest country we ever saw. The soil is of a rich, black, sandy loam. The country is rather rolling, and looks most pleasing to the human eye. The south fork of the Solomon river flows through Graham County, nearly directly east and west and has an abundance of excellent water, while there are numerous springs of living water abounding throughout the Valley. There is an abundance of fine Magnesian stone for building purposes, which is much easier handled than the rough sand or hard stone. There is also some timber; plenty for fire use, while we have no fear but what we will find plenty of coal.

Now is your time to secure your home on Government Land in the Great Solomon Valley of Western Kansas.

Remember, we have secured the service of W. R. Hill, a man of energy and ability, to locate our Colony.

Not quite 90 days ago we secured our charter for locating the town site of Nicodemus. We then became an organized body, with only three dollars in the treasury and twelve members, but under the careful management of our officers, we have now nearly 300 good and reliable members, with several members permanently located on their claims—with plenty of provisions for the colony—while we are daily receiving letters from all parts of the country from parties desiring to locate in the great Solomon Valley of Western Kansas.

For Maps, Circulars, and Passenger rates, address our General Manager, W. R. HILL, North Topeka, Kansas, until August 1st, 1877, then at Hill City, Graham Co., via Trego.

The name of our post-office will be Nicodemus, and Mr. Z. T. Fletcher will be our "Nasby."

REV. S. P. ROUNDTREE, Sec'y.

NICODEMUS.

18. Typical Nicodemus soddy with stone facing on one wall, ca. 1880. Permission of Kansas State Historical Society, kansasmemory.org.

19. Recruiting poster for Nicodemus, July 2, 1877. National Park Service.

20. Nicodemus general store and three residents, ca. 1885. Library of Congress.

21. Henry Williams and Reece Switzer, two early homesteaders at Nicodemus, Kansas, ca. 1880. Library of Congress. www.loc.gov/exhibits/african /afam010.html#obj3.

22. Early Nicodemus stone building first used as a general store, ca. 1880. Library of Congress, Prints and Photographs Division, HABS KS-49–10.

23. Nicodemus Blues baseball team, 1907. Permission of
Kansas State Historical Society, kansasmemory.org.

24. First district schoolhouse, Nicodemus, 2018. Author's collection.

then pardoned. He moved to Kentucky and migrated to Nicodemus as part of the Lexington contingent.

Niles would later be shown to be a big-time swindler, indications of which appeared as soon as he arrived in Kansas. In 1878 he had informed leaders of the supportive Black community in Leavenworth that he was the president of the Nicodemus colony and its authorized representative to receive their donations. That was false, and he was soon unmasked by W. H. Smith, the real president. The community's dilemma, however, was that Niles was the colony's most successful solicitor of aid. Hall accused Niles of taking some of the donated goods and selling them for his own profit, but even if he skimmed some off the top, Niles brought back the biggest contributions at the time when the colony needed them the most.

Unsurprisingly, Niles was involved in Nicodemus's first lawsuit. In 1881 he persuaded the Rooks County Bank to grant him a loan using fifteen hundred bushels of Nicodemus corn "piled up in a big shed" as surety. But there was no corn, and Niles was soon arrested. He was tried before a white Stockton jury, who listened to his eloquent and soulful defense lasting three hours. One juror held out in favor of Niles, thereby creating a hung jury. The irritated judge launched a second trial immediately, but this time Niles persuaded nine jurors to acquit him. The prosecution dropped the case.

Sometime later, Niles fled to Arkansas, where he again ran into legal trouble after passing himself off as an official with the power to certify homestead claims. He also sold corn whiskey without a license. He was sent to prison again. The *Chicago Conservator*, the Black newspaper, described him as "a bold, bad man," and Noble Prentice, a white reporter who visited Nicodemus in 1881, concluded that despite his many good qualities, Niles was not "loaded to the water's edge with scrupulosity." Historian Kenneth Hamilton called him "Nicodemus's most notorious confidence artist."[9]

But Niles was not quite done. He had long believed that former slaves should be compensated for their unpaid labor during slavery. Even while resident in Nicodemus he had given lectures in other towns on "colored people and the damages they received to life, person and property while in bondage." Originally a Republican, he abandoned that party in disgust and now he attempted to form a new party, the Indemnity Party, to advocate for compensation or what today we term reparations. He traveled to Washington, DC, to meet legislators and make speeches, but he was mostly denied access. Some credit him with getting the first reparations bill introduced into Congress. His Indemnity Party died stillborn.[10]

Nicodemus homesteaders had carried with them, in their vision of the new community they wanted to build, a deep determination to educate the colony's children. William Kirtley arrived in town with two Bibles, an elementary speller, and a dictionary. Jenny Fletcher opened a school in her dugout, probably as early as 1877, attracting between fifteen and forty-five students. John Samuels had learned his letters while enslaved in Tennessee, and he knew how important being able to read was. He volunteered on the committee to create Nicodemus's first public school.

Reverend Roundtree carried the most visible reminder of the evils of slavery. When he was a child, his owner's son was teaching him to read. The owner caught them, and he branded Roundtree's cheek as punishment. Ever after, Roundtree carried a scar in the shape of an *o* on his face. Kirtley, Samuels, Roundtree, Fletcher, and others knew from personal experience just how important education was to their dreams.

In 1879 Abram Hall, ever Nicodemus's most thoughtful and eloquent writer, presented a paper on education to Topeka's St. Johns Literary Society. The *Colored Citizen* reprinted his talk, titled "Our Needs," in full. Hall started with this challenge: "Who is there among you that is in any manner conversant with the present status, mentally, morally, and materially, of the Negro race in the United States, can rise in his place and truthfully assert they are not *mendicants on the bounty of their fellow races*? And who is there among you . . . does not feel his cheek burn and his ears tingle with shame at mention of it?"[11]

Surveying Black people's needs, Hall pointed to the many aching voids in Black life that needed to be filled, "so many obstacles to surmount, so many requisites to be supplied." He lamented that "Our needs, as a race, are almost as numerous as the sands upon a seashore." In the presence of them, he said, one hardly knew which to take hold of and which to withhold from. His fellow homesteaders surely agreed with his gloom: in 1879, they had barely survived two hard winters, and the first Exodusters started trickling into Kansas, starving, homeless, destitute.

Yet even in the face of so many desperate needs, Hall remained insistently positive. He found hope in the student burning the midnight oil, the craftsman teaching the apprentice, the avenues of trade (occupations) newly opening up. He said, "The race, once famous, now ignoble, but purified, let us hope, by the red sea of oppression through which it has passed" was, in his view, rising and making its way toward a better condition of things.

And of all the desperate needs, all the deficits under which Black people suffered, which was the most urgent? "We need first of all: Education; for it is the key which will unlock the door of caste, of trade, and consequently of wealth, will bring us home, and will make those homes the abode of intelligence."[12]

Nicodemus residents faced a financial obstacle in establishing a public school. Graham County, including especially Nicodemus Township, was populated largely by homesteaders, most of whom had not yet proven up their claims. Until they got their patents, the government still owned the land, making it exempt from taxes. So neither Nicodemus nor the county had a big enough tax base to fund a school. Nonetheless, Nicodemus people believed so strongly in education that they found a way to open Graham County's first public school in 1879.

Nineteenth-century Black homesteaders mostly saw *land* as the key to unlock the door to wealth and freedom, but they didn't disagree that education was also important. Lulu Craig, who grew up in Nicodemus with her homesteader parents, became a teacher for most of her adult life. Her granddaughter Alice McDonald remembered: "She [Lulu] was a strong strong believer in the fact that we needed to go to school and get an education. And Grandmother Craig pushed pushed pushed education so within the family group there are a number of us that are teachers cause Gram was a teacher and I was a teacher and Doris was a teacher and Darlene was a teacher and so she pushed it and it sunk into all of our heads to get out and get an education so that you could have a career."[13]

Beyond education, Nicodemians began to fill other gaps in community life. Thorton and Elvira Williams, like others living on their claims, came to town to worship and take part in church activities, bring their children to school when they didn't have a neighborhood school, socialize with cousins and uncles and aunts, sell their produce and buy supplies, and join in joyous community celebrations. They particularly looked forward to the Fourth of July and Emancipation Day festivities.

The community filled its Fourth of July with powerful oratory, music, races, ice cream, baseball, boxing matches, games, and other diversions. The event promised such a good time that it drew many outsiders, as many as two thousand people in 1886. William Sheppard, the white man who shot Erasmus Kirtley, brought beer and liquor to sell in Nicodemus because he knew there would be a big crowd and people would be joyous and thirsty. Revelers enjoyed, according to the relentlessly boosterish *Western Cyclone*, an "excellent [dinner] such as only the ladies of Nicodemus are capable of serving" and then listened to I. V. Flynn's "very eloquent speech." After the Webster String Band performed excellent music, "the young folks then enjoyed themselves dancing, swinging, eating ice cream drinking lemonade &c."[14]

The most important event of the year was Emancipation Day, sometimes known as "Demus [Nicodemus] Day" and later renamed Homecoming. Residents celebrated it around August 1, honoring the date in 1834 when the British Empire abolished slavery. According to a report in the *Western Cyclone*, Emancipation Day 1886 attracted between one and two thousand people to town.[15]

Organizers filled two or three days with nonstop events. Baseball was a central feature, the Nicodemus Blues typically fielding a very strong team. As the 1939 poster announced, baseball started a day early that year, because the event attracted so many teams—Hutchinson, Colored Monarch, Norton League, Bogue, WaKeeney, Nicodemus, and Old Hickory—that they needed extra time to get all the games in. They promised the crowd "fast, classy games each day!" There were also three boxing matches each day. There was platform dancing every afternoon and evening, and horse shoe pitching with cash prizes every day. The Hill City High School Band performed. The Dixie Melody Entertainers, a "mixed group of ten colored dancers," presented a floor show the final day. Families shared foods prepared specially for the day. Left unsaid, because everyone knew it, was that there would be many treats for the children—games, races, candy, ice cream, and other delights.

Among the most anticipated events for the adults were the speakers. Orators ranged over the injustice and miseries of slavery, the joys and opportunities of freedom, and the progress Black people had made in the years since emancipation. Demus Day continues to be observed—the community celebrated its 144th Homecoming Emancipation Day in 2022.

12. Handbill used to invite former residents to a homecoming celebration at Nicodemus, July 31–August 1, 1939. From *Promised Land on the Solomon: Black Settlement at Nicodemus, Kansas*, fig. 3–3. U.S. Department of the Interior, National Park Service, 1986.

Residents created civic and social activities during the rest of the year as well. They formed a literary society, organized an investment club, established sewing circles, and held dances in a grove outside of town. The AME and Baptist churches organized many of the events, sometimes as church functions, but more often the churches simply provided the most convenient place for committees and volunteers to meet and plan.

Two newspapers, the *Nicodemus Enterprise* and the *Western Cyclone*, competed fiercely even as both enthusiastically boosted Nicodemus. Two local white men, H. K. Lightfoot for the *Enterprise* and W. R. Hill for the *Cyclone*, edited the papers. Lightfoot charged Hill, the dodgy townsite speculator, with deception. According to Lightfoot,

Hill bought the *Cyclone* just so he could use it as a shill for Hill City's bid to be the county seat. The *Cyclone* struck back, calling Lightfoot a "political prostitute."[16]

One amenity absent from the town except during celebrations was any sort of pleasure establishment. The *Western Cyclone* claimed that the town had "no wiskey shops, billiard hall or other gambling hole" and that Nicodemus residents were "moral, refined people" with "no drunkenness or rowdiness, no cussing or whopping." The town's leaders, its investors, and most residents were determinedly "dry," favoring temperance and opposing Demon Rum. The town charter prohibited saloons and liquor stores, and when people bought town lots, they were required to sign a covenant preventing them from selling alcohol at their place for five years. Dry sentiment echoed arguments heard throughout much of Kansas and indeed wherever the Temperance Movement was strong, and town leaders reinforced the idea that alcohol consumption eroded the town's moral character.[17]

Nicodemus residents and certainly its boosters prized the fact that Nicodemus celebrated being a peaceable, law-abiding, morally upright, and racially harmonious community. Its newspapers found no crime or violence to report. There were, however, a few incidents. In April 1886 Rev. John Anderson and Deacon J. Joseph got into a fistfight over interpreting a Biblical verse. At the 1887 Emancipation Day celebration, a white man and white woman got drunk in a hotel and were charged with disorderly conduct. The same day two Black men, Clay Bradford and Allen Thomas, got into a dispute about Bradford's wife, pulled out their pistols and exchanged shots. One of their shots wounded a bystander. And to finish the day, two visitors to town got into a fistfight for some unknown disagreement. The white man hit the Black man, then the Black man knocked out the white.[18] Yet such incidents were infrequent.

The newspapers in the neighboring (white) towns of Millbrook, Wildhorse, and Webster made a big deal of the fights at the 1887

Emancipation Day celebration, suggesting that Nicodemus was a dangerous place. The *Millbrook Times* described the fight between Bradford and Thomas under the headline, "Bloody Work at Nicodemus!" The *Nicodemus Enterprise* leapt to the community's defense, pointing out that each of those towns had seen far worse violence themselves. The *Enterprise* generously provided a list of the worst examples. Why, it wanted to know, were these towns "howling" about one fistfight when in fact "a more peaceable set of people were never together than those who dwell in and around Nicodemus."[19]

By the 1880s Nicodemus became a thoroughly biracial community. African Americans constituted the overwhelming majority, but whites participated in all aspects of town life. White shopkeepers opened businesses in Nicodemus. C. H. Newth opened a drug store, A. L. McPherson opened a bank. S. G. Wilson operated a general store, and R. E. Lewis sold farm equipment. Blacks and whites who lived in and around Nicodemus created a remarkable fabric of racial cooperation, not just being civil to each other but working together, serving together on town committees and in town leadership, lobbying together, and in other ways collaborating for the common good. Racial collaboration began with W. R. Hill, a white man, joining with W. H. Smith, Reverend Roundtree, and other Black investors. Hill turned out to be unscrupulous and quickly fell out of favor, but these experiences modeled interracial collaboration.

Blacks and whites cooperated in almost all community activities. The Emigration Association, the Land Company, the School District officers, the Literary Society, the Cornet Band, the baseball club, the Grand Benevolent Society, the Daughters of Zion, and other community organizations all included white members. At the 1887 Fourth of July, Black speakers carefully alternated with white speakers: W. Cotton (white) opened the program, speaking on "The Past of Kansas." Samuel Garland (Black) followed, addressing "The Future of Kansas." Next came A. L. McPherson (white), H. C. Hawkins

(Black), C. H. Newth (white), Clark Samuels (Black), Hugh Lightfoot (white), and H. S. Henrie (Black). White businessmen joined Black town leaders to lobby the railroad companies to build their tracks to Nicodemus. Blacks and the relatively few whites lived, worked, socialized, politicked, and recreated together harmoniously.[20]

But while white residents of Nicodemus Township were clearly friendly to African Americans, others in Graham County were not. The white towns immediately surrounding Nicodemus were frequently hostile to Nicodemus and its residents. One nasty incident occurred in December 1880 in Roscoe, a town six miles northwest of Nicodemus. A Boston investor was building a large flour mill, employing both Blacks and whites to construct it. The white carpenters hosted a dance for themselves.

Midway through the dance, John Niles, the fiery Nicodemus leader well attuned to affronts and accompanied by perhaps twenty-five Black mill employees, attempted to join the party. They were asked to leave, and the managers of the mill then closed the building. But after some time elapsed, the managers decided the African Americans had gone home and they reopened the building to continue the party. Niles and his group returned, however, and found the doors closed. They began stoning the building and kept it up until the windows and sashes were completely shattered. They then shot into the building, and whites inside returned fire. The *Roscoe Tribune* labeled it "A Disgraceful Riot" and blamed Niles and his followers.

County towns disparaged one another because they all competed for the same resources—they struggled to attract outside investors and new settlers, obtain a rail link, and gain government jobs and business. The competition got fierce and vicious, including between white towns. Millbrook promoters accused W. H. Hill of trying to steal their businesses for Hill City after a cyclone flattened much of Millbrook.[21] Some participants tried to stir up racial animosity as a way to advance their towns' chances.

Residents of nearly every town on the central plains understood that its prosperity and future growth depended largely on two factors: whether it attracted a railroad line and whether it became the county seat. In the 1880s Nicodemus strenuously competed for both. The dispute over the county seat remains somewhat murky. In 1879 Abram Hall led a campaign to organize Graham County, which up to then had its law enforcement and other official business administered by neighboring Rooks County. State officials needed a formal count of residents to see if Graham had the requisite 1,500 residents to be organized. Governor St. John, though he appointed Abram Hall to take the census, disappointed Nicodemus leaders when he named Millbrook rather than Nicodemus as the interim county seat.[22]

After Hall's census proved Graham was ready to be organized, St. John fixed June 1, 1880, as the election date to choose the county seat. This set off a furious battle among the towns. The winning town would benefit, both immediately from construction of a county court house and other facilities and in future by all the jobs that county administrative work would generate. It would gain trade brought in by residents of other towns coming to do their official business. The sheriff's office and courts would be located in town. So, too, the winner would enjoy the convenience of being able to record their deeds and do other official transactions nearby. And the town would win the prestige of being the county seat. The winner would be put on a path to sure economic benefits and town permanence.

Hall originally hoped that Nicodemus would win the designation. In 1878 he wrote, "Nicodemus has hopes of proving to be the dark, yet winning, town in the race. She will certainly command the entire Negro vote of the county, and the white vote in her immediate vicinity." Gettysburg Township, on the far western side of the county, tried a different tack. As the (white) *Millbrook Times* put it, "They have a brilliant set of wire-pullers over in the Gettysburg alkali sands. First they cursed the black man from way back, and lost no opportunity to swear that if they couldn't get the county seat without the d—d n—r they didn't want it." Subsequent experience, however, chastened the wire-pullers: "Two elections were held [which McCabe won] and they began to get their eyes open to the fact that the white people of the county were disposed to deal justly with their dusky brethren and that the Gettysburg idea of making a war of the races had no sympathy with the people."[23]

But by 1880 the Nicodemus leaders realized their town lacked the votes to win the designation. In just a few years, the county's demographics had changed dramatically: white homesteaders were flooding into other parts of the county, dramatically reducing Nicodemus's share of the total vote. So Hall and McCabe switched their support to Roscoe, a nearby white town. It had only been platted the year before, but Roscoe boasted the new flour mill that employed a number of Nicodemus residents. Just then John Niles's battle at the Roscoe mill occurred, and however people assessed blame for it, it cost Roscoe many votes in the Black community.

Graham County voters split their ballots among Millbrook, Hill City, Gettysburg, and Roscoe, none gaining a majority. Each town's advocates leveled charges of falsified resident lists, forged signatures, and voting fraud. In a typical case, three cowboys from Sheridan County stopped to rest in Gettysburg and agreed to sign a petition to Congress asking for loans for farmers. But the petition was a fake, and someone tore their signatures off the petition and added them to Gettysburg's vote for the county seat. Officials threw out the results.

They ordered a new election, which was again marred by fraud. Graham County needed four elections to finally determine a result. Nicodemus voters' refusal to vote for Roscoe ensured that in the end Millbrook was named the permanent seat. But in the high plains, "permanent" is relative; in 1887 a cyclone flattened Millbrook and commissioners moved the county seat to Hill City.[24]

The second significant event for Nicodemus's future occurred between 1886 and 1888, when community leaders campaigned to persuade a railroad to build tracks to and through town. In December 1886 they started negotiating with the Missouri Pacific Railroad. W. W. Fagan, a company official, told the town that the Missouri Pacific was considering two routes west to Denver, one through Stockton that would also pass through Nicodemus and the other further north through Lenora, which would bypass Nicodemus. The railroad demanded a subsidy from the Graham County townships of $132,000, of which Nicodemus's share would be $18,000.

The town named Z. T. Fletcher and his brother to be the Nicodemus negotiators, and they got the subsidy reduced to $16,000. On March 22, 1887, the town voted eighty-two to eight to authorize issuing bonds in that amount. Expecting the company to build the line to Nicodemus by December, residents giddily watched for signs of the new tracks. But in September the Missouri Pacific dashed their hopes, rejecting their financial offer and informing them it was now building the alternate northern route.

Residents' hopes soared again, in February 1887, when the Santa Fe Railroad informed them that it proposed to run its tracks along the Solomon from Stockton through Nicodemus. In March residents got further good news when the Central Branch of the Union Pacific said it would have a train in town by fall.[25]

Nicodemus churned with excitement at the prospect of a rail connection. Inflated hopes set off an exuberant economic boom. Several white and Black businessmen moved to town and opened new enterprises. The *Nicodemus Enterprise* and *Western Cyclone* repeatedly reported on the imminent success of the railroad initiative and the new stores and offices popping up on town streets. They recorded with pride the scramble for town lots, with their shockingly (and pleasingly) high prices. They noted the many new migrants arriving to boost the town's population. Both the town and township grew significantly from about 250 Black people in Nicodemus Township (including the town) in 1880 to perhaps 400 or even 500 over the following decade.

By the mid-1880s, the town developed many thriving businesses, as suggested in figure 13. It had three general stores, two implement dealers, a blacksmith shop, hotel, livery stable, physician, stone mason, harness maker, barber shop, real estate broker, and loan company. Z. T. Fletcher and Bill Harris operated stores with fuller lines of groceries, including bacon, salt pork, tea, coffee, salt, corn meal, hominy, molasses, and candy as well as other staples like bar soap, tobacco, and coal oil. Shoppers still found flour hard to come by: Fletcher and Harris bought their supply from flour wagons that only passed by at irregular intervals, so they frequently ran out. (Alternatively, some men walked all the way to Ellis, returning with flour sacks on their backs.) Z. T. Fletcher also presented himself as a lawyer, offering to place the legal notices required for proving up and signing his advertisements "Z. T. Fletcher, Atty."

By the summer of 1887, when the Memphis reporter George Washington Jones visited, the signs of growth were everywhere. The town added another general store, two grocery stores, two drug stores, another blacksmith shop, a second hotel, a law firm, another livery stable, two millinery stores, and other businesses. It built two solid church buildings and had a $1,500 school building under construction. A group of Black and white businessmen formed the Nicodemus Land Company to broker property deals, profiting from the frenzied buying and selling of town lots and farmland.

Some residents began to be concerned with how the town looked. They complained that the old soddies and dugouts still scattered around did not properly present the town's new prosperity. They called for removal of the ruins and for the town to adopt measures to beautify its appearance.

13. View of Nicodemus street, showing Stone First Baptist Church and Williams General Store, ca. 1885. Permission of Kansas State Historical Society.

The *Enterprise* declared that the town was enjoying "a boom, not a boom of the Mushroom variety, but a genuine old fashioned boom, the variety that last long." The *Cyclone* reported that the town was growing modestly but confidently asserted that growth would speed up "with a heavy emigration and a railroad in the spring."[26]

The Santa Fe, however, also chose to bypass Nicodemus with its line. The Union Pacific continued to run surveys and make plans during most of 1888, including requesting that Nicodemus provide it with a financial subsidy, for which the town still had its $16,000 bonding authority. But for reasons not entirely clear, the railroad chose to stop building its line when it was still six miles south of Nicodemus, terminating at Bogue. One theory is that the Union Pacific—"a land company with a railroad side business"—was heavily involved in land speculation in the area and stood to profit more by platting its own town. Bogue, south of Nicodemus, became its railhead. Bogue, however, did not enjoy the expected bonanza either; by 1940 its population had only grown to 157 persons.

The double defeat of the county seat and the railroad stopped cold the development boom in the town of Nicodemus. The over-inflated balloon had been pricked, and all the newspapers' hot air escaped. People sensed immediately that their excitement and high hopes, their fevered speculation, and the businesses they started or expanded in anticipation of the coming growth, could not be sustained. They began to move out. Black businessmen moved to Bogue, taking their stock of goods and in some cases even moving their frame buildings. The whites moved to Hill City or places farther away, some leaving the county entirely and returning to Topeka or farther east. A. L. McPherson, the town's biggest property taxpayer, closed his Bank of Nicodemus. The town emptied out, and only a few Black people stayed.[27]

The town's leaders, likewise discouraged, stopped even trying to promote Nicodemus. Abram Hall had left years earlier, to take up editing newspapers in St. Louis and Chicago. E. P. McCabe moved to Oklahoma. And John W. Niles absconded to Arkansas. All saw greater political or personal opportunities elsewhere. Most historians, having misidentified the community as a "town," largely lost interest in its subsequent fate. They missed the slower and less visible development occurring in the countryside that would determine the community's longer-term future.

The dream of Nicodemus as a center of significant Black political influence and culture disappeared. Like other towns in the Great Plains which failed to get a rail line, Nicodemus could no longer serve as a regional market city, ceding to Bogue and Hill City and Stockton the role of middleman bringing in supplies and shipping out wheat and hogs. And without being the county seat, Nicodemus got no boost from local government. The dual setbacks ended the chance for Nicodemus to be a growing city with new residents bringing vitality to its business, commerce, politics, and culture. The town's population dwindled and nearly disappeared.

But while the *town* of Nicodemus declined after 1888, Nicodemus Township, the *rural community* of homesteaders, persevered. Most migrants had come to find land, and they had turned their claims into successful farms. True, their success had attracted shopkeepers, lawyers, land agents, even a bank, and those people had left, but the farmers remained. Few of the settlers had bought memberships in the town company, which was bad news for the investors, but when the newcomers spread across the landscape on their claims, it was a good sign for the survival of the colony.

By 1899 Nicodemus residents had earned 114 homestead patents, making them owners of about 18,115 acres. The Black population of Nicodemus Township peaked at 501 in 1907, and in the 1910 federal census, it registered 347 inhabitants despite the undercount. It still had 207 Black residents as late as 1940. Although weakened by the demise of the town, the Township's population persisted for nearly a half-century after 1890. It was a remarkable success.

Area farmers experienced good times when Great Plains agriculture thrived and struggled when the hard times came. The Mitchell family, displayed in their finery and with a solid frame house and outbuildings in the background, showed the possibilities. The period from 1900 to 1920 saw mostly prosperous years, capped by the excellent conditions at the end of the decade when wartime demand caused wheat prices to shoot up to historic highs and adequate rainfall produced plentiful harvests.

Unfortunately, the war-fed price boom ended in 1921, and Nicodemus farmers like most farmers in the Great Plains struggled during the 1920s. The rains came in some years but left corn and wheat parched in others. Prices for wheat and other farm produce bobbed up and down but mostly declined. Then hard times were replaced by true disaster—the 1929 stock market crash, the collapse of the national economy, and the onset of the 1930s droughts. Chicago

14. Mitchell family on their homestead outside of Nicodemus, ca. 1885.
Library of Congress, Prints and Photographs Division, HABS KS-49–5.

Board of Trade wheat prices fell from around a dollar a bushel in
the years between 1925 and 1930, to sixty-eight cents per bushel
in 1931, to just thirty-eight cents in 1932 and 1933. In Kansas the
1931 average wheat price of thirty-three cents per bushel was the
lowest on record.

The 1930s drought cut farmers' crop yields. Yields fell from
16.3 bushels per acre in 1928 to 9.1 bushels in 1931 and remained
low throughout the decade.[28] Farmers had little wheat to sell, and
what they did sell brought very few dollars. The Dust Bowl storms
arrived, blowing in thick layers of black, heavy topsoil from far-off
plowed fields. The dust smothered fields, farm equipment, barns,
houses, cars, livestock, and babies in cribs. When farmers tried to
make up their farm losses by seeking employment elsewhere, no
one was hiring.

By 1935 Nicodemus had suffered grievously under the heavy blows. Two young Black sociologists, Isabel M. Thompson and Louise T. Clarke, visited the famous town to see how it was faring. They called their article "Ghost Town—Almost." They reported, "Population—76; number on relief—72." They found only three small stone buildings, a church, a hall, and a store. The store, they said, was very small and meagerly stocked, because all marketing and trading had moved to Bogue. "The small frame buildings that could be seen were sadly in need of repair. . . . [It was a] desolate, weed-grown settlement."[29]

Thompson and Clarke were clear on the cause of this devastation: business collapsed nationally in 1929, and that collapse came to northwest Kansas in the form of collapsed wheat prices. Almost all the young people left Nicodemus trying to find jobs elsewhere. Adding to the suffering, they said, was the freak sideshow of weather conditions that nature brought to western Kansas—droughts in 1932, 1933, and 1934, followed by the devastating dust storms in 1935. "Entire families deserted this unproductive region."[30] Few could survive in such calamitous conditions. And few were left in Nicodemus.

When Nicodemus homesteaders succeeded in becoming landowners, did they also gain freedom? Of course, owning their small farms on the western Kansas plains could not change the racism of the nation or even the prejudices of many white Kansans. The neighboring city of Stockton during some years evidently had a "sundown" law which required Black people to leave town before sundown. When McCabe ran for statewide office, many Kansas newspapers viciously caricatured him with racist cartoons and slurs. When Nicodemus residents traveled outside their community, they were subjected to all the restrictions and humiliations of a segregated and racist society. As we now know, overturning our nation's pervasive racism, an ongoing struggle still, would require many more years and much more heartbreaking sacrifice.

Yet in other ways, they did find freedom. They clearly determined the important decisions within Nicodemus, exercising full self-government in their own community. Such control was unthinkable in the South. They were less successful in determining decisions which affected the settlement but were governed by outside groups, whether railroad officials selecting track routes or Graham County voters choosing their county seat. Even here, Nicodemus residents participated actively—through voting, lobbying, and holding office—in Graham County politics. McCabe, Hall, and Niles all held county office. Other Nicodemus residents elected or appointed to Graham County positions included John DePrad, J. R. Hawkins, and J. E. Porter, who served as court clerks. George Washington Jones, the Memphis lawyer and journalist who migrated to Kansas, became county clerk and the county's first district attorney. Daniel Hickman was chairman of the board of county commissioners. W. L. Sayers and John Q. Sayers served as county attorney, and the brothers became practicing attorneys in Hill City.[31] And at times Nicodemians exercised substantial influence within the Kansas Republican Party by participating in party conventions and voting.

Black homesteaders flexed their political muscles in a colony-threatening case in 1884. Henry Miller, a white land speculator in Stockton, discovered that the Nicodemus Townsite Company had negligently failed to complete its federal paperwork to gain ownership of the townsite. Miller contested the company's unfinalized claim, and he filed a Timber Culture claim on the land himself. If his claim had been granted, all the business owners and residents of the town would have had to pay Miller rent for their "own" places or even be evicted. Miller's contest panicked the Black settlers, who feared losing all they had built. Z. T. Fletcher joined with C. H. Newth, a white businessman, and others to form the Committee of Nicodemus Concerned Citizens.

The committee approached their congressman, Lewis Hanback, for help. Hanback, a white Republican first elected just two years before, agreed to use his influence. He arranged for an expedited hearing of the case before the United States Land Commission. Miller failed to show up for the hearing and lost his contestation by default. Hanback then persuaded the Land Commission to permit the Nicodemus residents to refile their townsite preemption claim, even though the town didn't yet meet the law's population minimum. They soon received title to their land.[32] Although at one level this episode revealed a politician simply doing ordinary constituent services, it was in fact a barometer of the political pressure Nicodemus residents could exert—they had induced a white congressman to intervene on their behalf against a potentially influential white businessman.

Black homesteaders also gained the right to organize their schools and educate their children as they wished. They cherished this right because literacy had been so cruelly forbidden in slavery, and they were reminded of it whenever they glimpsed the brand on Reverend Roundtree's cheek. Missives from their kin still living in the South renewed their determination, as they heard of whites undermining or even burning down Black schools. If education was, as Hall argued, "the key which [would] unlock the door of [racial] caste," then their newfound right to educate their children according to their own precepts was indeed a real gain in freedom.

Black homesteaders largely lived in peace, left, in Robert Knox's phrase, to "enjoy in peace and happiness by [their] own fireside the earnings of [their] daily toil," another important freedom. They initially had to defend themselves when cowboys and their rancher employers resisted closing the open range, but these conflicts were soon settled. There were a few other incidents, like the wounding of Erasmus Kirtley, the killing of John Landis, and the scuffles at the 1887 Emancipation Day. But there is no evidence of any systematic terrorism and intimidation of the kind so regularly visited upon Blacks in the South. No burned barns, no trampled crops, no mutilated livestock, no beatings or intimidation at voting places, no night riders, no jailing of Black people on trumped-up charges. No conspiracies, or at least no successful ones, by officials to cheat claimants out of their land. No regime of white assaults, rapes, and violence intended to cow Black people into subservience.

One mark of the growing equality that Nicodemus residents achieved was how western Kansas newspapers referred to them. Every little town had a newspaper. (Nicodemus had two.) Most were outrageously sensational and vitriolic, and they followed the nearly uniform convention of identifying the race of any Black person mentioned in a story. But many white editors of these papers gradually dropped the practice: Nicodemus people became people instead of "colored people" or some worse descriptor.

The *Western Kansas World*, billed as "The Official Paper of Trego County," ran this item of interest on September 24, 1887: "Z.T. Fletcher of Nicodemus gave us a pleasant call on Thursday. He and two other men were on the hunt of three boys, one belonging to Mr. Fletcher, one to A.L. McPherson and the other to 'Jack' Lovelady. The boys were reported to have been in Millbrook Wednesday night. From there they went north in some farm wagon. Two of the boys are fifteen years old and the other twelve."[33]

While the *World*'s readers might guess that Fletcher was Black because he was from Nicodemus, the biracial nature of the community meant this assumption was not certain. McPherson was the white banker. And what about Lovelady—was he African American or white? The fugitive boys were a mixed-race group, but apparently that didn't matter.

Not all editors adopted the practice. H. R. Cayton was a young Black man who traveled to Nicodemus to invest in real estate and the loan business. On a hot July day in 1887, he made a trip to Stockton to buy some pigs, during which he encountered W. L. Chambers, the white editor of the *Rooks County Record*. They had words. The next week Chambers printed an editorial in which he used their confrontation as evidence of how lawless Nicodemus was. He described in minute detail Cayton's hair, color, and race. Cayton responded in the *Nicodemus Enterprise* and *Western Cyclone*, calling out Chambers for "the deep-seated prejudice of this miserable puke."[34]

Another indicator of growing racial acceptance was signaled by the voters of Graham County who elected McCabe and others to county office. In 1880 whites in the county outnumbered Blacks 3,774 to 484, yet they elected McCabe to be County Clerk. Historian Kenneth Hamilton notes, "The county-wide election of Afro-Americans indicates the lack of intensive white racial hostility present in the county."[35]

Angela Bates, the Nicodemus descendant and longtime leader of the Nicodemus Historical Society, characterized Nicodemus as "a place they could experience real freedom."[36] The homesteaders acted on the same irrepressible urge to be free that motivated the later freedom-seekers of the Great Migration, and they risked disruption, dislocation, and leaving behind all that was known and familiar to find freedom.

Yet if we ask how, exactly, owning land is linked to freedom—what is it about land that leads to freedom?—it feels as if we are trying to grasp a handful of air. Does land ownership create independence? Does owning land allow one to retreat and shelter from society (including especially its racism)? Is land a power base? Does owning land confer standing in society? All these and other answers seem plausible but partial, failing to account fully for the Black homesteaders' profound belief that owning land would bring freedom.

We begin to gain insight into how homesteaders linked land and freedom from the homesteaders' own experiences. When cowboys sought to drive them out, Nicodemus homesteaders stood firm defending *their own land*. They gave no quarter. When they sought their congressman's intervention to assist them before the U.S. Land Commission, they exercised political clout made cohesive by being a *landed* community.

Whether we can explain it or not, they believed that owning land brought freedom. It propelled Black homesteaders to leave familiar surroundings, undertake enormous risks, endure years of struggle and hardship and disappointment, and ultimately experience the joys of great achievement. They owned land!

Today, Nicodemus is experiencing a rebirth of sorts, though probably not revival as a population center. Instead, Nicodemus is a National Historic Site. People are rediscovering its history, reconnecting with its thousands of living descendants in the Nicodemus diaspora and introducing new audiences to the Black homesteaders' dramatic story.

The Nicodemus Historical Society leads a campaign to restore the community's five historic buildings. They sit scattered among a few low frame houses, some long mobile homes arranged diagonally on corner lots, several new and somewhat anachronistic small houses, and the brick-faced "Nicodemus Villas" built for low-income retirees. The most prominent historic structure is Township Hall, which the WPA constructed in 1939 and now serves as the community's visitor center. The St. Francis Hotel, a collapsing two-story building dating to the 1880s, first served as a hotel, then successively a post office, school house, stagecoach station, and family residence. The District Number 1 schoolhouse, built in 1918, is owned and used by the local American Legion post. The Old First Baptist Church, completed in 1907, shows hard wear: a windstorm in the 1930s blew off its bell tower, and today temporary struts prop up its east wall, mocking the flying buttresses of gothic cathedrals.

The fifth and oldest historic building offers a glimpse of a hopeful future. Built in 1885, the African Methodist Episcopal (AME) Church is the only building owned by the National Park Service (NPS), which recently completed a simple but stunning renovation. Here the visitor can begin to imagine the homesteaders' joy, the exuberant songs and preaching, the delight in meeting old friends, the wiggly children dressed in Sunday finery being shushed on hard pews, the companionship, the homesteaders' pride in accomplishment and in this community that brightened their lives. The renovated church shouts out joy and hope.

Hundreds, sometimes thousands, of descendants return at the end of every July for Emancipation Homecoming Day. Writers, filmmakers, reporters, and artists show growing interest in Nicodemus. PBS has produced several short programs on the colony. Theater companies around the country mount Pearl Cleage's critically acclaimed play, "Flyin' West," set in Nicodemus, and Ruby Dee discussed the play in a Theatre Conversation at the Kennedy Center. Descendants and other visitors can see in Nicodemus's buildings and programs and growing visibility what Angela Bates and the Nicodemus Historical Society have achieved: they have brought the homesteaders' story to life.

Other Black people, seeking a way out of lives stunted by southern prejudice and violence and determined to build better futures for themselves, struck out on their own to claim land. Henry Burden of Virginia was one of the first to do so.

5

Henry and Mary Burden's Flight to Freedom

By his patient toil, his correct habits, and his unyielding integrity
he amassed a comfortable competency and was a striking example
of what a man willing to work can accomplish in Nebraska.

—*The Wilber Republican*, October 15, 1913, referring to Henry Burden

Henry Burden left Lincoln, Nebraska, on a bright spring day in
early April 1870. He traveled twenty-five miles southwest, probably
by team and wagon, to Crete, a recently settled village of about a
thousand people, in nearby Saline County. He may have sent his
heavier goods on the train, over tracks laid just the previous year.
If so, he collected his freight at the Crete depot, because the tracks
stopped there. Burden then took his team and wagon another ten
miles over prairie trails, really just two ruts in the grass, to Pleasant
Hill, an even-newer settlement of about a hundred people. From
Pleasant Hill he still had another two or three more miles farther
south to go, this time with no markers to guide him through the raw
prairie except perhaps a game trail. When he reached his destination,
still in Saline County, he staked out an eighty-acre homestead. He
formally filed his claim on April 8, 1870.

As he carted his wagonload of tools and provisions, Burden surely
also carried with him an exhilarating and terrifying mixture of hopes,
fears, doubts, and dreams. He was representative of a small group,
about a third of Black homesteaders in the Great Plains, who home-

steaded alone. They did not join colonies or other groups of Black people but simply set out across the prairie to find and claim land. Some were truly on their own; Burden, so far as we can tell, had no kin or Black friends nearby. Robert Anderson and Oscar Micheaux, whom we meet later, homesteaded far from other Black people. Others chose remote locations where they had relatives living dozens of miles away, one or two days' travel in the raw country. Joseph Speese homesteaded in Blaine County, Nebraska, sixty miles northwest of his nearest relatives in Westerville. James and Melinda Suggs homesteaded in Phillips County, Kansas, forty miles north of their friends in Nicodemus. George Washington Carver homesteaded in company with white friends.

Burden was also in service to—though he probably didn't think of it this way—the immense number of Black people in the South who desperately wanted to escape their intolerable living conditions yet lacked the means and knowledge to leave. He and Anderson, Speese, Micheaux, and others tested whether the West and its promise of owning land could be their new Promised Land. They spread the word about homesteading in the Great Plains to people back home in Arkansas and Tennessee and North Carolina through informal networks, letters and postcards they sent to kin, and occasional visits the more successful made to the South. Anderson visited Kentucky and Arkansas, Suggs preached in several states, Micheaux toured Georgia and was well known in Chicago. By their own success, all advertised the opportunities to own land.

Burden chose to file on eighty acres, not the usual 160 to which homesteaders were normally entitled. We don't know exactly why. Perhaps he didn't find another eighty acres of high-quality land available that pleased him. More likely, the Land Office determined that his claim lay within the boundaries of the federal grant to the Burlington and Missouri River Railroad. The government gave companies huge subsidies in the form of land—every other section out to ten miles on each side of the proposed rail line—to stimulate railroad building. Within that band, settlers could either purchase railroad land or file homesteads in the government-retained alternate sections. But the law assumed that the government's sections, now being closer to a railroad affording cheaper access to markets, would be more valuable, so it made its homestead grants less generous. Outside the band, homesteaders could choose to purchase or "commute" their claims for $1.25 per acre, but in the retained sections of railroad grants, the price was $2.50 per acre. In these "double minimum" lands, the government allowed homesteaders to claim only eighty acres. Virtually all the claims around Burden's were also for eighty acres, except a few larger ones, such as that by Henry Baumer, which was obtained using agricultural college scrip.[1] Burden's place was likely double-minimum land.

As a Black man, Burden was unique in Saline County. Not rare—unique. The 1870 census reported Saline contained 3,106 people, with none of them Black (Burden likely arrived after the count). Surrounded by a sea of grass and with white people as his only neighbors, with no house on the property yet, with the tough prairie sod to break before he could even begin to farm, he must have felt very, very alone. But remembering how far he had come would have inspired him because he was standing on ground that would soon be his own. He was going, quite literally, from being owned to owning.

Burden was born into slavery around 1842 in Petersburg, Virginia. During the war, the rebel government drafted slaves to construct Confederate Army fortifications. In late 1864 and early 1865 the Union armies tightened their siege of Richmond, including Petersburg. Burden's owner took him and some other enslaved men to work on General Lee's trenches. Burden was probably about twenty-one but may have been as young as seventeen.[2] The men were camped so close to the Federal lines that they could see the Union soldiers' camp fires. One night Henry escaped to northern lines, accompanied by—the stories differ—either a few others or perhaps as many as two hundred other Black men.

Burden joined the Union Army. He was officially listed as having been enrolled by Captain Irving Bean in Milwaukee on February 13, 1865. Burden may have traveled to Wisconsin, but more likely Bean or perhaps Bean's agent, serving as one of Wisconsin's roving recruiters, signed him up right there in Virginia. When a recruiter persuaded a man to sign up, the state got credit for him against its draft quota. Henry was credited to the "2nd Ward, City of Racine, Wisconsin." He earned a one-hundred-dollar enlistment bounty, of which the Army paid him $33.33 immediately.[3]

Burden served as a private in Company B of the Seventeenth Regiment of the U.S. Colored Troops. He had joined just as the war was ending, and his regiment was assigned various guard duties. He did not fight in any battles. The army mustered the Seventeenth Regiment out on April 25, 1866, in Nashville, and Henry was honorably discharged after fourteen months in the service.[4]

Now released, Burden traveled north. He spent two years in Wisconsin. Then in 1868 he moved to Lincoln, Nebraska. He secured a job at the Atwood House, a leading Lincoln hotel a few blocks from the state capitol.[5]

But Burden had bigger dreams, inspired by the Homestead Act. Perhaps he heard about the law in Wisconsin, and that motivated his move to Nebraska. Or he may have heard about it in Lincoln, watching trains arrive every day offloading migrants on their way to claim homesteads. *The Nebraska State Journal*, Lincoln's local newspaper, filled its columns with their stories. Wherever he got his information, he was fired by the idea of owning his own farm. He saved what he could from his earnings at the hotel and perhaps retained some of his soldier's bonus as well, and after two years, he was ready to homestead.

He filed on rolling grassland just south of Pleasant Hill. Standing on his land, he was perhaps overwhelmed by the serenity, the loneliness, and the excitement of that moment. Whites he did not yet know filed neighboring claims, on parcels still a long walk away. He likely lived in his wagon or a tent that first summer. He faced years of grueling labor to turn his prairie patch into a place that offered shelter from the burning summer sun and frigid winter blizzards and food grown in his own fertile fields. If he fell sick or a horse kicked him or he dropped a heavy stone on his foot, he would be his own doctor. He had deep wells of determination and courage to face alone such unnerving prospects because this was his chance to own his own land.

Just four years later, by April 1874, Burden had built "a house thereon 14 X 16 with 2 doors and 2 windows, [and] said house is built of pine lumber and is good and substantial." He also constructed an eight-by-twenty-foot frame granary and a stable. Being able to afford lumber instead of sod to build his house and barn showed that he must have saved a considerable sum from his prior work. Henry dug what was described as "a good well." He planted twenty-five apple trees and other "forest" trees. He was cultivating about thirty acres, a very large tract.[6] He also worked a limestone outcropping on his land, developing it as a quarry. He cut stone blocks and sold them to nearby families, who used them as foundations for houses and barns.

He finalized his homestead claim on April 21, 1874, becoming the first African American in Nebraska to prove up. He was not able to read or write, a lingering scar from his slave days, so he signed his homestead documents with an X. To serve as his witnesses, he called on neighbors William Elert and Ferdinand Sukraw, two white men who homesteaded nearby. Elert, born in Germany, arrived in Saline County in 1870 and farmed with his wife Olive. Sukraw had been born in Prussia and homesteaded a bit north of Burden's place.

25. Henry Burden.
Permission of Elizabeth
Burden and Burden family.

Just a year prior to witnessing for Burden, Sukraw's household suffered a sensational tragedy. His wife's brother, Fred Shultz, was part of a crew harvesting grain, but Schulz had difficulty keeping up. When others scolded him for it, he said he was sick and had taken some medicine but that he was still feeling poorly. He said he would go to the house and take some more medicine. After he had been gone a short time, an old man, a relative working on the crew, went to see why Schutz hadn't returned to the field. Sukraw's young daughter ran out to meet him, screaming, "Fred struck Ma and cut her head off, all but a piece of skin." The old man found the woman's body, head severed just as the girl said. Shocked, the men in the crew gathered up some clubs and weapons and found Shultz hiding in a field. Before they could capture him, he stood up, drew a knife, and cut his throat from ear to ear.[7] Sukraw was left with no wife and five young children to raise.

Soon after making his Saline County claim, Burden filed a second claim on eighty acres in nearby Polk County. He used his "additional soldier entry" privilege, a new benefit Congress had just passed in 1870. It allowed veterans to file for the full 160 acres even on double-minimum lands. The General Land Office (GLO) circular instructing local land agents about this benefit was issued on August 23, 1870.[8] That Burden, isolated on his claim and unable to read, learned about the new benefit is astonishing. The nearest land office was in Lincoln, and there's no evidence Burden traveled there. But he somehow developed an information network, perhaps relying on his white neighbors. Learning of the new law, he quickly grasped its implications for him, and he filed his Polk County claim. How he managed to fulfill the residency requirement is unclear. In any event, he received his patent on March 10, 1876. Soon after getting title, he sold the property, most likely because it was too distant for him to farm it himself. He received a handsome $2.50 per acre for his claim.

In 1873 Burden married Eliza B. Hill. He was now about thirty years old and as far as we know, had been alone ever since he fled Confederate lines and certainly since filing his claim. Where he met her or how he knew her is unknown. Eliza brought welcome companionship to the isolated farm. She also provided much-needed help with the farm work. Even as hard as Henry worked, he would have been very hard pressed to construct his house and barn, break thirty acres of sod, prepare and plant and harvest such big fields, dig a well, and plant an orchard by himself. We lack a good inventory of his farm equipment and livestock, but it's doubtful that he had a surfeit of machinery to work with. He may have hired help in turning over the sod, but certainly he did the rest himself. Now joined by Eliza, he would have continued to do the heaviest work, but she likely helped him in many chores. Unfortunately, she seemed not to have a strong constitution. In 1876, after three years of hard work on the farm, she died in childbirth. The baby also died.

Henry suffered many calamities and hardships during the mid-1870s. He lost his wife and child, with all the wrenching emotional trauma that it must have inflicted. A devastating tornado hit Saline County in May 1872. It evidently did not destroy Henry's buildings as it did so many others', but it likely damaged his crops. He woke up on Easter Sunday 1873 to one of the worst blizzards in the state's history. It raged for four days and created staggering snow drifts, which were exceptionally dangerous for his livestock. On October 14, 1873, a calamitous prairie fire, begun by migrants camping along Swan Creek, swept through the county from south to north, driven by fierce winds. A woman and four children perished as they attempted to outrun it. We do not know if it burned Burden's crops or hay, but it surely at least raised his anxiety. On July 25, 1875, heavy rains produced unprecedented flooding throughout Saline; it filled Turkey Creek just west of Pleasant Hill from "hill to hill." All these natural calamities occurred while the country dealt with the repercussions of the deep 1870s depression, set off by the Financial Panic of 1873. The panic squeezed credit, making it virtually impossible for farmers like Burden to obtain a loan.

But the worst trouble was the arrival of the grasshoppers, locust plagues dealing truly biblical devastation. Billions of ravenous insects blackened the skies like enormous storm clouds, and when they landed, they gobbled up crops and anything else edible. Protection or defense against them was hopeless. At first, they came only one or two at a time, here and there, looking almost like flakes of snow. But they were the advance skirmishers of an advancing phalanx.

Soon locusts came in thicker and faster, and they were followed by vast columns, black in the sky.

Hungry insects rained down in unimaginable numbers. They rattled on the roofs and against walls and windows, they fell in the fields, in the pasture, and in the water. They covered everything and everywhere. Within a couple of hours, every tree and bush, building, fence, field, and road was completely covered by a throbbing mass of insects. They consumed everything, crops and gardens and grass and trees, even wooden shovel handles and harnesses and ropes. When farmers tried to shoo them away, the pests refused to be scared and instead attacked the clothes on their bodies.[9]

During the 1874 plague, locusts devoured the entire corn crop in Saline County. They returned in 1876 and again destroyed all the crops and trees. They would have found Burden's newly planted fruit trees to be especially delicious. Farmers still had to feed their livestock, despite ruined pastures, and many were forced to buy hay, if they could find any for sale and had money to pay for it. Some residents relied on outsiders, kin back east or aid societies, to send them food to tide them over the winter. Many lost everything and simply gave up, returning east.[10] Henry Burden somehow held on.

A friend helped Burden through the hard times by loaning him money. Soon after Eliza died and when Henry was very poor, George Hastings supported him. Hastings, a white man, was a partner in the Pleasant Hill law firm of McGinty and Hastings, and he later became a judge. Hastings advanced Burden some money; how much is unknown. They put it officially in the form of a written loan contract, perhaps to spare embarrassment on both sides. But given the county's dire circumstances and especially Burden's poverty, Hastings undoubtedly considered it more as neighborly aid than a financial investment. In any event, it helped Henry get through the crisis. This was also the time when he sold his Polk County land for $400.

In about 1878, Henry married Mary Barbour. Like Henry, Mary was born into slavery, in Alabama, probably about 1847, and so she was a few years younger than he. After emancipation, at the age of perhaps eighteen or twenty, she found her way to Cincinnati to a halfway house set up to assist freedpeople adapt to their new circumstances. Superintendent J. K. Barbour, a Black war veteran, arranged for her to be educated, and he also adopted her. In 1877 or 1878, Barbour and his wife moved to Exeter, Nebraska, and Mary moved with them. Exeter was twenty-five miles west of Pleasant Hill. The Barbours' neighbors, perhaps with some matchmaking in mind, arranged for Henry to meet Mary.[11] Once introduced, Henry apparently became an eager suitor.

By marrying twice, Henry Burden distinguished himself from most other solo Black homesteaders. Surrounded by white people and often rooted on their own farms, unaffiliated Black homesteaders had great difficulty meeting potential spouses. Most lived alone and endured social isolation and psychic depression. Henry, by contrast, was able to marry soon after filing his initial claim and married again shortly after his first wife died. He seems to have escaped the loneliness that so afflicted others. He must have been an attractive catch, both his personality and his industriousness pleasing women.

Henry and Mary had eight children: George Hastings, John Jerry, Joseph, William, Franklin, Henry Jr., Mary, and Martha. They were all educated in the Pleasant Hill public schools. His marriage success undoubtedly helped him attain other achievements in life.

The Burdens apparently lived harmoniously with their white neighbors, although not entirely without incident. The teenagers, especially the girls, occasionally squabbled, as teenagers do. Not enough is known to determine whether the trouble was racially tinged or just ordinary adolescent quarrels. And when Henry went to join the United Brethren Church, one of the parishioners objected. Burden responded, "If you don't want me, I don't have to join." But

26. Henry and Mary Burden with their children.
Permission of Elizabeth Burden and Burden family.

the congregation overruled the objector. Henry became a lifelong member of the church and served as the treasurer of its board of trustees. The Burden family became faithful attenders.

Many of the Burden's neighbors were Czechs. Mrs. Frank Pisar, the Burdens' adjoining neighbor in section twenty-two, would cross the fields to visit Mary and have some female companionship. Their visits apparently satisfied both, even though at the start Mary spoke no Czech and Mrs. Pisar spoke no English. Soon enough, however, Henry and perhaps Mary, too, learned some Czech. Their children, who played and went to school with Czech children, picked up Czech as well, and it was claimed, they "spoke the language as if they had been born to it."[12]

Mary was known to be an excellent baker of white bread, and the Czech women living around her specialized in rye bread. They occasionally exchanged loaves, creating a treat for both families. Ray Krivohlavek recalled that at neighborhood social events, after all the feasting and games and excitement had tired out the children, his parents and the other parents would put all the assorted kids, Black and white, to bed together. The *Dorchester Leader* reported, "During all the time the family lived on this farm south of Pleasant Hill, work was freely exchanged with the neighbors, and the family was well-liked and respected by everyone who knew them." The Burden and Nerud families remained friends long after Henry died and his farm was sold. During the summer of 1940, Frank Burden and his family from Lincoln twice visited the Albert Nerud family in Saline.[13]

For much of their time on the farm, Henry and Mary were nearly the only Black residents in Saline County. In 1880 the census reported that the county contained 14,483 white persons and 8 "Colored" people. Among those eight were three Burdens.

In 1890 Burden doubled the size of his farm when he purchased the eighty acres lying just to the south of his Saline land. He finally owned 160 acres, and a pond as well.

Henry and Mary lived together on the homestead shown in the photograph until she died. Although we lack details, it is reasonable to assume that she, like Eliza, Henry's first wife, died in childbirth. Childbirth complications were an exceptionally dangerous killer of women. Mary was apparently in good health otherwise, but she was forty-eight and had given birth every other year for sixteen years—in 1879, 1881, 1883, 1885, 1887, 1889, 1891, and 1893. She died in 1895.

Henry was left with eight children to raise, ranging in age from two to sixteen. He continued to farm, and his older boys undoubtedly

27. Henry and Mary Burden with seven of their eight children, on their homestead in Saline County, ca. 1892. Permission of Elizabeth Burden and Burden family.

helped him. But now he had many homemaking duties as well. *The Crete News* commented that "Henry Burden kept the family together, gave to those children a fair education, always provided them with a comfortable home, and was a father and mother both to them."[14] It was said the children never missed church on Sunday. The *Nebraska State Journal* in 1902 enthused, "His children have been educated at the public schools and they have been so well brought up and are so bright and well-behaved that they are admitted and welcomed to all the social intercourse among their neighbors."[15]

Henry remembered that old "loan" he had received from George Hastings, now retired Judge Hastings, back in the hard times of the

28. Henry Burden Jr. with Pleasant Hill High School classmates.
Permission of Elizabeth Burden and Burden Family.

1870s. Henry and Mary had named their first son George Hastings Burden in honor of his friend and benefactor. In the intervening years, Pleasant Hill had failed to attract either a rail line or the county seat, dooming it to stagnation, and Judge Hastings had moved his legal practice and his family to Crete. More successful now, Henry had the means to make good on the loan. So he traveled to Crete to look up the judge and repay his old debt.

Hastings expressed great surprise and said he was not expecting repayment. But Burden insisted. Hastings had lost track of the loan documents, and together they began searching for them. After some considerable effort, they finally found the papers eleven miles away

29. Three Burden brothers and Bert Nerud skinny-dipping.
Permission of Elizabeth Burden and Burden family.

in Wilber. They had been stuck in a pigeonhole of the judge's office
desk in the old Pleasant Hill Courthouse, and the desk had been
moved to Wilber a dozen years earlier when the county seat switched
towns. Burden paid the judge and officially cleared his "debt."

During these years, Henry and his children appear to have been
well integrated into the community. He was a member, surely the
only Black member, of the F. J. Coates Post #107 of the Grand Army
of the Republic in Dorchester. He was an officer of his church. His
children went to the Pleasant Hill public school. There is a joyous
picture from around this time of three Burden boys, older teenagers, and a similarly aged Bert Nerud, skinny-dipping and horsing
around in a stream on a hot summer day.

Henry Burden resided on his claim for forty-three years. He died
in 1913. The Saline community responded to Henry's death with a
tremendous outpouring of respect and sympathy. Even discount-
ing for the adage, "speak no ill of the dead," and for the laziness

of obituary writers who ease their task by copying off others, the response was astounding. All the local papers—*The Crete News, The Friend Telegraph* (in Friend, Nebraska), *The Crete Democrat, The Dorchester Star, The DeWitt Times Union*, and more—reported his death, usually as a major news story on page 1 as well as in a more stylized obituary. Typical headlines were "Henry Burden, An Old Land Mark Gone" or "An Old Landmark Gone: Another Pioneer Gone to His Long Home."

The funeral on October 13 attracted a huge crowd of mourners. "Many Cretans and people from other parts of the County attended the funeral Monday. . . . The funeral procession to the Pleasant Hill cemetery was one of the largest ever seen in the county," reported the *Crete Democrat*.[16] The *Dorchester Star* noted that Burden's funeral was attended by the entire community and that mourners paid tribute to his many sterling qualities and worth. "No person ever passed beyond in this county who was more sincerely mourned by a larger number than was Henry Burden."[17] Judge Hastings gave the funeral oration for his friend, recounting his life and accomplishments. (In 1940, Attorney Robert R. Hastings, the judge's son, would give a "beautiful and touching address" at the funeral of Henry's son, George Hastings Burden.)

The community sentiment can be gleaned from the news reports— all the papers wrote of Henry's life in effusively complimentary terms, praising him for being an honest and kind man. *The Crete Democrat* remembered that when Mary died, Henry became solely responsible for raising the small children, and he nurtured them so well "that all are good citizens."[18] The *Wilber Republican* extolled him: "By his patient toil, his correct habits, and his unyielding integrity he amassed a comfortable competency and was a striking example of what a man willing to work can accomplish in Nebraska." "Henry Burden," it said, "was kind, polite and obliging, almost to a fault, honest and true as the needle to the pole, and his unswerving honesty, his integrity, his abhorrence of all that was mean, dishonest and vicious gained for him the reputation which extended far beyond the boundaries of Saline county."[19]

The respect and admiration for Henry Burden at his death was surely sincere and deep, but it came as no surprise. He had been similarly praised in print long before, including this description in a Lincoln—*Lincoln*, thirty-five miles away—newspaper eleven years earlier: "Henry Burden is a very interesting man when you consider what his life was at the beginning and what he has made of it. From the degradation of his slave life as a boy to the beautiful life he now enjoys on this beautiful farm, all his own, with his good wife and bright children, educated and respected. . . . The business men of Crete know Henry Burden and speak of him, not only with respect but with admiration for what he has achieved and what he is as a citizen."[20]

Indeed, the community had long esteemed this clever, hard-working, and upstanding man of such exceptional character. They respected his many achievements, but even more they admired the worthy man he was and the exceptional life he led. The outpouring at his funeral simply restated their admiration.

His passing, however, raised the problem, a common one, that apparently none of his children wanted to farm. In a pattern typical of other Black homesteaders (and white ones as well), the parents' commitment and sacrifices to educate their children produced children who sought better opportunities elsewhere. George Hastings Burden homesteaded for a short time in South Dakota, then returned to work in town at Pleasant Hill. Mary Burden, Henry's daughter, lived for a time in Wilber. At the beginning of World War I, Franklin Burden joined the Army along with some friends from Pleasant Hill. The Army shunted him off to a Black unit, but undeterred, he advanced to the rank of corporal and fought in three major battles in France. But none seemed interested in taking on Henry's farm as their life's work.

Hastings & Ireland, Attorneys

In the District Court of Saline County, Nebraska.

George H. Burden
                    Plaintiff

vs

NOTICE

John Burden, Joseph Burden, William Burden, Frank Burden, Mary Burden, and Martha Burden,
                    Defendants.

Notice is hereby given, that under and by virtue of an order made by said court in the above entitled cause, I. W. S. Collett, the duly appointed, qualified, and acting referee in said cause, will on the 25th day of July, A. D. 1914, at the East Door of the Court House in the village of Wilber, Saline County, Nebraska, at One o'clock P. M. of said day, offer for sale at Public Auction to the highest bidder for cash the following described real estate, to-wit:—The South Half (S½) of the South West Quarter (SW½) of Section Twenty Two (22) and the North Half (N½) of the North West Quarter (NW½) of Section Twenty, Seven (27) all in Township (7), Range Three (3) East of the 6th P. M., all in Saline County, Nebraska.

                    W. S. COLLETT, Referee,
First Pub June 18 to July 23.

30. Notice of legal action in which George Hastings Burden seeks to force sale of Henry Burden's farm, July 2, 1914. newspapers.com.

31. Henry Burden's house, on display at Saline County Historical Society Museum. Author's collection.

With no one stepping forward to take over the farm, the siblings wrangled over its disposition. As shown in the legal notice, George Hastings Burden sued his siblings to have the farm sold. He won in court, and the judge ordered the farm to be auctioned off. Frank Kupka bought it.

There was no official appraisal of Henry Burden's estate, and it is not known what it brought at auction. But the farm was quite valuable. One newspaper commented in 1902 that it was worth $50 per acre, or $8,000. *The Crete Democrat* noted at Henry's death, eleven years later and after it had become more valuable, that Burden "le[ft] a fine 160 acre farm and other property, all worth $25,000."[21] Simply correcting for inflation, that estimate would value Burden's estate at $670,000 today.

In following years the farm passed to other owners. One of them demolished the add-ons to the house, moved Henry's original building farther back on the property, painted it red, and used it as an outbuilding housing livestock. Still later, the Saline County Historical Society claimed the house, moved it to its museum in Dorchester, repainted it its original white, and now proudly presents it to the public as a reminder of and fitting tribute to Henry Burden. One can still see the window trim which he carved with a pocketknife.

Henry Burden was among the first unaffiliated Black homesteaders, but others followed. Like Burden, Robert Anderson and others grabbed at the opportunity homesteading offered, some becoming lifelong farmers and ranchers, others using their claims as assets to give them a leg up on other ladders of success. Few forgot their struggles or the thrill of owning land.

6

Homesteading Alone

I belong to the black race and am not ashamed of it. I have
seen considerable trouble and hard times, but . . . I have had
some mighty good times and have enjoyed life immensely.

—ROBERT ANDERSON, Black homesteader in Nebraska

James and Melinda Suggs homesteaded by themselves in Kansas,
though like many migrants, their journey was not direct. James and
his twin brother, Harry, were born into slavery in August 1831 in
North Carolina. When Suggs was three years old, his owner sold him
away from his parents and brother. After being sold a couple more
times, he wound up with a new owner named Suggs on a plantation
in northern Mississippi near the Tennessee border. James Suggs
grew up on that plantation. He was not allowed an education. But
wanting to learn, he would challenge the owner's children when
they returned from school, "Bet you don't know how to spell horse."
So challenged, they would spell the word he wanted to know. Bit
by bit, he stole his learning.[1] He trained as a blacksmith and was
sometimes rented out. He remained in Mississippi through the first
couple of years of the Civil War.

Suggs gained his freedom by fleeing the plantation when General Grant's army came into the vicinity. Slaveowner Suggs told his
slaves to hide all his cattle, horses, and moveable property into a
cane break, where the Yankee troops couldn't find them. But when
the federals arrived, one of the slaves showed the soldiers the secret
cache. James decided this was his chance for freedom, and he fled

to Corinth, where on February 1, 1863, he joined I Company of the Fifty-Fifth Regiment of United States Colored Troops.

Army camps were pestilential cesspits, and in 1864 Suggs contracted "tubercular consumption"—tuberculosis. He was sent to the hospital, recovered, and was discharged. Two months later he enlisted again, this time in Company H of the Fifty-Ninth United States Colored Troops. He served until he fell sick again, this time with fever and a painful abscess on his chest. He was discharged July 30, 1865, in Memphis.[2]

His wife, Malinda Filbrick, was born on April 5, 1834, in Alabama, enslaved to the McArthur family. McArthur was an old man who drank and gambled a lot and frequently whipped his slaves, including Malinda's mother. When he died, Malinda and other slaves were divided among McArthur's sons, also heavy drinkers and gamblers. Malinda's new owner fell into debt and sold her to the Filbricks. Mrs. Filbrick was described as a good Christian woman who didn't believe it was right to own slaves, an attitude highly unpopular in Alabama. She took a great interest in Malinda, including teaching her to read.[3] But neighbors angered with Mrs. Filbrick's antislavery beliefs forced her to leave the South. Mr. Filbrick then sold Malinda to the slaveowner Suggs.

Within the brutal conditions of slavery, James and Malinda, now both with their owner's last name Suggs, found comfort and love in each other. They had four children before James made his escape to the Army. The slaveowner Suggs worried that Malinda and her four children would join James in freedom, so he sent their two oldest children away to Georgia as hostages.

After the war, James's first thought was to reunite his family. He went north with a (white) officer of the Fifty-Ninth Colored Troops, a Captain Martin. They considered it too dangerous for James to return to Mississippi, and so Suggs asked Martin to help him recover his family. Martin already had a business trip to Mississippi planned, and he agreed to help Suggs. He easily found Malinda and the family, the two older children having returned from Georgia. He brought them north, and James, Malinda, and their children were reunited.

Suggs continued to work as a blacksmith, but at some point he heard the call to preach the gospel. He had been converted while still enslaved, and now took up his new calling. He preached for three years as pastor of a Free Methodist Church in Princeton, Illinois. He also toured, preaching at churches and camp revivals. He preached to the settlers at Nicodemus, and when he saw how poor they were, he traveled back to Illinois to solicit aid on their behalf. During 1878, 1879, and 1880 he traveled widely, preaching and appealing for aid for the Nicodemus Colony and for Kansas Exodusters. In 1879 the Free Methodist denomination issued him a certificate, endorsing him as an official collector of donations. Though never ordained, he became known as Reverend Suggs around this time.

He continued to tour widely and preach often, occasionally preaching at Nicodemus. *The Lawrence Tribune* called him "a noted colored evangelist from Illinois, who seems to be a revivalist of more than ordinary power." *The Beloit Courier* printed a letter from "A Citizen" (likely white) describing Reverend Suggs as not learned and having a penchant for making grammatical mistakes when speaking but whose sermons were powerful: "There is something in them that draws you to him with a cord of love. I would rather hear him preach than all the Dr.——— you could stack to Heaven."[4]

The problem was that when the Lord called, He didn't pay much. Worshippers didn't always respond with generous offerings. After leaving his Princeton parish, Reverend Suggs did not have a regular position, preaching only as a guest pastor on tour and at camp revivals. To provide more reliable support for his family, he entered a 160-acre homestead claim on February 21, 1884. He chose a location forty miles northwest of Nicodemus, in Phillips County, Kansas. He soon moved his family from Illinois to live with him. He built a two-room stone and frame house and sod stable, dug two good wells, and planted fruit trees. He seeded corn and wheat on the twenty acres he broke. He proved up his claim just two years later, using his military service to obtain three years credit toward the residency requirement. He listed four Black men, John Finley, Saul Washington, Henry Howard, and Henry Beachman, as his witnesses.[5] Suggs was fifty-five.

Reverend Suggs continued to preach as well as farm. The homestead supplied his family's material needs, while preaching served his higher calling. One morning he joined several other evangelists preaching at a large tent revival in Phillips County, just six miles from his home. He had been asked to exhort the young people, which he did at some length and with considerable success. As he stepped off the stage, someone told him a man wished to see him on the other side of the tabernacle. Reverend Suggs, always ready to provide private spiritual counseling, walked over to see him. But when he arrived, he was met by Phillips County Sheriff Woods and a detective, J. A. Rhodes, who read him an arrest warrant. They claimed Reverend Suggs was in fact Harrison Page, a man wanted for an 1878 murder in Illinois. Rhodes slapped handcuffs on Reverend Suggs, and he and the sheriff marched him out to the astonishment and dismay of the large camp audience.[6]

Phillips County did not have a lockup, so Rhodes and Woods took Reverend Suggs to Osborne City, in the next county over, which had a county jail. They locked him up while they waited for the legal papers to extradite him to Illinois.

The camp meeting was abuzz over the arrest of this renowned and much-admired Free Methodist pastor whom they had heard preach for years. Soon Reverend Suggs's friends began to organize his defense. They obtained a letter from Dr. Richard Edwards, a Congregational minister in Princeton, Illinois, testifying that he knew Reverend Suggs and that Reverend Suggs had been serving as a Free

Methodist pastor in that town when the alleged murder took place. They contacted E. P. McCabe, the State Auditor and Nicodemus resident, for help. The *Phillipsburg* (Kan.) *Herald* detailed Reverend Suggs's extensive reputation and achievements and declared that it was preposterous to arrest a man of Suggs's wide acquaintance and exemplary record as the alleged Harrison Page.

Reverend Lee, a white preacher at the camp, obtained a writ of *habeas corpus* in Phillipsburg. The county sheriff brought Reverend Suggs, after two terrifying nights in jail, before the Probate Judge of Osborne County. Reverend Suggs, whom others described as "dark as the ace of spades," argued he was not Page, identified as a "copper-colored mulatto." He proved to the judge's complete satisfaction that this was a case of mistaken identity. The Judge released Reverend Suggs unconditionally.[7]

Rhodes, it turned out, was a bounty hunter rather than an actual officer of the law. Reverend Lee now went to Squire Dickey, justice of the peace in Phillipsburg, and obtained an arrest warrant for Rhodes for kidnapping. Rhodes was captured and returned to Osborne, where the sheriff put him in jail. After a few weeks behind bars, Rhodes apparently got his case dismissed. But the *Phillipsburg Herald* still wasn't happy with the affair; its editor complained that Sheriff Woods' failure to scrutinize Rhodes' authority before issuing an arrest warrant had wasted a good fifty dollars of county taxpayer money.[8]

Reverend Suggs returned to his homestead and to preaching. The next year, along with several other evangelists, Black and white, he preached at another camp revival, where his popularity was if anything even greater. The daily crowds ran into the hundreds, and the camp's pavilion was many times filled to capacity. He continued preaching and farming until late in life. He died on May 22, 1889, at his son's home in Orleans, Nebraska.[9]

George Washington Carver, the internationally celebrated plant scientist, homesteaded in Kansas. He began life as an enslaved person owned by the Carver family in Missouri. He was born in 1861 or 1862, in the midst of the Civil War, when murderous partisan marauders laid Missouri raw. While George was still an infant, Confederate raiders attacked the Carver farm and kidnapped George and his mother. They took them to Arkansas to be sold. Moses Carver, owner of the kidnapped slaves, sent a man to recover them. He was only able to find George. George's mother had already been sold, and George never saw her again. When the tracker brought the baby back to the Carver farm, George was dehydrated, malnourished, and sick with the then-deadly disease of whooping cough. Susan Carver, Moses's wife, nursed him back to health, but the whooping cough damaged his vocal cords, leaving him with what was throughout his life described as a girl's voice.

After emancipation, the white Carvers decided to raise George and his brother, Jim. A childless couple, they were also raising several orphaned children of Moses's brother. They moved George and his brother into the "big house." George was frail and sickly, unable to work in the fields, so he did light household chores. Still, growing up on a farm, he learned a lot about plants, raising animals, and how to farm. He developed a talent for making plants thrive under his care, talking to them and seemingly having them answer back. He became a kind of plant doctor for sick plants in the neighborhood, all presaging his later career as a plant scientist. Sarah also taught him spinning, knitting, and fine needlework—arts he would pursue throughout his life. Moses was illiterate, but Sarah taught George to read, using an old Webster's speller, the only book in their home. A local schoolteacher also tutored George, after he finished his day teaching the white kids. Everyone could see that George was, as one of Moses's nephews described him, "the smartest boy I ever saw in my life."[10]

The white Carvers' support had limits, however, and they would not pay to send George to school. When George was about ten years old, with the Carvers' approval but likely determined to go with or without it, he walked eight miles to Neosho and the Neosho School for Colored Children. He arrived after dark and spotted a barn he decided to sleep in. In his good luck, the barn belonged to a Black family, Andy and Mariah Watkins, who agreed to let him live with them in return for chores.

Carver also talked his way into the Neosho School and attended for three years. By then he discovered that the poorly educated teacher had little left to teach him, and he was ready to move on. Meanwhile, the Watkinses, who were childless, had become so attached to George that before he left them, old Andy Watkins made out a will leaving all his property to George. (Carver never received any property, other than a large and much-revered Bible, because Mariah lived to a very old age and died destitute.)

When he was thirteen, George heard about a family moving to Kansas and hitched a ride. He took turns walking alongside the two wagons, so heavily loaded that not everyone could ride. They landed at Fort Scott, in the southeast corner of Kansas near Missouri and Arkansas. George worked at any job he could, also always trying to attend school. He rarely had the opportunity to attend regularly, and he remained itinerant for much of his early life. While in Fort Scott, George, who had never seen a whipping and rarely even witnessed a fight, watched in horror as a vicious white mob brutally beat and lynched a Black man and then burned his body.[11]

Carver worked his way north from Fort Scott to Olathe, near Kansas City. For a time the teenager lived with a Black family, the Seymours, and then moved with them to Minneapolis, a largely white town in central Kansas. Not yet twenty, he opened a laundry business using several loans from white bankers, who already must have been able to see the potential in him. He seemed to move easily

32. George Washington
Carver in 1906.
Tuskegee University
Archives and Museum.
Wikimedia Commons.

in white society, making friends mostly with white kids, being a
frequent dinner guest in white homes, and attending high school
(grades eight through ten) with mostly white students. He graduated
and was ready to move on.[12]

While in Olathe, he had worked for and become friends with the
Beelers, a white family of apple growers in the area. The Beelers' son,
John, about George's age, moved west to found a town, creatively
named Beelerville (later Beeler), in Ness County. Carver soon joined
Beeler in the new town.

In 1886 Carver, about twenty-five, decided to settle down. He filed
a homestead claim near Beelerville and became a farmer. Just eighty
miles straight north, Nicodemus was entering its boom period, but
Carver evinced no interest in joining the colony, although he knew
about it and later corresponded with Nicodemus resident Lulu Craig.
Carver now became part of a close-knit group of young Beelerville

men, all the others white, who homesteaded, worked to build the town, and joined together for literary and musical entertainments.

He built a fourteen-by-fourteen-foot sod house and whitewashed the walls with lime. He equipped it with a cookstove, bed, cupboard, two chairs, a table, washtub, ironing board, and flat iron. With few trees on his claim, Carver fed weeds, sunflower stocks, and dried cattle dung into his stove. The last, he remembered, left a steady stink around the house. Carver kept a garden, planted hundreds of fruit trees, and worked on the nearby Gregg-Steeley ranch to earn additional money. Mrs. Steeley, George Steeley's mother, didn't allow Carver to sit at the table during meals, and Carver's status on the ranch only improved when Mrs. Steeley returned to her own home.[13]

The Beelerville group, which included John Beeler, George Steely, Thomas Gibson, Bird Gee, and Carver, all claimed homesteads. Gibson died, and his widow Eliza inherited his claim. All the others, including Eliza, chose Carver to be a witness at their proving up. Carver chose George Steely and John, Elmer, and Bolivar Beeler as his witnesses.[14]

Carver found wresting a living on the Kansas plains to be difficult. He especially struggled in the severe winter of 1886–1887, when temperatures dropped to minus sixty-eight degrees. (This was the same winter that, hundreds of miles to the north, killed most of Theodore Roosevelt's cattle and destroyed his dream of being a western rancher.) The next spring and summer, grasshoppers reappeared, and while they weren't the enormous plagues of the mid-1870s, they nonetheless devoured Carver's crops.

Part of Carver's lack of farming success, surprising for someone so skilled in nurturing plants, can be traced to his continuing and unrelenting curiosity. His intense desire to know and to learn often led him to activities or trips during which he neglected his farming chores. In December 1877 the Beeler Literary Society elected Carver as its Assistant Editor (Elmer Beeler was Editor). In February 1888 the society presented a public program featuring, among others, Carver and Elmer Beeler singing a duet. In March, he joined John Beeler, Gee, and Steely in a plan to demonstrate tree growing for the public; Carver committed to planting one thousand trees. In September he went with John Lindell to the Castle Rock geological formation and returned with a full load of geological specimens. He also made sketches of the Castle Rock scenery which he intended to paint on canvas at home.

When Carver at some point lost all his household goods, presumably to theft, his curiosity was again to blame. The *Ness City Times* chastised him for his wandering ways, cautioning him to "Make your residence more continuous, young man."[15]

This was a small community, and Carver seemed to fit right in. The "Beelerville Buglings" column in the *Ness County Times* frequently reported on his activities. It informed its readers when he had some of his prairie acres broken, when he was improving his claim, and when he brought down the house with his "hoss" story at the literary society meeting. The *Ness City Sentinel* even published, in August 1886, a reminder telling him, "Geo. W. Carver, call at the post office, and get your trunk."[16]

Solo homesteaders, white as well as Black, suffered profound loneliness and depression from the extreme isolation of the prairie, and Carver was no exception. Later, Ole-and-Sven jokes or Garrison Keillor stories about "funny" Norwegian bachelor uncles play off this real-life circumstance, just as, more grimly, admissions to hospitals for the insane and high suicide rates documented it. But Black single homesteaders suffered the worst isolation. They lived solitary lives in a society that largely prohibited interracial marriage, and they had few opportunities to meet eligible partners of their own race. The result was that many lived their lives, or most of their lives, alone. James Suggs arrived in the Great Plains with his wife, Henry

Burden found two wives. But most, like Carver and Oscar Micheaux, whom we meet later, endured painful loneliness for many years.

Carver never found companionship on the plains. He may have been bisexual or gay, his intimate relations being veiled throughout his life. He had a friend in John Beeler and became close to the other young men living near the Steely ranch and Beelerville. They played music together, forming a quartet for which Carver played the organ, guitar, violin, and accordion, and they enjoyed many other projects and ventures together. Even with these friendships, Carver found life on a homestead to be lonely, which perhaps explains his frequent wanderings. Carver never did find a life's companion.[17]

Driven perhaps by his loneliness and intensely curious nature and facing locusts in the summer and punishing freezes in winter, Carver decided to give up farming. His plan seemed to be to turn his principal asset, his homestead, into cash and then invest the cash in furthering his education. He borrowed $300 from the Bank of Ness County, spending some of it to commute his homestead and saving the rest for school fees. He later erased the debt by selling his homestead to the banker's son for one dollar, the deal including the bank forgiving his loan.

He left his homestead with cash in his pocket and moved to Iowa, where he enrolled at Simpson College in Indianola, Iowa. He finished his education at the Iowa State Agricultural College (now Iowa State University). He began his distinguished career in science at the Tuskegee Institute, working with Booker T. Washington, and he became one of the most recognized names in American history. Carver's migration from slavery in Missouri to freedom in the West concluded with a return to the Jim Crow South. Ness County today claims Carver as one of its original homesteaders and honors him with a stone marker, surrounded by fencing to keep out wandering cows, set on the northeast corner of his former farm.[18]

Robert Anderson, after a long journey, both geographically and spiritually, also homesteaded in Nebraska.

He was born enslaved on a Kentucky farm on March 1, 1843. Late in his long and eventful life he reminisced about the hymn "I was once in bondage, but now I am free." He disavowed being religious or even being much of a singer, and he interpreted the hymn's words differently from what its author intended. Anderson recalled, "I once was in bondage, a slave in the old days preceding the Civil War, and owned but owning nothing, valued in dollars and cents as any other chattel, to be bought and sold, traded or worked, even as a horse or cow, as the financial needs or desires of the owner dictated."

He spoke these words as an old man, contentedly surveying his vast ranch. The hymn's refrain begins "I am dwelling now in Canaan."[19] Anderson had found his promised land in Box Butte County, Nebraska.

Anderson, like Henry Burden, James Suggs, and George Washington Carver, homesteaded alone, not associated with any colony. In the Great Plains, unaffiliated claimants constituted nearly 29 percent of all Black homesteaders, amounting to roughly one thousand individuals. Solo Black claimants likely gained title to about 220,000 acres. Most were men. Women, if never married, widowed, or abandoned by their husbands, were eligible to homestead, but they did so more frequently as members of a colony than by themselves. Including all family members, perhaps as many as four thousand to five thousand Black people lived on the farms of unaffiliated homesteaders.[20]

Anderson was born the property of the Robert Ball family of Green County, Kentucky. Ball operated a marginal farm worked by a small number of slaves and an overseer. Anderson's earliest recollections were of the slave quarters, where there were no luxuries, no conveniences, and no privacy. The conditions were wretched, he said, not because his owner was exceptionally cruel, because Robert Ball was not. Rather, slaveowner Ball "merely followed the custom of the times, a time when owners thought their Black slaves needed no more care than a hog or cow and sometimes got considerably less than a horse."[21]

Anderson's mother cooked for the Ball family, and her job gave her certain privileges compared to the men, women, and children who sweated in the fields. Her position benefited little Robert as well, as he sometimes enjoyed delicacies surreptitiously slipped out of the kitchen. His father was owned by a neighboring farmer named Anderson; he was called Anderson's Billy, or Bill Anderson. Both mother and father, Robert claimed, were "pure blooded African Negroes and there is not a drop of white blood in my veins." His owner, Col. Ball—the self-bestowed rank a southern courtesy title—was originally a stonemason before moving to the farm. The little boy became his owner's favorite, and he showed his esteem by giving the boy his own name, Robert Ball. (Robert would later change his name to Robert Anderson).

Robert grew up around farming, and he learned to raise flax and hemp and other crops through experience in the fields. He also worked in the main house, a rough, unpainted structure looking nothing like iconic antebellum mansions. He relished those times when his owners required him to serve food at their table, because he was able to sneak a few bites for himself. He would carelessly on purpose drop a biscuit on the floor, which then none of the whites would eat. He would usually get spanked or have his ears boxed, but he always got the biscuit.

He particularly loved cake. One evening when Mrs. Ball was hosting a social gathering, Robert helped serve. At some point while talking with her guests, Mrs. Ball held up a piece of cake. He saw this as an opportunity and pretended that he thought she was holding out the cake for him. He snatched the piece and thanked her for it.[22] Anderson's early experiences taught him to work for *and take* what he felt he deserved.

Col. Ball's wife was universally hated by the enslaved people on the farm. When Robert was six, his mother in some way upset her, and she demanded that Col. Ball get rid of Robert's mother. Although Col. Ball was reluctant to do so, his wife prevailed, and Ball sold Robert's mother to a slave trader who took her to work in the Louisiana cane fields. Robert never saw his mother again. Although Col. Ball did not believe or practice beating his slaves, his wife and field overseers did. On one occasion when Col. Ball was away, Mrs. Ball confronted Robert in the dining room over some perceived infraction. She whipped the fourteen-year-old boy within an inch of his life. Robert was transferred to field work, where overseers beat him.

In 1864, when Robert was twenty-one, he decided what he deserved was his freedom, and he snatched it just as he had snatched that piece of cake. The Union Army controlled most of Kentucky by then and Confederates had little presence. Instead of running away, Robert approached Col. Ball and told him he wanted to join the Union Army. Ball, though angry, told him that he needed to decide for himself what to do. Almost immediately, Robert said his good-byes. One evening, wearing all the worldly goods he possessed, he slipped through the fence and escaped the farm. He enlisted in Company G of the 125th Colored Infantry, U.S. Army, as "Robert Ball." A few months later, Lee surrendered to Grant at Appomattox Court House, effectively ending the war. Robert had not fought in a battle.[23]

Robert spent the next years in the Colored Infantry, stationed at Fort Bliss, Texas, along the Mexican border, and at Fort Leavenworth, Kansas. His unit skirmished with American Indians in both locations. On maneuvers he saw how much good land was available for those willing to claim it, and he yearned to own his own farm. Like so many others of his generation, he saw owning a farm as his opportunity to become independent and free.

He mustered out at Jefferson Barracks, Missouri, in 1867. The army paid him more than three hundred dollars in backpay and unpaid enlistment bonus, a very handsome sum—nine years later, Henry Burden was delighted to sell his whole eighty-acre Polk County claim for four hundred dollars. Robert returned to Kentucky, but he found conditions there harsh. War had completely disrupted the local economy, creating chaos. Landowners had little money to hire workers, and freedpeople scrambled to support themselves. Many landowners expelled their now-freed former slaves, turning them out of their homes and casting them adrift.[24]

He changed his name, becoming Robert Anderson. He moved to Iowa and used his army pay to buy some property. But he failed to inspect the ground before he purchased it. What the shady real estate broker promised as "fine farming land" turned out instead to be rough, unusable, and worthless. Robert was now broke again.

He worked for a time, making bricks used to construct Tabor College in a town that was well known as an important stop on the Underground Railroad. Then he worked for a farmer for three years, again saving his money. In 1870 he bought a team and wagon, intending to go west and homestead. He arranged a freight contract to carry goods to Lincoln, Nebraska, which paid for his trip.

After delivering his load in Lincoln, he continued west and filed an eighty-acre homestead claim in Butler County, Nebraska, just south of the Platte River. He felt he was now well on his way to achieving his dream of owning his own farm. He proved up his claim, listing three potential witnesses: George Mattingly, Jacob Nelson, and Charles Fredrick. Mattingly was a twenty-seven-year-old Black farmer, Nelson and Fredrick were both white. At the land office, Anderson called Mattingly and Nelson to testify. The GLO issued his patent on April 1, 1875, an April fools prank cruelly presaging his experience.[25]

Anderson also filed an eighty-acre claim in Lancaster County, closer to Lincoln, on August 22, 1874, the very day he proved up his first claim. He received patent on the Lancaster claim in 1876, likely using his military service as time toward the required residency period. He now owned 160 acres.

But 1874 to 1877 were difficult years. First came terrible locust plagues. Insects rained down on Anderson's farm just as they did on Henry Burden's place sixty miles to the south. Anderson remembered these bitter years as a time when grasshoppers came and ate up everything. Four years of drought followed the locusts, and the sun burned up everything he planted in the fields. "A great many times during my years on that homestead, it was a case of jack rabbit or no breakfast. It wasn't so bad in the summer time, but in the winter it was pretty hard to live at all." He lasted on the land until 1881, and then lost it. He had worked for three years in Iowa, saved his wages to invest in his Butler and Lancaster County farms, and put in eleven years of sweat and toil on them. But just as when the real estate man cheated him out of his army pay with worthless Iowa land, Robert now walked away from his Nebraska homesteads broke, having lost everything he had.[26]

He moved to eastern Kansas and hired on as a cook in a railroad camp, then for three more years worked as a farmhand. He was thirty-eight and illiterate, not being able even to write his own name. One winter, he went to school for three months, the only formal education he ever received, but as smart as he was, he evidently learned quickly. And he had learned from life.

With all his setbacks and failures, he still burned with desire to own his own land. He could never shake that dream he had formed in the army to be independent, not a hireling. He was convinced that owning land was his ticket to independence. He returned to the West, locating in the Lawn Precinct of Box Butte County in far western Nebraska.

In deciding to homestead alone, Anderson had chosen the hard path of making his way in an all-white society, virtually without Black friends, associates, or allies. He and other solo Black settlers

33. Robert Anderson on his ranch in Box Butte County, ca. 1915. Permission of History Nebraska, RG2973, PH02–01.

needed to be tough and single-minded, so that hurtful abuses and humiliations would not distract them from the prize of owning land. More than that, they had to learn to rely on their white neighbors, as those neighbors might rely on them, for all manner of help. They traded labor and shared machinery, and they socialized together to break the awful loneliness of the plains. Never did Black homesteaders depend on their white neighbors more than during that critical moment in the land office when they proved up.

The GLO required as part of proving up that each claimant advertise in local newspapers the names of four potential witnesses and actually call two of them to the land office to testify. Witnesses certified, under penalty of perjury, that the entryman had met all the homestead law's requirements—that the homesteader had constructed a dwelling and resided for five years on the claim, had taken no absences longer than six months, had plowed at least ten acres, and had made other required improvements to the land. Friends or acquaintances who lived far away, such as kin living in a distant

Black colony, could not provide credible testimony that the claimant hadn't left his land. Only nearby neighbors were in a position to vouch for the claimant's residency. For solo Black homesteaders, usually the only nearby neighbors were white.

If a witness lied or simply failed to show up at the land office, the Black homesteader would be out of luck—denied his patent, five years of sweat and labor down the drain. A prejudiced witness who didn't want a Black family in his neighborhood or who might covet the claimant's land for himself could do great damage. Solo Black homesteaders needed white witnesses they could trust to show up and speak the truth, affirming they had fulfilled all the homesteading requirements. We found no instances of white witnesses failing to testify for a Black homesteader who called them or of a Black home-steader losing his claim because of it. But solo Black homesteaders needed a great deal of faith in white neighbors while proving up.[27]

Anderson had already used up his homestead eligibility with his Butler and Lancaster County claims. The GLO issued its patent on the former to "Robert Anderson, alias Robert Ball," and its over-worked clerks may have failed to connect those claims to this new arrival in Box Butte. Whatever the explanation, in 1891 Anderson became owner of 159.5 acres through a cash sale, likely a commuted homestead claim. In 1894 he proved up a 160-acre claim under the Timber Culture Act. This law required him to plant ten acres of trees, which he did. He also built a two-room sod house. He remembered later how he cut the sod into large pieces and laid them on top of one another to make the side walls of his house. He fashioned his own window and door frames.[28] To help pay construction costs, he earned extra money working on the Burlington Railroad. The bottom line was that he was finally a landowner again.

Now well tutored in the cruel Great Plains climate, Anderson survived the lean years of the 1890s drought. He raised a small amount of wheat, had a good garden that he carefully watered from his well, and stocked his table with rabbits and grouse. He kept going, doing every task on the ranch that he could do himself. He added a few head of horses and a cow. He built frame additions to enlarge his sod home and attached a barn. "I was indeed a king" he later wrote fondly of that time, "I learned that the soil would raise anything if properly cared for."[29]

But Anderson more than survived, he thrived. He watched as drought, just like the one in the 1870s that had dried up his crops and squeezed him off his Butler County homestead, now drove his neighbors off their Box Butte land. Confident that rainfall would return, he purchased their failed farms. By 1896 Anderson owned 480 acres, some of which he plowed to raise wheat and oats. He continued purchasing his neighbors' land, increasing his holdings to 1,280 acres in 1902 and 2,080 acres by 1918. He raised cattle and bred horses, turning most of his ranch to pasture. He sold fresh berries and fruit in the nearby town of Hemingford. As soon as he reached town, customers rushed to his loaded wagon to buy what they wanted; afterward, Anderson took any remaining produce to be sold in the grocery store.[30] The agricultural boom during the Great War benefited Anderson, making his operation highly profitable.

Anderson's large property, a combined farm and ranch, required enormous labor to operate. He ran cattle and cared for up to fifty horses, plowed, planted, and harvested a quarter-section of grain fields, fed chickens and pigs, nurtured fruit trees and berry bushes, and maintained barns, fencing, and outbuildings. He drew on his own great capacity for work but needed more. He and his neighbors, Constantine Klemke and Joe Bartos, regularly helped each other with jobs like threshing and stringing fences that required more than one person. During times of peak work, especially foaling and threshing, he hired temporary workers, but the pool of available farmhands was shallow. Increasingly, he came to rely on his relatives, particularly his nephews, who came to stay at the ranch.

Anderson grew into a shrewd businessman, learning hard lessons from his costly earlier mistakes. He remembered his purchase of worthless Iowa land. He recalled when he lost his savings, $1,600 carefully hoarded during three years as a Burlington Railroad cook in Kansas. He had wanted to invest to get a good return, and so he loaned the money to an acquaintance. The man promised a handsome payoff, but unfortunately the fellow disappeared with Anderson's savings, never to be seen again. Years later, when Anderson took out a bank loan to purchase farm equipment, he had a strong suspicion that he was charged an "awful" interest rate.[31] Whether or not the banker had given him an unfair rate, Anderson's distrust tells us much about both his shrewdness and his vigilance in dealing with white businesses. These experiences taught him hard lessons, indeed.

Through it all, he accumulated property by being highly disciplined, personally abstemious, and plowing his profits back into his expanding ranch. He amassed a significant fortune during the opening two decades of the new century. His land, only a small part of which was mortgaged, was appraised at $61,000 in 1920; corrected for inflation, that would equal about $892,000 in 2022. With buildings, machinery, livestock, and all the other appurtenances of his ranch, his operation was worth well over a million dollars in today's money.

He became prominent and admired in his community. He "was very well liked. You couldn't help but like him," remembered H. Wildy, an acquaintance. Neighborhood children, like those of the Klemke and Bartos families, loved him for bringing them candy and playing games with them. He was respected for his pioneer status, his military record, and his farming and ranching success, all attributes that went far with rural people.[32]

The *Hemingford Journal* regularly reported the comings and goings of this familiar and admired figure. Its "Lawn" column recorded when he was sick and wished him a speedy recovery. The *Journal* noted when one Anderson nephew returned east after working a year on Robert's ranch and another arrived to take his place. It reported Anderson's trip with Matt Beaumont to the county fair. It reported his return to Hemingford after a trip on legal business to Alliance, the county seat. It commiserated when he had the misfortune to have his team run away, damaging his harness, spring wagon, and fence. It reported the good news that he found his wandering hog. It hailed his return to Hemingford after spending the winter in Arkansas with relatives and touring elsewhere in the South. And it printed an unusual public thanks, after the paper's editor had found himself one evening seventeen miles from town without transport; Anderson gave him a lift, letting the man avoid a long and lonesome walk home.[33]

Anderson became color-bearer for the Hemingford post of the Grand Army of the Republic and carried the flag at Fourth of July festivities. He served as a member of the program committee planning Memorial Day ceremonies. He was a member of the Masons and the Methodist Episcopal Church. When the occasion was right, he showed himself to be a dapper dresser, with a high white collar and tie, three-piece suit, and a handkerchief peeking from his breast pocket. Anderson had finally found great financial success and a measure of freedom in the Great Plains. He claimed, "It was to that determination [to own land], formed when a soldier, that I owe my independence today."[34]

In 1920, at the age of seventy-seven and after thirty-six years of farming and ranching in Box Butte County, Anderson retired. He sold all his livestock, farm machinery, wagons, and other equipment at a public sale. He leased his land to George Jessen, and Anderson lived with Jessen and his wife in an impressive new frame house Anderson built to replace the ranch's old sod home. Mrs. Jessen did Anderson's laundry and cooked his meals. He began traveling widely, to visit relatives and also to see the country. He even visited

Cuba and Mexico. He returned to Green County, Kentucky, and revisited the Ball farm where he had been enslaved.

Despite his prominence, he faced incidents that marked the racial boundaries within which he lived. He was known around town as Uncle Rob. While the local papers typically identified him just as "Rob. Anderson" or "Mr. Anderson," sometimes it was "Uncle 'Rob' Anderson" and in two or three stories even as "Zip Coon." He made a trip with two white ranchers to sell their cattle, and in Omaha they discovered that restaurants and hotels would not serve all three—where the white men were welcome, Anderson was not. They decided to stay together, and after much searching, finally found establishments that would serve them all. One Memorial Day, visitors to Hemingford used a racial slur to object to a Black man carrying the flag, inflicting a humiliation and marring the day even though local residents rushed to defend him.

Robert Anderson lived most of his life alone, but in 1922, at age seventy-nine, he traveled to Arkansas, where he met Daisy Graham. She was twenty-one and an impoverished teacher, the daughter of destitute parents. He fell in love with her, and while she didn't love him, she was awed by his wealth. In the hardscrabble Jim Crow South, she saw it as a good option to marry a man whose fortune would provide her an escape and perhaps a lifetime of financial security.[35] Robert and Daisy were soon married, and they returned to his ranch.

When Daisy and Robert arrived back in Box Butte, he took her to the Hemingford Hotel for a celebratory dinner. The new manager, not knowing who they were, refused them service. Even after someone informed the manager that Anderson was one of Box Butte's most prominent citizens, he refused to let them enter. The Andersons left humiliated and angry.

Daisy Anderson did not share her husband's frugal and self-denying ways, or maybe the old man simply wanted to dote on his young wife. Daisy's parents and two brothers came to live permanently at the ranch, and other relatives showed up as well. During the 1920s they mortgaged more and more pieces of his land to support a much fancier lifestyle. While Robert never felt the need to purchase an automobile before he got married, between 1923 and 1930 the Andersons bought several expensive Buicks from Russell Miller, the local dealer.

Daisy took over full management of the ranch as Robert declined. Farmers faced increasingly hard times in the 1920s, and Daisy made several costly investments to expand farm operations. Unfortunately, they failed to pay off. In 1928 she took out a new mortgage for the huge sum of $28,000. Robert found the prodigal mindset hectic and bewildering. Baffled by the changes, he could not halt or even slow the family's economic descent, and perhaps didn't try. He was old and tired, and though saddened by the family's new easy come, easy go style of life, he accepted it fatalistically.[36]

During these years, Robert recalled for Daisy his remembrances of his life, and she wrote them down. In 1927 they published *From Slavery to Affluence: Memoirs of Robert Anderson, Ex-Slave*. Daisy would publish multiple editions of the little book over the coming decades, adding her own life story and her increasingly bitter reflections on America's race relations.

In 1930 Robert, Daisy, her brother, and a friend were returning by automobile from Arkansas. In eastern Nebraska, they flipped their car over. The other passengers survived, but Robert died on the way to a Lincoln hospital. He was eighty-seven years old.

The banks foreclosed on Robert Anderson's now-mortgaged land. Daisy Anderson, propertyless, moved to Strawberry Park, Colorado, near Steamboat Springs. She lived out her life in straitened circumstances, finding it hard to support herself.

Homesteading offered a path for enterprising but penniless Black individuals to own land, accrue some wealth, and gain a measure of

34. Robert Anderson, ca. 1920. Permission of History Nebraska, RG2973, PH02–02, 104122.

independence. Some, like Robert Anderson, stayed on their farms as their life's work. Others, like James Suggs, relied on their homesteads to support their families while pursuing other callings, in his case preaching the gospel. Still others, like Carver and Micheaux, used the assets they accrued by homesteading to fuel their success in other occupations. The "success" of their homesteading venture was thus not whether they remained on the land and launched successful multi-generational farming enterprises—some did— but rather, in a racist society in which they were poor, success was defined by whether they were afforded opportunities to rise above their poverty. For many, it proved to be a rewarding and perhaps crucial step in their personal progress.

Among the new freedoms Black homesteaders exercised, they cherished most owning land. Being a landowner gave them standing. Robert Anderson summed up the profound wisdom of his hard-won and remarkable life:

I belong to the black race and am not ashamed of it. I have seen considerable trouble and hard times, but there was always a consolation in thinking that it was not as bad as it might have been. I have had some mighty good times and have enjoyed life immensely. I have found that happiness and enjoyment is where we make it, and there is a heap of satisfaction in knowing that I did my best. I have worked hard with honest and earnest intent, and feel that my labors have been rewarded. I have always tried to be fair and honest in my dealings with others and have always tried to give an honest day's work for an honest day's pay. I have friends all over the United States, and cannot help but feel that every one in Box Butte County, and western Nebraska, regardless of color, is my friend and I am proud of it. I always try to attend to my own business and never interfere with any one else. After all is said and done, I find that there is no greater rule for making and holding friends, for happiness and contentment and real enjoyment of life, than in doing unto others as I would like them to do unto me, and try to do it just a little bit better.[37]

As Anderson accumulated his fortune and enjoyed his independence, 150 miles east of Box Butte a group of Black homesteaders was similarly motivated by the dream of land and freedom. They prepared to try their luck in the Nebraska Sandhills, starting a new settlement called DeWitty.

7

DeWitty and the Sandhills

We had two big problems, the dirt and the flies. Summertimes
we twisted newspapers and lit the top. . . . The flame burned the
wings off the flies and then they were swept up and burned.

—AVA SPEESE DAY, daughter of DeWitty homesteaders

On April 11, 2016, a crowd gathered at a pull-off on U.S. 83 in
Nebraska's remote Sandhills. Pickups and parked cars lined the
side of the road. The crowd included both Black people and whites,
nearby neighbors, and some folks from as far away as Kansas and
California. They came to dedicate a historical marker for DeWitty,
a Black homesteader colony in Cherry County.

A white Washington-based author, Stew Magnuson, initiated the
idea of a marker, and DeWitty descendants Joyceann Gray, Catherine Meehan Blount, and Denise Scales quickly joined the effort.
Organizers hoped they might attract a dozen or two attendees; so
when 250 people showed up, everyone was surprised. Ralph Edinger,
an elderly white man from the Cherry County Historical Society,
stepped forward to welcome people. He started by confessing, "I
am completely overwhelmed by the size of this crowd."

Little wonder. Cherry County is larger than Connecticut, but it now
has only three thousand inhabitants outside Valentine, its county
seat. The U.S. Census Bureau designates an area as "unsettled" or
"frontier" if it has fewer than two residents per square mile; rural
Cherry County is far below that, only *half* a person per square mile.[1]

When the formalities were over, the crowd reconvened in the Brownlee Community Center, eleven miles up the road. The Ladies of Brownlee served what everyone agreed was a delicious lunch. Sonny Hanna, scion of white ranchers, led a tour for descendants to visit the lands their Black ancestors had once homesteaded and are now owned by ranchers. Some celebrants went to look for their ancestors' graves.

What the crowd came to honor has disappeared. There remain no buildings or other physical reminders of DeWitty, aside from a foundation and some artifacts. Yet descendants had already started probing DeWitty's history, and the marker dedication sped up their efforts. Artes Johnson and others formed the nonprofit Descendants of DeWitty and launched a website featuring photos and videos.

One video of that day shows relatives searching for the graves of the homesteaders. Joyceann Gray, upon finding the grave of her ancestor Goldie Walker Hayes, says, "We've come full circle, that's what we've done here." Johnson and archeologist Bill Hunt look for the grave of homesteader William P. Walker in the Brownlee cemetery. The gravestones are hidden under a heavy carpet of prairie grass mixed with some poison ivy. Johnson calls out, "Ok, Grandpa Walker, where you at? Where are you, sir?" Finally, they discover a stone, pull away the tangled roots that cover it, and sweep off the dirt. They pour water on the stone, and then emerges the name, WALKER. Family members raise shouts of joy amid their tears.[2]

Catherine Meehan Blount has developed a lively website, filled with photos, stories, genealogy, poetry, and insightful musings. Joyceann Gray published *Our DeWitty: And Now We Speak*, creatively reimagining the stories of DeWitty women. Descendants Denise Scales, Avis Roper, Delbert DeWitty, and others perform a dramatic play reenacting DeWitty times, which they present at museums and public schools and colleges. Family members began searching attics and closets for old photos and letters. Some reached out to

Buxton, Ontario, an ancestral stopping point for escaped slaves, where William P. Walker raised his family before his first wife died and where relatives still live. Having hit this rich and personal vein of history, descendants find each discovery urges them to do more.

Yet as Roper and Scales wrote in an insightful essay in *Black History Bulletin,* "The compelling question is, how do we harness the forces of scholarly and popular history, preservation, genealogy, teaching, and writing to discover, understand, document, preserve, and teach the significance of Black family settlement in the Great Plains?" Breaking into scholarly and popular history is particularly necessary, they argue, to remember people in remote or less populated spaces like the Great Plains who were previously neglected and left out of the history books.[3] Indeed it is.

Leroy Gields filed a 160-acre homestead claim on June 12, 1902, in Cherry County. On July 16, 1904, he filed for an additional 480 acres under the just-passed Kinkaid Act. One month later his sister Matilda Robinson filed a Kinkaid claim adjacent to his. She had already claimed a 160-acre homestead near Overton, Nebraska, 150 miles to the southeast, so her new claim was limited to 480 acres. Together, their 1,120 acres in Cherry County raised the flag for the new opportunities under the Kinkaid Act.

Congress acknowledged that the standard 160-acre homestead was too small to support a family in the drier regions of the West. Representative Moses Kinkaid of Nebraska—another Moses promising land!—proposed legislation allowing 640-acre claims, and in 1904 Congress approved his bill. The new law restricted the larger claims to an eight-million-acre region of western Nebraska, centered on the Sandhills region. In a provision that would be key to DeWitty settlers, the law also allowed homesteaders who already had proved up or commuted 160-acre claims to file for an additional 480 acres, as Gields and Robinson did.

Kinkaid opportunities attracted other Black homesteaders. The largest group came from Overton, Nebraska, in the Platte Valley, in what would be their second migration. They initially lived in Buxton, Ontario, where they or their ancestors who had escaped slavery could be safe beyond the reach of the Fugitive Slave Law. They had created a workable multiracial community there, but in the 1880s some wanted to return to the United States and take up homesteads. William P. Walker, whose parents had escaped from slavery, and the Meehans, Crawfords, and Rileys, about a dozen families in all, left Canada in their first migration and settled near Overton.

The families had prospered in Overton. It was a friendly town surrounded by more people on farms than in town, a place where the Black migrants worked hard and obtained a good living. William P. Walker filed for a 160-acre homestead and proved up in 1890. Three years later he proved up an additional eighty-acre Timber Culture claim. William Crawford owned his own house, though it was mortgaged, and in 1889 purchased eighty acres, perhaps commuting a homestead claim. Charles Meehan proved up his 156-acre homestead claim in 1890. The families worked other jobs as well. Meehan, for one, worked as a traveling salesman, making a circuit of the nearby towns of Cozad, Platte, and Ringold; locals called him "the soap and lace man."[4]

The families rooted themselves in the community, building lives filled with all the normal rhythms of joy, triumph, and sorrow. The local paper, the *Alfalfa Herald*, reported when William Crawford felt it was time to build an addition to his house. It recorded that George Riley drove to Lexington and Dennis Meehan was absent from school. It noted twelve-year-old Rose Meehan's victory in the girls' hurdles race at the big 1903 Fourth of July celebration. It shared the news that Albert Riley attempted to turn a handspring and cracked one of the bones in his right foot. C. H. Walker placed a notice in the *Herald* announcing that his "Chestnut sorrel Poney mare . . . branded on the left shoulder With letter Q" had gone missing. William P. Walker advertised that he had lost a horse. And the *Herald* mourned with others when Mrs. William Crawford died. The entire community sympathized, it said, with Mr. Crawford and his children during their bereavement.[5] The *Alfalfa Herald* was mostly filled with news about white people, but it chose not to identify the race of any individuals in its stories, nor did it ever allude to the mixed-race Meehan marriage.

The Black families in Overton sensed that as the bold new century opened, they should seize new opportunities opening to them. Ava Speese, later Ava Speese Day, remembered that when her grandfather, Charles Meehan, and others heard about the Kinkaid Act, they investigated and were excited by what they found out. They decided to migrate a second time.[6]

The families' main reason to leave Overton was land. They would be starting all over, and they were not young—Charles and Hester Meehan were then fifty-one years old, William P. Walker was sixty-three, William Crawford was sixty-six. But the Kinkaid Act offered them acreages three or four times what they owned in Overton. So too, they may have wanted to move to where their children could claim land when they came of age, because the region around Overton was getting filled up.

And they may also have had a deeper reason to move. The new colony offered *community* as well as land. Overton was a region of mixed-race settlement, where Black homesteaders were interspersed with a larger number of white settlers across the big landscape. Joyceann Gray, the DeWitty descendant, noted that this left "individual Black families lonely, with other nationalities and skin colors surrounding and isolating them for many miles."[7] The ambiance of the town was that of a white community, as reflected in the school, the town leadership, and the columns of the *Alfalfa Herald*.

While Overton accepted its Black minority, its makeup nonetheless made it difficult for Black residents to establish and maintain distinctly Black institutions and a Black community. The African American church had to draw parishioners from a very wide catchment area, forcing worshippers to travel inconveniently long distances to attend services. In a more homogenous Black colony, residents could more easily organize their church and control the schools. They would be freer to create their own community institutions and leisure activities, their own baseball team and dances. Community life in general might be safer, more convenient, more fulfilling. The Sandhills would be their new promised land.

Bonanza ranchers and the federal government had recently fought a bitter dispute for control of the region. Ranchers wanted to run their cattle on the open range, and they strung barbed wire to enclose huge swathes of public land. The federal government, after years of lax enforcement, began insisting that ranchers obey the 1885 Van Wyck Law, which forbade fencing public domain. This was the range wars come to western Nebraska.

Bartlett Richards owned the huge Spade Ranch and attempted to enclose over two hundred thousand acres of public land for his own cattle. In 1905 an Omaha grand jury indicted him, and at trial he was found guilty. Federal judge William Munger sentenced him to a small fine and six hours in custody. Bartlett served his sentence at the Omaha Club, a fine dining and watering hole.

Bartlett's sentence outraged President Roosevelt, who ordered the Justice Department to send a new prosecutor. In 1906 federal officials charged Bartlett and other Spade officials with conspiring to defraud the government by filing phony homestead claims and suborning witness perjury. The trial generated national headlines, and the judge this time sent Bartlett to jail for a year. Ranchers and lawmen began tearing down the illegal fences. Conviction of Bartlett and other ranchers opened land to homesteaders. The DeWitty migrants hoped, as the *Omaha Daily Bee* put it, to settle on "land a huge part of which was thrown open to settlement as a result of the recent prosecutions of land grabbers by the United States government."[8]

The Overton folks would be leaving behind, again, a settled and familiar life to set up in a wild and remote region. They did not set up a formal colony organization as the Nicodemus investors did, but they must have informally agreed among themselves to migrate together. The dozen Walker-Meehan-Riley-Crawford families who formed the core of the group knew each other well.

They worried about getting their federal paperwork correct because ownership in the Sandhills was confused. White settlers had earlier made 160-acre claims and then abandoned them. The status of that land was unclear. Then there were the phony homestead claims engineered by the Spade owners; now that they had been convicted, what was the legal status of that land? The migrants didn't want to file on contested land and build successful farms and then have some prior owner come along and invalidate their titles. And they wanted to make sure they met any new requirements imposed by the Kinkaid Act.

They requested advice from D. Clem Deaver, head of the Burlington Railroad's Landseekers Information Bureau. The Burlington had already sold all its own land, and it assigned Deaver to promote settlement along the railroad's right-of-way in hopes of increasing rail traffic and company revenues. Deaver took the train from his office in Omaha to Halsey, Nebraska, to meet with the Overton folks.

He came away highly impressed. "These people have struck on a fine plan, it seems to me," Deaver informed *The Omaha Bee* in April 1907. He found them to be intelligent, of high moral character, and with great ambition. He liked how they organized their settlement scheme in a businesslike way. "They wanted me to help them locate the cancelled [revoked] sections in the immediate vicinity of their colony and to get other good colored persons to join them." The *Bee* emphasized that these folks were, as it flashed in its subhead, a "Clean

35. Charlotte and William P. Walker (*left*) and Hester and Charles Meehan. Courtesy of Great Plains Black History Museum.

Set of People." It complimented the group for attracting a colony of men and women who were honest, thrifty, and ambitious. Deaver opined that the colony "will be no place for the sluggard, the parasite or the immoral man. The procession will move too fast for him and the atmosphere will be too uncomfortable for his happiness."[9]

Deaver may have been reassuring the *Bee*'s white readers that the settlement would be a righteous and self-supporting addition to the state. This was a familiar theme, assuaging fears that migrants might become costly dependents of state largesse. Earlier, the Nicodemus founders had stressed finding "people with means." Their unease with people who lacked means (the Exodusters) reflected concern about the quality of people joining their community as well as subtle class differences among migrants. And nearly simultaneous with Deaver's comment, Black recruiters for the Sully County colony in

South Dakota promised to bring in only the "better class of intelligent negroes." Deaver reminded readers that "We have in Nebraska several settlements of white people of different nationalities and every one of them is prosperous."[10] The Black colony, he insisted, would be no different.

The Meehans led one group which arrived in the Sandhills in 1907. Hester Meehan, a Black woman, was married to Charles Meehan, a white man. They moved to DeWitty with their six surviving children; the older ones were in their twenties and thirties, but Gertie was fourteen, and William just ten. Charles had been abandoned as an infant and raised in mixed-race settlements of Round Eau and North Buxton, Ontario. Hester was born in Round Eau. They played together as children in North Buxton. Charles believed himself to be Irish, and later his grandchildren would remember how he playfully assigned an Irish name to each of them.

Catherine Meehan Blount discovered, however, a different ancestry. Blount, the youngest of the Meehans' forty-four grandchildren, used DNA evidence to learn that Charles' biological family was actually the German-Jewish Himmelreich (later changed to Heavenrich) family of Detroit. The Heavenrichs were prominent and prosperous clothiers with a significant dry goods trade. Charles apparently never knew of the Heavenrichs or his connection to them. The "soap and lace man" had thus unknowingly entered a trade eerily similar to that of his biological family.[11]

Meehan, along with Robert Walker, Albert Riley, and brothers Maurice and William Brown left Overton in June. They drove wagons carrying their families and goods up to remote and largely roadless Cherry County. A month later William P. Walker led a second group including the William Crawfords, George Rileys, and other families, traveling by rail and then making the last thirty-five miles in wagons. Soon after arrival, they all staked Kinkaid claims northwest of Brownlee.

They settled along both sides of the North Loup River. The Gields and Robinson claims would form the eastern outpost. Others concentrated their claims in a band, about fourteen miles long and three miles wide, running from Dennis Walker's homestead on the northwest to the farm of Edward Hannahs on the southeast. What later became the tiny crossroads village of DeWitty was eleven miles northwest of the white town of Brownlee, and thirty-seven miles south of Valentine, the county seat. The migrants brought with them the fruits of their successful farming in Overton. Deaver reported, "Three [rail] carloads of goods for this settlement were shipped to Thedford, last week. The shipment consisted of homestead goods, farm implements, horses, cows, hogs, chickens; one family having three crates of chickens."[12]

The settlement grew in phases, with distinct family groups or individuals arriving from across the country. In 1906 three Black filers made Kinkaid claims. Then, in a flurry, eleven claimants filed in 1907, including the Walkers and Meehans. In 1908 three more filed, in 1909, six more, in 1910 another six, and in 1911, twelve more. Christopher Columbus Stith and his wife Margaret (she was William P. Walker's daughter), the Chester Curtises, the W. H. Murphys, and others came from Lincoln, stopping first in Valentine to file their claims and then going south to DeWitty. Families from Overton continued to move in as well. Six single women—Matilda Robinson, Sarah V. Curtis, Sadie Selby, Arnetta Hayes, Charlotte Conrad, and Peryle Woodson—filed their own claims. As Walker descendant Joyceann Gray observed, "Women wore six shooters and rode horses as well as any of their male counterparts."[13] From Gields's first filing in 1902 through 1911, forty-three Black claimants filed entries.

DeWitty's population peaked in 1915 at around 150 residents. Not surprisingly, the number of residents closely followed the number of homestead claims occupied, including both those already proved-up and ones in the process of being finalized. Families remembered differently the community's size, some claiming the population rose as high as 185 or 200, while others estimated no more than 85. Reverend Burckhardt, the colony's ecclesiastical leader, claimed there were 150 souls in the immediate vicinity. Ava Speese thought about forty families lived in DeWitty at any one time, though as many as one hundred families may have come and gone over the years.[14] We examined decennial censuses, land tract books, memoirs, and other materials to identify 155 Black people who lived in DeWitty. But our figure is likely an undercount, and our best estimate is that between 175 and 200 Black people lived in DeWitty at some point during these years.[15]

The families spread out across the vast treeless landscape, where the huge dunes create an undulating, bumpy horizon. They lived on their claims to fulfill the law's residency requirement. Some claimants, like Charles Murphy, filed for the full 640 acres allowed by the Kinkaid Act. Others, like the Meehans and Walkers, had already proved up 160-acre homesteads elsewhere and so were limited to 480-acre claims. Proved-up DeWitty homesteads averaged 508 acres and in total amounted to 29,464 acres. Some residents may have filed claims which they failed to prove up (but in the meantime, controlled the land for five or seven years), or purchased or leased additional lands. DeWitty settlers likely owned or controlled 35,000 to 40,000 acres in all. Long distances separated farm families, as their big properties spread them apart.

DeWitty became a rural neighborhood, a locus of concentrated Black homesteading. Almost all residents were farmers, and DeWitty never developed as a "town." Few residents clustered around the general store and post office, and the settlement was never incorporated. Despite the distances between farms, DeWitty nonetheless grew into a true community, bonded by kin ties, shared histories, church and communal events, and the common struggle for survival. It included all the Black residents nearby (and at least one prominent white man, Charles Meehan), giving DeWitty its distinct identity. Many residents were related: William P. Walker, whose first wife died and left him with three children, married Sarah Riley, widowed with three children of her own. They went on to have four children together. Residents worked hard to build community-enhancing institutions, especially schools and churches, which strengthened communal affiliations.

Beyond their own community, residents considered as "local" the nearby white-owned ranches and the region south of DeWitty, including the towns of Brownlee, Thedford, and Seneca, with which they conducted business on a regular basis. By contrast, Valentine, farther away to the north, required a trip on horseback of several hours to reach. It was largely outside their orbit, even though the *Valentine Democrat* occasionally carried a "DeWitty" column in its "All Around the County" feature. DeWitty residents typically traveled to Valentine only to do official business at the courthouse.[16]

Some Black families, the Emanuels, Meehans, Walkers, and others, came to DeWitty already experienced in farming. D. Clem Deaver enthused, "One most excellent feature of this colony is that several of the pioneers are practical farmers. They . . . have learned the lessons of frugality and industry, as well as the methods of successful farming."[17] Other families including the Prathers, Stiths, and Selbys came to DeWitty as novices in farming.

But none of the settlers had experience farming in the Sandhills. It is a geologically and topographically unusual region of enormous sand dunes covered with a thin layer of topsoil and grass. The topsoil provides little nutrition to growing crops, and rainfall drains quickly through the underlying sand. The soil wears out after a few years. The new migrants needed to learn, and learn quickly, how to grapple with the region's peculiar climate, soils, and hazards. They learned through trial and error which crops would grow and which did poorly. And always they were subjected to farmers' luck: whether the rains came at the right time, whether they avoided hail and grasshoppers, whether the cows calved successfully. As with white claimants, some prospered and did well, while others did poorly.

In 1912 Miles H. DeWitty and his brother erected a sign on the front of a small frame building announcing, "DeWitty Bros., General Merchandise." Inside their store they also opened a U.S. Post Office. They placed their building on Miles's Kinkaid claim about a mile south of the North Loup River, roughly in the center of the band of Black farms. The store offered a limited inventory of items for sale, much of which DeWitty had purchased at the Brownlee general store. The settlement had no official name, so DeWitty, a Texan with Texas-sized self-assurance, named it after himself. Lacking competitors, the name caught on. In 1916 Dennis Meehan won appointment as DeWitty's second postmaster, and he immediately renamed the community "Audacious." Although the new name better expressed the community's pioneering aspirations, by then "DeWitty" was in common use, and it stuck.[18]

The new arrivals set about their most urgent task, building shelters. Some built frame houses, but most used sod. Soddies were both cheap and practical. Lack of trees except for the occasional cottonwood meant local lumber was scarce and building a frame house expensive. When owners could afford it, they made the walls of sod but used boards for the roof and floor. A family stockpiled any boards to be used, as well as window and door frames, the latter often being homemade. Then a team of men would cut the sod, haul it to the house site, and lay it like bricks. Four men could construct a substantial sod house in three or four days. Charles and Hester Meehan proudly pose at Christmas 1913 with nineteen of their children and grandchildren. Their substantial sod house stands immediately behind them, and a sturdy sod barn can be seen in the background.

36. Charles and Hester Meehan with family members, DeWitty, Christmas 1913. Permission of Catherine Meehan Blount.

If the family lacked money for a board roof and floor, they made do with dirt floors and a roof constructed out of tree boughs overlaid with sod. Some, like DeWitty resident William Crawford, lived in half dugouts at first, open air style, until they got their sod houses built. The Stiths moved to DeWitty in the summer of 1914 and lived in tents until they could finish their soddy.[19]

Sod houses with their thick walls were said to be cooler in summer and warmer in winter than poorly insulated frame houses. But they weren't perfect: "We had two big problems, the dirt and the flies," recalled Ava Speese. "Summertimes we twisted newspapers and lit the top. . . . The flame burned the wings off the flies and then they were swept up and burned." Charles Meehan astonished other settlers by plastering the entire inside of his soddy. "No one had a home as easy to keep clean as grandma [Meehan]"[20]. Still, some homesteaders built wood houses right away, and most who lived in soddies moved out of them as soon as they could afford to build a proper frame house.

Sod houses made for close quarters. Ava Speese described her family's home: "The folks' bed and dresser were in the southeast corner. Behind the door was a high cupboard. The north end was the kids' beds with the chiffonnier [a high dresser with a mirror] as a divider. A window in the north wall later became the door to a lean-to kitchen. Between the beds was space for table and chairs, cook stove, heater, and the organ." Along with the sod house came a root cellar, dug deep as a room, the excavated dirt used to build up the ground around it. The builder then roofed it over and piled dirt on top. The cellar remained warm enough in winter to keep the stored jars of canned tomatoes and beans from freezing, and cool enough in the summer to prevent food from spoiling.[21]

Wood was so scarce that if someone left the colony, he sold his roof and floor. The buyer hitched a four-horse train to the floor and dragged it out from under the walls, which promptly fell down. Next, he hitched on to the roof and pulled it over the floor. Then he set off across the prairie to where he wanted to build his house. Settlers in DeWitty who could afford lumber had it shipped by rail to the depot in Seneca, about thirty-five miles away. Then they hauled it back to their building sites by team and wagon. Some homesteaders were reluctant to build wood structures until they learned at proving-up the exact boundaries of their claims.[22]

DeWitty residents, like most homesteaders, farmed to support their families. Fields averaged about twenty acres, and a few farmers planted as many as forty acres. Almost all farmers grew corn as their principal crop, because they could use it both as feed for livestock and at the dinner table. They put up large amounts of hay, as the Ed Hannahs family is shown doing in the photograph. They needed hay during the winter for draft animals, cattle, and riding horses, and some made a profit selling it as well.

37. Ed Hannahs family haying at DeWitty, ca. 1915.
Permission of History Nebraska, RG2301, PHOI–022, 22320.

Dan Meehan grew cane, which he processed in a little mill he
constructed. He hitched horses to walk round and round, crushing
the stalks; then he boiled the juice in a big iron cauldron. He sold the
molasses. Others tried sorghum. Some grew oats. But many found
that the most reliable crop was potatoes, which could survive despite
the harsh conditions. Some farmers reported yields of five hundred
or six hundred bushels to the acre during the first few years.[23]

Families also raised cattle, chickens, pigs, and brood mares,
sending their cattle and horses to market in Omaha via the rail
connection in Seneca. They broke the mules to harness, then sold
them. They sent cream from their dairy cows to be sold in Seneca
or Thedford. They relied on hogs as their main source of protein,

but they also hunted grouse, prairie chickens, ducks, geese, rabbit, and occasionally deer for meat. Women and children often fished along the North Loup River.[24]

They also made good use of local berry patches. Every fall a group of the men and sometimes a group of women would take two or three wagons and go several miles up into the Wamaduze Valley northwest of the settlement and pick wild plums, grapes, cherries, and chokecherries to make into jelly and jam. They'd stay for three or four days, sometimes a week, to harvest the fruit.[25]

The families perpetually lacked cash. During their first few years, farmers found that raising crops and livestock, gathering local fruits, and hunting and fishing would feed their families, but those activities did not earn them much cash to purchase supplies. Even when they skimped, they still needed money to buy tools, building materials, plows to break the prairie sod, fencing wire, coats and shoes, some food items, and other supplies. Some families had arrived with savings, but most families needed income from off-farm jobs to survive.

Some DeWitty men took employment as carpenters and masonry workers throughout Cherry County. Albert Riley and two to three of his neighbors would go out and build a sod house for which they charged fifty dollars a house. They built eighteen or twenty sod homes in the area. A. P. Curtis worked for the railroad while maintaining a family home in DeWitty. Several men, Charles Speese among them, freighted ("drayed") for people and hauled coal for the school district.[26] Others hayed the county roads. They rented or leased their pastures to ranchers, who paid them thirty-five dollars a month to use the land during winter. Ava Speese's family, despite having only eighty acres, rented out hay and cropland the entire time they lived in Nebraska. Some DeWitty settlers even resorted to leasing out their entire homesteads.

Most residents who worked outside DeWitty found jobs at the nearby white-owned ranches. The Hanna and Faulhaber families employed Black men as wranglers, handymen, and cooks. Albert Riley worked as a farmhand for the Triple-L ranch, and William Ford walked fourteen miles from his home to the Lee ranch and back each day to work. Some white ranchers employed entire families: men worked with the animals or in the barns, while women cooked in the bunkhouse kitchens and their daughters washed dishes. Chris Stith cooked on the Box T Ranch's chuck wagon on cattle drives and during branding season. Other times he and his wife Maggie both worked in the kitchen of the ranch house.[27]

Together, Black DeWitty residents and white landowners developed a mutually dependent and mutually beneficial economy. The DeWitty people relied on white ranchers to employ them, and they earned the cash they desperately needed, especially before their fields produced saleable crops or when drought or insects left them little to harvest. Reciprocally, the ranchers benefited by employing trustworthy workers who, because they also farmed in the area, were more likely to be reliable and work responsibly than was the case with transient hands.

Their relationship of mutual dependency was not equal, but it appears to have been largely nonexploitative. In the South, white landowners ruthlessly exploited Black farm laborers because the laborers worked on the landowners' land and had no alternative way of earning a living. By contrast, in DeWitty Black people seeking ranch jobs were themselves *landowners*. If they felt exploited, they could return to work their own farms.

We don't know how much the Hannas, Faulhabers, and other ranchers paid their Black employees, and undoubtedly workers and bosses experienced the normal employee-employer irritations over wages and other work matters. But their relationship had few of the exploitative features that characterized the southern system—unlike in the South, it did not involve credit relationships, sharecropping, or wages paid in a form that could only be spent in a landowner-owned store. In DeWitty residents continued to work jobs on the ranches throughout the colony's existence, suggesting that they had the power to bargain for acceptable employment terms.[28]

DeWitty residents did most of their doctoring themselves. Doctor Roth, the nearest trained medical person, was a full day's ride away. Home doctoring was typically women's work. Sandhills author Mari Sandoz notes about wives among (white) homesteaders, "Particularly important was her place in accident or sickness, with doctors so few and far between." So it was for Black women as well. Hester Meehan served as midwife for the entire colony, except during her own eleven births, when Charlotte Walker attended her.[29]

As rural people, they were familiar with binding up injuries and nursing fevers, using goose grease, castor oil, hydrogen peroxide, Spon's Distemper Cure, turpentine, and lots of Vaseline. Corina Walker, William P. Walker's daughter, was one of DeWitty's healers. She combined modern remedies with traditional cures. Sixth-generation descendant Wayne Brown recalled, "She had a special mix that my Grandmother Betty [Corina's granddaughter] understood. And when you would get sick, Grandma would always slip you a little bit of something and would say it was from that time in DeWitty." They had trained themselves to be doctors, whether ministering to sick horses or sick people. As Brown noted, "That's always stuck out to me that these people brought a little bit of Africa with them. . . . They came with their own solutions to get through, with medicine and salve and husbandry."[30]

Black girls and boys, like their white counterparts, contributed crucial labor to the endless work of running a farm. For the photo, Edna Brown Jackson showed off the prize Hereford calf she nurtured. Ava Speese worked under the hot summer sun, "Picking potato bugs and burning them." Many years later, Lena, the oldest Speese daughter, grimaced as she remembered, "We always had a large potato patch, and, oh, my back hurt so from carrying those

38. Edna Brown Jackson with her calf, on Maurice Brown's homestead, DeWitty, ca. 1915. Permission of History Nebraska, RG2301, PH02–02, 22169.

potatoes when we picked them in the fall." An excellent rider, she also helped herd the cattle on horseback, usually riding bareback. Inside, she helped with the cleaning and washing and ironing and taking care of babies.

Older male children helped their parents in winter cut heavy blocks of ice from Buffalo Creek and pile it up in the icehouse. They carefully covered the ice with straw, and it kept perishables cool in the spring and summer. Throughout the year young adults fed and tended livestock, and in summer they joined the grownups in haying. Younger children milked dairy cows, starting with an Armour's or Swift's two-pound lard pail and later moving up to a five pounder. They helped to wean piglets by feeding them in a bowl or pail, and they'd pull weeds for pig feed. After school, they'd bring in enough water to fill the boiling pan for washing dishes and keep bringing it in until the rinsing was done.[31]

Early one bright autumn morning, Charles Speese took some machinery out to where he was working in his field. He also needed the team and wagon that day, so he left instructions for his daughter Lena to get her little brother Clifford and drive the wagon out to meet him. When the children got to the wagon, Lena found the family shotgun lying in its well. Somehow the gun's hammer got cocked. Lena didn't know how to uncock it except by pulling the trigger, so she pulled it. The shot blasted out just over Clifford's head, missing him by inches. Lena said, "We didn't tell our mother about that until we were grown."[32]

From early spring until snow covered the ground, children were expected to find "Hereford coal" for the stove. Rattlesnakes sometimes hid under the warm cow patties, so parents instructed their children to first take a stick and turn the chip over before picking it up. They loaded the chips on a wagon and hauled them home. Best was when they found a patch no one else had discovered, so they could go back and load up several times until they had picked it clean. Ava Speese remembered, "We once picked six loads in a day, loads with double sideboards."

Back home, they stacked the chips near the kitchen ("but not too near") for further drying. When it rained, neighbors up and down the valley cried out, "Cover up the chip pile!" Regardless of what they were doing at that moment, they dropped everything until they covered the pile. Collecting cow patties was a chore that seemed never-ending.[33] But children's work freed their parents for the heavy field work or to take off-farm jobs.

Initially, DeWitty residents conducted most of their personal business in Brownlee, a tiny settlement—its population peaked in 1940 at eighty-six residents—which nonetheless featured a bank, blacksmith shop, livery barn, drug store, and general store. The

Brownlee store carried yard goods, a few dresses and blouses, over-alls, and work shoes. But DeWitty residents like other homesteaders made extensive use of the Sears, Roebuck and Montgomery Ward catalogs to purchase clothes, household items, fruit, tools, farm implements, seeds, and even baby chicks. Their goods came on the railroad and were delivered by Rural Free Delivery mail. They bought heavy goods that they couldn't get in Brownlee, like lumber and coal, in Seneca, then hauled them home.[34]

The DeWitty homesteaders insisted that their children be well educated. Their commitment came in part from their own experiences because many of the homesteaders were well educated themselves. Robert H. Hannahs and his wife Rosetta both were literate and certainly wanted their son Herbie to be educated. William P. Walker had served as postmaster, among other positions, in Buxton. Charles Meehan had been a traveling salesman. Both jobs required not just literacy but *facility* with words and numbers. They needed to read Post Office or company policies, record and keep accounts, correspond with customers and vendors, and do other tasks drawing on a variety of mental skills. And they retained that memory of when learning to read was denied during slave days, so for them, education was part of being free.

No schools existed in the North Loup valley when they arrived, and the newcomers soon got to work organizing them. Descendant Joyceann Gray noted that all children "got an education, some more than others but each had a choice in that. All the children were encouraged to choose their own path after basic education was firmly in place."[35]

The parents' commitment also coincided with deeper channels in African American thought. However they felt about the debate between Booker T. Washington and W. E. B. Du Bois, they were surely *aware* of it. Du Bois and Washington differed on the purposes of schooling and whether to prioritize higher levels of education. High schools were just becoming more common in the nation, and only a small minority of the population, Black or white, had graduated that level. Some homesteaders sided more with Washington's idea of basic schooling, self-help, and building self-reliant Black communities, while others favored Du Bois's call for higher education for the talented few to support political and legal activism, challenge Jim Crow, and end disenfranchisement and discrimination. Regardless, *both* visions required Black people to be educated.

The homesteaders established legally recognized school districts to create a taxing authority and to formalize the construction and management of neighborhood schools. Each district had a one-room schoolhouse. Residents formed school Districts 108 and 113 in April 1908, District 110 in February 1909, and District 164 in March 1911. As the rural community attracted new settlers and its own children grew to school age, the residents altered the school district lines to meet the fluctuating number of students enrolled.

Teachers had to accommodate to the facilities available. Belva Spicer, a DeWitty teacher in the Kidderville District (District 164), started the school year meeting her class in an abandoned sod building across the river from the Curtis house. She had an old horse which she rode to and from school. Ava Speese remembered "There was no bridge so the river had to be forded every day." As winter approached, Spicer moved her class into the Curtis home. She portioned off one end of the rectangular sod house for the school, the teacher standing at the front of the house and double seats set out for her sixteen students. When the snow and ice melted, they moved back across the river again.[36]

Fernnella Walker, Goldie Walker Hayes, Esthyr Shores, and William Meehan, all community residents, took their turns teaching.

39. Fernnella Walker with her class at DeWitty School, ca. 1915.
Permission of Joyceann Gray.

Goldie's school rooms were always very clean, with carpets on the
floors and white curtains at the windows. She collected the best
books and equipment that she could persuade the school board to
purchase. DeWitty teachers evidently provided high quality instruction—at least no parents left complaints about them.

Talented and exuberant young poet Bill Meehan, at age nineteen
and before he became a teacher, included in his poem, "Nebraska,"
the line, "And when it comes to training, we've the very best of
schools." That may have been a boast about Nebraska, not necessarily DeWitty, but in another poem, "On the Banks of the North
Loup River," he wrote specifically about his home community. In
one stanza, he expressed both his impatience as a child for school
to open and his relief when it did:

Here we had no school for ages,
but a good school now we have,
On the banks of the North Loup River,
where the school less days are past.[37]

The DeWitty schools carried students through eighth grade, sometimes a bit more, so children either stopped then or had to go elsewhere to attend high school. Brownlee apparently didn't have a high school either, so DeWitty kids went to Thedford or Seneca. Both towns were far enough away that their mother or another adult, with students in tow, lived in town during the few winter months when school was in session. When Rosetta Speese's children finished tenth grade at DeWitty, she took Ava, Howard, and Lena to Seneca, but school authorities told her they did not have room in school for her children. The Thedford school sent word that it would welcome them. Rosetta and the children moved there, all of them living in three small rented rooms. She gave birth to twins that winter, and the older children attended school with no difficulty. For several years, they stayed in Thedford each winter.

DeWitty parents were also keen to encourage the children's at-home learning. They diligently combed libraries and state agencies to acquire educational materials to enrich the home environment. They persuaded the state library to mail them books on loan. The Speese children remembered receiving "books galore." They read the entire *Encyclopedia Britannica*, the poetry of Paul Lawrence Dunbar, classics, and autobiographies.[38]

Parents enjoyed playing instruments and made sure their children had the chance to develop their musical talents. Children joined in the family's music making from a young age. Charles Speese had an excellent singing voice and considerable experience in performing publicly. At home, he and Rose wore out two pump organs and a piano while living in their little DeWitty sod house. Community activities always included music as well. At neighborhood socials and dances they usually had an orchestra, a violin, guitar, mandolin, and piano, and they sang with the same exuberant spirit with which they played baseball.[39] They filled their church services with music, the choir and accompanists typically setting high standards for musical quality.

They also encouraged other forms of creativity. William Meehan began writing poetry at age seven. By thirteen he could render a distressing childhood accident involving an ax into a rueful and self-mocking narrative poem. By nineteen, he was writing lyrical verses about his mother, the beauty of the Sandhills, and pride of place. Ava Speese Day also became a writer.

According to their children and grandchildren, the most important legacy the homesteaders gave them were the values, life habits, and grit which the older generation taught by example. Herbert Hannahs, Lena Speese, Mildred Meehan, Ellen and Estyr Ford, and the other students in teacher Fernnella Walker's classroom drew deep life lessons from observing their parents' hard work, resilience, dignity, and sense of personal worth.

While important to DeWitty parents, schooling may have reflected one boundary to racial mixing in Cherry County. DeWitty leaders created Districts 113 and 110 in areas that included both Black and white children, pioneering integrated schooling four decades before *Brown v. Board of Education*. Don Hanna Sr., his brother Francis, and the Pedersen children were among the white students learning side-by-side with Black children in District 108 under the tutelage of a Black teacher.

After a year, however, school authorities redrew the boundaries of the district, and the District 108 school merged with Goose Creek School District (District 127). The change separated Black and white children. It is unclear whether whites, Blacks, or both pushed for the change, but rarely is this sort of segregation coincidental. In the

41. William "Bill" Meehan, age eighteen, DeWitty resident and poet, 1915. Permission of Catherine Meehan Blount.

1918

42. (*opposite top*) Charles and Rosetta Speese with their children, Howard, Ava, Lena, Celeste, and Clifford, DeWitty, 1917. From the collection of Katannah Day, daughter of George and Lena Speese Day, via Jeffrey Gilchrist. Permission of Catherine Meehan Blount.

43. (*opposite bottom*) Charles Meehan with team at DeWitty, ca. 1914. Permission of Catherine Meehan Blount.

44. (*above*) Boss Woodson and his sister, Nora Woodson, in DeWitty, ca. 1918. Permission of Joyceann Gray.

45. (*opposite top*) Fernnella Walker on horseback in
DeWitty, ca. 1918. Permission of Joyceann Gray.

46. (*opposite bottom*) Maurice Brown in chaps in DeWitty,
ca. 1918. Permission of Joyceann Gray.

47. (*above*) Community celebration at DeWitty, ca. 1914.
Permission of History Nebraska, RG2301, PHOI–024.

48. (*opposite top*) DeWitty residents fishing along the North Loup River, Nebraska, ca. 1920. Permission of History Nebraska, RG2301, PH01–011.

49. (*opposite bottom*) Novella Selby as a baby, with unidentified woman, DeWitty, ca. 1922. Permission of Catherine Meehan Blount.

50. (*above*) Robert Hannahs family in DeWitty, ca. 1915. Permission of History Nebraska, RG2301, PH3–03, 22372.

51. Fernnella Walker Woodson with baby, Charles Woodson, in DeWitty, ca. 1920. Permission of Joyceann Gray.

1960s geographer C. Barron McIntosh studied the redistricting, meticulously looking for evidence of racial motivation. He concluded, "One might detect a bit of racial discrimination in the exchange of land between District 113 and 110, and in the apparent exclusion of sections three and eight, both occupied by Black[s], from District 100 when it was formed. However, no written or oral evidence has been recorded to verify such an assumption." Despite repeated tries, McIntosh found no direct evidence of racial discrimination, nor did DeWitty residents complain of discrimination.

In another ambiguous case, Seneca school officials may have denied enrollment to the Speese children because of racial prejudice. Howard was fourteen, Lena thirteen, and they were ready for a higher grade than the DeWitty school offered. Charles had ridden his horse the long trip to Valentine to present their case to the county school board, and he obtained approval for them to enroll. But the children spent only one day in Seneca before the red-faced superintendent pulled them all out of class. He informed them that they couldn't stay because the Seneca school was full. Family lore says that a white family that moved into Seneca the next day had no trouble enrolling their children.

The Speese family returned home. Soon the Thedford superintendent sent his message that they could enroll in the Thedford school. Rose enrolled them in Thedford right away. But both the school redistricting and the Seneca incident raise strong suspicions about whether whites were blocking Black children from entering their schools.[40]

Children and grandchildren of DeWitty homesteaders took to heart their elders' exhortations to become educated. Amos Walker, William P.'s oldest child, graduated from the University of Nebraska in 1899 with a degree from its Teachers College. William P.'s daughters Fernnella and Goldie graduated from Kearney State Normal School (now University of Nebraska at Kearney) and also became teachers. His daughter Sweet studied at Douglass Hospital in Kansas City, Kansas, a facility opened in 1898 to serve the Black patients who were largely excluded from the city's segregated hospitals. Sweet became a nurse.[41] William (Bill) Meehan was a teacher and aspired to become a lawyer. Chris and Maggie Stith's son, Dwight, became a doctor. Charles and Rose Speese's daughter Norma became a nurse and professor. The roll of DeWitty descendants' educational achievements goes on and on.

When asked how the homesteaders became so committed to education, descendant Wayne Brown observed, "You know, as I scrub through the history, I can't find where they learned this lesson, but it seemed that education was very important to the Walker family, from Goldie to Fernnella and to the sons as well of [Miles] DeWitty. I mean, education was the key."[42] Abram Hall would have smiled in agreement.

Much of DeWitty's social life revolved around church. Initially Sunday services were held in private homes. Community members held a fundraiser to finance a church building, and it was said that everyone pitched in, even those who could not donate money. They converted a sod schoolhouse, located about five miles from DeWitty's store, into the new church. Photos show white neighbors working alongside their DeWitty counterparts. Congregants made the furniture, and the congregation acquired a pump organ and two stoves. The County Judge of Cherry County donated a large Bible.

The St. James African Methodist Episcopal (AME) Church opened in 1910 and could hold 120 parishioners. Reverend O. J. Burckhardt, originally from Lincoln, was the first minister and lived in William Steadman's home until the community built a parsonage. Reverend Burkhardt never filed a homestead claim, intending instead to focus on meeting his parishioners' spiritual needs, but later pastors both preached and homesteaded.

DeWitty residents affiliated with various denominations, but most supported the local church by attending services and making donations during offerings. The large Kinkaid claims spread families across a wide expanse, and some parishioners traveled long distances, as much as ten or more miles, to attend. Community members worshipped on Sundays, ate big meals and socialized together, and then about three o'clock rode home. Bible school, baptisms, choir practice, and other services kept the church busy during the week.[43]

The residents undoubtedly organized their own church because, being in charge, they liked it better. But they were also unwelcome in neighboring white churches, marking another boundary to racial mixing. Lena Speese remembered one Sunday when she and several of her younger siblings wanted to go to the white church in Brownlee. Their mother, Rose, permitted them, even though she knew they weren't wanted there. "The way we were treated there, we got snickers and looks and hunches [moving her shoulder as if to bump someone] . . . we never went back again. That is one of the worst feelings in the world, to know that you're doing what you should do, but that no one appreciates it." Lena lamented, "This is part of growing up Black."[44]

Homesteader families organized many activities to have fun and draw the community together. The local barber, R. H. Hannahs, hosted a big picnic for other DeWitty homesteaders on the first Sunday of August. They filled the day with speeches, food, and games, and sometimes a rodeo. Don E. Hanna, a white rancher, recalled the talented musicians who added liveliness and energy to local cultural life: Turner and Joe Price, Boss Woodson, Mac Boyd, and Herbie Hannahs played for dances from Broken Bow to Alliance. Joe Price had a "Big Band" that traveled the United States.[45]

DeWitty folks were passionate about baseball and rodeo. They supported their town baseball team, the "Sluggers," which usually

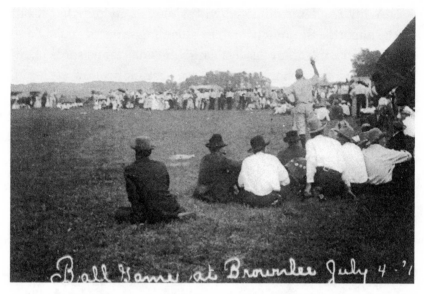

40. DeWitty Sluggers vs. Brownlee team, baseball game, at Brownlee on the July 4, 1914. Courtesy of Denise Scales.

drew a crowd. The team suffered very few losses between 1910 and 1920. Coached by DeWitty settler George Riley, the Sluggers were well known throughout the region. Ava Speese recalled, perhaps somewhat romantically, that the Sluggers would let the opposing team win right up to the bottom of the ninth and "then come way back and defeat the heck out of them." It seemed not to matter which team they played, Brownlee or Seneca or Thedford. Hanna, the white rancher, remembered their star players, especially Joe and Turner Price, and how the team beat everybody around. "They played everybody and beat everybody."[46]

The community also made a big deal of rodeo. DeWitty people raised horses and regularly worked with them and around them, so it was natural they should want to show off their horse skills. They loved to perform and compete at rodeo. As descendant Wayne Brown put it, "some of the best pictures are when I see African-American women holding their guns at the gunslinger position. I'm a former police officer. So when I see them at gunslinger position, I was like, 'Oh my goodness, these ladies knew how to throw down.'"

Brown noticed something else: They knew how to dress up and be fancy. "You would see them on a black horse, a woman with a black fur, with her black hat. You know, that's the Cadillac of DeWitty. And so you knew she was showing what she could do. She was going all out. So they knew how to dress and have fun and party, and they sure loved to rodeo and gunsling."[47]

DeWitty and Brownlee always celebrated a big Fourth of July together. Children ran foot races and ate ice cream made from ice cut during the winter. Ava Speese remembered Bert and Ida Morgan, two local white residents who always stopped and filled the children's pockets and aprons with candy and gum and Cracker Jacks. In 1925, the year that Ava's family left for South Dakota, they hauled lumber from Wood Lake to make the floor for the July Fourth dance. Five hundred people joined the dance that night. Still, some racial boundaries remained: Mamie Faulhaber, wife of rancher Carl Faulhaber, remembered that the communities "had a dance for black and another dance for white."[48]

DeWitty parents worried about the limited pool of local marriage prospects for their children. Families of the homesteader generation had so frequently intermarried that their children had lots of cousins but a very limited selection of appropriate marriage partners. And despite the modeling of interracial marriage possibilities by Charles and Hester Meehan, they did not consider their Black children marrying whites to be a possibility. Young people in the next generation typically had to leave the community to find a connubial partner.

DeWitty residents developed quite harmonious relations with their white neighbors. Each group had its own affairs to tend to, and they understood the racial boundaries, schools, church, and marriage chief among them. Episodes like those at the Brownlee church and the Seneca school were not common, mainly because the communities knew the informal rules of separation, and they had their own institutions. DeWitty homesteaders did not experience racial violence, and they found in Cherry County a site where they staked their claims without intimidation or interference. They were not subjected to racial assaults, destruction of property, or other crimes or acts of terrorism or racial hatred. At least, we have not found any suggestion of such acts in any of the interviews, diaries, letters, books, or other written or oral sources we have examined. Moreover, there is much evidence of interracial cooperation, intermingling, and mutual benefit. DeWitty residents apparently found their white neighbors to be mostly neighborly.

The oral tradition handed down in descendant families corroborates these friendly and cooperative relations. Delbert DeWitty, speaking at the 2016 dedication of the historical marker, observed, "Good people, that's what was so fantastic about this [DeWitty] experience, you can imagine what our . . . ancestors went through now, between the DeWitty and the Brownlee, and the cooperation . . . I grew up in Tulsa, Oklahoma, and the riots of 1921 depict the tension and the hate within our society at that time, and the uniqueness of this [DeWitty] environment to me is what's breathtaking, the camaraderie is to me the special thing."[49]

William Meehan grew up in DeWitty. At age nineteen (in 1916), he wrote a paean to Nebraska that included these lines: "The people are progressive, and cooperation rules." Wayne Brown observed, "From all the family stories, they [my DeWitty ancestors] got along with their neighbors . . . I'm a former attorney and I, I looked, I was like, I've got to find a lawsuit, I've got to find a hanging or something had to happen between, you know, the white neighbors and the Black neighbors. But from everything that I have been able to find, they had a good relationship with their neighbors."[50]

DeWitty homesteaders could never fully immunize themselves from the vicious national and even state tides of racism. If they traveled to Omaha or Denver, or maybe to Seneca and Valentine, they found themselves back in the segregated and prejudiced society that reflected life in America. In 1919 in Omaha, a mob lynched Will Brown, a Black man accused of assaulting a white woman.

Even in Cherry County, racial violence was not unknown. In 1911 near Cody, four white men lynched a Black ranch hand, Charles P. Sellers. (We discuss this killing in the appendix.)[51] And in Empire, Wyoming, just across the Nebraska border, sheriff's deputies killed Baseman Taylor, a man who was related to several DeWitty settlers. (We consider this murder in chapter 10.) Taylor's death would certainly have become known to DeWitty homesteaders because of Taylor's kin ties.

So when Black DeWitty farmers and neighboring white ranchers lived peacefully together, helped each other, and played games together, they accomplished something quite remarkable. The DeWitty folks, dispersed across a vast landscape, had placed themselves in highly vulnerable situations. They opened themselves to violence against themselves and their property of the kind whites routinely visited upon rural Black people in the South. But instead they seemed to enjoy genuine mutual respect.

One point of vulnerability was that a prominent DeWitty couple, Hester and Charles Meehan, lived for two decades as an interracial couple in open defiance of Nebraska's 1855 anti-miscegenation law. The law prohibited marriage between whites and Blacks. It dated back to Nebraska's territorial days, when slavery was legal throughout much of the Union, and there is little evidence that the law was ever enforced. In fact, Nebraska recognized interracial marriages if legalized outside its borders.[52] Still, if some hate-filled white person wanted to harass the Meehans or harm the DeWitty community, he could easily have made trouble for them by complaining to authorities. No one did.

So too, the geographical isolation of Black farms meant they and their crops, barns, and livestock would have made easy targets. Malicious white neighbors bent on using violence to drive them out could have done great damage by assaulting them or mutilating their cattle or burning their barns. Residents would have found it difficult to organize a collective defense in these circumstances. But we have no reports of any such violence or attempts at intimidation.

DeWitty residents homesteaded at a time of intense conflict between (white) ranchers and *all* homesteaders, white or Black, over access to public land. The migrants arrived in the Sandhills just as Bartlett Richards went to jail and other ranchers fumed at having to tear down their fences on public land. They were hardly in a mood to welcome competitors for the grass. The murderous "Johnson County War" in nearby Wyoming reflected this tension.

Yet in DeWitty there was little conflict. William P. Walker triggered the only incident when he had his homestead surveyed and fenced. Very soon, the rancher whose spread lay next-door showed up, irritated and accompanied by several tough cowhands. Walker sensed danger and remained calm.

"We know you had your claim surveyed," the rancher said, "and some of my ranch boundaries are over on your claim."

Walker jumped in before the man could say more. "Well, now, everything is all right, we can work out a way to settle things. Why don't you just pay me in hay for my land each year?"

The rancher, taken aback, readily accepted this proposal. The tension evaporated, and he left with his men. Walker had averted violence without so much as a scuffle, and he had fully preserved his Kinkaid rights. Although on this occasion a white rancher confronted a Black homesteader, the quarrel was about access for grazing cattle rather than racial differences, and it was peacefully settled. Homesteaders recorded no other confrontations with surrounding ranchers.[53]

Despite all these *potential* sources of conflict, *actual* conflict was absent. Relations between Black DeWitty residents and their surrounding white neighbors, including in particular the Hannas and Faulhabers, remained friendly and even mutually supporting. As we have seen, many DeWitty residents worked on the ranches to earn extra cash, apparently without undue discord or strife. The groups played sports together, occasionally volunteered together on community tasks like building the DeWitty church, and socialized together. After baseball games, the opposing teams and their supporters often enjoyed a big picnic together.

And they depended on each other, as neighbors do. Charles and Hester Meehan moved away to Illinois, and in 1923 Hester died while she was visiting friends in Alliance, Nebraska. That morning, Rosetta Speese, their daughter still living in DeWitty, received the telegram with the awful news. Rosetta, her sister Gertie, and daughter Ava prepared to leave immediately for Alliance.

But just then the clouds opened, and it began to rain heavily. Rosetta's husband, Charles, feared the weather was too severe for their horse and buggy. So he set off on horseback to ask Don Hanna Sr. to drive them to the railroad in Seneca in his automobile. Hanna quickly agreed, and he drove to the Speese house to gather up the women. They drove the next two hours over muddy, rutted roads to Seneca. With money given him by Charles, Hanna bought the women's tickets to Alliance and got them settled on the train. As Ava reflected, "Neighbors were neighbors and did what they could for each other."[54]

The good will that DeWitty and Brownlee residents fostered during these years continued well beyond the 1920s. When Ava Speese Day and her husband Lee returned to the abandoned settlement site in the 1960s, Don Hanna Jr. drove them around. Lee was unable to "get over how nice the white people in the Sandhills and [Gillette] Wyoming were to us." Ava simply told him it had always been like that: "Neighbors; like people think the word really means." In 2016 that good will was renewed at the historical marker dedication, with Black and white descendants intermingling, sharing family stories, and enjoying one anothers' company together.[55]

DeWitty—despite its new name Audacious—ultimately disappeared from the Sandhills. Its homesteaders faced the same daunting challenges that afflicted other homesteaders in the region, and they suffered similar fates, mostly from similar causes. The period from 1907 to 1920, years during which DeWitty had grown, was a wetter time in the region, despite sparse rainfall in some years. And nationally, American farmers enjoyed good markets for their crops and prosperity. World War I and the two years following brought extremely high crop prices and profitability. Nineteen twenty-one, however, was a bad year: corn and wheat prices sagged sharply, and farmers entered a period of agricultural depression that extended throughout the 1920s.

Cherry County, containing DeWitty, reached its highest population count in the 1920 census; it has suffered depopulation ever since. Of the seven counties abutting Cherry County, five reached their population peaks in 1920, one in 1890, and one in 1930. Black *and* white homesteaders struggled after 1920, and many were forced off their land.

DeWitty and all of Cherry County turned out to be largely unsuitable for row-crop farming. Soil quality was poor, and rainfall even in nondrought years was slight. Unsuccessful crops forced Charles Speese to move his family away from DeWitty in 1925. Speese's story was typical of settlers who came to Cherry County seeking a better life but were driven out by the harsh conditions. The poor returns devastated their ability to pay taxes and repay their mortgages.[56]

Although the Kinkaid Act encouraged them to farm, farmers found the poor soil of the Sandhills defeated their efforts. Historian W. D. Aeschbacher noted that by 1920 the pattern of ranching which extends to the present was fairly well established. Most of the region had become privately owned, with little remaining public domain, and the ranchers' ranges were largely fenced. "Any illusions that farming would displace raising cattle in the area had been dispelled."

Former DeWitty resident Albert Riley Jr. agreed with Aeschbacher when he recalled, "It would have been better if the land had never been broken up. This land would raise good crops for a few years and then, after cropping, the wind would blow and ruin the land." Riley said that DeWitty homesteaders didn't have land enough or hay enough to run cattle and be successful at it. Riley's own parents sold their land and returned to Overton, a climatological region to which they were more accustomed. Riley himself remained in DeWitty for a time after they moved away, but he also eventually sold his land. He moved to the Fort Niobrara Wildlife Reserve, where he worked for twenty years.[57]

President Theodore Roosevelt had insisted that the Kinkaid Act would bring farmers to the Sandhills, and he was correct. What he didn't promise and couldn't ensure was that once there, they would thrive. The farmers did not outlast the ranchers. A few Black homesteaders tried to transition to big-time ranching; we know that the Speese and Taylor families, when in Overton and later in Empire, owned cattle herds. And descendant, Joyceann Gray, observed that her ancestors "were mostly cattle ranchers and raised horses. The land was best for that."[58] But most DeWitty residents lacked sufficient capital and access to borrowing to allow them to scale up to profitable ranching operations.

In 1925 William Henry Sirrell and Charles Speese both picked up their families and left DeWitty for Sully County, South Dakota. They wanted better schools, especially high school, and a better way of life, where the soil produced more bountiful crops of wheat and flax. Other families, including Chris and Maggie Stith's family, had no choice but to rent their land to ranchers and move away; the Stiths went to Kansas for work. James Griffith and his family returned to Saskatchewan, Canada. By the end of the decade, only a handful of DeWitty settlers were left.

DeWitty descendants point to a bittersweet connection between education and DeWitty's dissolution. They believe that the homesteaders increasingly saw educating their children and grandchildren as their primary goal. Joyceann Gray, the DeWitty descendant, noted that the community "was not built to last." Catherine Meehan Blount, another descendant, echoed Gray's assessment, and added, "it [DeWitty] was meant to educate their children. DeWitty provided a better life for their children."

DeWitty homesteaders, though they may have started with the dream of creating a permanent farming settlement, came to see their great venture in a new light. DeWitty would serve as a way station in an historic process that opened greater opportunities for succeeding generations to use their talents and pursue their dreams. As descendant Wayne Brown put it, "Education was the key. Some of the families say that DeWitty wasn't supposed to last for a long time, it lasted for 30 years, but it was a purchase. It was a purchase in American freedom. And in that freedom, they purchased education."[59]

The homesteaders made great sacrifices to fulfill their commitment to education. They took valuable time away from urgent farm tasks to organize school districts, build schools, recruit teachers, and supply school needs. Despite their desperate lack of cash, they taxed themselves to pay teachers and buy books. Their sacrifices are what made the schools possible. And they succeeded, setting the next generations on the path to success.

The homesteading generation worked to ensure that their children and grandchildren would be well educated, but that created the same Hobson's choice that afflicts so many farm families. Educated children do not, in general, become farmers. For the sons and daughters to use their educations obtained at such cost and hard work, they had to leave the farm. They became teachers, pharmacists, insurance agents, lawyers, nurses, writers, police officers, and a bewildering lineup of other callings. People in these occupations usually do not carry the family farm into the future. And to complete this bittersweet irony, their children's successes were exactly what the homesteader generation wanted for them. The farming generation's deep commitment to educating their children produced children who were not interested in farming.

The Great Depression further damaged the few remaining farmers' ability to make a living. There was always the mortgage, sometimes more than one, to pay. Banks in the 1930s in western Nebraska had little money to lend anyway. DeWitty homesteaders sold out to the adjoining ranchers. Or they simply walked away from their homesteads, and the holder of the mortgage took the land and in turn sold it to the ranchers. According to Ava Speese Day, fourteen of the DeWitty Kinkaiders' places were sold through a sheriff's deed, a process that included a public auction for back taxes and mortgages owed. By 1936 nearly all of its settlers had sold out to ranchers, reportedly at good prices, though any farmland in mid-1930s didn't bring much. Everyone moved away.[60]

Peryle Woodson, the last African American Kinkaider remaining in DeWitty in 1940, married and left the area. She leased her land to white rancher Don Hanna. After her death, her husband willed it to their children, who continued to pay taxes on the claim until 1993. The family later sold the land to Don Hanna III.

DeWitty residents experienced the soaring hopes that homesteading gave rise to, they suffered the sacrifices and disappointments it extracted, and they relished the achievements it made possible. They also provide a model of relations between African Americans and their white neighbors that was surprisingly harmonious and mutually beneficial. Thus, DeWitty's story also reveals much about the decency of their white neighbors. At its core, however, the DeWitty saga is about Black homesteaders successfully building a community and a new life for themselves in the extremely challenging physical environment of the Nebraska Sandhills.

Among those who tried but ran out of luck in the frustrating fields of the Sandhills were Charles and Rose Speese. But they were just one branch on the tree of the audacious Speese family.

8

The Speese Family Odyssey

We hear that Charles Speese has sold out his first class farm . . .
No one in Westerville holds a better record than Charlie
Speese and we are sorry to lose him. There are many white
families we could spare in preference [to] the Speese family.
—*Custer County Chief,* February 28, 1908

At a late-1970s evening gala, Norma Speese-Owens was surrounded
by international nursing students. They had come to the United
States to be trained to care for cancer victims, and they had come
specifically to learn from Speese-Owens. And no wonder: She was
an eminent tenured professor in New York University's (NYU's)
nursing program and part of a research team at the Sloan Kettering
Cancer Center. What the students may not have known was that
she was also the granddaughter of Moses Speese and Susan Kirk,
an enslaved couple. In the 1870s, newly emancipated but not really
free, Speese and Kirk escaped their new oppressors secreted under
loads of hay. They left North Carolina to homestead in Nebraska,
launching a new life for themselves and creating opportunities for
descendants like Norma.

The Speese odyssey, which had NYU as but one of its destinations,
began in much less exalted surroundings. Moses Shores was born
into slavery about 1795. As was common among slaves, he was given
the last name of his owner. Slave states did not recognize marriages
among enslaved persons, but Moses and his wife in fact, Fanny, had
a child, Jeremiah, or Jerry. Moses or perhaps Fanny and Jeremiah

were sold away. Now separated from Fanny, Moses then found a second wife, Hannah Webb. Moses and Hannah produced at least two children, one of whom was Moses Speese, whose surname would eventually come from his last owner.

Speese was born in 1838 in Fayetteville, North Carolina. He was taken or sold to a different owner in Yadkin County. Like his biblical namesake, Moses Speese would lead his family out of calamity and oppression, in his case away from the horrors of the post-war South and to the new promised land of Nebraska. He remained in North Carolina after emancipation, and like so many freedmen, he shared the joy and soaring hopes of freedom.

Moses Speese then experienced the terrible crushing destruction of his dreams. He got caught in the claws of the post-war system of sharecropping and debt peonage. A landowner would agree to let the sharecropper farm his land for a share, usually half, of the harvest. In the one-sided contract, the landowner directed the farmer what to plant, when to plant it, how to harvest it.

Moreover, the sharecropper typically was also required to purchase his farming supplies, food, clothing, and other necessities at the land-owner's store, at prices the landowner set and using credit for which the landowner kept the books. The landowner charged unconsciona-bly high interest rates, but in truth, given the sharecroppers' illiter-acy, he could charge any rate at all to keep the sharecropper in debt. The result was that every year sharecroppers fell farther and farther behind, with only mounting debts to show for their toil and sweat.

Owing the landowner money, the sharecropper could not leave—his debts tied him to the land in a relationship scholars have termed *debt peonage*. Debt peonage turned out to be nearly as oppressive as slavery. In Moses's case, the landlord charged him for goods he did not even order or receive. By the early 1870s, Moses Speese saw that all his hard work in the fields only produced more debt, and his chances of bettering his life were evaporating.

Speese mentioned to his landowner that he was interested in the government's offer of free land in the West. The landowner, enraged, told him he could leave but his wife, Susan Kirk, and their three children would have to stay as collateral for his debts. (Moses and Susan's first four children had been born during slavery and either died or been sold away—in any event, *lost*.) Speese had a supportive neighbor, whether white or Black is not known, who in 1871 or 1872 hid him under a load of hay and took him to a railroad stop in the next county. The neighbor bought him a ticket, and Speese sped on his way to New Castle, in the middle of Indiana. The Speese odyssey, the family's part in the great migration, had begun.

Moses labored at numerous jobs in New Castle and saved his money, all to reunite his family. He regularly sent payments to his Yadkin County neighbor, and by 1873 he had saved enough to rescue Susan and the children. Following the same subterfuge, hiding Susan and the children under a load of hay, the neighbor transported them to a railway stop. They escaped, traveling to New Castle and joined Moses.

Moses Speese's father, Moses Shores, had seen both his second and third wives, Hannah Webb and Patsy Davis, die during slavery, and he now reunited with his first wife, Fanny Shores, Moses Speese's stepmother. The Shores soon joined the Speeses in New Castle, as did several of Moses Speese's siblings—his brother Josiah Webb, his half-brothers John Wesley Shores and Jerry Shores and their wives, and half-sisters Mary Hauser and Lizzy Stimpson. Their slavery-derived different last names would confuse researchers, courts, journalists, and even family members for decades.[1]

Now gathered, the Speeses and Shores looked west. Moses Speese still wanted some of that free government land, and in 1880 he led the large extended family to Nebraska. Only Moses and Fanny Shores— Moses was eighty-five—stayed behind. The migrants stopped for two years in Seward, a German immigrant town just west of Lincoln.

Moses hauled freight with his team and wagon. But most of the land around Seward had already been claimed, so they moved on.

In 1882 Moses and the family settled in Westerville in Custer County, Nebraska. Here they found land still available for home-steading, and several family members filed claims. Their homesteads clustered near each other in the sixteenth and seventeenth town-ships of ranges seventeen and eighteen west. Moses Speese filed a 158-acre homestead claim and a 160-acre timber culture claim. His brother Josiah Webb filed on 160 acres. His half-brother Jerry Shores claimed a 160-acre homestead, and his other half-brother, John Wesley Shores, filed two claims, totaling 320 acres, one of which may have been a purchase.

Two of Jerry's children, Minerva Shores and William Shores, were old enough to file their own claims. Minerva got 160 acres, and William 175 acres. Moses's oldest child, William H. Speese, was technically too young, at eighteen, to file but somehow also managed to enter a 160-acre claim. While all their homesteads were raw land requiring hard labor to make productive, family members now had claims to nearly fifteen hundred acres of fertile prairie. Moses and Susan built their first house on their own land.

For the next twenty-five years, the families prospered in Wester-ville. They worked hard and were evidently quick to learn how to use their new land effectively. The four half-brothers, Moses Speese, Jerry Shores, John Wesley Shores, and Josiah Webb, all did well, becoming increasingly known and integrated into the life of the region. As most homesteaders did, they worked their farms and also picked up off-farm jobs to earn cash. In 1883 the Westerville Methodist Church hired Moses Speese and his sons to help build its new house of worship, and they worked other jobs as well.[2] His younger sons, John Wesley (sixteen), Joseph (fourteen), Radford (ten), and Charles (one), were too young to file their own homestead claims yet, but they were clearly in waiting.

Solomon Butcher photographed Jerry Shores's family in 1887, and Moses Speese's family in 1888. Butcher himself tried to homestead, but he quit after only two weeks. It was too hot, too dirty, and too buggy for him. He then turned to photography, at which he succeeded brilliantly. In the 1880s he roamed Custer County photographing the settlers. He typically arrayed his subjects standing or sitting in front of their sod houses, with a background carefully arranged to show their material possessions in full view—teams and wagons, pigs, cows, dining room table and chairs.

When Butcher photographed the David Hilton family, Mrs. Hilton insisted that the men haul her pump organ out of her house to be in the picture and that her sod house *not* be in it. She wanted her friends back in Boston to know that she still played the organ but not that she lived in a dirt home.[3] Butcher's glass plates, once nearly thrown out, now constitute our most precious photo documentation of the period.

Butcher's photographs of the Shores and Speese families display their prosperity. They are less prosperous than some of the white homesteaders Butcher photographed but clearly more prosperous than others. The Shores family is arrayed in front of their large, well-built sod house. Jerry sits with his wife Rachel, their daughter Minerva holding her baby next to her husband, Reverend Albert Marks. Their son James is standing, holding a dog. They look well fed and healthy. In the background we see some of their possessions: two substantial and well-built sod buildings, a team and wagon with an additional horse, barrels, a grindstone, and other equipment used in household and farm chores.

In the Speese family photograph, Moses sits with his wife Susan, four sons, and a daughter (the other woman is unidentified). They too look well fed, well clothed, and healthy. They sit in front of a large, well-built sod house. In the back we see a couple of outbuildings they've constructed. Directly behind them they've parked a

52. Jerry Shores family on homestead, Custer County, 1887.
Permission of History Nebraska, RG2608, PHO–1231, 10527.

53. Moses Speese family on homestead, Custer County, 1888.
Permission of History Nebraska, RG2608, PHO–1345, 10963.

rather fancy carriage, certainly not something used on the farm. They have two teams hooked to farm wagons. By 1885 the Speeses had three cows that annually produced three hundred pounds of butter and seventy chickens which yielded 1,800 eggs for sale. They enjoyed bigger crop yields per acre than many neighbors.[4] These are all signs that Moses Speese and Susan Kirk had become quite successful farmers.

Aside from the people, however, the most striking feature in the photograph is the tall, sturdy derrick behind the house. The Speeses not only have a well; they have a windmill to pump their water. Many homesteads did not yet have a well, and most that did, didn't have a windmill. Having both was a huge advantage. Nor was the Speeses' windmill some jury-rigged homemade mechanism, but rather a top-of-the-line Halladay Standard. That model was the first self-regulating windmill for pumping water. When it had pumped the water tank full, it turned itself off. This feature was enormously helpful, because the windmill could be left unattended to pump on its own when the family was away for a few days. The U.S Wind Engine and Pump Company in Batavia, Illinois, sold many Halladay Standard windmills across the Great Plains.

Moses Speese likely ordered his windmill from a Halladay catalog or perhaps a traveling salesman who carried miniature samples. The manufacturer fabricated it at its plant and freighted it in pieces by rail to the Speeses. Moses and his sons assembled it themselves. Moses likely paid about seventy dollars for it, a significant investment, consuming perhaps a quarter of one year's crop revenue. The device meant that the wind, which central Nebraska has in abundance, drew the water, eliminating an arduous and tedious daily chore. Depending on the flow in the well, the windmill could pump enough water for personal and household use and also for watering the livestock and vegetables in the garden.[5]

Moses Speese and Jerry Shores waited their full five- or seven-year residency period to prove up, so they obtained their homesteads free. Others in the family chose to "commute" or pay cash for their claims. Sometimes it made sense to commute—one benefit was that the owner could then mortgage his or her land.[6] Commutations, like the windmill, signaled a substantial level of material prosperity, because to commute the claimant had to come up with two hundred dollars in cash.

To the modern eye, the Speese and Shores dwellings and possessions might seem meager, even suggesting poverty. But the settlers did not necessarily see them that way. When Butcher photographed the (white) Ira Watson family in Custer County in 1886, the family sat in front of a sod house smaller than those of the Speeses and Shores, beside a well with no windmill. But Mrs. Watson has her arms proudly, almost defiantly, folded, and she betrays a sly smile, as if to say, "Yes, you're right, our place *is* pretty sweet!"[7]

The Shores and Speeses were clearly more affluent than the Watsons. Just seventeen years earlier, Moses Speese and Susan Kirk had hidden under a load of hay to escape their North Carolina tormenter amid mounting debts and brutal peonage. To them, their Custer County property must also have seemed pretty sweet.

Much later, Mrs. W. H. Hodge of Westerville recalled the Shores and Speeses in a feature for the *Custer County Chief* called "Pioneer Story of the Early Settlers." She wrote, "Two of our neighbors were colored families. 'Uncle Mose' and 'Aunt Susie' Speese and their family of six sons and one daughter, lived west of us. 'Uncle Jerry' and 'Aunt Rachel' Shores and their family of one daughter and two sons lived to the south. . . . Both families were as fine neighbors as any one would want."[8]

As the farmers' hard times of the 1890s turned into the better times of the 1900s, the Speese sons increasingly came to the fore. Moses Speese died in 1896, at the relatively young age of fifty-eight.

54. Ira Watson family on homestead, Custer County, 1886.
Permission of History Nebraska, RG2608, PHO–1003, 2892.

By then, the Speeses and Shores had either proved up or purchased 1,453 acres in Custer County. We do not know if any of their land was mortgaged, or if mortgaged, how draining the interest was. But it was not so burdensome that the banks repossessed any land.

Among Moses's sons, the oldest, William H. Speese, purchased his claim on June 4, 1890. But W. H. does not appear to have been cut out for farming, and he later appears as "Rev. W.H. Speese," preaching in Omaha and Iowa. Moses's timber culture claim, settled on August 30, 1894, was the last of the clan's land claims to be proved up in the county. As Custer County filled up, the sons found there was little additional land left to be claimed.

The Speeses's life in Westerville was filled with the usual troubles and small triumphs of rural life. In 1899 John Wesley Speese entered a Burlington Railway contest for the best letter on the state of Nebraska; he won five dollars when his essay was chosen as one of the top entries out of 223 submitted. On August 7, 1903, Charles placed a notice in the *Custer County Chief*: "Strayed—From my place on Aug. 3rd, one gray mare, aged 5 years, branded circle R. Liberal reward will be paid for the location of the same. Charles Speese." On December 27, 1907, in the nearby town of Dunning, Radford entered a contest to guess the number of seeds in a gourd sitting in a store window. He guessed 426, which turned out to be the exact number of seeds, and he won a sewing machine. At the next Fourth of July celebration in Westerville, Charles won an athletic contest, and the newspaper recorded his win.[9]

The extended family showed off its growing prosperity in two big weddings. On April 22, 1900, Maggie Shores wed Baseman Taylor. The Shores hosted the ceremony at their house. Fifty guests showed up, including most of the Speeses. Other guests traveled from far away. A correspondent for the *Custer County Republican*, probably Susan Kirk herself, wrote that the wedding was so impressive it threw all other topics of conversation into the shade. The visitors were extremely generous, she reported, offering gifts that included many useful, beautiful and ornamental items, but she couldn't list them all because that would have occupied too much space in the paper. Kirk wrote, "[Rev. Kyle] tied the knot that completed the act of welding two loving souls into one and two throbbing hearts to beat in loving unison, which we hope may continue through all the vicissitudes of a long and happy life."[10] Tragically, these hopeful wishes would not be realized, and the two throbbing hearts' marriage and lives would end disastrously some few years later.

The second wedding, on Thanksgiving Day 1907, matched Charles Speese of Westerville with Hannah Rosetta Meehan of the tiny emerging settlement that would become DeWitty. He was twenty-five, she just sixteen. This too was a big wedding, what with the Speeses becoming increasingly well-known Westerville folks. Charles and Rose, as she was known, would produce seventeen children.[11]

The Speeses and Shores attracted attention and admiration for their musical talent. Their music may have had roots in slave days, when Black people salved their wounds and sadness with gospels promising salvation. We have no record of Moses Shores, Moses Speese, or Susan Kirk being musical, though perhaps they were. Their grown children, however, made themselves into accomplished violinists, pianists, and singers. They had some classical training, obtained where is not clear, and they formed a touring concert group. They adopted different names for their group over the years, achieving their greatest prominence as the Speese Jubilee Singers.

The Speese Singers put on sophisticated, high-culture performances of vocal and instrumental music, touring the area. The *Custer County Chief* announced in January 1896 that "Our colored troupe" was embarking on a month-long tour of central and western Nebraska. On January 3, the *Sherman County Times*, published in Loup City, carried the notice that the group would appear at the town's opera house that coming Friday evening. It listed the prices

55. Charles Speese and Hannah Rosetta "Rose" Meehan at their wedding, Westerville, 1907. Permission of Bellevue Collection, Perkins Library Special Collections, Hastings College.

of admission as twenty-five cents for adults and fifteen cents for children. The group also performed at the Loup City Methodist Church on January 10 and in Alliance on February 3.[12]

But some western Nebraska audiences apparently expected African American performers to put on minstrel shows with stereotypical lowbrow, slapstick parody. The Alliance paper, like Loup City, called them "the Speese jolly jubilee singers." A performance in St. Paul, Nebraska, particularly flopped, the audience demanding a minstrel show.

The Speeses adjusted to the more vulgar tastes of their white audiences, sometimes billing themselves as the "Speese Minstrel Show" or "The Slave's Children." They omitted their previous classical-themed playlist. At Fullerton, the newspaper announced, "Speese Bros' famous Down South Colored Comedy Company will hold the boards at Sheaff's opera house on next Monday night, March 2. They will be assisted by the Tabor College Jubilee Singers."[13] Their tour of the region showed both the possibilities and limits for Black performers in central Nebraska. Being pressured into performing minstrelsy must have been a bitter pill for the talented and classically inclined Speeses.

The Speese brothers, later joined by sisters and female cousins who were equally talented, performed to make money and also, one imagines, for the joy of performing (when white audiences appreciated their talents). They were apparently very popular, according to the *Custer County Chief.* In what one hopes they appreciated as a delicious irony, the Speeses used their earnings from entertaining mostly uneducated white audiences to pay for their college tuitions.

The Speeses would continue to make music and perform publicly most of their lives. Solomon Butcher photographed the nattily dressed group in 1909 at the Lexington, Nebraska, Business College. In 1913 they performed at the dedication of the new Goshen County, Wyoming, courthouse in Torrington. They performed at church dedications in Prairie Center and Red Cloud, Wyoming. On July 27, 1921, a group out of the Black colony at Empire, which the *Henry Dispatch* called "Taylor's-band-of-singers," performed in Torrington. They were special guests as one of the Chautauqua attractions. On July 22, 1923, the *Morrill Mail* announced that "the Speese colored male quartet will entertain at the Dutch Flats M.E. church" in Nebraska.

Charles was still performing even late in life. On January 15, 1954, he sang at a public concert as a member of the Grace AME Radio Choir in Casper, Wyoming. Other members of that choir included Margaret Speese and Howard Speese.[14]

As successful as their farms and life in Westerville were, Moses and Susan's children looked farther west for their land and future.

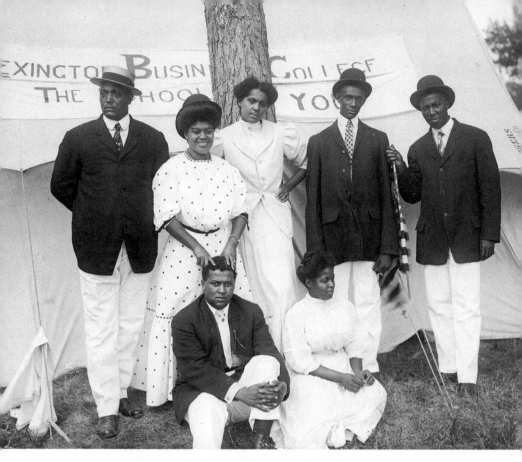

56. The Speese Jubilee Singers, Lexington, Nebraska, 1909. Permission of Bellevue Collection, Perkins Library Special Collections, Hastings College.

Joseph Speese moved to Blaine County, a more remote region bordering Custer County on the north, where he homesteaded in 1903. The *Sandhills Brewster News* recorded his arrival: "J.S. Speese of Halsey, who is honored with the distinction of being one of the only two colored men in Blaine county, was in town Monday on business." It elaborated that Mr. Speese and his brother had recently moved from Westerville to the Sandhills "to engage in the cattle business and," that he was "well pleased with his new location." The brothers' mother, Susan (Kirk) Speese, proved up on a 160-acre homestead in Blaine County on October 16, 1907. Joseph proved up his claim on March 3, 1908.

Radford Speese, Joseph's brother, on September 12, 1910, bought an isolated tract of ninety-four acres in Sioux County, still farther west and abutting the Wyoming border. He paid $1.25 per acre.[15]

Charles Speese, the youngest brother, began liquidating the family's holdings around Westerville in preparation for moving west. The *Custer County Chief* lamented on February 28, 1908: "We hear that Charles Speese has sold out his first class farm of 320 acres to some ranchers from Wyoming; consideration, $50 per acre. No one in Westerville holds a better record than Charlie Speese and we are sorry to lose him. There are many white families we could spare in preference [to] the Speese family."

Charles, or perhaps the Speese and Shores families, reaped a tremendous windfall from this sale. The property may have been Moses's original land, his homestead claim and timber claim totaling 320 acres. The sale cleared $16,000 (worth more than $500,000 in 2022) at a time when the annual earnings of nonfarm workers averaged just $600 per year.[16] And this was just one sale—the family still owned at least 1,133 acres in other Westerville properties. If those acres sold at the same $50 each, they would have brought $56,650 (worth nearly $1.8 million in 2022).

The Speese siblings, now more affluent, had bigger plans. Radford, Joseph, William, John Wesley, and Charles formed Speese Brothers, a land and cattle operation. (Their company would likely not have included their remaining brother, Earl, who had a lifelong debilitating disease, probably epilepsy, and was described as crippled; he died in 1907 in the Lincoln Hospital for the Insane.) Sometime in 1908 Speese Brothers bought a 2,500-acre ranch at Wet Sheep Creek near the village of Henry, in Scotts Bluff County, Nebraska, bordering on Wyoming. The *Mitchell Index* reported, "The purchasers are colored men, five brothers, prominent and wealthy ranchmen of Blaine County. They expect to stock the place with sheep."

Joseph visited the Sandhills town of Brewster in June 1908 on business. The *Brewster News* described his excitement: "J.S. Speese . . . is highly elated over his prospects on a new ranch he has recently bought on the western border of the state." Whether in the cattle business or sheep raising, or both, the affluent Speese Brothers appeared well on their way to even bigger success.[17]

Soon, however, they somewhat abruptly bailed out on Nebraska. They continued to own property in the state for a few years, but they set up shop in Empire, a new Black colony just then taking shape over the state line in Wyoming. We do not know the cause of the Speese Brothers' rash move, only that it was ruinous. Todd Guenther, the most perceptive historian of the Speeses and Empire, suggests their decision was driven by a combination of factors—worry over a Nebraska Supreme Court decision concerning slave marriages and inheritance rights, frustration with inadequate funding of Nebraska schools, and perhaps an unsated yearning, an urge felt by so many young men of the time, to "go west." Yet none of these causes, nor all of them together, fully explain the brothers' decision.

Josiah Webb, one of the original four half-brothers, died in 1904 without a will and without children. Webb left what the *Custer County Chief* described as a fine farm of 160 acres near Ansley, Nebraska. Several of Moses Shores's heirs appealed to the Nebraska Supreme Court to decide who should inherit his estate. Half-brother Jerry Shores was also dead, but his children claimed the estate or part of it, too. The children of the other two half-brothers, Moses Speese (dead) and John Wesley Shores (who may have been dead) also claimed the farm. The heirs of Moses Speese and John Wesley Shores initiated the case against Jerry Shores's heirs.

The case would eventually evolve, however, so that it pitted the heirs of Moses Speese against the heirs of his two half-brothers, Jerry Shores and John Wesley Shores. Throughout the legal process, the courts and especially the newspapers reporting on the case, got tripped up by the confusion of last names.

The Court's decision on which heirs should inherit turned on the touchy issue of whether Moses Shores's cohabitations with three women under slavery constituted official marriages. The relationships were never bigamous, because Moses only lived with the next woman after his previous partner was sold away or died. If they were legal marriages, then the heirs of all three of Josiah Webb's half-brothers would be entitled to inherit. But if they were not legal marriages, then Josiah Webb would be considered illegitimate and by Nebraska law his estate would revert to his mother (dead) and her heirs, that is, only to Moses Speese's surviving children.

The marriages were certainly not officially recognized in North Carolina in the 1850s, because the state did not recognize any marriages among enslaved people. But slavery, as usual, created horrific dilemmas impossible to solve: If the Nebraska Supreme Court deemed the marriages legal, was Moses Shores's first marriage to Fanny dissolved when she was sold away? Unless the answer was yes, his later marriages would have been bigamous. The court either had to accept the antebellum slave-owners' racist law or make new laws recognizing the marriages and accept its unknown ramifications.

The court chose the former option, declaring Moses Shores's cohabitations not to be marriages recognized in Nebraska law. It therefore awarded Josiah Webb's estate entirely to Moses Speese's children, that is, to Joseph, Charles, and their siblings. The court's shocking acceptance of the discredited Slave Power's law, the disrespect it implied for Moses Shores's marriages, and the assertion that the four half-brothers were all illegitimate, undoubtedly distressed all of Moses Shores's grandchildren.

Still, it is difficult to see why this case would cause the Speese Brothers to leave Nebraska abruptly. After all, Nebraska law certainly recognized their *own* marriages as legal, their children as legitimate, and they could pass their estates on to their children without dispute. Moreover, Moses Speese's heirs had initiated the suit *and won it*. The Speese siblings would inherit Josiah Webb's farm. Still, even the winners must have found repugnant this regurgitation of slavery's utterly evil impact on its victims.[18]

The Speese Brothers may have left Nebraska in part due to their irritation over inadequate funding for Nebraska schools. They set a very high priority on educating their children, and Nebraska schools, entirely locally financed, were chronically underfunded. One event may have been particularly galling. Some whites, to raise money for a nearby rural school, put on a minstrel show in blackface, mocking Black stereotypes. The Speeses were appalled. Still, for people as sophisticated as they were, who could bill themselves as the Down South Colored Comedy Company or the Speese Minstrel Show or The Slave's Children to contend with *and profit from* prejudiced white audiences, this incident, while discouraging, seems unlikely to have pushed them out. And as for funding, they could hardly have expected more generous school budgets in Wyoming.

Perhaps, finally, they were simply gripped again by the yearn to go west. But they had already just gone west. Their move from Westerville to Blaine County and then further west to Thomas and Sioux counties had already moved them into much less settled territory.

Whatever combination of irritants and attractions motivated them, the Speeses decided to shift their operations across the border to the new Black colony of Empire. In the summer of 1908, Radford and Joseph drove a line of heavy wagons trekking west, leading a buggy, cows, horses, pigs, and perhaps two dozen Speese, Taylor, and Shores kin. Charles Speese and Otis Taylor soon arranged for their families and goods to travel by rail to Torrington, the depot nearest Empire.

We discuss the history of Empire later, but Wyoming turned out to be a terribly unfortunate place to land. The Speeses found the first decade to be moderately rewarding, but that was deceptive, with more rain and higher crop prices than usual. When normal weather—dry and subject to extremes—returned, and crop prices in 1921 sank through the floor, they struggled.

So too, the white people around Empire proved more racist and hostile than the migrants had encountered in Nebraska. The Speeses got into minor disputes with neighbors, trading accusations of stolen tools, downed fences, and worse. On February 15, 1911, the *Natrona County Tribune* reported, "Charles Speese of Sheep creek, arrested recently charged with cattle stealing, and who was bound over for hearing Jan 12 at Torrington, has disappeared and his bonds forfeited."[19] Charles! Partner in Speese Brothers, faithful church choir member, upright owner of substantial assets, earlier described as wealthy and praised as having a record second to none in Westerville, now arrested for cattle theft! The case was eventually dismissed, but it nonetheless reflected the high level of unneighborly tension. Soon, things would turn far worse, even deadly.

By the time Empire dissolved around 1920, the Speese brothers had lost most of their assets. The capital so patiently built up during the Westerville years was gone. The difficult times in Empire turned relative against relative, friend against friend, in disputes that frequently ended in lawsuits. Everyone recognized the Empire experiment had failed, and it was time to get out.

Charles and Rose returned to Nebraska with their children. But instead of going back to Westerville, where they still had relatives but now no longer owned any land, they joined the growing Black colony at DeWitty. Rose, whose parents Charles and Hester Meehan had led one group of early settlers to DeWitty, had many relatives there whom they hoped would be helpful.

The Speeses' problem was that after Empire, they had few assets and they had mostly used up their rights to claim government land. Charles had proved up on a 320-acre Enlarged Homestead claim in Empire. He believed he should have been permitted under the special provisions of the Kinkaid Act to claim an additional 320 acres. Already in 1912, barely three years into his stay in Empire, he wrote to the Alliance and Valentine land offices in Nebraska asserting his Kinkaid right, but the officials disagreed. In 1920 he wrote again to the General Land Office, seeking clarification of his rights and asserting new rights under the 1916 Stock Raising Homestead Act.[20] He wanted to relinquish (abandon) his earlier claim. But he received no relief, and despite his efforts, he was out of options. He wound up filing on only eighty acres in DeWitty.

Charles, who had recently dealt in hundreds of acres and with his brothers run big herds of cattle, was reduced to farming one-eighth of a section. The family's precipitous decline showed in their housing as well. In Empire they built a spacious, multiroom house; in DeWitty, they lived in a small, crowded soddy.

The DeWitty years, though hard, were nonetheless rewarding. Charles worked his farm and took other jobs when available. He grew potatoes and other crops and occasionally hunted, fished, and collected wild fruits. Rose raised chickens and vegetables, but mainly focused on her growing brood of children. Norma was born there, as well as Lela, Homer, and Francis.

By 1925 Charles and maybe Rose, too, were once again fed up with the hard livelihood, the inadequate schools, and their poor prospects in the Sandhills. They moved to a Black colony in Sully County, South Dakota, seeking better land and better schools and a better life. The Blairs, McGruders, and other Black homesteader families had settled in Sully County as far back as the 1880s, and the Speeses went to join them. Once again, they likely had relatives, the families of William Day and William Davis, who encouraged them to come. The Speeses spent the next seventeen years in the Sully County colony.

Charles' land problem was even worse in Sully County than it had been in DeWitty. He had now completely exhausted any rights to claim government land. And the hard years in DeWitty surely left them with few savings. So in Sully County Charles was reduced to *leasing* eighty acres. Ever resilient, Charles and Rose and their large family somehow made it work.

They would have limited resources for the rest of their lives. The 1940 Census lists eight children living at home, all eight going to school, and the oldest, Norma and Francis, in ninth grade. The parents separated sometime in the 1940s. Rose moved to Minneapolis, where she joined several of her children. She died in 1966. After they split, Charles headed back to Wyoming and wound up in Casper, where for a while he worked as a janitor for the Consolidated Royalty Company. He died in 1970.

Despite the hard times they lived through, and the hard luck that was visited upon them, despite the many barriers and obstacles placed in their path, despite their disastrous decision to move to Empire, Charles and Rose nonetheless bequeathed to their children a precious legacy. They endowed their children with education, a capacity for hard work, their moral values, and a deep sense of self-worth. Their daughter Ava, who married Lue Day in 1931, was a successful homemaker and sometime author. Numerous others of their many children and grandchildren served honorably in the military—Ava's brother Benjamin, a World War II vet, is buried at Fort Snelling National Cemetery; Richard M. Speese, their grandson, served in the Navy during the early days of the Vietnam War. Many others made successful if unremarkable lives for themselves. Norma Speese-Owens made good on the discipline and educational commitment that Rose instilled in her during their years in Sully County by becoming a nurse, professor, and cancer researcher.

Moses Speese hid under a load of hay to escape his North Carolina oppressors. He would have been so proud *but likely not surprised* at the things his descendants could achieve when given the chance.

After they left DeWitty, Charles and Rose joined the Sully County colony. The founders of the colony had homesteaded in the region some forty years earlier, bringing with them their own high hopes and dramatic histories.

9

Opportunity in Sully County

Ben Blair, who is locating many colored people at Fairbanks,
was in Pierre yesterday. He has a thousand acres of
growing crops, and stated they were the best ever.

—*Pierre Weekly Free Press*, June 13, 1907

In 1882 Benjamin Blair, the son of formerly enslaved parents, traveled with his brother, Patrick, to scout out opportunities in Dakota
Territory. His father, Norvel Blair, was unhappy with their life in
Illinois and instructed his sons to assess whether they should homestead out west. Benjamin and Patrick arrived in Sully County, in the
center of what seven years later would become the state of South
Dakota. The county lay about twenty miles north of the tiny developing settlement of Pierre. The Blairs found the region promising,
and when Sully County opened to homesteading in 1883, they filed
claims. Their father Norvel joined them a year later, filing his own
claim and purchasing land as well. In so doing, the Blairs became
the first residents of what would later sometimes be called the Sully
County Colored Colony.

Norvel Blair was the patriarch of a large family. He had been born
into slavery in Tennessee in 1825. He described his first owner as
an "orphan girl" named Mary Keteral. When he was eight years old,
he was sold to Urich Lyson, who then sold him to Adam Dixon,
who later swapped him to Gulley Wilson for another slave. He was
shuttled from Tennessee to Arkansas and back to Tennessee. Upon

emancipation, Norvel got himself to Saint Louis and then moved to Grundy County, Illinois.

In Illinois, Blair worked as a farm laborer, then rented a farm himself, saved his earnings, and bought land. He continued to raise profitable crops and engaged in various other ventures. He was especially skilled at breeding and training fast horses. His children worked jobs that also contributed to the family's growing prosperity. Their success, however, raised jealousy among neighboring whites and attracted the greedy. Illiterate, Blair trusted a white lawyer, a well-known Republican, to handle his deeds and mortgages. But the man cheated Novel out of much of his property.

Blair started over, renting a farm, and over several years, by working "night and day" and evidently being an excellent farmer, he again accrued considerable property. But his prosperity attracted the attention of another white lawyer, this time a Republican judge. Blair's son Ben warned him not to trust the judge, but Norvel saw promise in people. He wrote, "[I] could not believe that [the judge] would wrong me and my family when he knew how hard I had worked and he professed to be such a good friend of the colored race."[1] Norvel was again maneuvered into a welter of mortgages and lawsuits. The judge and his son defrauded Norvel of most of his property. After fifteen years of hard labor in Illinois, during which he had been extremely productive, he and his family were left with little to show for it.

Norvel published a book, likely written down by Benjamin, who was well educated, called *A Book for the People!* It carried the long subtitle *To Be Read by All Voters, Black and White with Thrilling Events of the Life of Norvel Blair, of Grundy County, State of Illinois. Written and Published by Him, and with the Money He Earned by His Own Labor, and Is Sent Out with the Sincere Hope That if Carefully Read, It Will Tend to Put a Stop to Northern Bull-Dozing and Will Give to All a Free Ballot, without Fear, Favor or Affection and Respect.* "Bull-dozing" was the term used to describe southern Democrats' use of violence to intimidate Black voters; here Blair turned it against northern Republicans.

Norvel related in bitter terms how his family had been shamefully robbed by reputable Republicans. He wanted to tell both the Blacks and whites of America about the deceptions of the Blacks' so-called "friend," the Republican party. "I say here that they are not the friends of the colored race and that they are entitled to no credit for the freedom of our race."[2] Norvel's anger over being cheated in Illinois caused him to send Benjamin and Patrick to find better opportunities in the West.

Only recently wrested from the Sioux and minimally organized, Dakota Territory was beginning to attract migrants. Some focused on Sully County and especially on the town of Fairbank, platted in 1883. The Chicago and Northwestern Railroad (C&NW) wanted to extend its tracks westward across the Missouri River and on to the Black Hills. Fairbank sat on the river's eastern edge. The railroad's surveyors found Fairbank to be a favorable spot for a crossing, with a hard rock river bottom and a gradual incline up the west bank. Word quickly spread that Fairbank would be the crossing point.

The news set off a speculative frenzy. A land company circulated a plan purporting to show the coming tracks of the Dakota Central Railway (a C&NW subsidiary), with a depot right in Fairbank. Railyards and warehouses would occupy the land between the depot and the river. Speculators—both "reputable men" and get-rich-quick unknowns—worked the town. They bought, sold, and resold 395 Fairbank lots while waiting for confirmation of the Dakota Central's plans. As the first on the scene, they drooled over the coming big windfalls. The bolder ones, convinced this was their big opportunity, even constructed buildings. Benjamin and Norvel Blair bought some of the town lots.[3]

Unfortunately for Fairbank and its giddy speculators, the C&NW chose a different route. It placed its terminus in Pierre instead of

Fairbank. Now bypassed, Fairbank was further diminished when county voters chose Onida as the county seat. Real estate values in Fairbank collapsed through the floor overnight. Most of the fortune hunters departed, much poorer than they had arrived.

The Blair family, however, stayed on and survived the bust. They built a substantial house outside town on Norvel's homestead claim in section one of Fairbank Township. They apparently bought some of the town lots being abandoned. They acquired more farmland and soon set about creating a profitable farm operation. Norvel and his children Edith, Winnie, John Wesley, Mary Elizabeth, Benjamin, Lucy, Seymour, and Patrick all filed homestead claims. Some took advantage of the changing laws and filed more than one claim. Between 1887 and 1908, members of the Blair family finalized fifteen claims in Sully County, including homesteads, enlarged homesteads, and timber culture claims. They proved up one claim in Hughes County and possibly purchased land in Faulk County. Their claims amounted to 3,001 acres of fields and grazing land and they may have purchased other land outright.[4]

Norvel, now in his seventies, focused his energies on farming, horse breeding, and accumulating land. He had brought from Illinois his string of Morgan horses—Morgans were favored as general riding horses, as coach horses, for cavalry, and for racing. Norvel and his sons built growing reputations for their fast horses. Black jockeys had been prominent during slavery, and after the Civil War Black jockeys won eight of the first sixteen Kentucky Derbies. While they had a storied history as jockeys, Black Americans less often owned the horses they raced. The Blairs were different. One of their horses, Johnny Bee, held the record for the fastest horse in the state from 1907 to 1909. "Racing horses is a fine sport for any man," Norvel declared, "as it teaches him how to be a good winner and a good loser, and if you can't be both you should never race horses."[5]

Between their arrival in 1882 and when Norvel turned eighty in 1905, the Blairs stuck to building their own farms and businesses. They were among the very few Black homesteaders in Sully County or indeed South Dakota. By the end of the 1880s, only the Davis, Day, and Howard families joined them as African American homesteaders in Sully County. Norvel's children proved to be energetic entrepreneurs during these years. Sons Benjamin and Patrick operated a livery in Fairbank while also farming. Daughters Mary Elizabeth (known as Betty) and Winnie for a time operated a restaurant and bakery in Pierre.

By the turn of the century, the Blairs had established themselves as highly successful if relatively isolated farmers. Benjamin, or Ben, emerged as the recognized family leader. In August 1893, referring to Ben, the *Pierre Weekly Free Press* reported that "three train loads of fat cattle were shipped to Chicago. . . . Marriott, Wimmer, Ducheneaux, and Blair were the principal shippers." In June 1904 it reported that Benjamin "was down from Sully over Sunday." It continued, "He says there is a large acreage of crops of all kinds in his country and that they are all looking fine." In June 1907 the paper commented, "Ben Blair . . . was in Pierre yesterday. He has a thousand acres of growing crops, and stated they were the best ever." In August he was back in town "for harvest supplies." In December 1908 the *Free Press* reported "B.P. Blair, P. Sorenson, Wm. Joiner, and Wm. Davis [Joiner and Davis were also African American] were down from Fairbanks Friday. Mr. Blair made two shipments of hogs to Sioux City markets."[6]

Farming success, always respected in rural areas, increasingly thrust Benjamin into the role of community leader. In 1896 Fairbank voters elected him as the first African American school board member in South Dakota. He was then chosen as chairman of the Fairbank district school board and served for ten years.[7] He began thinking about how he could more actively promote Sully County as an African American settlement site. As an increasingly prominent representative of his race, he wanted to help Black people share what he saw as Sully County's exceptional economic opportunities. And as an entrepreneur, he also likely saw opportunities for profit.

The first local notice of Ben's efforts was a sensationalized headline in the *Pierre Weekly Free Press*. "'Coon' Colony: Ben Blair Seeking to Colonize Negroes in Sully County; He Plans for a 'Darkville' Near or At Old Fairbanks Town." This story reproduced word-for-word, without citation—small-town editors often did so—an ordinary *Des Moines Register* article about Ben Blair's visit to Iowa to recruit settlers. But the *Free Press* added its own racist headline. The headline must have distressed the Blairs, who didn't normally see such naked racism in the local press.

The headline was even out of character for the *Free Press*. The word "coon" appeared as a slur in the paper only twice, never in a headline, in the seven years between 1902 and 1908. Typically, the paper was very respectful, using the labels "negro" or "colored people" and not printing racial stereotypes or gross caricatures. The *Register* article itself used much more respectful language to describe how Ben had been "in conference with the most prominent negroes in the state [Iowa], spending three days in going over his plans."[8] Two months later, the *Free Press* more respectfully noted, "B.F. Blair of Fairbank, Sully county, who is working up a colored colony for that section, says he is receiving a great many inquiries from all over the United States from colored men. They want to know what the situation is, and he has assurances that a number of them will come out to look over the country this fall."[9]

Part of "the situation" potential migrants likely wanted to learn about was the state of local race relations. Despite the initial racist headline, Black-white relations appear to have been quite good. The Blairs had operated their farms for twenty years without any reported racial incidents. Author Betti Vanepps-Taylor noted that "Dakota

Territory [earlier] lifted its whites-only restrictions on franchise and education."[10] Black journalist Kate D. Chapman in 1889 described her hometown: "Yankton has a mixed population of five thousand inhabitants, about sixty of whom are Afro-Americans, who are all more or less in a prosperous condition. The schools, churches, and hotels are thrown open to all regardless to color, and . . . the feeling that exists between the two races is friendly in the extreme."[11]

Black residents also did well in what W. E. B. Du Bois, writing at just this time, called "civic equality." They had access to and participated in the courts: Benjamin Blair was called to serve on a U.S. district court jury for a case in Deadwood. Black people voted and participated in politics: Benjamin later served as a precinct delegate to the Democratic convention for Sully and Hughes (Pierre) counties, placing a candidate in nomination for U.S. Senate. Ben's sales pitch to potential colony recruits likely was made more attractive by what many perceived to be a racial climate more tolerant to Black advancement than elsewhere in the country.

Benjamin initiated a more formal recruitment effort in July 1906, when he traveled to Yankton to meet with other Black South Dakotans and Reverend John C. Coleman, an AME pastor from Pennsylvania. They organized the Northwestern Homestead Movement (NHM), with a stated purpose of "bringing a better class of intelligent negroes from the southern states to South Dakota, to file on land in colonies and in the case of those having the means, to buy land outright." Dr. Coleman became president of the new group, which included the Link Brothers Organization, already in the business of recruiting southern Blacks for migration to South Dakota. The NHM was headquartered in Yankton, Kate Chapman's hometown, which was considered the gateway to South Dakota. It already had an active, though small, Black community.

The Northwestern Homestead Movement envisioned establishing four African American colonies in the state. It advised new arrivals that they could obtain land by making homestead claims, by purchasing land if they had sufficient cash, or by participating in a building-and-loan program it intended to initiate. Good land for homesteading was becoming available in central South Dakota, so NHM proposed locating its colonies there. Ben on behalf of the Blair family pledged 1,700 acres to build an agricultural college to teach Black farmers advanced agricultural techniques useful in the Great Plains.[12]

The local press greeted formation of the Northwest Homestead Movement with very favorable reporting. The *Pierre Weekly Free Press*, abandoning its earlier name-calling, headlined a long and respectful article, "Negro Colony in South Dakota: Project Includes Establishment of Agricultural Colleges to Teach the Colored People Farming." It quoted Reverend Coleman: "The negro must become an independent citizen if he is going to remain in this country. No servant people can obtain a permanent footing in any country unless they secure means for an independent existence, and for such existence they must follow agricultural pursuits. . . . I am advising the industrious class of negroes . . . to take up homesteads." Ben's recruiting paid off. In April 1907 he returned with a number of Black families who intended to settle in Fairbank Township.[13]

The other three proposed colonies never got started, and Ben Blair never opened his agricultural college, but Sully County apparently got a boost from the NHM effort. Once again the Blair entrepreneurial energies helped drive the project. Betty Blair, Benjamin's sister, saw business opportunity in the colony effort, and she became a land locator and sales agent for the King Real Estate Company of Iowa. Blair had "considerable drive and sales skill." Black resident Fern Barber remembered Betty: "Like most land agents she was pretty good at embellishing a tale; she went back east to recruit buyers and even got them to believe there weren't any flies in South Dakota."

Betty Blair successfully brokered a number of land deals for Black newcomers. In her first one, in 1908, she located William Davis on 160 acres, probably the northeast quarter of section twenty-one in Fairbank Township. These were boom years in South Dakota land speculation; Davis sold his quarter-section in 1918, clearing a $5,000 profit (worth nearly $100,000 in 2022). Blair apparently also profited handsomely from her land sales during the boom, and she was credited with assisting most of the Black families joining the Sully County colony to find land, contributing to the success of the colony itself.[14]

Black families acquired land mainly through homesteading, and some also purchased or leased land. William Fairchild filed a homestead claim in 1905 or 1906 and proved it up in 1911. Dock Palmer proved up his claim in 1911, Green Windsor in 1912 and another with his wife Mary in 1925, William Davis and John Joiner proved up their claims in 1914, William Day and Rob Fields in 1914, George Howard in 1917, H. C. Thomas in 1915, Elmer Figgins one in 1917 and another in 1923, Allen Florence in 1914 and another with his wife Emma in 1922, Ed Gorham in 1920, and William Nash in 1922.

John and Ellen McGruder's purchase of a huge ranch opened a new phase in the development of the settlement. They arrived in 1908 with several children and considerable wealth. Both Ellen and John had been enslaved near Bethel, in northwest Missouri. After emancipation, John had prospered in various enterprises around Bethel. He even purchased part of the farm where he had been held enslaved. The McGruders shifted operations to South Dakota, and working through Betty Blair, bought the 1,200-acre Lytle Ranch. They allegedly paid $35,000 for it, though the financial arrangements are unclear.

The McGruders ran three hundred head of cattle, three thousand sheep, and thirty race and work horses. John purchased a large steam tractor with Scotch plow bottoms for breaking prairie. He employed the tractor in his own fields and broke sod for other farmers in Fairbank and Grandview townships. The *Okobojo Times*—Okobojo was a Sully County town, now-defunct—noted that the "plow operators passed through town Wednesday with the big monster, on their way to Hughes County to break a large acreage for newcomers."[15] Cecil Leo McGruder, John McGruder's great-grandson, remembered the steam tractor. He admits it "wasn't used much by the time I can remember, because as one neighbor told me, after hauling 10 wagons of coal, it would take one of the wagon-loads of coal just to get the [tractor] back home."

John McGruder died in 1916. By then the family had mortgages on the land, and Ellen was unable to keep up the payments. She lost their original place.[16] Despite the setback, she persisted and filed her own Enlarged Homestead claim for 283.5 acres. She worked tirelessly on her claim and received her patent for the land in 1920. Son William and his wife, Meta, farmed a half-section in Grandview township, while sons George and James each filed on 160-acre homesteads.[17]

The Sully County colony's population likely peaked at about 125 residents. The exact number remains unknown, with different observers offering varying estimates. John Andrews, E. L. Thompson, and others conventionally claimed a Black population of 200, but that is perhaps an exaggeration. Betti Vanepps-Taylor puts the figure at 80, which is more probable but perhaps low. The census, which often undercounted Black people, registered 54 African Americans in both 1910 and 1920. A peak population of around 125 seems more plausible, given that 22 different individuals proved up homestead claims, and others bought land, as John McGruder did, or leased land, as Charles and Rosetta Speese did. Still others may have resided in what remained of Fairbank city, doing town jobs rather than farming. Adding all these claimants, buyers, lessors, and their families, suggests a peak population of about 125.

Black residents of Sully County probably owned or controlled around ten thousand acres. The *Onida Watchman* in 1907 asserted that members of the colony owned thirty-five thousand acres, but unless members had major holdings outside of Fairbank, Troy, Pearl, Little Bend, and Grandview townships, that appears to be exaggerated. We know that the Blairs (three thousand acres) and McGruders (two thousand acres) had large holdings, but most other families owned a quarter-section, with a few owning twice that. Counting claimed, proved-up, purchased, and leased land, total Black-controlled land likely amounted to about ten thousand acres.

The Sully County homesteaders made education one of their top priorities. Norvel Blair was illiterate into his forties but apparently learned to read and write after that. His sons were already well educated in Illinois schools when they arrived in South Dakota. The Blairs participated in founding and operating the Fairbank schools because they wanted the family's children to be educated. They also knew that to attract new Black residents they would need to offer good schools. Rose and Charles Speese were examples of that, because they moved from DeWitty in part to find good schools for their children. They were especially concerned with finding a high school for the older children, including Ava and Norma.

The McGruders, too, ensured that their children would be well educated. Cecil Roosevelt McGruder was a young boy when his father, William, moved to Sully County. Cecil Roosevelt attended the Grandview Township school in Okobojo through the eighth grade, along with his siblings Juanita, Albert, and Louis. Cecil Roosevelt's nine children attended the Fairbank School through eighth grade and then went to live with families in Pierre, trading housework and childcare for room and board while they attended high school. One of Cecil Roosevelt's children, Cecil Leo, joked in his yearbook that he "never let his studies interfere with his sleep," but joking aside, the McGruders took education seriously. When the one-room Fairbank elementary school closed in the 1960s, Cecil Leo didn't want to see the building fall apart, and so he acted. "It always looked

57. Children at the Fairbank School, Sully County, 1933.
Permission of Jeanettee Parton.

like a big old building to me when I was going to school, I went up
to measure the thing and took my stack mover [a heavy trailer used
to move stacks of hay] and hauled the thing home. Slid it on and
took it home. When you're a little kid, things look big."[18]

Several of Cecil Roosevelt's children attended college at the Northern State Teacher's College in Aberdeen, including Linda, Wayne,
Marion, and Maxine.

The McGruders' hours out of school in the evening were often
spent making music. Cecil Roosevelt played the violin, and all of
Cecil's children joined in. Elnora, Herman, Wayne, and Marion
played guitar, and Leo was the drummer. Other times they passed
the hours simply visiting with neighbors. Cecil Leo remembered
that the Blairs kept a parrot, with the imaginative name Polly, as a

Northern State Teachers College
Aberdeen, South Dakota

Date 10-21-65

This is to Certify that

Marion McGruder

Is a Student at Northern

And Classified as a /Freshman

On September — 1965

MARION McGRUDER

58. Marion McGruder's student identification card, Northern State
Teachers College, 1965. Permission of Jeanettee Parton.

pet. Cecil Leo as a youngster used to "pick on that parrot something
terrible." With an almost mischievous smile he remembered sitting
at the Blair's table with a pencil lying within arm's reach and Polly in
a cage nearby. He reached out and "picked up the pencil and [Polly]
started screaming, 'Betty! Boy! Pencil!'" If Cecil Leo's infectious
laugh is testimony, those were good times.[19]

Early Black settlers in Sully County and people later recruited for
the Sully County colony remained active in the region well into the
twentieth century. The commemorative volume, *75 Years of Sully
County History*, published in 1958, notes, "The McGruders are the
only ones left of the Colored Colony, the others having moved to
various parts of the country following the 1930 depression years."
Maxine McGruder, great-granddaughter of John and Ellen McGruder,
was said to be (in 1953) "the only Negro teaching at a white school
in South Dakota." A few homesteader descendants continue to live
in the Pierre area.[20]

Black migrants, during the exploration and testing that preceded
the Great Migration to northern cities, made Sully County another

migrant destination. They took great risks and persisted through years of backbreaking labor to achieve big results. For a time, the Blairs, McGruders, Days, Speeses, and others created prosperous livelihoods for themselves, educated their children, and looked to the future.

Their future in farming eventually turned out to be bleak, as the farmers' depression of the 1920s gave way to what in the southern plains were called the "Dirty Thirties" and in the northern plains "them dry years." Crops withered, and prices sagged. The Sully County colony did not survive the hard times, but by then most of its children, now educated, made meaningful and fulfilling lives for themselves elsewhere in the Great Plains and the nation. Still, the land yielded up its blessings. Jeanettee Parton, a McGruder descendant, mused, "My family sacrificed everything for their land. Success was born and found in the land. Everything we had came from the land."[21] And if the metric is, as it should be, the successful lives of the Sully County descendants, those sacrifices paid big dividends.

Today, the Sully County colony is marked only by two physical remembrances: a headstone carrying the single word "Blair" in a small cemetery on private property, tended by Roger McGruder and the (white) landowner; and an historical marker on the grounds of the Sully County courthouse in Onida. We initiated the campaign to erect the marker, working with the McGruder family and the National Trust for Historic Preservation's African American Cultural Heritage Action Fund, which paid for it. The Sully County Board of Commissioners enthusiastically approved its placement. Black homesteader descendants Roger McGruder and Leo L. McGruder helped unveil it in October 2020. The marker concludes,

> Though most community members left during the Great Depression, these homesteaders remain a powerful reminder

59. Black homesteader descendants Roger McGruder and Leo L. McGruder unveil historical marker at the Sully County Courthouse in Onida, commemorating the Black homesteader community of Sully County. 2020. Permission of *Onida Watchman*, DRG Media Group, Pierre.

of generations of African Americans who sought opportunity in the Great Plains and pursued their dreams of land ownership, entrepreneurship, and civil equality.

While the Sully County homesteaders enjoyed substantial success, Black migrants in Wyoming, who started with such excellent prospects, endured a harder fate.

10

Tragedy and Failure at Empire

Hotels are public utilities, and as such should be open to all the
public. . . . It may be a breach of propriety for us to tell the public
of our discomfort due to discrimination, nevertheless we felt it
our duty to do so, and duty knows not the laws of propriety.

—RUSSEL TAYLOR, Empire homesteader

Radford Speese flicked the end of his whip on the horses' rumps,
encouraging them to pull his heavy wagon west. He led a caravan,
wagons weighed down with carpenters' tools, farm implements, and
household goods, and carrying perhaps twenty people. They headed
to Goshen County, Wyoming, just across Nebraska's western border.

The party included several intermarried Speese, Shores, and Taylor families—Joseph Speese, John Wesley Speese, Baseman Taylor,
and their families. Baseman's wife, Maggie Shores, had recently died,
so his family consisted of just himself and his six-year-old daughter,
Elsie. Sixteen-year-old Rose Meehan drove one of the wagons, then
quickly hopped the train back to Westerville in time to marry Charles
Speese. Soon enough, Charles Speese and Otis Taylor, with their
families and household goods, traveled by rail to Torrington, the
nearest stop, and then took teams and wagons the remaining seven
miles to join the little community. There, in 1908, they established
the new settlement of Empire.

Exactly why they left Nebraska isn't clear, but certainly part of
their motivation was to take up the government's new offer of bigger
homestead claims. In 1904 Congress created a buzz when it passed

Nebraska Congressman Moses Kinkaid's bill. It authorized claims of 640 acres, but this privilege was limited to a special region in northwest Nebraska. Many land seekers speculated that Congress would soon extend the fix to other areas in the interior West, and they weren't wrong. Wyoming's Congressman Frank Mondell, chair of the Public Lands Committee in the House of Representatives, had just such a plan. Congress passed his Enlarged Homestead Act in 1909.[1] It permitted 320-acre claims in marginal lands throughout the West. Just as there were "Kinkaid claims" in the Sandhills, Charles Speese called his Wyoming filing under the Enlarged Homestead Act a "Mondell claim."

The Speeses, Shores, and Taylors may have seen this opportunity coming and migrated west to get a jump on the competition. The site they chose in the North Platte Valley was Spoon Hill Creek (later renamed Sheep Creek). It lay right along the eastern edge of Wyoming. Henry Cunningham, a white rancher in Spoon Hill and an agent for the Empire Land and Cattle Development Company, wooed them to this spot.

The Speese Brothers already owned a nearby ranch straddling the state line. Joseph was excited that while the ranch's barn and seven hundred acres were in Nebraska, his house would be in Wyoming, which would mean that his kids would go to Wyoming schools.[2] Otis and Sarah (Speese) Taylor moved into a house thought to be exactly on the border, with a wall separating the western Wyoming room from the eastern Nebraska room.

The newcomers joined a few other scattered Black settlers, including Rosengrant Peyton, a homesteader out from Wisconsin, and Jim Edwards, a big cattle rancher who lived sixty miles north of Empire. But few other Black people lived in eastern Wyoming, and even whites were pretty sparse in 1908. This was raw country—Torrington itself had popped up only in 1900. The Speese brothers and other new settlers spread out across the landscape on their claims, which they supplemented with purchased land. The town they created remained rudimentary.

The Empire builders harbored big hopes for success in the Equality State. They seemed well-equipped to achieve it. They had been financially successful in Nebraska, so they had capital to invest. They had created a supporting community for themselves in Westerville, within of course the constraints imposed by the era's racist mores, and they carried with them to Wyoming the supportive bonds of a ready-made community.

And unlike many homesteaders, they had extensive farming experience. Historian Todd Guenther observed, "These young, black men and women who came of age around the turn of the twentieth century . . . pulled calves in the snow and drove their stock to railheads for shipment to eastern packing houses. They raised good mules that were marketed in Omaha."[3] They became intimately familiar with the peculiarities of the Great Plains climate and soils, knew which crops did well, studied fluctuations in eastern markets, and made informed decisions. They brought skills and capital to their new venture and were flush with confidence. They had succeeded before, and they fully expected to succeed again.

Their investable capital came from selling their cattle and successful farm properties in Nebraska. In December 1907 Charles Speese sold the family's Custer County cattle herd. The following March, Baseman Taylor sold his livestock, farm equipment, and household goods. Also that month, the Speeses sold three parcels in Custer County, netting $12,000. In January 1909 Otis Taylor and Charles Speese returned to Nebraska to sell the remainder of their stock and equipment.

Now they could plow those proceeds into the farms, cattle, and houses at Empire. Charles Speese and Otis Taylor each claimed 320 acres of Enlarged Homestead land. Joseph Speese made a Desert Land claim of 160 acres, both near Spoon Hill Creek. They also purchased some 800 acres of Cunningham's farmland, and they owned the ranch straddling the state line. The Speese brothers' investment in their Wyoming properties probably exceeded $20,000 (worth more than $615,000 in 2022), a huge sum. Having capital was a big advantage, giving firm foundation to their soaring aspirations.

The Empire residents' financial status was reflected in the houses they built. No one mentions dugouts, and most didn't use sod. Instead, they built solid frame farmhouses, constructed of lumber ordered in by rail. Even the few who did build soddies, as Charles Speese did when he constructed his big five-room sod house, added a shingle roof.[4] On January 20, 1910, the *Torrington Telegram* reported that Radford Taylor "brought back a load of lumber with which to complete his house." Otis and Sarah Taylor's house, the one on the state line, had been started some years earlier by two white sisters. The Taylors added on to it, creating a comfortable two-story, eight-room house.[5] Others lived in houses less elaborate but still substantial, especially for homesteaders. Most completed their homes by late 1909 or early 1910.

Their affluence also meant that they, unlike many homesteaders, did not need to be in a rush to plant their first crop so they could eat. While they were hard workers and eager to get going, they were driven by ambition, not looming hunger. In 1911 the Speese brothers sought to purchase a cattle herd, as can be seen in the ad Joseph placed in the *Brewster* (Nebraska) *News*. Buying two hundred cow-calves at once would have been an expensive deal, and certainly would have jump-started their cattle operation.

We do not know the exact population of Empire, which fluctuated over the years. Typical families were very large. Russel and Henrietta Taylor had seven children. Charles and Rosetta Speese at that point had six kids. The settlers proved up ten homesteads in all, and with their large families, we estimate that perhaps sixty people or so lived on those claims. Other residents purchased their land or leased it

Wanted to Buy.

I want to buy 200 calves, cows with calves by their side or yearlings.

J. S. Speese.   Box 162

Terrington, Wy.

60. Notice placed by Joseph Speese in the *Brewster News*, August 25, 1911, 5. newspapers.com.

or didn't farm at all, and they added more people to the population. Perhaps eighty or a hundred people resided in Empire at its peak.[6]

Empire residents aggressively filed claims for nearby public lands, perhaps reacting to the parade of new land-seekers who arrived daily to stake claims. The Enlarged Homestead Act, like the Kinkaid Act, attracted many whites scrambling to get the bigger tracts it permitted. The 1877 Desert Land Act also authorized larger claims, but it required installation of expensive irrigation works. And later, in 1916, the Stock Raising Homestead Act would authorize claims of 640 acres (later reduced to 320 acres) in regions considered so dry as to be good only for grazing. Empire residents used or tried to use all these laws. Russel Taylor filed a homestead claim in 1913 and another claim, probably an Enlarged Homestead claim, in 1914, for a total of 321 acres. His wife Henrietta Taylor filed for an additional 200 acres, but she never patented that claim.

Charles Speese vigorously pursued his rights under various legislative acts, although he was not always pleased with the GLO's response. In 1912 he wrote the GLO about what he considered his rightful claims. He noted that he had "perfected title" or proved up on 320 acres in Wyoming under what he called the "Mondell act" (the Enlarged Homestead Act) and wondered whether he wasn't still eligible to claim another 320 acres in Nebraska under the Kinkaid Act.[7]

The law allowed a homesteader who had already proved up a 160-acre homestead under the 1862 Act to claim an additional 480 acres under the Kinkaid Act. Charles had already claimed 320 acres under

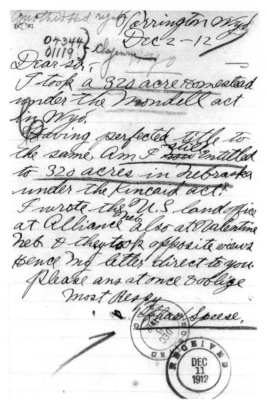

61. Charles Speese's letter to the General Land Office, December 3, 1912. National Archives and Records Administration.

the Enlarged Homestead Act. He argued that if the GLO applied to his situation the logic that permitted 160-acre claimants to file for an additional 480 acres, he should be able to claim 320 acres under the Kinkaid Act. But the Alliance, Nebraska, land office rejected his request. Describing himself as a "much wronged homesteader," he protested to Washington that the local land office was unjustly ignoring his rights.

Lizzie Speese, married to Charles's brother Joseph, also pursued her rights under the changing legislation, though perhaps she was somewhat confused about which legislation applied. On November 14, 1916, she filed for 320 acres under the Desert Land Homestead Act, the maximum allowed to an individual under that act.

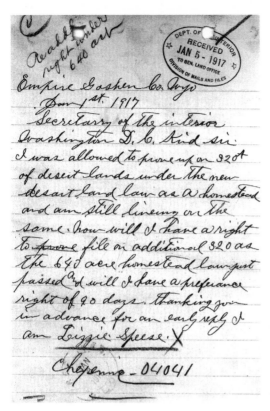

62. Lizzie Speese's letter to the secretary of the interior, January 1, 1917. National Archives and Records Administration.

Then on December 29, 1916, Congress passed the Stock-Raising Homestead Act, which allowed entrymen to claim 640 acres of land that was too dry for crops. Just two days later, on New Year's Day 1917, Lizzie wrote from Empire to the Secretary of the Interior asking him to clarify whether she was now eligible to claim an additional 320 acres, since she had only claimed 320 acres. The GLO denied her appeal. She signed her letter with an X, suggesting she was not literate. Nonetheless, like her brother-in-law and other relatives, Lizzie kept a sharp eye on how new laws and regulations affected her rights to claim federal land.

Empire farmers needed to adapt their farming knowledge to eastern Wyoming's dry, sandy soils and sparse rainfall. They had moved deeper into the rain shadow of the Rocky Mountains, which made Empire drier than Westerville. They tried a variety of crops, including potatoes, corn, and barley. Most had vegetable gardens and raised chickens and livestock. In 1912 Joseph Speese won first place at the county fair for his sweet corn, popcorn, potatoes, millet, cucumbers, muskmelon, and field peas.[8] But to raise such crops they needed to irrigate their gardens, and they also needed water for household use and for their livestock. Wells were the only reliable source of water. Unfortunately, the water table was highly variable and often deep. Miles Speese finished digging a well for the H. L. Watson family, not striking water until he reached a staggering 163 feet.[9]

Russel Taylor moved to Empire in 1911 and quickly became both its educational and religious leader. He had graduated from Bellevue College, a Nebraska institution then run by the Presbyterian Church. He also studied at Lane Theological Seminary in Cincinnati, which was affiliated with the Presbyterians and whose first president, Lyman Beecher, was the father of Henry Ward Beecher and Harriet Beecher Stowe. Lane Seminary hosted several famous antislavery debates in the 1830s. The debates were so controversial they set off protests that nearly wrecked the school. Cincinnati was too close to slave-state Kentucky for antislavery opinions not to be dangerous. The school was still controversial for its liberal racial views when Russel attended just before the turn of the century.

After studying at Lane Seminary, Russel spent a decade in New Market, Tennessee, working as a Presbyterian missionary to freed-people. Later he traveled the country as chair of the Freedmen's Bureau of the national (northern) Presbyterian church. When Russel and his large family moved to Empire, they moved in with his brother Otis and sister-in-law Sarah, taking up lodging in the Nebraska room of their house that straddled the state line.

Russel's extensive travel gave him wide experience and national contacts, creating a prominence few homesteaders enjoyed. He was

63. Russel Taylor, ca. 1915. Permission of Bellevue Collection, Perkins Library Special Collections, Hastings College.

much better known outside Goshen County than in it, as people in Torrington seemed not to notice or care about him. He was Empire's most eminent citizen and the obvious choice to write the "Empire Items" column for the *Goshen County Journal*. He became, in effect, the person who spoke for the colony in public. He brought enthusiasm and a vision for what the community could be, alongside a pugnacious insistence on standing up for his community's rights.

At just this time another Wyoming homesteader, Elinore Pruitt Stewart, came to national attention for her letters to *Atlantic Monthly*. A white woman, she and her daughter settled across the state in Sweetwater County, where she filed a homestead claim. She married Clyde Stewart, a dour Scotsman, also a homesteader. Recording her experiences in her *Atlantic* letters, Elinore projected a no-nonsense approach to the rigors of frontier life. But with her toughness came a charming literary side as well. She modeled the grit, determination, honesty, and inherent uprightness that delighted Eastern readers and that those easterners associated with winning the West.

Many years later, historian Sherry Smith uncovered the rest of Elinore's story. Elinore filed her homestead claim as a single woman and married Clyde Stewart the next week. She worried enough about a possible contest to her dubious claim, now that she was married, that she relinquished her claim to her mother-in-law. The mother-in-law, when she received patent, promptly sold it to Clyde. Although never detected by the GLO or its agents, Elinore's transactions arguably constituted fraud of the homesteading marital rules. In any event, Elinore's readers and critics alike so loved her stories that Houghton Mifflin, in 1914, published them as a book, *Letters of a Woman Homesteader*. The book became a classic and is still in print.[10] In 1979 Hollywood retold the Stewarts' story in a powerful film called *Heartland* starring Conchata Ferrell and Rip Torn.

Over in Empire, Russel Taylor soon mobilized thirty residents to found Grace Presbyterian Church, the community's first congregation. He served as its pastor. The church initially held services in people's homes, then in Empire's new school building, and finally in 1915 in its own building. Officially Taylor was assigned to Grace Church by the Wyoming Presbytery's Board of Home Missions, which paid his salary. This arrangement relieved his congregants, many of whom were cash poor, from having to tithe to support him.

Taylor still traveled occasionally for the national Presbyterian church to continue his mission work among freedmen, and he maintained ties with the majority-white Presbyterian governing bodies in both Nebraska and Wyoming. In 1912 women of the First Presbyterian Church of Omaha prepared a Christmas box for "the home mission pastor and his family at Empire, Wyoming." The ladies collected clothing as well as other items thought to be useful.

Taylor thanked them in a letter the women considered "so filled with appreciation, couched in such touching words [that] the full meaning of the Biblical injunction 'Cast your bread upon the waters' was forcefully revealed."[11]

Taylor obtained a fourth-class post office for Empire in April 1912, with himself as postmaster. In rural communities, the post office frequently operated out of a private home or store. Russel ran his post office from his residence in the "Nebraska Room" of Otis's house. This meant that the Wyoming settlement's post office was actually located in Nebraska, which was certainly unusual and perhaps illegal. However, obtaining a post office for Empire placed the settlement on a more official basis.[12] Taylor also farmed his claim.

Empire residents soon finished their first tasks—filing claims, building houses, getting their farms going, starting a school, erecting a church, and obtaining a post office. They were then able to turn to longer-term concerns. Unfortunately, they confronted three great obstacles that cast a dark shadow over the community's development.

The first source of trouble was the hostility of surrounding whites. The Speeses and Taylors had been sold on the Spoon Hill Creek area by Henry Cunningham, a white man who seemed genuinely committed to bringing long-term Black residents into the area. Other whites, however, appeared less keen on their arrival. The locals might have been unfriendly to any large group of new arrivals. Ranchers opposed all homesteaders, who closed the open range and competed for the sparse grass. And would-be white homesteaders competed with everyone to get their claims filed on the available government land, which was rapidly filling up. But the ranchers and other whites undoubtedly reacted more harshly because these newcomers were Black.

Ranchers began to blame their Black neighbors whenever stock or tools went missing or fences were downed. In 1909 the Speeses leased some of their cow pastures to prominent white rancher Yorick

Nichols. By the start of the next year, they had fallen out, both sides charging the other with theft of hay, stock rustling, and threatening to shoot each other. They launched a series of lawsuits. Usually Nichols or other whites sued the Speeses, other times the Speeses sued them. In February 1911 Charles Speese was arrested for "cattle stealing" and bound over for hearing in Torrington. The charge was soon quashed. In 1912 and 1913, Squier Jones sued John Wesley Speese for stealing hogs and for unpaid debt.

Torrington Justice of the Peace James Jackson heard most of the cases in this ongoing feud. John Wesley Speese, the family's attorney, several times requested changes of venue because he believed Jackson was "biased and prejudiced." Still, the Speeses seemed to win more often than they lost. In one case transferred for trial to Gering, Nebraska, a district court jury, according to the *Mitchell Index*, "awarded the plaintiffs [Speese Brothers] something like twenty-three hundred dollars."[13]

But the continuing string of cases created worries and must have been emotionally exhausting, even when the Speeses won. And Empire residents endured other irritants as well. Torrington was not alone in discriminating against Black people, but it was one of the worst. Restaurants, hotels, schools, even some stores refused to serve African Americans. Russel Taylor wrote numerous letters to the *Torrington Telegram* and other papers protesting that he and other Empire residents were citizens and should be served. Outraged at one incident, Taylor railed about it in his "Empire Items" column printed on the front page of the *Goshen County Journal*:

> Our teacher, Miss Rose Hutchinson, accompanied by Mrs. H. L. Speese were in Torrington Saturday looking for a place where the former might board during her attendance at the county Teachers Institute. To our surprise we were informed that she was unable to find such accommodation. It has also come to

our ears that one of our citizens out here was recently refused lodging in one of the Torrington hotels although he was compelled to stay all night there in order to attend to some business with one of the foremost business men of Torrington the next day. Though he had money to pay his way he was forced to stay all night in the livery stable with the attendant there.

We do not feel that the true people of Torrington approve of such as this. We believe that when they know the true status of affairs they will see that such offenses do not occur again. The state of Wyoming is too broad and too liberal to tolerate such narrowness.

Hotels are public utilities, and as such should be open to all the public.

—RUSSEL TAYLOR

The *Journal*'s editor, in the next issue, took Taylor to task without ever mentioning his name:

We are not sure whether it was Ben Franklin or Horace Greeley but some wise man once gave the following advice to angry people:

When something happens to make you angry or provoked at someone, don't go and have it out with him while your mind is unbalanced by these disturbing emotions, but write a letter to the offender. Pour out all the indignation and spitefulness you feel in your heart. Put it down on paper in black and white. Then lay that letter in your desk until the next day. Let your mind become cooled and calm equilibrium regained by the restoring power of sleep. Then pick up your letter and read it. Nine times out of ten you will blush with shame at your own letter and will destroy it, thanking God that you did not send out a letter which would have served to shame you for days or years to come.

But Taylor did not back down, responding in his column the following week: "It may be a breach of propriety for us to tell the public of our discomfort due to discrimination, nevertheless we felt it our duty to do so, and duty knows not the laws of propriety." It is doubtful that Torrington hoteliers and restaurant owners changed much, despite Taylor's stated optimism. Nor did area whites improve their attitudes.[14]

Empire's school was the second great arena of controversy and conflict. Like parents in other Black colonies, Empire parents cherished their ability to shape their children's education. The whole Speese-Shores-Taylor migration to Wyoming may have been motivated in part by dissatisfaction with Nebraska schools.

And the families aspired to more than just the lower grades. Some of Moses and Susan Speese's children had attended Tabor College in Iowa, an institution that welcomed Black students as a continuation of its long-standing commitment running back to when it was a stop on the Underground Railroad. William H. ("Henry") Speese graduated from Tabor in 1895 with a bachelor of literature degree and eventually became an Episcopal minister in Ohio. John Wesley Speese was a law graduate of Kansas Wesleyan University in Salina, Kansas, and had apprenticed with a lawyer in Topeka. Russel Taylor graduated from Bellevue College. In 1910 only 2.4 percent of eighteen to twenty-four-year-olds were enrolled in college, and several Speeses and Taylors were among them.[15] For the parents, education was a precious birthright they were determined to bequeath to their children.

They came into conflict with the local school board soon after their arrival in Empire. The school board authorized a new school building for Empire, one Russel Taylor later called "one of the very best buildings in the county among rural schools." In 1909–10 the community had hired a young Black woman, Sallie Thistle, to be the teacher in their one-room schoolhouse. So far, so good. But things soon began to sour.

Taylor had been expected to be the teacher in 1910–11, but he was delayed on his mission work in Tennessee, so the board hired a young white woman, a Miss Daniel, to teach the Empire students. The residents protested, and the board dismissed Daniel and rehired Thistle. Thistle's return temporarily restored the peace, but both Empire parents and the board now harbored deep distrust of each other. It would only get worse.

Taylor finally arrived to assume leadership of the school in late 1911. At first the Empire school served only Black children, but Taylor opened it to whites as well. Wyoming state law prescribed separate schools when there were fifteen or more Black children in a district. However, segregation was rarely enforced in practice. The law's purpose was to keep Black kids out of white schools, but at Empire it would have meant keeping white kids out of a Black school. Several white parents enrolled their children in Taylor's school, but other whites soon pressured them to withdraw them. The Empire school reverted to being *de facto* all Black.

The school enrolled twenty-two students for 1912–13. Parents wanted to be sure it was a Black person instructing their children. Taylor later wrote that in all his years in school, no white teacher or schoolbook had ever taught anything about, or were even aware of, the accomplishments of Black people.[16]

In 1914 Empire parents again found themselves embroiled with the school board. This time the quarrel was over the recent school census. Then as now, the county allocated funds to each school for its operations depending on how many students the school enrolled. It determined enrollment by an annual census. The *Torrington Telegraph* published an article called "Facts about the School Census" which praised the care that enumerators took and the accuracy of their count. Taylor objected in his *Goshen County Journal* column, saying "We have no doubt but that the law on this matter is all right, but like some other things in our school supervision it is not carefully administered."

He went on to accuse the four enumerators, who certified their results under oath, of at least malfeasance and possibly corruption. He faulted the previous year's count. For the 1913 census, he claimed, the clerk of the school board met a fifteen-year-old Empire girl in the sand hills and questioned her about the number and ages of Empire's school children. Her answers constituted the board's only source of data, and parents complained that the census-takers missed at least one child who was of school age and therefore reduced Empire's school budget proportionately.

The 1914 count, according to Taylor, was even worse. There was in fact no census conducted at all. Taylor questioned everyone in Empire except one family, and no one could recall ever speaking to an enumerator. What, he asked, was the purpose of the enumerators' sworn oaths attesting to the accuracy and completeness of the school census? Taylor continued, "If these enumerators are paid for their service and we presume they are, and since the very foundations of our schools financially rest on this enumeration it seems to us that it should be guarded with zealous care."[17]

It may seem that Taylor was engaging in an ordinary school funding dispute of the kind that may be found in many communities. But here the wound went deeper—what was so hurtful was the officials' brazen *disrespect* and *disregard* for the Empire community.

In August another conflict over teacher selection erupted. Empire parents—including six Taylors, two Speeses, and one other parent—representing eighteen students presented a formal protest to the board. They declared that for the past three years they had enjoyed the effective service of a teacher with the second-highest professional certificate granted in the state. But, they complained, the board ignored their wishes and went out of the state of Wyoming to recruit a teacher. The new teacher was "of tender years, of little experience, and of an inferior grade of certificate." This was not a question of race—both the teacher being let go and Miss Hutchinson, the new teacher from Kansas, were Black. Rather, the issue was quality and once again the board's studied and offensive disregard of the parents' wishes.[18]

Joseph Speese and Russel Taylor traveled to Torrington in December to put their concerns directly before the board. They were at pains to disavow any animus toward Miss Hutchinson: "Our teacher is a good girl, and conscientious in her work." But, they said, she was unable to properly control the school or do the work. "We doubt if there is a school in the county where dissatisfied patrons having students in the proportions we have, eighteen out of twenty-two enrolled, whose dissatisfaction is as ignored as is ours." Taylor reported that two board members were inclined to listen, but the third told them their complaints were without any weight because the petitioners were prejudiced. This sent Taylor off on an extended exegesis on the meaning of the word "prejudiced," but as usual, he and Joseph Speese obtained no relief.

The Empire community's school wars sharply contrasted with the experiences of Black homesteaders in Nicodemus, DeWitty, and Sully County. In those communities, Black people controlled the local schools—they made the decisions of which teachers to hire and how the schools would serve local families. They were not without conflict over school taxes, interaction with county boards, and arranging for high school enrollment. But the schools themselves were run by community members, a power that residents highly prized. In Empire, white board members exercised more intrusive and biased oversight and simply dismissed community concerns.

The third and crushing controversy involved Baseman Taylor, Russel's brother. Baseman had married Maggie Shores, John Wesley

Shores's daughter, in their fancy Westerville wedding, but she died in 1906. In 1910 Baseman sent his young daughter, Elsie, back to Nebraska to be cared for by her maternal grandparents, John and Millie Shores.

Baseman declared he was tired of farming and done with it. He supported himself instead by working odd jobs in hotels in Torrington and Henry. He resided in a shack on several acres, with few tools or other possessions. He was the least successful Taylor or Speese, and he suffered for years from poverty, depression, and other psychological problems. He became increasingly isolated and led a precarious existence.

By 1912 Baseman had become paranoid and actively aggressive. Russel and others worried that he was a physical threat to their families and neighbors. In thinking about what to do, they may have remembered Earl Speese, the brother of Russel's wife, Sarah. Earl had been sent to the Nebraska State Hospital for the Insane in Lincoln, though he may have had epilepsy rather than mental illness. Earl ultimately died in that hospital, but the Speese family never voiced any criticism of it, believing it was the right place for him. Russel may have had this experience in mind when he asked a court to declare Baseman incompetent, expecting that his brother would be sent to Wyoming's State Hospital for the Insane in Evanston.

The Goshen County sheriff and deputies took Baseman into custody, treating him roughly. They apparently injured Baseman's head, and he began having seizures. Lacking a jail, the deputies took him to be held in the Torrington Hotel. (The hotel seemed to have no objection to housing Black prisoners, though it had refused to lodge Empire's prim young teacher, Miss Hutchinson.) Baseman refused to keep quiet in the lobby, and the deputies repeatedly struck and brutalized him. Hotel guests and staff looked on in shock.

Baseman continued to be loud and disruptive, and the deputies took him to an upstairs room. They shackled him to the bed and continued to torture him, choking, burning, and beating him. They kept him in the room, apparently with no plan to transport him to the Hospital for the Insane. They inflicted numerous injuries, and at some point they damaged his trachea. Baseman Taylor died after three days of beatings.[19]

The county prosecutor refused to charge the sheriff or his deputies with any crime. His decision came despite the presence of numerous witnesses, all white, who had been in the lobby and volunteered to testify to the deputies' prolonged abuse of Baseman. The *Torrington Telegraph* ascribed Taylor's death to his preexisting medical or neurological condition; *The Goshen County Journal* failed to report it at all.

Baseman's killing shocked and disheartened the whole Empire community. They had left Nebraska perhaps in part because of dissatisfaction with the racial climate, and now they had tragic evidence that Wyoming, the Equality State, was worse. In Westerville they had not been subjected to any similar act of violence, but in Empire one of their own—a Taylor married to a Shores—had been openly killed. It was the worst assault and only fatal attack on a resident of any of the Black homesteader communities we studied.

Russel Taylor was especially traumatized by his brother's murder. Perhaps he was so shattered because he was the one who called in the sheriff in the first place, so he may have felt personal guilt. Perhaps he was humiliated because, despite his own prominence, the deputies felt free to abuse Baseman anyway. Perhaps he grieved because, despite his many attempts, he was unable to obtain any *post facto* justice for Baseman. It was hard to accept there would be no redress or accountability for such an egregious and public act of official cruelty. Russel lodged a wrongful death lawsuit and repeatedly filed legal complaints, seeking to have charges brought against the deputies and sheriff. But John Wesley Shores, the family attorney, advised him that his actions were unlikely to succeed, and he was ultimately forced to drop them. All that was left was tragedy and sorrow.

After a decade, the great Speese-Shores-Taylor migration to parlay their Nebraska success into a Wyoming "empire" looked increasingly shaky. They continually quarreled with nearby white ranchers, the white school board, a Torrington court they felt was biased against them, and hotels and restaurants that wouldn't serve them. They grew frustrated that they could not determine who taught in their own school. And wresting a living out of the dry Wyoming soils proved much harder than expected. They were particularly discouraged by the meager results in the fields. The harsh, dry, unforgiving climate, with an average rainfall of only about fifteen inches per year, punctuated by periodic droughts, allowed only a small margin for success.

As sometimes happens in small groups under pressure, Empire residents began fighting each other. It started in church. Grace Presbyterian, in a sense, served as the community's "established" church. Russel Taylor, its pastor, was its dominant figure, and he was not hesitant to promote himself as well as his church. His "Empire Items" columns frequently praised church events, with only the thinnest veneer disguising his own self-congratulation. "Russel Taylor has signed a contract with an Eastern Publishing House"; "A very impressive and edifying service was held at Grace Church on Sunday"; "We were pleased to have so many of our young people accompany us Sunday . . . many expressed themselves as being helped by the sermon." His leadership may have worn thin.

In addition to being self-promoting, Russel was frequently absent—away on trips for the national church's Freedmen's Bureau. Grace Church suspended services during his travels. And this combination, or perhaps other factors such as the practical one of how far members had to travel to attend, opened the way for competitors. Reverend Haycraft was a white preacher who had worked

64. Sheep Creek Baptist Church of Reverend Haycraft, with mixed-race congregation, near Empire, ca. 1920. Permission of Todd Guenther, courtesy of History Nebraska.

with Minerva Shores's husband, Reverend Albert Marks, back in Westerville. He migrated to the area and opened the Sheep Creek Baptist Church of God, an integrated church.

Reverend Currens, also white, opened the Sheep Creek Presbyterian Church just on the Nebraska side of the state line. It too was open to both Blacks and whites. Because of the location of Currens's church, it was sanctioned by the Presbytery of Nebraska, whereas Grace Church was part of the Presbytery of Wyoming. Both new churches drew off members, including Speeses and Taylors, from Grace Church. Congregation members not only attended the Sunday service but participated in a whole range of other activities, including potlucks, socials, dances, Bible study, and summer camps. Each church became a social web and sometimes even an economic and political network as well as a religious brotherhood. Competing churches tended to splinter the community.[20]

Toward the end of the hot summer of 1914, Russel Taylor reported in his column, "Shortness of the grass is making cattle especially rogueish, and this is causing some unpleasantness between neighbors." Mary Speese pressed charges against Otis Taylor for driving her cattle from what she insisted was their home range. The dispute wound up splitting other Speeses as well, with Radford and Charles supporting plaintiff Mary while Joseph testified for defendant Otis. Four days later, Otis filed a suit against Radford, accusing him of "uttering and useing obscene and licentious language in the presence of Sarah Taylor, a female." Sarah, Otis's wife, was Radford's sister.

Russel's trauma and continuing obsession over Baseman may have contributed to the settlement's fragmentation because he would have been the natural leader to mediate such internecine disputes. But Russel had become increasingly distracted by his pursuit of justice for Baseman and neglected his role as community leader.

Whether discouraged by continuing racism, disturbed by internal tensions, or disheartened by how hard it was to succeed at dryland farming at Sheep Creek, residents began departing Empire for new opportunities. Charles and Rose Speese left in 1915, moving to the larger Black community of DeWitty. They wrote letters back to kin and friends at Empire, saying conditions were better at DeWitty, with a better social life, more political clout, and more potential spouses for their children.

In the next few years, others departed as well. Some returned to Nebraska. Some Empire residents moved a few miles south to lands they hoped would give them better access to irrigation water from Wyoming's new Interstate Canal. By 1920 Empire had largely emptied. Houses erected with such high hopes and expense were left abandoned and soon fell apart. Russel Taylor sold his tractor, a La Crosse Happy Farmer 12–24, "all in A-1 condition, having plowed only 240 acres last summer." It was available "cheap if taken soon."[21] Cultivated fields returned to rangeland to be used by ranchers for grazing their cattle. In that year, the census recorded only twenty-three African Americans remaining in Empire, and by 1930 only four Blacks lived in all of Goshen County.

Russel Taylor returned to Omaha, where he affiliated with the Seward Street Methodist Church in North Omaha, the city's Black neighborhood. In 1922 he conducted a one-hundred-voice choir in a program put on by the Colored Commercial Club of Omaha for a large audience in the City Auditorium. The choir sang southern gospels, to which the audience responded with thundering applause. In 1924 he ran in a crowded field for a seat on the board of the Omaha School District. He attracted 4,630 votes, but he needed nearly thirteen thousand to win one of the six open seats.

Taylor refused to keep quiet. In 1925 he wrote a lengthy letter to the *Omaha Daily News* decrying those who tried to oppose capital punishment based on the Bible. He declared that many Biblical verses say that "penalties and punishments are to be inflicted for the breaking of [the Ten Commandments]. And [that] in every instance the death penalty is demanded for the breach of [the Sixth Commandment]."

Just two months later, Taylor organized a rally, attended by four hundred persons, which raised $135 for the defense of Dr. Orlon Sweet and others who were on trial in Chicago, charged with murder for deaths that occurred during "racial disturbances." Black communities across the nation considered the prosecution unfair and wrong. In 1928 Taylor wrote to the *Omaha Evening Bee-News* complaining that "a colored student, though highly efficient in the game, was removed from the basket ball team of Central High" because of "the refusal of the [St. Joseph, Missouri] team to play so long as the colored player remained on the other team."[22] Taylor's passion for racial justice and his demand to be heard remained as strong as ever.

The migrants had carried such high hopes to Empire, but all they got back was hardship, financial loss, conflict, and tragedy. The

Speeses suffered financial disaster, losing nearly all the wealth they had built up in prior years in Westerville. Charles and Rose Speese and their six children—they would go on to have ten more surviving children—returned to Nebraska, but they lacked the ample bankroll they had so confidently carried to Empire. They moved from their commodious house and lands in Empire to a tiny sod dwelling on eighty acres in DeWitty to start over yet again.

Today the only physical reminder of Empire is a historical marker adorning a rest stop on the interstate and a small sign at a nearby museum. The place where Empire's faithful gathered to worship and its children struggled over their school lessons is a privately owned pasture. We obtained a grant from the National Trust for Historic Preservation's African American Cultural Heritage Action Fund to pay for erecting a marker, and we worked with Dan Bach of the Wyoming State Parks, Historic Sites, and Trails to design the sign and obtain official approval. Today, a handsome marker beckons to travelers who stop at the Dwyer Junction Rest Area on I-25 near Wheatland, about fifty miles west of the colony's actual site, to learn Empire's story.

If the Empire homesteaders served as scouts for the Black multitudes in the South seeking escape, they had proven that eastern Wyoming would be no promised land for them. When Empire was abandoned, those multitudes had already turned their eyes and hopes toward northern cities.

As the Empire settlers suffered tragedy and failure in Wyoming, an enthusiastic and hard-charging solo homesteader was finding success in South Dakota. He pleaded with other Black men to come take up the opportunities he saw around him. He not only succeeded at homesteading but he retold his own homesteading story in books and films for decades, becoming one of the founders of America's independent Black filmmaking industry. His name was Oscar Micheaux.

11

Oscar Micheaux, "The Homesteader"

Jews, Germans, Swedes, Arabs, Southern whites and
Irish Were All on Hand to Get Land. Negroes Should
Not Wait for Cities to be Built, Then Try.
—subhead in the *Chicago Defender* above Oscar Micheaux's article

The eager land seeker perched on the buckboard's bench next to
Slater. He had hired Slater, a land locator, to find him a homestead
claim. They had journeyed this October day to the far western edge
of Gregory County, South Dakota, where only game trails marked
the prairie. The horse struggled to pull the wagon through the undulating grasses, even though the autumn chill had already left them
withered and dry. The land seeker was the only Black man for miles
around, and had he ever caused a stir when he had arrived in town!
He declared his intention to buy a relinquishment, but nobody
believed he really had the money. Slater had reluctantly taken the
job of finding a claim for the man, but he expected he would never
see a commission.

They traveled some miles across the newly opened Rosebud reservation lands, finally coming to a plateau where the grass, the soil,
and the lay of the land appeared entirely different from any the
Black man had yet seen. Small streams emptied into a larger one,
winding along like a snake's track. "It was beautiful," the land seeker
exclaimed. "I was carried away by the first sight of it."[1]

Oscar Micheaux, who later became a novelist and the first great
African American filmmaker, homesteaded in South Dakota. He

65. Newspaper advertisement for first showing of Oscar Micheaux's *The Homesteader*. Wikimedia Commons, Micheaux Book and Film Company.

purchased a relinquishment in Gregory County in 1904, and he sedulously claimed more land over succeeding years. He left with a broken heart.

Micheaux was marked, haunted almost, by his homesteading venture. He retold his experience again and again in novels and movies. His first books, *The Conquest: The Story of a Negro Pioneer* and *The Homesteader*, started the pattern which he carried through in subsequent books. And he wrote, produced, and directed more than forty movies, many of which focused on his homesteading life—how many is uncertain, because many of his early films have been lost. He made some of the first "race films," produced specifically for Black audiences and employing only Black actors. An early film was *The Homesteader*, a full-length, eight-reel, all-Black-cast movie.

Critics labeled Micheaux the most successful African American filmmaker of the first half of the twentieth century. He died in 1951, and in 1987 Hollywood honored him by placing a star on its iconic "Walk of Fame." The star reads "The Father of Independent Black Filmmaking."[2] Even though he left South Dakota after a decade, his homesteading experiences were so powerful that he returned to them repeatedly in his writing and films. In many ways, homesteading kept his creative juices flowing through his whole life.

His novels and movies were intensely autobiographical. *The Conquest* (1913) and *The Homesteader* (1917), as well as his movie *The Homesteader* (1919), all presented, in the most thinly disguised form, his own life experiences as a homesteader. In *The Conquest*, the principal character, a Black South Dakota homesteader, is named Oscar Devereaux (Devereaux was Micheaux's middle name). In his novel *The Homesteader*, the Black South Dakota homesteader is called Jean Baptiste. As critic Leathern Dorsey noted, "When the story begins, Jean Baptiste is given a full pedigree, which is remarkably similar to that of Micheaux." In both novels, the character's wife is named Orlean, just as Micheaux's actual wife was, with only her maiden name slightly altered—McCraline instead of McCracken. He even builds his late-in-life novel, *The Wind from Nowhere* (1944), around his homesteading life. All his biographers use his novels as their principal sources for information about his life.[3]

He was born in 1884 in southern Illinois. His parents had been enslaved in northwestern Kentucky, and when freed they moved across the Ohio River. His father, Calvin Michaux, was illiterate, but his mother, Belle Gaugh, though uneducated, treasured books and encouraged Oscar's ravenous love of learning. Calvin farmed a forty-acre plot near Metropolis, not far from Cairo. He grew wheat and corn and owned some livestock. He increased his holdings to eighty acres and did well. Oscar later said that his father was ranked as "well-to-do, that is, for a colored man."[4]

Micheaux was the fifth child of thirteen, and the children, especially boys, were expected to help out with the interminable farm chores. Oscar later admitted that his brothers did most of the field work, as he found it "too cold to work in the winter, and too warm in the summer." He did better at selling the family goods at the local market.[5]

While selling vegetables, Oscar began developing his outgoing, pleasing personality. "I met and became acquainted with people quite readily," he remembered. He greeted each prospective customer with a special greeting that usually brought a smile and nod of appreciation as well as a purchase. One time, one of his brothers complained about how Oscar was getting out of all the hard work and said he'd run the vegetable stand instead of Oscar. But he found himself tongue tied in front of white customers and decided working in the fields was easier. Oscar quickly learned how to use flattery and how pleased even important men's wives were when he bowed and gave a pleasant "Good Morning!"[6] He boldly hailed the town's leading white people by name, apparently in such a charming way they were entertained. He was learning to be comfortable with white people and interact easily with them.

Metropolis was a Jim Crow city, described as a small southern town in a northern state. Illinois law guaranteed Black children an education but left it up to each locality to decide whether schools would teach Blacks and whites together or separately. Metropolis chose segregated schools. Four teachers taught all the grades in the black school, and in 1896 the district graduated its first Black high schoolers, including Oscar's older sister, Ida—a major achievement. In 1900 only 6 percent of seventeen-year-olds of all races graduated from high school. Oscar attended the "colored" elementary school, for which his parents paid school fees. He claimed he got good grades, but his rebellious and free-thinking ways caused his classmates to nickname him Oddball. He griped that he was continually critiqued for talking too much and being too inquisitive, saying "About the only thing for which I was given credit was in learning readily."[7]

He left before graduating high school. Despite the poor facilities and ill-prepared teachers, Oscar left school with an insatiable appetite for reading and learning.

Oscar's father, though he owned a fair amount of land, was land-poor. Oscar described farming around Metropolis as unrewarding and slow, hard work. Calvin fell farther and farther behind, trying to make mortgage payments, pay school fees, and support his growing family. Like others, he heard the siren song of the West. Calvin's older brother Andrew had homesteaded in Kansas and prospered, eventually owning seven hundred acres. His younger brother William and other relatives homesteaded there as well. In 1900 William died and left part of his estate to Calvin. With this unexpected windfall in hand, Calvin packed up the family and moved from Metropolis to Great Bend, in central Kansas.

By then Oscar had already left town. He disliked farm life and felt that the parochial culture of Metropolis offered few chances to realize his big (if still unformed) ambitions. At sixteen years old, he hopped a train going north. He stopped a couple of times to pick up jobs along the way. He worked for some weeks in a hot and noisy foundry and got sick. Later he bailed water in a smoky coal mine, lasting only six weeks in that job. His eye, however, was on Chicago. His brother William worked as a waiter on a train, and according to letters home, he was flush with cash and enjoying the high life in the big city at night.

Oscar arrived in 1902 to find Chicago to be the busiest, most congested place he'd ever seen. Even though it was mostly a white city, thirty thousand Black people also lived there. That was many more Black people than he had ever seen.

The glitzy life William had boasted of turned out to be a sore disappointment. William had quit his waiter job in a fit, and so far hadn't found another one. He was broke, living in an ugly little flat, drinking away his savings, and had no plan or thought for the future. Oscar was appalled, and after staying with his brother for a short time, soon moved to his own place. He found a variety of jobs, trying out work in the stockyards and in a steel mill and at a shoeshine stand, but he didn't stay long in any of them.

Micheaux tried to land a job as a Pullman porter, one of the elite positions open to African American men at the time. He showed up at the Pullman hiring office twice a week. But he could never get past the chief clerk because he had no experience as a porter and no one on the inside to recommend him. He changed his plan of attack. He waylaid the hiring superintendent just as that official arrived at work, and Micheaux presented his case. Just eighteen, he must already have exuded charm and intelligence, because instead of being brushed aside for his impudence, the superintendent called him into the office and asked for his references. Oscar got the job.

Micheaux's successful ploy earned him a plum position. Pullman porters were known to earn exceptional wages, especially if they excelled at eliciting tips.[8] Portering was clean though exhausting work. Oscar refined his ability to appeal to the wealthy and indulged white men he served. While his relationship with patrons was undoubtedly never equal—he was, after all, Black and a porter—neither did it appear to have been overly subservient. He developed a crafty ability to talk easily with affluent passengers in a manner they enjoyed. He quickly learned that what most of them really liked was to hear themselves talk, so he became an attentive listener.

In addition to tips, passengers gave Oscar valuable cast-off clothing, bottles of whiskey, newspapers, books, and other items discarded during travel. He was not a drinker; so he sold the whiskey or traded it for something he could use. But the newspapers and books, now there was a prize! He consumed them thoroughly. VanEpps-Taylor argues that his years of portering "provided Micheaux with the equivalent of a college education."[9]

For Oscar, the job's best benefit was the travel to all parts of the country. The young man from Metropolis visited the nation's true metropolises—cities like Philadelphia and Washington and San Francisco and all the open spaces in between. He especially enjoyed the long hauls across the middle of the country, seeing the vast plains.

Oscar grew disappointed with his earnings. Pullman required him to pay for his summer and winter uniforms and for train meals out of his wages. Tips perhaps tripled what was left in his wages after the company's deductions. But at the end of the month, his take-home pay was not the bonanza people thought Pullman porters made.

In response to the company's stinginess, trainmen developed an elaborate system of embezzlement known as "knock-downs." When passengers boarded outside of Chicago, they bought their tickets from the white conductors. The conductors simply pocketed part of the fares and reported less to the company than they actually took in. Black porters got a share of the take as payment for keeping quiet about it. In response, the company sent undercover "spotters" to ferret out the cheaters. Spotters and trainmen played cat-and-mouse, as the conductors and porters watched carefully for which passengers might be agents. Micheaux participated in the scheme, though he eventually decided it was greedy and inhuman, corrupting even the porters.

With wages, tips, and knock-downs, Micheaux cleared about two hundred dollars a month. And because he was extremely frugal, a habit he would continue his whole life, he accumulated two thousand dollars or more in savings. But after a couple of years of portering, Micheaux found it difficult to shake his farm roots.

The farmer's son who shirked working in the fields and fled his hometown now dreamed of owning his own farm. Riding the rails across the plains between Chicago and Denver especially fired his imagination. He wrote, "During the summer it is one large garden farm, dotted with numerous cities, thriving hamlets and towns, fine country homes so characteristic of the great middle west, and is always pleasing to the eye." He especially liked the lands between North Platte, Nebraska, and Julesburg, Colorado, where the yearly rainfall was insufficient to mature crops but the short buffalo grass fed the ranchers' herds winter and summer.[10]

It was perhaps fortunate that his eye began to wander, because on a long run to Portland, Oregon, a spotter caught a conductor and Oscar pocketing fares. Both were immediately fired. With characteristic panache, Micheaux made a beeline for the company's Saint Louis office, where he again applied for a porter's job. He was careful to submit only non-Pullman employer references. Again he landed the job. Pullman's Chicago headquarters, to whom the spotters reported, apparently never figured out that Oscar was back on their payroll. But his portering days were drawing to a close.

In 1904 Micheaux learned that President Roosevelt had declared part of the Rosebud Reservation in South Dakota open for homesteading. The federal government freed up land by making allotments of reservation land, usually 160 acres or more depending on the size of the family, to individual Native families. When it finished assigning allotments to all the families, the government still had many acres of reservation land left over. It declared the unallotted land to be "surplus" and paid the tribe for it. According to the Dawes Act, "the sums agreed to be paid by the United States as purchase money for any portion of any such reservation shall be held in the Treasury of the United States for the sole use of the tribe or tribe's Indians to whom such reservations belonged." (Corrupt BIA officials embezzled the funds, most of the entrusted money disappeared, and the tribes gained little benefit from it.) The president then "opened" the surplus land for homesteading.

66. Oscar Micheaux
at about age thirty.
Photographs and Prints
Division, Schomburg
Center for Research
in Black Culture, New
York Public Library.

On the freed-up reservation tracts, the government granted settlers land under homesteading rules, limiting each claimant to 160 acres and requiring the usual residency on the land. And in addition, it charged homesteaders a per-acre fee. On the Rosebud, Congress set the fee at four dollars per acre, requiring the entryman to pay one dollar at initial entry.

The portion of the Rosebud Roosevelt opened could accommodate 2,400 homesteads. Micheaux, now twenty, traveled to Chamberlain,

South Dakota, to register his name. He found the town awash with land seekers, both men and women, as well as agents, locators, notaries to help prepare applications, confidence men, pickpockets, and women selling sandwiches and other services. They all crowded into a hurriedly built collection of shacks, a few buildings, tents, and privies. More than 107,000 people had turned up to apply for the available slots.

On July 28, 1904, the General Land Office held its lottery to determine who would win the right to claim a homestead. Micheaux was disappointed when his ticket, number 6,504, was drawn. He realized his chances of getting a claim were hopeless. He returned to Saint Louis to resume his work as a porter, but he continued to dream of owning land in the Great Plains.[11]

In October, Micheaux contemplated returning to South Dakota, thinking that some of the lottery winners would not really want to farm and might be willing to relinquish their claims for cash. Selling or purchasing a relinquishment was technically illegal, because if one relinquished (abandoned) a homestead claim, the land was supposed to go back into the pool available for others to claim. However, claimants sold relinquishments quite openly, even posting ads for relinquishments in the local land office. The seller obtained his payment and arranged with his buyer to be in the land office when the relinquishment was recorded. Having obtained access to a claim, the (new) entryman still had to fulfill all the requirements of proving up, including residency.

Micheaux rode the train from Saint Louis, carrying $2,500 in cash. At Omaha he boarded a Chicago and Northwestern special packed with people excited about the opportunities on the Rosebud. He was the only Black passenger and an object of great curiosity. They crossed the Missouri River, and everyone got off at Bonesteel, the temporary end of the rail line.

After several refusals, Micheaux found a locator named Slater willing to take him seriously, and together they traveled by horse and wagon westward. Bonesteel is in the far southeast corner of Gregory County, and Micheaux wanted to find a claim on its western edge, where he thought the land would be cheaper and the soil better. Along the way, they passed several nascent towns. Each hoped to be on the path of the railroad's coming westward extension, and each was gearing up its campaign to become the permanent county seat. Micheaux and Slater reached the plateau with land so beautiful it "carried [Micheaux] away." Nearby they could see the rudiments of a new settlement called Dallas. Slater knew the original claim holder wanted to sell the land as a relinquishment. Excited, Oscar returned to Bonesteel.

The next day, October 14, 1904, he purchased the relinquishment for $375 and paid his land locator $80. He formally entered his homestead claim at the land office. He paid his initial $160 toward the full price of $4 per acre, or $640. Having missed the planting season, he returned to Saint Louis to continue working for Pullman.[12]

Micheaux returned to South Dakota in April 1905 to farm his homestead in earnest. This time, Bonesteel was abuzz with the rumor that the hamlet of Dallas, right next to Micheaux's claim, was likely to be selected as the next railhead past Bonesteel. His visit the previous autumn, brief as it had been, apparently left a strong impression among the locals. Everyone now thought it was *highly suspicious* that Micheaux had insisted on claiming land so far away as Dallas—how had he known to go there? A rumor spread that he was a man with *inside* information.

When the stage pulled up in front of the Bonesteel post office and Micheaux descended, Slater was right there to meet him. Slater was now desperate to be in business with this obviously well-connected, or at least prescient, man. Oscar was all of twenty-one years of age.

Slater took Micheaux to be introduced to the postmaster. Then he took him to meet Ernest A. Jackson. Jackson was both the bank president and the leader of the townsite company promoting Dallas. He and his two brothers were big land investors and maintained a close relationship with the head of the c&nw railroad. Micheaux and Jackson shook hands, and Micheaux immediately liked him. "I admired him," he recalled, "I could see at a glance that here was a person of unusual aggressiveness and great capacity for doing things."[13]

Jackson invited Oscar to have dinner at the hotel he owned, quite a contrast to when, a few years later, Robert Anderson and his new bride were turned away from the Hemingford Hotel dining room. Jackson asked Micheaux if he'd like to sell his claim, for twice the money he paid for it several months earlier. Oscar declined, saying he'd come to farm. Micheaux and the Jackson brothers became friends—perhaps Micheaux used some of the charm and ease he developed while portering to form this alliance with the most powerful men in the area.

Oscar withdrew $500 from Jackson's bank, using his savings in a Chicago bank as security. He purchased a team of horses and a wagon, lumber to build a cabin, and other supplies. He departed Bonesteel for his claim, holding his head high. He was filled with the thrill of being a landowner and seeing his dream come true before his eyes. This was the glorious start to his whole new life!

Unfortunately, his team only made it two miles out of town before breaking down. Later, Micheaux ruefully recalled how he didn't know much about horses when he started homesteading. He got swindled by an "unscrupulous rascal" who tricked him into buying one horse "so awkward he looked as though he would fall down if he tried to trot" and another which had "two feet badly wire cut." He later told how nearby residents in Dallas would swap stories about his poor horse judgment, telling traders who arrived with a lame horse to trade to "go over to the sod house north of town and see the colored man."[14] Oscar returned to Bonesteel with his broken-down team, got two better horses, and next day, bowed but not defeated, he started again for his claim.

He hired a sod mason for three dollars a day, and together they built a low sod house, fourteen by sixteen feet, with a hipped roof. He dug a well, added a fourteen-by-sixteen-foot granary, a barn, and a shed. But he had a great deal to learn. His ignorance of horses continued to cause him problems, and mules were no better. Farmers around Metropolis used mules, because they believed mules capable of doing more work than horses and they ate less grain. But Oscar's first mule team, Jack and Jenny, were lazy and balked. He whipped them, but it didn't seem to improve their performance. He traded Jack to a passing dealer for a different mule, but that one was lazy *and* malicious.

He had trouble finding the right plow, not realizing that prairie sod required a special "breaking plow" that would make a long, slanting cut, severing the grass roots and neatly turning over the slice. He tried to break all his land at once, creating a mountain of work, rather than doing as other homesteaders did, breaking manageable patches of forty or sixty acres at a time and leaving the rest for next year. He conducted his trials and errors in full view of his curious neighbors. As one commented, "You can't find a better metaphor than a Pullman porter pushing a plow. He must have gone through the agonies of hell."[15]

He carefully rotated his crops, probably to learn what would grow well and also to maintain soil quality and respond to fluctuating crop prices. On the first tract of prairie he broke, he planted corn (1905), wheat (1906), flax (1907), oats (1908), and corn (1909). He faced many hardships on his farm, horses straying, drought, grasshoppers, hail, stripe rust on the wheat, and deep snow drifts which often killed livestock. He worried about what price he would get for his bags of wheat and flax. And like everyone, he feared prairie fire. One fire destroyed much of Dallas and appeared ready to consume Oscar's fields when at the last moment, a shift in the wind averted disaster.

In 1906 he paid $3,000 for a relinquishment some miles away, north of Gregory, increasing his holdings to 320 acres. His goal was to own a thousand acres. He broke and planted increasing amounts of land each year, totaling 120 acres by 1908. His acreage didn't compare with the massive "bonanza" farms up in the valley of the Red River of the North, where owners hired platoons of farm hands to plant wheat on thousands of acres. But Oscar's farms measured up quite favorably with those of other homesteaders. He invited his sister, Olivia (Olive) Michaux, and their maternal grandmother, Louisa Goff, to join him and file claims as soon as the government opened up more of the Rosebud in nearby Tripp County.[16]

Micheaux may have planned from the beginning to commute his claim, since he had already paid the first $160 installment the very day he filed on the land in 1904. Coming from life as a successful porter, he was confident he could raise the additional cash necessary to prove up. By July 20, 1909, he had gathered the remaining $480. This suggests that he might have earned some money during winter months when he left his claim, or perhaps his farm had become quite profitable.

For proving up, he listed in his legal notice four white men as potential witnesses: local real estate agent Wilford Standiford and farmers Samuel Osler, William T. McGuire, and Thomas Reynolds. He called on Standiford and Osler to provide affidavits. The only other Black man nearby was the local barber, and Micheaux said he didn't care for him. The proving up went smoothly even though Micheaux had misplaced his receipt for the $160 installment he'd paid in 1904.[17]

Slowly Oscar earned the respect of the farmers around him. They could see he worked incredibly hard, always a winning trait in farming communities. He plowed straight furrows, he planted efficiently, and his fields produced bountiful crops. Unheard of, Oscar used eight horses to pull a binder with a seeder hooked on behind. Don Coonen, a neighbor, marveled at the innovation: "Harvesting and seeding at the same time was an innovation all his own."

The neighbors found Micheaux to be an interesting man to talk to. He always seemed willing to help when they had a task that required an extra hand. He occasionally hired himself out to other farmers. His neighbors' dismissive laughter eventually turned to grudging respect, then to acceptance, and finally to admiration, when they realized that he had broken many more acres of prairie than most of them had.[18]

He was proud of his land and became an eloquent booster for all the region's opportunities. Locators and land agents began bringing new white prospects by to talk to him, because his visible success and positive outlook "sold" the country well. Since he had worked as a porter and traveled so widely, neighbors considered him a "railroad expert." When they fretted about which direction the C&NW would choose for extending its all-important tracks, they sought his views.

Promoters of Burke, Herrick, Gregory, and Dallas competed fiercely to obtain the railhead for their town. Bonesteel and Fairfax joined the fight for the permanent county seat. Landowners knew their acres would be worth a lot more if they were near the railroad and a lot less if they were far from its tracks. Micheaux's claim was halfway between Dallas and Gregory, which meant he had less to lose. Some wondered if his choice of location didn't confirm their suspicions that he had insider information from people high up in the railroad management when he chose it.

Micheaux did not take a direct role in the disputes among towns, but he did have a front-row seat, given him by his continuing friendship with the Jackson brothers. The Jacksons, early promoters of Dallas, had significant holdings in Bonesteel and other towns as well, and they bought up huge tracts of land throughout the county.

As the current began running in Gregory's favor, business owners in Dallas started physically moving their stores the five miles across the prairie to Gregory. Soon the only buildings remaining in Dallas were owned by the Jacksons: a two-story bank, a two-story hotel, a saloon, and some smaller structures.

Ernest Jackson had taken a long absence from the area. It turned out he had been plotting strategy with his family and business backers in Omaha and Des Moines. In Chicago, he had persuaded his friend, the head of C&NW, to show him the railroad's still-secret plans. The company had chosen the Gregory route, not Dallas. With this foreknowledge, which he carefully withheld from everyone, Ernest now "magnanimously" offered to join up with Gregory and move his buildings there. But Gregory's leaders were confident of their coming victory and spurned Jackson's offer. In Oscar's words, Gregory had just made "the most stupid mistake of her life."

Jackson was outraged. He hitched seventy-six horses together and pulled his bank across the prairie, seemingly ready to enter Gregory. But when the procession got within a half-mile of town, Jackson veered off. He set up "New Dallas" on a hill just outside Gregory and opened his bank for business. When the C&NW line arrived, both Gregory and New Dallas were ready to compete for the widely anticipated next boom in neighboring Tripp County.

Afterward, Ernest Jackson regaled Oscar with the insider story of the whole struggle. He told him about his contacts, his holdings, his strategy. Micheaux listened with great interest, and he retold the whole episode in graphic detail in his novel *The Homesteader* and elsewhere.

Micheaux was pleased with his growing land empire, but increasingly he felt tortured by loneliness. All through his early years in Chicago and working for Pullman, he seems to have had no serious romantic relationships. He entered homesteading alone as well, without a female partner and choosing to locate among an almost uniformly white society. His skin tone was said to be coffee with cream, and he could not, nor did he ever try, to "pass" for white; in his creative works he often disparaged those who did. Now, on the farm, especially during the long winters, loneliness swept over him. He decided it was time to marry.

Unfortunately, he had fallen in love with someone unattainable. She was white. In both *The Conquest* and *The Homesteader*, Micheaux describes her at length under the rubric of "The One True Woman." She apparently returned his affection. Scholars haven't identified the real "Scottish Girl," but they have little doubt she existed. She was blond, twenty years old, and lived with her widowed father and siblings on a neighboring farm. She hadn't finished high school, but she was an avid reader. She and Oscar shared reading and discussing the books and magazines he had collected.

He saw, with some dread, his growing affection for this young Scottish girl. On one occasion he was at her house and they were reading a volume of Shakespeare. She sat at a table holding the book while Oscar stood over her. She stopped reading and looked up, their eyes met, and Oscar kissed her twice on her upturned lips. He said, "Without any intention of being other than kind, I found myself being drawn to her in a way that threatened to become serious. . . . I found myself on the verge of falling in love with her."[19]

Her father and brothers were close friends with Oscar and worked alongside him. Oscar employed one brother for a time, and Oscar sometimes bunked at their place. Although it was never put to the test, the girl's family did not appear opposed to such a marriage.

It was Oscar who drew back. He knew how dangerous such a liaison could be. It was not only against custom, after the South Dakota legislature passed an anti-miscegnation law in 1909, also illegal. He had always been opposed to Black people marrying whites, saying they were disloyal to the race. An example was right before him: his dislike for the Black barber in town stemmed partly from the barber having a white wife. He also felt having a white wife would destroy any chance he had to influence other Black people. So Oscar knew he could not marry the Scottish girl.

Still, it was hard. "I hated to give up her kindness and friendship. I would have given half my life to have had her possess just a least bit of negro blood in her veins, but since she did not and could not help it any more than I could help being a negro, I tried to forget it."[20] Judging by all the times in his novels and films that he returned to his sadness over "The One True Woman," he never did forget.

With a rather businesslike approach, Micheaux turned to finding a Black wife. He was lonely, but also he saw in marriage a great opportunity to acquire more land. He worried that Roosevelt would soon open Tripp County and all the land would be claimed quickly. He had used up all his eligibility to enter a claim, but his sister Olivia and grandmother Louisa Gough could file. And so could a wife, if he could find her quickly enough.

His wife would need to file her claim in her maiden name before they married to make it legal, or at least legal enough. In preparation, Oscar had already paid $1,200 for his future bride's relinquishment. But he would forfeit his money if she didn't file before the deadline. So Oscar needed to find his bride right away.

There were three candidates. The first, Jessie, was a young woman he had known in school. They had corresponded over the years, and he had visited her from time to time. They had developed a sort of unspoken understanding that they were engaged. But every time Micheaux got close to making the engagement official, he backed away. Now, his letter proposing marriage arrived too late, and Jessie married someone else.

The second was someone he never met, a daughter of Junius Groves. Groves, a Black farmer, owned five hundred fertile acres and was known as the "Potato King of Kansas." His daughter and Oscar exchanged some letters, and he was intrigued, but again his ambivalence caused him to be dilatory. On one trip, he waited at the Omaha depot, expecting to receive a telegram from her encouraging him to come to Kansas for a visit, but it never came, and their relationship withered.

His third choice was Orlean McCracken, daughter of a well-known Chicago Methodist preacher, Reverend Newton J. McCracken. The Reverend was a big man, said to be a free talker but a poor listener. She was a twenty-five-year-old college graduate and teacher. He met Orlean the previous year. "I could not claim to be in love with this girl," he wrote. "Nor with anyone else, but had always had a feeling that if a man and woman met and found each other pleasant and entertaining, there was no need of a long courtship."[21] He was about to put that theory to a severe test.

After an exchange of letters, Oscar traveled to Chicago to propose marriage. He received a rude shock when he knocked on her door and recognized her mother—the wife of the Reverend McCracken he had seen years before in Metropolis. The reverend himself was away, but Micheaux remembered him from when Reverend McCracken had toured southern Illinois for the AME church. He and other church officials visited Metropolis, and they descended on the Michaux house for dinner. During dinner, when the pastors had seemed unconcerned about falling into the deadly sin of Gluttony, there had been a nasty blow-up. Young Oscar objected to something McCracken said. McCracken didn't expect to be contradicted, especially by a young boy, and took immediate offense. He sharply chastised Oscar, embarrassing his parents. Only at Orlean's front door did Oscar realize the connection: he was now proposing to make this puffed-up, self-satisfied, and bloviating pastor his father-in-law.

When Oscar later stopped to visit a friend in Chicago, he asked her whether she knew the reverend. She replied, "Yes, I know him and know him to be the biggest old rascal in the Methodist church.

He's lower than a dog, and if it wasn't for his family they would have thrown him out of the conference long ago, but he has a good family." She continued, "He has no principles and is mean to his wife, never goes out with her . . . but courts every woman on the circuit who will notice him . . . When he is in Chicago he spends his time visiting a woman on the west side. Her name is Mrs. Ewis."[22]

Oscar's friend's assessment fit precisely his own dim view of most Black pastors, whom he instinctively disliked as arrogant hypocrites. W. E. B. Du Bois, writing about the same time, caustically bemoaned that in the South both the Black and the white church "omits the sixth, seventh, and eighth commandments, but substitutes a dozen supplementary ones." Oscar had known some Black pastors who didn't always bear the best reputations, and in Dakota he read Black newspapers which frequently exposed immoral ministers. Still, he reflected, "It didn't discourage me when I learned [Orlean's] father had a bad name although I would have preferred an opposite condition."[23]

Orlean and her mother tentatively agreed to the engagement, but they needed her father, of whom they spoke with great awe, to give the final word. Reverend McCracken had now risen to be a presiding elder of the church and was on another tour and couldn't be reached. Oscar, growing frantic about losing his relinquishment deposit, asked Orlean to accompany him back to South Dakota. She could file on the claim and then they would be married.

Orlean and her mother agreed she could travel with a chaperone, if Oscar would pay their fares. Oscar, Orlean, and the chaperone took the train and soon arrived in Gregory. Orlean, Oscar's sister Olivia, and his Grandmother Gough all filed homestead claims.

When Reverend McCracken returned home and heard the plan, he erupted. He would allow the wedding, because he believed Oscar to be a wealthy landowner and because his own finances were chronically shaky. But he insisted Orlean return to Chicago and that they have the proper Chicago wedding that befitted his social standing. After some wrangling back and forth between groom and future father-in-law, Micheaux reluctantly agreed. He was irritated that he had to pay forty dollars for an engagement ring, which offended his chronic frugality. He regretted the eighty dollars he was forced to cough up each time someone took a round-trip from Gregory to Chicago or vice versa and expected him to pay. He was saving all his money to pay his mortgages, and these frivolous expenses didn't help. The whole wedding process was turning out to be more complicated and expensive than he had counted on.

Micheaux returned to Chicago at Christmas to make final wedding plans. Dinner at the McCracken house did not go well. Oscar was a devoted follower of Booker T. Washington's self-help philosophy, and he would later feature Washington's photo on the wall in many of his films. But Reverend McCracken was bitterly opposed to Washington and his ideas on industrial education. Oscar sat at dinner, seething but uncharacteristically stifling his own views.[24] Still, the wedding planning proceeded.

Oscar and Orlean wed on April 21, 1910, in Chicago. They left the same evening for South Dakota. Orlean, described as a shy "daddy's girl," was easily dominated by her father and unprepared to cope with his displeasure. She was used to city comforts and certainly was unprepared for life in a South Dakota soddy. As Micheaux wrote, "The girls in Chicago do not always understand the life out here." Biographer VanEpps Taylor commented that all of the accounts agree that Micheaux could hardly have chosen a poorer match.[25]

Orlean had a hard time adjusting to the homesteading life. She and Oscar had quarreled almost right after the wedding, and apparently they continued quarreling daily. She was lonely, unhappy, and disappointed that her new husband paid more attention to his farming than to her. He now farmed five scattered properties—in Gregory County, he worked his Dallas homestead and his relinquishment north of Gregory, and in Tripp County he had Orlean's, Olivia's, and Grandmother Gough's claims to farm. Oscar, the long-time bachelor, had faint experience in tending an emotional relationship that required him to give empathy and support, not to mention love. And Orlean's father proved to be very intrusive and damaging to the marriage.

The breaking point came when Orlean got pregnant. Oscar was away when she went into labor. She had a difficult, breech birth, and the baby was stillborn. By the time Oscar returned, the baby had already been buried. Orlean asked him to send a telegram to Reverend McCracken, stating, "Baby born dead. Am well." The reverend and Orlean's younger sister left Chicago immediately for Gregory, arriving the next morning. Orlean was depressed and sickly. Unfortunately, Oscar was extremely busy, having just hired a man with a steam engine to break two hundred acres of his Tripp County land, for which Oscar had to haul four tons of coal.

Her father commanded Orlean to return to Chicago. Oscar offered to pay their fares, but McCracken ostentatiously refused. Orlean privately informed Oscar that, at her father's direction, she had already withdrawn fifty dollars from his bank account. She departed with her father and sister for Chicago, and the marriage soon crumbled.

Micheaux's whole homesteading venture neared collapse. In part he had been *too* successful, or maybe just too ambitious, and he was now land-poor. He suffered stress and exhaustion from trying to farm five widely separated claims in two counties. He fretted over mounting bills coming due. He had mortgaged his own 320 acres for $7,600 and used $6,400 to purchase the relinquishments for Olivia, Louisa, and Orlean. And now he had Orlean's doctors' bills to pay on top of his mortgage payments, and he owed money to hired hands and suppliers. The nasty end of his marriage and the loss of his baby further depressed him.

He began to change his focus, whether because of his mounting troubles or from the excitement of new opportunities he perceived. He had always been a voracious reader. Friends described finding him in his soddy during those first winters in South Dakota, small stove struggling against the bitter weather outside and Micheaux in bed bundled under his covers with all his clothes on, only his face and a book showing. He believed strongly that he should try to influence other Black people, encouraging them to step up to Booker T. Washington's challenge of self-improvement. And he began writing.

He published his first article, "Where the Negro Fails," which appeared in two columns on the front page of *The Chicago Defender* on March 19, 1910. Micheaux saw wonderful prospects opening in the West and despaired that Black people were not taking advantage of them. Black men in particular were hemorrhaging opportunities that were likely never to come again. "Isn't it enough to make one feel disgusted to see and read of thousands of poor white people going west every day and in ten or fifteen years' time becoming prosperous and happy as well as making the west the greatest and happiest place on earth." He deplored the typical young Black man who failed to take up a homestead, instead sticking to places like Chicago. "He can give you a large theory on how the Negro problem should be solved, but it always ends that (in his mind) there is no opportunity for the Negro." He urged action: "The time is at hand—the Negro must become more self-supporting. Farm lands are the bosses of wealth."[26]

The article was notable for another reason—Oscar became Micheaux. In southern Illinois his family used the name Michaux, and his Kansas relatives continued to use that spelling. The Pullman Company enrolled him as "Oscar Michaux." He had entered his South Dakota land claims using it. But now he inserted the "e," perhaps to create a more interesting persona.

Micheaux published another long, front-page article in *The Chicago Defender* on October 28, 1911. It bore the heading, "Colored Americans Too Slow" and was subtitled "To Take Advantage of Great Land Opportunities Given Free by the Government." This time he reverted to "Oscar Michaux" and identified himself as "Government Crop Expert for Rosebud County," a perhaps self-endowed title. He lamented that "Jews, Germans, Swedes, Arabs, Southern whites and Irish were All on Hand to Get Land." And he insisted, "Negroes Should Not Wait for Cities to be Built, Then Try." He warned, "The white race will run you off your feet if you fail to get and own land."[27]

After informing his readers of the new land openings in Tripp County, Micheaux complained that "our people do not take the chance advantage that these openings afford as do the whites." He described the great inflation in land values during just his own seven years in South Dakota, and he asked, "What does this mean? It means that every one that came here five to eight years ago own farms that are worth from five to ten times their valuation in 1904. . . . Where have our people been with all their declamations and appeals for opportunities during this time?" His answer was that they were absent, and he commented, sarcastically, "Of course I know the whites have all the opportunity and the Negro hasn't the half."

Why were Black people not claiming their share? "There can be but one particular excuse and that is the personal bravery of an opportunity that only comes once." Then contradicting himself, he added, "I have always felt that the colored people have been held back largely by some of our social demagogues. I recall . . . a preacher, a presiding elder in the Methodist conference was very explicit in his determination to register for these lands, and . . . he was coming with a great following." Unfortunately, after his grand declaration, the elder then vanished. Micheaux concluded, "It's not the individual, but it's the cause that follow such pretentions that is detrimental to our young people." Even though Oscar never named him, his Chicago readers would have little trouble in puzzling out which elder he was talking about.

After his forays into journalism, Micheaux turned to writing novels and then filmmaking. He published his first novel, *The Conquest, The Story of a Negro Pioneer*, in 1913. It was (and is) seen as his own story thinly disguised as fiction. He published *The Forged Note: A Romance of the Darker Races* in 1915, a story about a Black homesteader who marries the daughter of a Chicago preacher. He published *The Homesteader* in 1917. It is a longer and more detailed retelling of his life story which he had already laid out in *The Conquest*.[28]

He began writing on his homestead, and then in 1915, after ten years on the farm, he moved to Sioux City, Iowa, to concentrate fully on writing. He had heavily mortgaged his properties, and in any event, he seemed psychologically drained and exhausted. He did not keep up the mortgage payments, and his lands were eventually foreclosed upon. His sister Olivia remained on her land, farming with her husband. He would then leave novel-writing to make films, only returning to novels, mostly pulp fiction, twenty-six years later.

Not unlike Willa Cather, Micheaux drew on his prairie experience over and over for *The Conquest, The Homesteader*, other novels, and for his movies, but unlike her, his work never gained great critical acclaim in his lifetime. It was largely dismissed by the big guns of the Harlem Renaissance, which left him irate. More recently, however, *The Conquest* and *The Homesteader* have risen in reputation, especially among historians, as invaluable first-hand accounts of the settlement boom and race relations.

Micheaux's filmmaking also met with mixed success. He released his first silent film, *The Homesteader*, in 1919. Micheaux financed its production by setting up a film company and selling shares of stock in it to the white farmers around Sioux City. As with all his films, it was made on a shoestring. Most of the actual filming took place in Tripp County. Unfortunately, we cannot judge the film's

67. Oscar Micheaux, the filmmaker, on location. Photographs
and Prints Division, Schomburg Center for Research
in Black Culture, New York Public Library.

quality because all copies have been lost. We do know it retold his
homesteading struggles and triumphs. He went on to make more
than forty other films, both silent films and "talkies," many of which
are also lost.

The Exile, running one hour and nineteen minutes, was his first
feature film with sound (see fig. 73). Micheaux filmed and released
it in 1931. In it, Micheaux again retells his South Dakota days, bas-
ing the film on his first novel, *The Conquest*. This film survives.[29]

Micheaux made "race films," films by and for Black people, when
few others did. Hollywood was then enthralled with D. W. Griffith's
Birth of a Nation, one of the most overtly racist films ever made, and
the studios were completely closed to Black writers and filmmakers.

Many acknowledge Micheaux, as his Hollywood star does, as the Father of Independent Black Filmmaking. Some even argue he was "the Jackie Robinson of film" and "the Black D.W. Griffith."

Phillip Lopate, writing in the *New York Times* in 2007, entered a dissenting view. "Micheaux was simply not a very good filmmaker, on any technical level," he sniffed. "Even his best pictures . . . suffer from hammy acting, preposterous melodrama, confusing continuity, stiff dialogue and clumsy lapses in film grammar." He quotes another critic who declared, "Micheaux's films define objective badness." Lopate patronizingly wondered why the self-taught Micheaux, working with penurious production budgets and segregated theaters, couldn't be like Spike Lee (a graduate of the New York University Film School) or French independent filmmaker Jean Vigo.

The film historian Charles Musser, professor of Film and Media Studies at Yale University, however, places Micheaux among the top ten filmmakers of the silent era—among such giants as Charlie Chaplin and Erich von Stroheim. Spike Lee also has a positive view of Micheaux, saying "Oscar Micheaux has been my idol. He inspired me to do my first film."[30]

Micheaux's real-life connection to the McCracken family had one last mile to go. A Tripp County banker contested Orlean's claim, alleging (probably rightly) that she had failed to reside on it for the required three years. Oscar obtained a ruling in her favor from the local land office, but the case was sent to Washington for adjudication. Before it was decided, Oscar's Washington lawyer informed him that the banker had made a secret trip to Chicago and met with Reverend McCracken. He persuaded the Reverend to sell him Orlean's farm for $300. Oscar was outraged—he had paid $2,500 for the relinquishment, another $500 in legal fees, and in any event the land was now worth double his investment.

Micheaux struck back. *The Chicago Defender* gave the sensational story front-page priority.[31] Its bold-type headline read, "Rev.

M'Cracken Sued for $10,000." The subhead was "Son-in-Law Wants $10,000 of the Doctor's Religious Funds for Taking Back His Wife's Affections." It further blazoned, "White Banker Hoodwinks Former Wife to Sell $6,000 Farm for $300 and Now He is Laughing—Rancher Becomes Angry." In his suit, Micheaux claimed that he and Orlean "lived together in peace and harmony, with no thought of separating. . . . Rev. McCracken came on two visits . . . and that while parading as a friend of his, [McCracken] chose a day when [Micheaux] was away; had his wife forge his name on a check for $50 and brought her to Chicago." Micheaux further claimed that McCracken's removal of Orlean created the only grounds for the banker to contest the claim.

Reverend McCracken, the self-proud presiding elder of the church, was greatly humiliated by the suit and news coverage, as Micheaux surely knew he would be. He and Oscar both hired lawyers, and sometime later the suit was settled privately. We do not know the settlement terms, because the relevant records do not survive, but certainly Micheaux did not receive $10,000. McCracken didn't have anywhere near that much, which Micheaux would also have known. One surviving scrap suggests that they may have settled the dispute for $300—the amount McCracken had received for the farm. By then, Micheaux was a fulltime cineaste, producing and directing films that told and retold stories of his homesteading days.

Micheaux, like Ben Blair before him, tried to persuade Black people, especially Black men, to seize the opportunities he saw opening through homesteading in the West. He was sure it offered an excellent chance to own land and build wealth. He thought the opportunities would disappear quickly, and he was right. He spent weeks in Atlanta and traveled to Roanoke and other cities in the South, selling his books, presenting his films, and spreading the word about homesteading. But by the time he was ready to show *The Homesteader*, conditions in the country had changed. Black people already found the war plants opening to them and big-city life beckoning. They joined the Great Migration heading north, instead of west.

As Micheaux was accumulating his hundreds of acres, another charismatic figure, O. T. Jackson, was dreaming of founding a Black homesteader colony in Colorado.

12

Sand and Success at Dearfield

In the evening after dinner mother read to us every night, or else
she'd play the piano or the organ and sang, she had a beautiful
voice. . . . And we were just a family. The thing they're trying
to bring to America now, we had then. We were a family.

—CARRIE WRIGHT, Dearfield descendant

Oliver Toussaint Jackson filled a room as fully as his illustrious
middle name suggested. A big man with a big voice and hearty,
friendly manner, he exuded energy. He had been born in Oxford,
Ohio, in 1862. His father and probably his mother had been enslaved
in Virginia. In 1886, the twenty-four-year-old moved to Denver,
bursting with ambition.

Just six years later, he had earned enough and saved enough to
buy a farm outside Boulder. He also began running the Stillman
Cafe and Ice Cream Parlor on Boulder's Thirteenth Street. In 1898
he switched to the Chautauqua Dining Hall, where he supervised
seventy people and possibly owned the food concession. He also
operated his own restaurant, famous for its seafood, at Fifty-fifth
and Arapahoe Streets. He closed his restaurant in 1907, when the
Boulder chapter of the Women's Christian Temperance Union—
fueled by Colorado's recent passage of women's suffrage—convinced
Boulder to go dry.

Jackson also began developing political ties. Surprisingly, he
affiliated with the Democrats. Most Black people, even those disil-
lusioned by the Republicans' abject failure to protect Black rights,

68. Oliver Toussaint Jackson, ca. 1910. Paul W. Stewart Collection, University of Northern Colorado Archives and Special Collections.

nonetheless disdained Democrats, whom they held responsible for violence and Jim Crow in the South and hostility to Black progress in the North. Even in Colorado, the national party's southern politics tainted Democrats. Jackson's political connections paid off in 1909 when Gov. John Shafroth appointed him to be the governor's official messenger. Except for a two-year lapse during the 1925–1927 term of Republican Clarence Morley, Jackson worked continuously in the governor's office until 1933.[1]

Being the governor's messenger gave Jackson both an income and political influence. Governors trusted him to deliver confidential messages, oral as well as written, conveying politically sensitive and perhaps even politically dangerous information. They needed to know that he would deliver his messages without disclosing the contents to other interested persons, including some who might be willing to pay him well for information. Jackson's long service in the position with no hint of scandal suggests he kept their trust. And upon that trust he was able to build political influence.

Jackson's political skills started with his impressive memory. He remembered the face and name of every person working in the capitol. He could recall the name of a statehouse visitor after just one introduction, even if he had not seen the person for years. In the 1920s and 1930s, newspapers described him as the "veteran negro messenger in the governor's office and known to thousands of people thru the state" and "a power in state politics, because of the regard in which he [wa]s held by the negro people."[2]

Jackson's restless mind turned to bigger ambitions, and he began thinking about building an all-Black farming community in Colorado. It was not an original idea. Black leaders had struggled for years to establish Black farming communities in Colorado with little result. That was surprising because the state seemed favorable to African American settlement. Its second Territorial Governor, John Evans, supported Black migration to help populate the state. When Colorado achieved statehood in 1867, its new constitution required that no "distinction or classification of people be made on account of color." Denver Mayor John Sopris, in office 1878–1881, welcomed Black migration, though with the equivocation that "they ought not be brought in indiscriminately." By 1910 Denver alone had a population of 5,476 Black people, and overall the state counted 11,453 African Americans.[3]

Yet even with these potentially favorable circumstances, Black leaders mostly failed in their attempts to establish Black farming settlements. Denver's Black leaders met in 1871 to consider colonization, but they made little progress. Independently, starting in 1872, an agent planned to bring one hundred African Americans from Georgia to settle in southern Colorado. In 1879 another group of Denver's Black leaders, this time under the leadership of Reverend Robert Seymour, tried to bring Exodusters stranded in Kansas but achieved little.

In 1902 Reverends Jesse Park and John Ford announced plans to create a Black agricultural community near Denver and another near Cañon City. That same year, Isaac B. Atkinson, founder of the Ethiopian Protective and Beneficial Aid Association, proposed purchasing four thousand acres of sugar beet land near Pueblo for settlement but failed to get his project going. In 1904 a group of well-to-do African Americans in Kentucky, Alabama, Georgia, and Tennessee planned to establish a farming colony near Craig, in northwest Colorado. They wanted a place "where there was more freedom of thought and their children would have an opportunity for an education." In 1906 Isaac Atkinson floated another proposal to borrow $10,000 from African American residents of Colorado to establish a Black colony on the outskirts of Denver.[4]

Most efforts failed. One that succeeded was a homesteader community in southeastern Colorado called The Dry. It had the benefit of local organizers, and several families (Lulu Craig among them) came over from Nicodemus. But other efforts left little trace. They lacked sufficient funds and were unable to find donors, banks, or charitable institutions to invest in them. Some faced local or political opposition. And they could not recruit enough Black families willing to undertake the hardship and risk of homesteading on the plains.

O. T. Jackson planned to succeed where others had failed. He was inspired by Booker T. Washington, who injected new energy into

Colorado's colony movement. Denver residents in 1908 formed a Colorado branch of Washington's Colored Men's National Business League, intending to establish a "negro colony in Colorado" in line with Washington's national self-help initiative. League delegates met in Denver in 1909 to explore how to form a district and town whose purpose would be to own land upon which to let homesteads.[5] O. T. Jackson and some of Denver's other prominent Black leaders formed the Negro Townsite and Land Company to purchase land for Black settlement. But Jackson's Black partners, especially those in the business community, distrusted his white and Democratic backing and withdrew their support. The company collapsed and was dissolved in 1910.

Undeterred, Jackson proceeded to a new plan. He eyed the large tracts of government land still unclaimed in Colorado's eastern plains that were available for homesteading. Homesteading had come late to Colorado, as land seekers first focused on the more attractive farming lands of Nebraska, Kansas, eastern Washington, and eastern Oregon. Only in the 1890s did significant numbers of homestead claimants begin entering the dry shortgrass prairie of eastern Colorado. Even as late as 1910, abundant federal land remained.

Jackson filed a Desert Land Act claim in 1910. He chose a spot near Greeley, in Weld County. Close to the South Platte River, it sat seventy miles northeast of Denver. He later converted his Desert Land claim, with its burdensome irrigation requirement, to a 320-acre Enlarged Homestead claim. He sold his Boulder farm to purchase an additional forty acres in Weld County. He was ready to launch his colony. Dr. Joseph Westbrook, a prominent Denver physician and early supporter of the project, suggested its name: Dearfield, "because the land will be dear to us."[6]

Jackson recruited nineteen settlers, who arrived in Dearfield in 1911. Jackson and his wife Minerva moved to Dearfield, although he continued as the governor's messenger in Denver. One of his early recruits was James Monroe Thomas. Thomas was born enslaved in Alabama in 1849. He lived for a time in Denver, working as a day laborer. He moved to Dearfield when he was sixty-one years old, on December 17, 1910. It must have been a chilly arrival. He filed his homestead claim in 1911. He lived in a "house tent" for nearly three full years, until he got his twelve-by-fourteen-foot, single-room frame house built in November 1913. He sent for his family to come from Oklahoma to join him.[7]

James Matlock came from St. Joseph, Missouri, to join the colony in 1911. He was seventy-two years old. He survived the first hard winter and soon had bountiful crops growing. Jackson described him "as hale and hearty as a man of 40."[8]

Another recruit was Joseph H. P. Westbrook, the Denver physician. Dr. Westbrook was born in Mississippi and graduated from Meharry Medical College. In 1907 he migrated to Denver and opened a medical practice and drug store. For a time, the Denver branch of the nascent NAACP lodged its headquarters in the reception room of Dr. Westbrook's medical practice, which he stocked with copies of W. E. B. Du Bois's *The Crisis* and other literature.[9] He joined the Dearfield community, providing medical care, though he didn't claim a homestead and probably didn't reside there.

Thomas and the other early settlers soon experienced the problems that plagued other plains homesteaders. Many were poor when they took up their homesteads. Some who filed claims only had cash enough to pay their fare and the cost of freighting household goods from Denver to Masters, the nearest rail depot. Others paid their fare as far as their money would take them and walked the rest of the way to Dearfield. Neighboring ranchers at first opposed the newcomers for fencing off public land which the ranchers had been using to graze their cattle. The settlers relied almost exclusively on a small creek and rainfall for their water.[10]

69. James Monroe Thomas on his homestead in Dearfield, ca. 1915. U.S. Department of the Interior, National Park Service.

The settlers suffered terribly during the first winter. Only two of the families had wood houses; the others lived in dugouts or tents, which provided poor protection against the howling winds and bitter winter cold. They scavenged firewood from along the South Platte River and in the coulees, but mainly they relied on cow chips and sagebrush for fuel. Three of the colony's six horses died. In spring, the homesteaders turned to constructing more permanent shelters. The prairie contained few trees big enough to saw into planks, and most homesteaders had little cash to purchase lumber. James Monroe Thomas did a bit better: he was able to construct a one-room wood shanty with windows, a barn, and a chicken house.

More families arrived to join the colony, among them Frank and Anna McPherson. Anna McPherson's mother, Harriet Bailey, was born into slavery on the Bailey plantation in Lauderdale County, Alabama, in 1841. After emancipation, she moved to Nashville, where Anna, her oldest child, was born. Frank and Anna married in 1888. They worked for a white family in Nashville, he as butler and cook, she as maid and laundress. When the family moved to Denver in 1903, Frank and Anna, accompanied by Harriet Bailey, chose to come along, making the family's own personal exodus from the Jim Crow South. They wanted to see, as their great-great-granddaughter put it, "what possibilities might open up for them in a different environment than such an oppressive system they were in in Tennessee." In Denver, they continued working for the family for a while. Frank took a slaughterhouse job. Then they decided to homestead in Dearfield.[11]

The homesteaders struggled to get cabins built and land under cultivation. Even Jackson, who had the benefit of a government paycheck, struggled early on to produce a working farm. He had land under cultivation each year starting in 1911, but it took him until 1913 to harvest crops he could sell.[12]

Some Dearfield residents emulated Jackson and kept their Denver jobs, while others sought work nearer their claims. Frank and Anna McPherson continued to live in Denver, traveling out to work their Dearfield farm on weekends and during enough months each year to fulfill the homesteading law's residency requirement. James Monroe Thomas hired on at a nearby ranch, a sign of the ranchers' softening attitude toward the homesteaders. Jackson noted in 1915 that the colony's main support came from employment by the white farmers and ranchers within ten or so miles of Dearfield. "This has been a great help to us and to them. We have cooperated with each other by exchange of work, the use of tools and horses, sharing our food and fuel, until now we are like one large family."[13]

Most of Dearfield's aspiring farmers had no farming experience. Only seven or so of the first sixty settlers had been farmers, and the rest had to learn quickly on the job. The knowledge they lacked most was how to get plants to grow in the dry climate and sandy

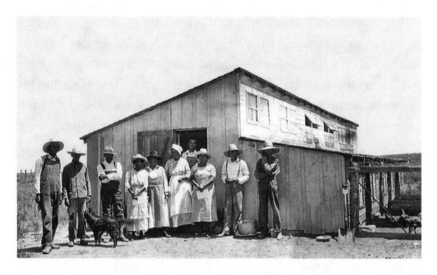

70. Poultry culling demonstration by county extension agent for local farmers, Dearfield, 1923. Photo courtesy of Weld County Government.

soils of the rolling prairie. Their fields carried only a thin layer of topsoil over a bed of sand. When a county extension agent visited Dearfield in 1917, he noted, "The sand is discouraging on the roads and it is a problem in the fields."[14] He may have particularly noticed the sand because his Ford got stuck in it, and he had to walk several miles to reach Dearfield.

The state agricultural college (now Colorado State University) in Fort Collins and the state normal school (now University of Northern Colorado) in Greeley helped. Dearfield residents attended educational meetings for farmers in Greeley and Fort Collins. The county extension agent advised them that they needed to try out crops suited to the sandy soil, such as rye, Sudan wheat, beans, corn, sweet clover for pasture, sunflowers for chickens, and potatoes. The recently established Cooperative Extension Service provided other advice, including helping them learn how best to raise poultry for market.[15] But there was a lot to learn.

Their main teacher was trial and error, a most unforgiving disciplinarian. During these early years, they struggled. James Monroe Thomas suffered losses especially when his corn crop was poor. He fed his family first, but the short crop meant he lost eight horses before proving up his claim. Jackson, too, acknowledged that the Dearfield farmers succeeded "without capital or any appreciable knowledge of dry farming."[16]

The homesteaders' trials were given front-page publicity. Booker T. Washington II visited Dearfield with his family, photographed in a melon field with Jackson. *The Modern Farmer*, the newspaper of the National Federation of Colored Farmers, highlighted the colony's progress. The federation published its paper in both Nashville and Chicago, emblazoned with its rallying cry of "Stay on the farm if you're on it! Go back to the farm if you're off it!" In 1930 *Modern Farmer* noted about Dearfield, "There were lean years in the early days of the settlement because the men and women who came to take up the land were not experienced in farming methods. . . . Year by year, however, their efforts counted for more, and within a comparatively short time the colony was an outstanding example of what can be accomplished by hard work."[17]

In spite of obstacles, the early settlers persisted and most stayed on their claims to fulfill the homestead law's residency requirement. James Monroe Thomas proved up in January 1915; Frank McPherson received patent in 1918. By 1915 homesteaders had constructed forty-four wooden cabins located out on their claims, and by one estimate they had put up over a hundred miles of fencing. The settlers broke sod to plant small gardens, and they cultivated squash, beans, corn, melons, and pumpkins. They raised chickens, ducks, and turkeys. They put up hay, both for their own livestock and for sale.[18]

They found that their biggest challenge was obtaining water. They needed water for household use, to grow vegetable gardens and fruit trees, to water livestock, and most ambitiously, to irrigate their

71. O. T. Jackson in a melon field with Booker T. Washington
II, his wife, Nettie Blair (Hancock) Washington, and their child,
Booker T. Washington III, Dearfield, ca. 1914. 3015.0001.2D,
City of Greeley Museums Permanent Collection.

parched prairieland fields. The community lacked the right to take
water from the South Platte River, because the State of Colorado
already closely regulated such withdrawals. Farmers at the Union
Colony (later renamed Greeley) in 1876 pulled out their guns to face
off against upstream irrigators around Fort Collins, fighting for water
taken from the Cache la Poudre River, a South Platte tributary. Both
sides armed themselves for battle, and only state intervention ended
the dispute. A stream near Dearfield lost its entire flow during most
of the year and was appropriately named Lost Creek.

Weld County co-ops and farmers associations, aided by local governments, built irrigation canals in a frenzy—the Bijou Canal, the
Empire Intake Canal, the Empire Reservoir, the Riverside Irrigation
District, all near Dearfield. But Dearfield farmers could take water
from these projects only if they bought in, and they usually lacked

the cash to do so. The right to water one eighty-acre field from the nearby Bijou Canal had cost $1,000 in 1901, and the price had gone up since.

But the real problem was that no one wanted to sell their water rights. Farmers had bought all the canal's water and the water in other irrigation channels when they first opened. If the water-rights owners were still farming, they needed the water for their crops; if they were selling their land, a water right boosted the sale price. So landowners held tight to their water rights. Moreover, Dearfield lands were elevated, some as much as three hundred feet above the South Platte, so even if they did manage to buy a water right, they would need to purchase expensive pumping equipment to lift the water to their fields.[19] Dearfield farmers were simply shut out of the irrigated farming business.

Residents dug wells for their household needs and for watering gardens and livestock. The earliest town well was dug by hand in 1912, and during the first years, residents relied on water from wells owned by O. T. Jackson, Dr. W. A. Jones, W. Moore, and W. Pritchette, all relatively affluent settlers. Then in 1914 James Matlock, O. T. Jackson's father-in-law, purchased a gasoline-powered boring rig. He drilled a town well, finding, as the *Denver Star* noted, "a fine flow of good soft water at 25 feet." The well was intended for use by anyone in the colony.[20]

Matlock then went into business drilling wells for farmers, and in the next couple of years, he completed dozens of farm wells. He generally struck water at a manageable twenty to thirty-five feet— James Monroe Thomas listed his well during proving up as "a 12' deep bucket well"—but it was highly variable and sometimes they found water only a long way down. Farmers erected windmills to pump the water.

Lacking both water rights and capital for field irrigation, they instead followed "dryland farming" methods. They adopted this approach out of necessity, but they may have gained confidence in it from national agricultural experts who touted it. Samuel Aughey, a professor at the University of Nebraska, and other experts promoted a theory that "rain follows the plow." They had observed a correlation, which turned out to be spurious, between plowed areas and rising moisture levels. When farmers plowed, they theorized, they permanently altered local climatological conditions in a way that triggered increased precipitation.

Farmers' groups organized Dry Farming Congresses, including in Denver in 1907 and 1915 and Colorado Springs in 1911, to promote dryland farming techniques. At the meetings, USDA experiment station personnel, national agriculture experts, and experienced dry farmers all testified to the techniques to be used and the crops to plant. Dryland farming, despite its unpromising name, was reasonably successful during the wetter years of the late 1910s. Unfortunately, the theory was false, and dryland farming left Dearfield farmers highly vulnerable during later dry years.

Between 1914 and 1921, Dearfield residents became increasingly successful. Typical was James Monroe Thomas, who had to borrow money to make his initial filing costing fourteen dollars. By 1913 he had his house built and crops growing in his fields. He was offered (and refused) $2,000 for his claim.[21]

The town of Dearfield was officially platted on 480 acres in February 1914. The nearest rail link, a Union Pacific track with a depot in Masters, was two miles away. Residents began opening or attracting businesses. They organized a company to manufacture concrete blocks, a lumber and coal yard, and a boarding house with a store attached. Others launched a hotel, a restaurant, and other businesses. Dr. Westbrook, the Denver physician, provided medical care until he resumed his fulltime Denver practice. He was replaced in 1914 by Dr. W. A. Jones, who doctored and farmed his 282-acre claim as well. Jackson attempted, unsuccessfully, to attract investors to open a bank. The *Denver Sun* in 1913 printed a major frontpage story extolling Dearfield's business opportunities under the headline, "Dearfield No Longer a Possibility, But a Reality. Farmers Making Good."[22]

Town leaders pleaded for more Black people to join them. In 1917 the Dearfield Agency, with offices on Arapahoe Street in Denver, ran ads in the *Denver Star* under the heading, "Negroes Farming in Eastern Colorado." It recounted how O. T. Jackson and others had found a twenty thousand-acre bloc of unoccupied federal land in Weld County and that sixty Black families had now taken up fifteen thousand acres of it, the remaining portion occupied by "a good class of white settlers." Moreover, there were, it said, five hundred Black families, encompassing two thousand Black farmers and farm hands, working in eastern Colorado. Their presence, the ads suggested, created a wonderful opportunity for Black entrepreneurs.

After some additional boosterism, the Dearfield Agency got to the point. "Now is the time for the young Negro to become interested in the Town of Dearfield. . . . We will give every inducement possible, for WE NEED YOUR BUSINESS NOW." It urged Black people to take up the opportunity to furnish the farmers with supplies and to handle their marketable crops. To bolster the colony's bona fides, it offered as references Colorado's governor, two ex-governors, a U.S. Senator, Denver bankers, and other notables—testament, no doubt, to Jackson's political connections made while serving as the governor's official messenger.[23]

Despite the agency's appeal, Dearfield remained mainly a community of farmers. Most Dearfield residents lived on their claims. After a visit, the Weld County extension agent noted, "It is a colony of farms and farmers. There is no town."

The extension agent said that while they faced many difficulties, the homesteaders "seem happy and hopeful." He was impressed with their good spirits: "They love the land; they have started here, and they mean to succeed. No one can refuse to take an interest in such spirit." He pledged to learn their needs and assist them by developing methods they could use to help them realize bigger returns from their lands.[24]

Within four years the community had attracted over one hundred residents, and then it doubled its population. Dearfield had around 230 inhabitants in 1920, according to census data. but if the census undercounted Black persons here as it typically did elsewhere, the true 1920 population might have been closer to 275 or even 300. That was a far cry from the nineteen hardy souls who came for the first winter, and enough to create a real sense of a growing community.[25]

Joseph Houston, one of the newcomers, promoted establishment of a nearby Black village called Chapelton, a few miles southeast of Dearfield. It served as Dearfield's twin, being both complementary and sometimes competitive with it. It never grew as large as Dearfield, but Chapelton eventually hosted a general store, and in 1917 it opened the colony's only U.S. Post Office. Chapelton had two churches and the community's first officially sanctioned school, opened in 1919.

Still, a visitor in 1917 reported, "About the grocery store there seems no greater settlement than at other points. The schoolhouse is a mile or more to the east and the church as far or further to the west."[26] No real boundary separated Dearfield and Chapelton, and anyway, neither Chapelton nor Dearfield ever formed much of a town.

The colonists came to own land rather than live in town. By 1922 forty-seven Black homesteaders had received patents to their claims, gaining ownership of 8,554 acres, and some in addition had purchased more land. Still others had filed on land which they intended to prove up but ultimately did not. In total, Dearfield residents likely farmed more than ten thousand acres and perhaps controlled as many as fifteen thousand acres.

By the time Dearfield (including Chapelton) farmers brought in their 1917 harvest, they had achieved substantial prosperity. Sixty or seventy residential families worked the land. Their 1918 harvest produced their first significant marketable crops, netting them over $50,000, or an average of $833 per farm (equivalent to just over $16,000 in 2022). The substantial payout allowed them to buy farm equipment, upgrade their stock, and make home improvements. Jackson valued Dearfield's total holdings at $432,500, possible if it also included the value of the community's livestock. The homesteaders had clearly created considerable equity for themselves—Jackson's figure would imply an average farm family's net worth of nearly $7,000 (equivalent to $136,000 in 2022) for the sixty-two claims. Quite a boost for people who, less than a decade before, had trouble paying their train fares from Denver.

Dearfield farmers had an even better harvest in 1919. The following winter the *Greeley Daily Tribune* reported enthusiastically on the colony's progress under the headline, "Dearfield Is Very Much on the Uplift Now." It enthused, "The colored population of Dearfield are alive and progressive."[27]

The 1920 crop was best of all. The *Fort Collins Coloradoan* head-lined its story, "Weld County Negroes Produce Record Crop in Dearfield District." Dearfield farmers had planted a third more acreage than in 1919, and 90 percent of their crops matured, as compared to just 60 percent during the successful previous year. The corn crop was especially good, so farmers planned to fatten many hogs over the winter for spring marketing.[28]

During the years from 1917 to 1921, World War I and the postwar collapse of European agriculture dramatically pumped up demand for Dearfield's products. Dearfield farmer Bert Griffith could look out proudly in 1918 at his twenty acres of corn, another twenty of beans, four acres of cane, a smattering of pumpkins and watermelons, eight pigs and a cow. Success like his was increasingly the rule in Dearfield.

Residents could now attend to other priorities as well. First among them was ensuring that their children were educated. Some Dearfield children attended nearby integrated schools. Residents also operated their own local grade school, which may occasionally have included white students. In 1929, although enrollment was down considerably, the Dearfield school still had twelve Black students when Red Cross nurses came for a public health inspection. The nurses gave the school a grade of "outstanding," praising the exceptional cleanliness, good manners, and well preserved teeth of the children.[29]

Black and white children remembered differently how well the integrated schools worked. Bertha Reed, a white student, later recalled, "The way I remember it, we were all good friends. It never made any difference whether we were Black or white." But Carrie Wright, a Black student, had different memories: "The little kids were mean at school. Tryin like we wanted to play and when they'd draw up sides, we'd be the last ones. And if they had enough, they wouldn't call us a'tall, and my sister and I sat on the steps. And umm . . . I don't know, I've always been a person that could adjust. It didn't worry me, I expected it. They acted that way all the time, if they'd been real nice, we'd have wondered what was gonna happen."[30]

Parents organized activities at home that supplemented formal schooling. In the 1970s Carrie Wright recalled, "In the evening after dinner mother read to us every night, or else she'd play the piano or the organ and sang, she had a beautiful voice. And either we'd have a concert or she'd read to us. And we were just a family. The thing they're trying to bring to America now, we had then. We were a family."[31]

Children who wanted to attend high school had to go farther away, most likely living with relatives in Greeley or Denver. Dearfield teacher Odessa McCollough even began planning for an "industrial agricultural college," but she never succeeded in opening it.

By 1914 Dearfield had added a church, the Union Presbyterian Mission Church. Reverend J. A. Thomas Hazell, whom Jackson described as "the only negro preacher who has taken an active part in the establishment of Dearfield," presided. Soon other churches sprouted: Chapelton had three churches, with AME, Baptist, and Presbyterian congregations. The Chapelton Presbyterian church was initially an offshoot of the Dearfield town mission, but by 1918 the Dearfield Presbyterians had moved their building to Chapelton. Churches not only called people to worship but served as the hubs for cultural and community activities. Residents also attended Pentecostal services and camp revivals, like those at which Reverend Suggs had preached, which remained highly popular.[32]

O. T. Jackson provided another center for community life at his Lunch Room and gas station. Located on Highway 34 right at the heart of the settlement, the Lunch Room was a convenient place for neighbors to gather and socialize. People sat around, inside and in good weather outside, to hear the latest news, discuss how the crops were doing, plan weekend visits, arrange to borrow tools or get help replacing fence wire, gossip about neighbors, drink morning coffee, and probably, for some, have lunch.

The town hosted an annual civic and political festival and a carnival, attracting prominent outsider orators. In 1917 Governor George Carlson, no doubt persuaded by his official messenger, came to Dearfield to be the featured speaker.

Dearfield residents' hard work and visible success produced growing esteem in the eyes of their white neighbors as well. The *Denver Post*, in 1917, reported under a headline "Negro Colony at Dearfield is Big Success" that "Farming Community is Prospering and People Are Industrious." "A Credit to Colorado" it continued, and "Value of Land and Improvements Is Steadily Advancing." The *Weld County*

News also praised Dearfield's success. It cited its two churches and school for "adding materially to the educational and moral standards of the community" and observed that "since the first filing within the colony [ten years earlier] there has been but one arrest for any offense of any magnitude and the offender in that instance was not legitimately a resident." Laced with condescension, these comments nonetheless reflected developing racial harmony. Local Black-white relations apparently lacked racism's frequent companions of unfair policing, trumped-up charges, and biased court decisions.[33]

The increasing harmony locally contrasted with the vicious racism growing nationally. Racial violence grew across the South, of course, but also in places like Indiana, which saw a resurgence of the Ku Klux Klan; in Omaha, which witnessed a brutal lynching in 1919; and in Tulsa, site of the horrendous 1921 Tulsa Massacre. Even in Denver, the Ku Klux Klan attracted thousands of members, including high elected officials, although its venom seemed mainly directed at Catholics and Jews.[34] O.T. Jackson experienced his only spell of unemployment during these years, when KKK-backed Republican governor Clarence Morley dismissed him. But two years later, Jackson was back on the job.

On the ground in Dearfield, African American homesteaders from the start had found off-farm employment with white ranchers and others, and their interactions appeared marked by growing cooperation. The Colorado Board of Immigration, in its four-page brochure "Dearfield Colorado Township and Settlement," observed, "Attracted by the success [of Dearfield], white farmers began moving into the territory to take advantage of the cheap lands offered for sale, and today there are both white and colored farmers working harmoniously together in the region, striving for the interdependence which successful farming brings to the people of both races."

Dearfield resident Eunice Norris observed that her fellow Blacks and the whites got along because "they didn't have time for trouble.

There was a spirit of helpfulness." Historian George Junne Jr. and his coauthors concluded that "the situation [in Dearfield] seemed to be the opposite of conditions in other parts of the United States."[35]

Dearfield reached its high-water mark around 1921. The value of the community's annual production reached $125,000. Its farmers' worked land worth over $750,000, and they also owned livestock valued at an additional $200,000. When farm equipment and buildings were added in, their assets amounted to over a million dollars. The average family farm was worth just over $16,000 (equivalent to $233,000 in 2022).[36] Dearfield was adding population, deepening its farming roots, building wealth, and seemingly positioning itself well for its future prosperity.

But the years of Dearfield's success had been characterized by both greater precipitation and higher crop prices than would be true for the next two decades. The relatively wet 1910s gave way to the drier 1920s and then the extreme drought of the 1930s. Dearfield's homesteaders lacked access to irrigation canals or other reliable sources of water, and so they struggled to survive even short-term dry spells and lacked the capacity to endure long droughts.

Equally devastating, crop prices collapsed after the war ended. Wheat prices had soared as high as $2.00 and $2.50 per bushel between 1916 and 1920. But they fell as quickly, hitting $1.00 per bushel between 1921 to 1924, and then collapsing again to below $0.50 per bushel in the early 1930s.[37] Prices of other food crops that Dearfield homesteaders produced—poultry, eggs, milk, and dry beans—collapsed as well.

Combined, the drought and price collapse spelled doom for marginal farmers, including those in Dearfield. Dearfield farmers suffered another blow when their off-farm employment dried up. White ranchers around Dearfield and Greeley were hit as hard by the bad conditions as Black farmers were, and they had less money for, or need for, hiring Dearfield residents. Banks responded to the depressed economy by calling in loans and refusing to make new ones, drying up credit just when it was needed most.[38]

Dearfield's population plummeted after 1921, as residents abandoned the community. They found the dry weather, low crop prices, loss of off-farm employment, and credit squeeze made surviving on the land impossible. Like many white farmers, they fled to the cities to seek work or relief. Few newcomers arrived, as migrants out of the South found opportunities opening to them in northern cities more attractive than homesteading. By 1930 the community had only four residents, a remnant of its 1921 level.[39]

The story of Dearfield as a prosperous, growing community offering expanded opportunities to African Americans was over. Many factors contributed to the colony's decline. Lack of access to irrigation water severely damaged the farmers' chances. Thomas Bailey, a Dearfield farmer who persisted longer than most, blamed the farmers' lack of experience. He said it "doomed the project." The *Greeley Daily Tribune* pointed to other causes, which afflicted white farmers as well, including "Drouth, grasshoppers, and depression."[40]

Unable to support their families, Black homesteaders sold their land to neighboring ranchers. They mostly sold out at the prevailing market price for land, but unfortunately no one was paying much for agricultural land during such hard times. The region was and is better suited for ranching than row-crop farming—at least until decades later deep groundwater wells, modern pumps, and center-pivot irrigation systems made irrigated fields more possible. Few Dearfield residents seem to have attempted ranching. With insufficient resources to begin ranching and drawing undue optimism from their past decade's experiences, they stuck with row-crop farming until their luck ran out.[41]

O. T. Jackson stayed on, trying desperately to revive his community. In 1927 when some two thousand delegates to the Negro Baptist Churches of the United States met in convention in Denver,

Jackson organized a day's excursion for them to the Platte Valley, with a visit and barbeque in Dearfield. In 1931 Jackson sent a circular to a Baptist group coming to Denver, describing Colorado as a "Land of Opportunity."[42]

He also continued to organize big Labor Day celebrations to which he invited his political friends. In 1930 he advertised a "barbeque feast . . . Good music selected by Morrison's orchestra, and a barn dance." The big feature, however, were the political speeches, starting at 6:30 PM. Jackson worked his political contacts, inviting all elected officials from Weld and five other counties, including Denver and Boulder. He encouraged former Dearfield residents to return for a Homecoming, and a local club organized an automobile excursion.[43]

When in 1931 workers finished paving Highway 34 between Greeley and Fort Morgan, leaders of the two towns agreed to stage their ribbon-cutting ceremony halfway between them, at Dearfield. Excited officials from both towns organized huge caravans to carry the crowds to the event. The Greeley newspaper anointed Jackson as the "unofficial Mayor of Dearfield" who would be there to welcome the visitors. Indeed, more than welcome: "O.T. Jackson, who owns the cold drink and ice cream business in Dearfield, . . . did a land office business, nearly every one of the 1,000 people present requiring refreshments on the hot [July] afternoon."[44]

But Dearfield had lost almost all of its people and the harsh climate was ravaging its abandoned buildings. Already by the time of the road dedication, the only occupied structures were Jackson's famous Lunch Room and filling station, along with his house and two or three others. The Greeley newspaper described Dearfield as "a decayed 'town' of three or four houses."[45]

Soon it would become a ghost town. In 1937 only two of sixty-seven original families remained. Jackson himself persisted in trying to revive Dearfield long after almost everyone else had left. He tried to market the area as a fishing and outdoors resort for Black

72. O. T. Jackson advertises to sell Dearfield in *Greeley Daily Tribune*, March 28, 1944, 7. newspapers.com.

tourists. He even tried, during World War II, to interest the U.S. Government in Dearfield as a possible internment camp for Japanese Americans. (The government instead opened Camp Amache, two hundred miles to the south, where it imprisoned more than seven thousand American citizens of Japanese descent. Camp Amache is now a National Historic Site.) None of Jackson's efforts to save Dearfield succeeded.

In 1944 Jackson placed a hauntingly heartbreaking ad to sell Dearfield. He found no buyers. He tried again in 1948, again attracting no buyers. He died later that year. Only Jennie Jackson, O. T.'s niece and caretaker, lived off and on in Dearfield until the 1970s.

Local enthusiasts now lead an energetic and ongoing effort to remember Dearfield's history and preserve it as an historic site. Filmmakers Donnie Betts, in *Dearfield, The Road Less Traveled* (1998), and Charles Nuckolls, in *Remnants of a Dream: The Story of Dearfield Colorado* (2018), have created documentaries telling Dearfield's story. Archeologist Robert Brunswig and Professor of Africana Studies George Junne Jr., both of the University of Northern Colorado, lead a preservation group working in association with the Black American West Museum in Denver. The Museum now owns much of the site.

They are in a race against time and weather to save the remaining buildings. The preservation group was developing stabilization plans and seeking funding to preserve Squire Brockman's house and blacksmith shop, but in June 2020 a violent storm blew them down. They sit now as heaps of gray, rotting boards.[46] The preservation group won major National Park Service funding in 2021 to stabilize and restore the two remaining structures. Representative Joe Neguse, an African American Democrat from Boulder, and Representative Ken Buck, a white Republican from Weld County, joined forces to try and win National Historic Site designation for Dearfield. Funding and political support offer hope that Dearfield will survive as a historical and cultural site.

Dearfield no longer has any residents, yet still it endures. "I think Dearfield is an example of dispelling every negative idea about who we are," observed Terri Gentry, great-great-grandchild of original homesteaders Frank and Anna McPherson. "Dearfield shows resilience, it shows energy, it shows intelligence, it shows innovation, it shows creativity, it shows a broad spectrum of perspectives about how you live your life." Gentry continued, "Slavery was designed to show us that we were not human, that we couldn't think for ourselves, that we couldn't do anything unless you are whipped or coerced to a particular behavior. Dearfield shows our humanity. It shows brilliance. It shows honoring and reclaiming some of the things that we had before we left Africa. It shows the strength, the risks, the ideas . . . For me, it's standing out there in the middle of nowhere looking up and seeing all the stars and recognizing that you're part of that."[47]

As Dearfield experienced its cycle of prosperity and decline, another colony, also led by a visionary Black man, took shape near Roswell, New Mexico. Its name, like those of Nicodemus, Dearfield, Audacious, and Empire, expressed its soaring aspirations. It was called Blackdom.

13

Struggles in the Desert at Blackdom

At first whites didn't mind [the Black homesteaders].
They were all from the North and they soon all moved
out and left the place to the Southerners. They didn't
like nobody. They was hard on us as they could be.

—ROOSEVELT BOYER, Blackdom descendant

Frank Boyer, like O. T. Jackson, wanted to establish a colony of Black
landowners, and like him, Boyer had difficulty getting it going.
But he persisted, and he succeeded in founding the community of
Blackdom, New Mexico. His promised land proved to suffer both
a harsh natural geography *and* an unfriendly social environment,
but it nonetheless gave shelter to weary migrants.

Boyer was born in Georgia in 1870, the fifth of seven children
to parents who previously had been enslaved. His father, Henry
Boyer, worked as a wagoneer for the U.S. Army during the Mexican-
American War, and he returned with stirring tales of land and opportunity in the West. In 1888 Frank Boyer joined the Twenty-Fourth
U.S. Infantry Regiment, a Black unit in the segregated Army, and was
sent out west. The Twenty-Fourth saw action in quelling revolts of
the Creek and Navaho tribes, and his unit was put to work building
Fort Huachuca in Arizona.

When his five-year enlistment expired, Boyer returned to Georgia.
With the help of a white judge who paid his expenses, he enrolled at
Morehouse College. He also proofread for the *Atlanta Constitution*.
After graduating with a degree in education, he studied at Atlanta

Baptist Seminary and Fisk University in Nashville. While in college he met and married Ella McGruder, a nurse and midwife.[1]

Boyer, now highly educated, became frustrated with the limited life prospects in the Jim Crow South and decided to return to the West. In January 1900 he and his friend Daniel Keys simply started walking. They left Pelham, Georgia, walking across the South toward the setting sun. More than once they were harassed and humiliated, and at one point some whites shot bullets near their feet to make them sing and dance. They worked odd jobs along the way. Frank sent some money home to Ella and their children and saved as much of the rest as he could. After traveling 1,400 miles, they arrived in Roswell, New Mexico. Boyer stopped there, while Keys continued west.[2]

In 1901 Boyer brought Ella and their children to join him. For the next two decades, they would be based in or near Roswell. Boyer worked a variety of jobs in Roswell, and at some point learned of land available under the Homestead Act. He and Ella decided to homestead, but Frank had bigger plans, too.

On September 9, 1903, Boyer and twelve other African Americans incorporated the Blackdom Townsite Company. The company intended "to establish a negro colony and to found and erect the town of Blackdom." It would purchase and settle land, build and operate irrigation plants drawing water from artesian wells, and in general "obtain control of a large body of land in the county of Chaves . . . and there to establish and maintain a colony of negroes." It pledged to build schools, colleges, and churches to improve and lift up the moral and mental condition of the colonists.[3] Boyer would serve as president.

The *Roswell Daily Record* printed on its front page the company's articles of incorporation, including its claimed capitalization of $10,000. But the paper also mocked as "Hot Air" the company's lengthy prospectus, which imagined that "There will be a population of ten thousand . . . and ten parks and ten commons and 120

83. Frank and Ella Boyer, ca. 1920. New Mexico State
University Library, Archives and Special Collections.

miles of streets surrounded by an eight mile boulevard, and after
it is thoroughly peopled there will be ten banks, ten bakeries, ten
bookstores, ten newspapers, 100 printers, 25 lumber yards, 250
carpenters, 500 cooks, 200 teachers, 100 preachers, 100 physi-
cians" and more.[4] These were exaggerated claims, to be sure, but
the *Record*'s mockery foreshadowed how some whites would not
welcome the new Black community.

The company's founding and its promise of an all-Black colony
made news across the country. The *Hamilton County* (Indiana) *Ledger, Boston Evening Transcript*, (Louisville) *Courier-Journal*, and nearly
a hundred other newspapers carried the story. Some interpreted the
$10,000 capitalization as evidence of the founders' seriousness.

Company officials chose for Blackdom a location about eighteen
miles south of Roswell, in the desert prairies of the Roswell Basin.

The basin consists of carbonate rocks, limestone and dolomite, and is marked by large caverns in the chalk formations. Rainfall and surface runoff form sinkholes. Just west of the Pecos River, this area averages only twelve to thirteen inches of rainfall annually and suffers recurring droughts. It is part of a larger region, sixty-five miles long north to south and seven to twelve miles wide, which parallels the Pecos.[5] Boyer and his associates had chosen a dry, forbidding landscape to colonize. They must have realized how difficult it would be to grow crops, and so they made explicit their expensive commitment to irrigate the proposed farms.

The Blackdom incorporators had mixed motivations. They viewed their proposed colony as a profit-making venture, perhaps through land speculation, which they did not see as being in conflict with helping fellow Black migrants acquire land. Unfortunately, the company lacked a detailed plan for how it would create the colony. It did not have the claimed $10,000 capitalization nor indeed many assets at all, and the investors sought buyers for the five thousand shares of company stock priced at two dollars each.[6] Company officials fought among themselves, further stalling progress. Their original plan to have thirteen company directors proved unwieldly, so in 1911 Boyer amended the articles to provide for just three directors: himself, his wife Ella, and one other.[7]

Boyer forced the changes because, after several years, the company had made little progress. It was able to persuade only a few settlers to move to Blackdom. Three homestead entries in the Blackdom area had been finalized by 1907, but only Isaac Jones was affiliated with the colony-building project. Between 1904 and 1908 five Black claimants, including Frank Boyer, proved up homesteads near Dexter, a neighboring (white) community.

Sparse rainfall may have slowed progress in attracting homesteaders. While 1904 to 1906 had been wet years, the years 1907 through 1910 were ones of drought. Precipitation in Roswell (the nearest station with weather records) averaged just 8.8 inches during this period, and 1910 was disastrous, getting only 4.87 inches. Rain as sparse as eight inches almost always meant dried-up plants, scanty or no crop yields, and little income for farmers. Frank Boyer's brother John observed that the land was most valuable for grazing, but livestock was expensive and John himself only grazed three hogs and a horse on his land. Farming for profit was nearly impossible in such difficult circumstances.[8]

What could save such parched fields, especially during drought years, was irrigation. And irrigation appeared possible, given the region's plentiful water from artesian wells. "Artesian" water—the name comes from the old Roman city of Artesium, today's Artois in France—is water trapped in an aquifer with an overlaying sheet of impermeable rock, putting the aquifer's water under great pressure. When the rock above the aquifer is punctured by a bore hole, water naturally spurts to surface, creating a flowing "artesian" well. In Roswell, artesian wells produced gushers of clear, pure water.

At Blackdom, however, the artesian water lay deep underground, hundreds of feet down, so driving a bore hole to reach it was expensive. The pressure was insufficient to raise water at that depth all the way to the surface, adding extra cost for the pumps necessary to lift it the rest of the way. But if artesian water was too expensive to tap, Blackdom farmers had a second option: alluvial aquifers. A separation barrier consisting of impermeable rock lay above the deep artesian water, and above that, at reachable depths, small alluvial aquifers formed. Blackdom farmers paid about $180 for drillers to reach the alluvial aquifers, and these wells provided sufficient water for household use, gardens, small orchards, and livestock. They did not supply enough water to irrigate fields.[9]

Frank Boyer drilled a deep well, which may have cost him four thousand dollars, likely exhausting his savings and credit. The necessary pumping and piping equipment to move water to the fields added more expense. In 1904, he petitioned Roswell water pump merchants Leary, Gill, and Marrow to provide him credit to purchase an engine to power his pump because he lacked the $160 to pay for it. He was not alone—none of the incorporators had the means to pay for deep wells and extensive irrigation equipment. The founders made little progress in establishing the colony during these years.[10]

Toward the end of the new century's first decade, Black land-seekers developed renewed interest in Blackdom. Their interest was reinforced by the spectacular rainfall of 16.37 inches in 1911, bountiful rains that rewarded farmers who had claimed land. They may also have sought refuge from the growing racism of Roswell's whites.

After the Territory's period of frontier lawlessness, ex-Confederate Captain Joseph Lea platted Roswell in 1885, and he established the New Mexico Military Institute in 1891. In the 1880s, however, Roswell and the surrounding region were mostly settled by northerners from Nebraska, Indiana, and Kansas. Relations between Blacks and whites, never equal, nonetheless mainly reflected a northern style of more tolerant separateness. "Jim Crow and its supporting institutions of the South had not fully developed in Chaves County," Blackdom historian Timothy Nelson noted. As a result, "racial tension in Chaves County at the turn of the Twentieth Century was comparatively milder than that in the South."[11]

This mild racial regime was about to change. Drillers made the spectacular discovery of plentiful sources of gushing artesian water, and railroaders laid new tracks connecting the city to the national network. White migrants flooded in. Roswell's population tripled, from 2,006 in 1900 to 6,172 in 1910. Most of the newcomers came from Texas and elsewhere in the South, and they brought with them southern attitudes regarding race.

The newcomers quickly changed Roswell's culture. Interactions more frequently featured racial taunts and anti-Black violence, and officials began more stringently enforcing vagrancy and other racial suppression laws. When Roosevelt Boyer Sr. (Frank's son) was asked how the whites treated them when the Blacks arrived, he responded: "At first whites didn't mind. They were all from the North and they soon all moved out and left the place to the Southerners. They didn't like nobody. They was hard on us as they could be."[12]

Blackdom descendant Rodney Bowe remembered being told about when his ancestors went into Roswell. He said, "The boys would be in the back of the wagon and they told them to be quiet don't say a word don't talk to anybody that you're not supposed to talk to. And they would cover them in the back of the wagon when they went into Roswell for fear of angering a white townsperson and getting the whole family in trouble. So when they would come in that was one of the biggest challenges that they had."[13]

The *Roswell Daily Record*, newly launched in 1903, signaled the new white hostility. In its first year it printed "The Roswell Negro." The item reported that a white visitor was repulsed by finding a Black person eating at table with white folks at a church festival. The newspaper defended Roswell by proclaiming that "there is just as little so called 'negro equality' in Roswell as you can find in any town of the south."[14]

John Henry Mullis was one of the white newcomers. Born in Arkansas, Mullis was a Democrat in the mold of southern Democrats hostile to Black equality. His politics fit well with the *Record*'s racial slanders and racial mockery. He was elected Roswell's mayor and provided an official face to racial oppression. He and the *Record* were simply local manifestations of the intensifying anti-Black venom in the nation at large, especially in the South. White southerners reasserted white supremacy in a spree of lynching and tightening of Jim Crow repression.

Black migrants, encouraged by the wetter weather and seeking relief from growing white hostility in Roswell, began arriving in

The Roswell Negro.

W. F. Pafford says he has all he wants of Roswell. While attending the fair there last week he dropped in on a church festival, thinking he would help along a good cause. About the first thing he ran up against was a sable son of Africa eating with the whites. This was more than Mr. Pafford could stand and he left, quietly informing the management that he did not go to Roswell to rob Roosevelt of his honors.—Claude News.

The above item which is going the rounds of the press does Roswell a gross injustice. In the first place there are but very few negroes in Roswell, and those who are here keep their places.

84. "The Roswell Negro," *Roswell Daily Record*, October 8, 1903. Newspapers.com.

Blackdom. They came by train, in wagons, on horseback, and even on foot in their quest to own land.

Between 1909 to 1916 the migrants filed homesteader claims, which they proved up between 1914 and 1921. In all, sixty-four individuals, including in some cases members of the same extended family, successfully proved up claims. Forty-two claimants each owned approximately 160 acres and thirteen became owners of 320 acres. At least twelve women homesteaded, some undoubtedly to increase the family holdings, but others on their own. Mittie Moore, Ella Boyer and Pernecia Russell each owned large tracts. In all, the claimants gained title to 13,056 acres.[15]

85. Blackdom farmers working in the field, ca. 1920s, including (*from left*) Loney K. Wagoner, three daughters of Joseph and Harriet Smith, and an unknown man. Permission of Historical Society of Southeastern New Mexico.

Claimants included the families who became the social and political leaders in Blackdom and made it successful. The Proffit family, migrants from Mississippi, entered four separate filings by different branches of the family, giving them control of 878 acres. The Collins family, also from Mississippi, proved up on 638 acres in three filings. The various Boyers, from Georgia, claimed 960 acres in six separate filings. George and Myra Wilson's family, from Missouri, claimed 800 acres in three filings, and the Smith family, possibly from Tennessee, 640 acres in three filings. The Ragsdale family from Mississippi accumulated 1,080 acres. Loney K. Wagoner from South Carolina claimed 636 acres. Leading all of them was the Herron family, from South Carolina, accruing 2,227 acres in nine separate filings. Historian Nelson concluded that "the importance of homesteading cannot be overstated as a major opportunity for Black people in Chaves County." It allowed Black people to invest and build capital, and obtaining "free" land was Blackdom residents' central motivation for moving to the colony.

One of the new claimants was Mittie Moore.[16] She was a phenomenon. Before moving to Blackdom, for a decade or more, she ran the most successful and well-known brothel in Roswell. Her establishment apparently catered to some of Roswell's most powerful men. Moore was so successful she was able to extend her control over much of South Virginia Avenue, known as Roswell's "Bawdy District." Local officials periodically raided her business, but their attacks never managed to close her down. Given her clientele, perhaps they had no intention of doing so. When hauled into court, Moore was adept in defending herself using the letter of the law. Judges regularly let her and her employees off with minor fines, a cost of doing business. Moore was little concerned with social acceptability, and she focused on ensuring that her business remained profitable and open. Which mainly it did.

What finally shut Moore's brothel for a time was the federal government. She became a casualty of President Woodrow Wilson's war on moral corruption. As the nation entered the Great War, the starchy and high-minded Wilson grew concerned to protect the moral health of the Army's new draftees. He saw them as naive innocents who would easily fall prey to and be corrupted by the lewd pleasures he was sure surrounded U.S. training camps. He was even more obsessed with the temptations his soldiers would face when they reached Old Europe. To protect them, he launched a "cleanliness" campaign to root out brothels, gambling dens, and other iniquitous places near training camps and mobilization centers.

President Wilson appointed Raymond Fosdick to lead the cleanliness campaign. Fosdick, later the president of the Rockefeller

Foundation, sought to introduce libraries, musical events, and athletic activities to dissuade the troops from their daily visits to local brothels. He promoted vocals and a "singing army" to distract men from vice. He saw boxing as an especially effective tool for tamping down hormonal urges. The Army employed a merciless and extreme strategy, as historian Zachary May noted, "to eliminate the source [of venereal disease], which included prostitution and red-light districts."[17]

Although Roswell's nearest Army training camp was at Deming, NM, 250 miles away, Mayor Mullis enthusiastically joined Wilson's cleanliness campaign. The mayor focused Roswell's enforcement, not coincidentally, on the African American neighborhood. They specifically targeted Mittie Moore's flourishing brothel and closed it down.

But Moore the entrepreneur had already begun exploring other options. She used her business acumen, developed in the brothel business, to acquire land in Blackdom. She may already have known Frank Boyer, because later she enlisted his help on a land claim. Known as Mattie Moore and Mattie Moore Wilson in Blackdom, in 1915 she filed on a 320-acre Enlarged Homestead claim. A couple years later, she filed a 320-acre Stock Raising claim.[18] With Boyer's help, she also pursued a homestead claim based on her assertion that she was the heir of a soldier who had made a claim before he died. Local land officials rejected this filing, and she pursued it up the chain. After several more appeals, the General Land Office in Washington finally dismissed her claim and closed her case. Still, her other, successful claims made her one of the largest landowners in Blackdom.

Blackdom probably reached its peak population of 150 to 200 people in 1918. As was true elsewhere in the Great Plains, its prosperity was strongly dependent on adequate rainfall. From 1911 through 1923, rainfall averaged 13.5 inches. Thirteen-and-a-half inches of precipitation put farmers right on the dry edge of crop productivity, but it was enough to allow them to harvest profitable crops. Another crucial factor was *when* the precipitation came—it was best if it fell as snow for the winter wheat or early in the growing season for other crops, but when it fell at other times of the year, it was much less helpful. Unfortunately, lack of rain was not the only danger: in 1916 a worm infestation destroyed the apple crop, and over time row crop yields tended to decline because of increasing alkalization of the soil.[19]

Many of Blackdom's homesteaders, including Mittie Moore and Frank Boyer, came to their land with little prior farming experience or knowledge. They had a lot to learn. Even those who had farmed elsewhere needed to stop using farming techniques they had found successful in more humid locations. Usually people arrived knowing how to grow cotton, but cotton would not thrive with so little water. Blackdom's farmers didn't plant cotton, according to former resident Lillian Westfield Collins. She acknowledged that they harvested some good crops in the early years because of wet winters, and that "some years they would have corn and such things as that. And that Kaffir corn." But they depended on rainfall for their moisture and weren't used to having to irrigate: "That was the thing they just couldn't seem to understand, that they wouldn't get enough moisture to raise their crops."[20]

Blackdom farmers gradually learned by trial and error new techniques that worked in the arid prairieland. They learned which crops to plant, when to plant, how to rotate crops to preserve soil fertility, when to cultivate, and (where possible) when to irrigate. But the trials that failed could prove costly. Crutcher Eubank, a migrant from Kentucky, started planting kaffir corn during the desert winter when he first arrived to homestead. Kaffir corn was a sorghum grain that was a predecessor to modern milo. Farmers believed it to be highly drought-resistant and used it mainly to feed livestock. But

86. Blackdom farmers harvesting crops, ca. 1918. New Mexico
State University Library, Archives and Special Collections.

kaffir corn is a warm-weather plant that needs to be planted when
the ground is warm, not in winter. Eubank harvested very little that
first year, and though he ultimately thrived, his costly mistake put
his farm in financial jeopardy for years.

Frank Boyer ran a large and successful alfalfa haying operation
on his farm at nearby Dexter. He also started a different kind of trial:
extending small loans to farmers. But during a dry year, 1917, he
overextended his resources when his debtors could not repay their
loans. He was wiped out, lost his haying business, and was forced
to move to Ella Boyer's desert claim near Blackdom. Trial and error
in such a variable climate could be devastating.

Blackdom's homesteaders began to prosper during these years.
They adjusted to the region's peculiar environment and learned

how to plant and harvest good crops. George Smith's father grew alfalfa and corn. At harvesting and haying time, as shown in the photograph, families joined together to share the work. Most farm families also put in vegetable gardens, raised chickens and hogs, and planted fruit trees for their own consumption. Some grew apples as a cash crop. They also benefited from high prices, thanks to wartime demand. The dozen or so leading families, many intertwined, extended their land holdings.

Blackdom also inched toward becoming recognized as an official "place." In 1912 Territorial Governor William Mills appointed Wesley T. Williams, a Blackdom homesteader, as a notary public. The same year federal judge William Pope appointed Williams as the first Black U.S. Commissioner, assigned to Blackdom and empowered to conduct preliminary investigations and issue search and arrest warrants. (The Roswell directory listed Williams as a laborer with a city residence; like other Black residents, his name had a small "c" in parentheses next to it.) In 1916 Blackdom's George W. Malone passed the bar, becoming the first Black lawyer in New Mexico.[21]

In 1912 the Post Office opened its Blackdom office, so residents no longer had to travel to Roswell or Dexter to do their mail. James Eubank, the first postmaster, initially delivered mail out of his small store, but residents soon constructed a stand-alone building to house their post office. In 1914 Eubank passed the civil service examination for fourth-class postmasters and was reappointed. The U.S. mail was a crucial community link, the means by which residents exchanged letters with distant family members, obtained newspapers, and received packages and goods ordered from Sears, Roebuck.[22]

While African Americans faced growing racism in Roswell, they got along much better with their white neighbors out around Blackdom. Lillian Collins Westfield was a toddler when she traveled with her family from Mississippi and arrived in Blackdom in 1908. She recalled that relations were good with the white ranchers. Some

73. Poster advertising Oscar Micheaux's 1931 film, *The Exile*. Wikimedia Commons. https://en.wikipedia.org/wiki/File:Micheaux_Exile.jpg.

74. Cecil Roosevelt McGruder with daughter Ann, Sully
County, 1941. Permission of Jeanettee Parton.

75. Blair family tombstone, private cemetery in
Sully County. Author's collection.

76. (*opposite top*) Dr. W. A. Jones with Mesdames Hicks, Rothwell, and Muse, outside Jones's clinic, Dearfield, ca. 1915. Paul W. Stewart Collection, University of Northern Colorado Archives and Special Collections.

77. (*opposite bottom*) Dr. W. A. Jones plowing on his homestead, Dearfield, ca. 1915. Paul W. Stewart Collection, University of Northern Colorado Archives and Special Collections.

78. (*above*) James Monroe Thomas haying on his homestead, Dearfield, ca. 1915. Paul W. Stewart Collection, University of Northern Colorado Archives and Special Collections.

Began its existence under very unfavorable conditions on July 3, 1901. The first officers elected to manage this little project were W. A. Jones, M.D., Pres.; A. A. Waller, Secretary and H. J. M. Brown, Treasurer. This set of officers has served the company unchanged, during the life of the co-partnership. The small loan business grew so rapidly and extensively that we were compelled to add the Real Estate feature with A. A. Waller as manager.

An immediate death was predicted for this little adventure. First, because it was a wide diversion from the line of business heretofore engaged in by the Negro; second, we were forced into competition with men of the other race who had years of experience in this line of business, and capital in unlimited amounts at their command with which to successfully put through any deal they could match; third, the lack of vision on the part of the Negro, to see and know that if he would have a representative in any line of business that he above all else must give him his full support. We can say of a truth that after 17 years of sticking, that the light is beginning to dawn. And by staying in the game and refusing to quit regardless of cost or conditions, we have encouraged others to enter the various branches of business knowing that every one that enters make it easier for the next. This little Company began business with the small sum of $250.00. They now own City property, both improved and unimproved, a ranch and stock, and today they are doing about $4,000 worth of business each month. It is our aim to please all the people, and we stand as your representative in this line of business in this community, and our future success will depend very largely on you.

The Colored American
Loan & Realty Co.

2636 Welton Street   Denver, Colo

PHONE CHAMPA 4 5 5

PATIENTLY PROGRESSING!

79. Advertisement for loan company that provided mortgages to Dearfield homesteaders, Denver, ca. 1915. Paul W. Stewart Collection, University of Northern Colorado Archives and Special Collections.

80. Unidentified Blackdom family in front of farmhouse, ca. 1920. Permission of Historical Society of Southeastern New Mexico.

81. Blackdom U.S. Post Office, ca. 1918. Permission of Historical Society of Southeastern New Mexico.

82. Blackdom resident hauling harvest to market in wagon, ca. 1915.
Permission of Historical Society of Southeastern New Mexico.

of the more affluent ones would bring clothing and other items to help the struggling homesteaders. Nearby ranchers permitted Black homesteaders who lacked wells to draw water freely from ranch wells or stock tanks.

During the annual fall cattle roundup, cowboys dropped in to eat with Blackdom families, sometimes unrolling their bedrolls and spending the night as well. When the homesteading family was away, they left their doors unfastened, allowing the cowboys to come in. Next morning, the cowboys pinned a note to the door saying, "I was here." Collins Westfield observed that "Most of the Caucasians [around Blackdom] had come from the South, but they were very nice. They were different from the ones we were used to."[23]

Community leaders sought to recruit more colonists by advertising nationally for interested families. On December 14, 1912, they advertised in *The Freeman*, a Black Indianapolis newspaper, reminding readers of the free government land available and asserting no Jim Crow. They appealed for five hundred Black families to join the colony.

Just a week later, Blackdom homesteader Lucy H. Henderson's lengthy letter to the editor appeared in the *Chicago Defender*, which gave it prominent placement. The paper headlined it "Free Land for the Race in Mexico"—the byline made it clear the land was in *New* Mexico. Henderson first disavowed any financial stake in attracting land seekers, pointing out the land was free. She then informed readers, "[There was] plenty of good farmland which the government is willing to give you for a very small entry fee and three years' residence." Moreover, she said, this land was equal to the best land anywhere and located "where the climate is ideal [and] there is no 'Jim Crowism'." Here, she said, "the black man has an equal chance with the white man."

But Henderson, like Micheaux, saw the opportunities quickly being gobbled up by white settlers who were flocking in every day.

WANTED!

500 Negro families (farmers preferred) to settle on Free Government Land in Chaves County, New Mexico. Fertil soil, ideal climate. No "Jim Crow" laws. For information write Jas. Harold Coleman. Blackdom, New Mexico.

87. Blackdom's advertisement to recruit families, in *The Freeman* (Indianapolis), December 14, 1912. newspapers.com.

Within the past ten days in her neighborhood, she warned, eight white families from Kansas and Iowa had filed on 1,280 acres and in the past four months whites had taken up 16,000 acres. If Black people were going to get their share, the time was now. "Your future is in your own hands," she insisted.[24]

The Blackdom Townsite Company officially platted the town in 1920. Its plan showed a large public square in the town center, flanked by Lincoln and McDonald Avenues and Douglass and Turner Streets, all surrounded by 120 commercial and residential lots. The town already had a schoolhouse, a store, a church building, a pumping plant, and what locals termed an "office building," probably containing land sales and legal offices. But despite the grand design, and the dreams that lay behind it, the town never developed in reality. "The townsite plan filed in 1920 existed only on paper," observed Blackdom historian Austin J. Miller. The Blackdom community ranged out several miles and consisted of scattered families on homesteads. As in other homesteader colonies, the community's vital heart was in the countryside.[25]

Like Black and white homesteaders elsewhere, Blackdom's homesteaders needed to find off-farm work to survive. In good years, a marginal homestead might not provide a full living for a family, and in bad years even thriving homesteaders needed other income. At DeWitty and Dearfield, homesteaders found work on surrounding white-owned ranches, the men as cowhands and carpenters, the women as cooks and cleaners. But at Blackdom, there were very few jobs nearby—Roswell, eighteen miles away, held most of the available jobs. Many Blackdom claimants held on to their Roswell jobs.[26]

When Blackdom's men and some women worked and lived in Roswell, however, they reduced their presence in and commitment to Blackdom. Their absences emptied out the community. It slowed their farm-building and detracted from the time they spent with neighbors at community events. Isaac Jones, one of the incorporators, made little progress on his homestead for months, because he continued working in Roswell. John Boyer, brother of Frank, filed an initial homestead claim in 1905, but he kept his job in Roswell as a janitor. His employment provided the income needed to build his homestead and feed his family, but working in Roswell limited how much effort he could put into the Blackdom community. Crutcher Eubank put in his initial filing in 1906, but to keep his family fed, he left the homestead for weeks at a time to work in nearby towns or Roswell.[27] The Blackdom families who continued to maintain a residence in Roswell were simply less available to attend church, support the school, or participate in community-building social activities.

As families slowly began populating Blackdom, community leaders turned to making good on their promise to provide education to the residents' children. Some older folks had been forcibly denied education under slavery, and younger people had parents and other relatives who had been deprived. They prized education as a mark of their freedom as well as a prerequisite to self-help. Blackdom parents demanded a school for their children.

Blackdom was part of the school district of Greenfield, a neighboring white settlement. Its school board turned away Black children, unwilling either to integrate its own school or build a separate school in Greenfield for Black children. Blackdom leaders instead persuaded the board to purchase building materials for a school in Blackdom, and residents constructed their own school, which opened in 1910. The residents' attitude toward segregated schools is unknown, but Roosevelt Boyer Sr. recalled about his father, Frank Boyer, "Dad wasn't use to negroes going to school with whites so he didn't fight it. Better for Black children to be in their own school. He got a teacher from El Paso."

Blackdom's school housed grades one through seven in an open, one-teacher room. The community petitioned the state's Superintendent for Public Instruction for help with curriculum materials and paying the teacher. They argued that Blackdom was the only exclusive Black settlement in New Mexico and that its residents had taken up ten thousand acres of homesteaded land, pointedly declaring themselves to be significant stakeholders in the region. The superintendent's response is unknown. Over the years the community employed a number of teachers, some from the community itself. A Miss Maise came from Louisiana and Lloyd Allen from Oklahoma; but Jarves Eubank, Ester Herron, George Malone, James Eubank (Crutcher Eubank's son), and Loney K. Wagoner, a local homesteader and head of a large family, came from the community itself. Blackdom's last teacher, Cora Vandenbon, arrived in 1926.[28]

Blackdom colonists, like many rural families, did much of their doctoring themselves. They patched up each other's wounds, nursed children with fevers, splinted broken bones, and prescribed long bedrest for injured backs. They applied a mixture of folk remedies rooted in herbs, kerosene, and Epsom salts supplemented with purchased elixirs like Vaseline and castor oil. Without telephones, Blackdom neighbors set up their own signal system: a white flag meant someone was sick or injured and called neighbors to come and help. Most responded eagerly, assisting with the washing, cooking, and other chores or if need be, fetching the doctor. To handle the most dangerous threat to women's health, childbirth, the community supplied its own midwives. For other serious cases, residents called in a white doctor from Dexter or Greenfield.[29]

Blackdom's families came together to worship and socialize at church. They built a small Baptist church, completed in 1909, which also served as a schoolhouse until the new school was built. The congregation grew too large for the first church, so in 1915 residents organized a campaign to pay for constructing a bigger one. The *Artesia Pecos Valley News* reported, "A number of negroes from the Blackdom settlement up the valley came to Artesia Saturday afternoon and put on a very creditable performance in the Corringhall that night. The receipts went to the building fund of the Blackdom church." The troupe gave concerts up and down the valley.[30] They applied their funds to help construct a $1,000 church building, which they called the Second Baptist Church.

Most residents belonged to the community's only church, even though they were Methodists, Catholics, and Seventh Day Adventists, as well as Baptists. Hobart Boyer, Frank's and Ella's son, remembered that Sunday School was especially lively. "When we'd go to discussing the Bible, everybody would start picking it apart!" Pastors, some resident and others called out from Roswell, presided over church services. Monroe Collins, of the prominent Collins homesteading family, was a deacon of the church, and Tom Collins one of the preachers, as was one of the Proffit brothers.[31]

Residents could hardly wait for their community celebrations and festivals, times of great excitement and joy. The celebrations broke up the long and monotonous months on the farm. One was Emancipation Day, celebrated on Juneteenth. Another was July Fourth. Organizers invited whites as well as Blacks, and visitors from Roswell, Carlsbad, and elsewhere flocked to Blackdom to share the good food, games, music, speeches, dancing, and fun.

Blackdom residents loved baseball, and they turned out in good-sized crowds to watch their team's games. The field was open prairie,

88. William Proffit residence at Blackdom, ca. 1920.
Permission of Historical Society of Southeast New Mexico.

with no backstop. Blackdom usually played Black teams from Carlsbad or Roswell, but for big celebration days they might schedule several games, including white teams from Dexter and Greenfield. One Juneteenth, after the feast and wanting more action, the Blackdom team challenged the whites present to form a team. W. E. Utterback, the white team's catcher, remembered trying to block Blackdom's big first baseman, David Proffit, whom they called Y.Z., as he came barreling around third and headed home. "I made the mistake of trying to block this Y.Z. from home plate. He came in head first and skinned my shin bones about a foot. By the way, we lost the game."[32]

After the Emancipation Day game, attendees of both races shared the feast. Nearby cattlemen gave them two or three fat steers, which they roasted over open fires. The celebrants watched boxing matches and enjoyed the music and dancing.[33] "Kids would dance," George Smith recalled. "Mothers take their kids to the dance. They wouldn't let 'em go by their selves to a dance or anything like that. Women would take their kids."[34]

Residents also put on a big community Christmas celebration. They set up a tall tree in the schoolhouse. Families gathered to hear a program of Bible storytelling, sing gospels and Christmas carols, exchange gifts, and enjoy a big feast. With families widely distributed on the land and many maintaining residences in Roswell as well, the community's celebrations took on special importance for building neighborly camaraderie. Even so, social life suffered. Most people attended church, in descendant George Smith's opinion, because oftentimes there wasn't much else to do.[35]

Lack of access to water haunted the colony. Before 1920 farmers were favored with wet winters, which helped the crops, though 1909, 1910, and 1917 had been dry years. The real problem was that they could not afford to drill deep wells nor buy irrigation equipment. For household use, vegetable gardens, and watering stock, many families took water (with permission) from the ranchers' stock tanks and hauled it home in barrels by team and wagon. But for crops in the fields, relying on dryland farming put them at great risk when snowfall and rain failed.

Mittie Moore moved to her claim in November 1915 when she was thirty-six (or possibly thirty-eight) years old. Five years later at proving up she listed her farm as having a "House one-room 14x14 and porch, four wire fence around the farm, Chicken house." Her witness, Erastus Herron, described how "no more than 20 acres [out of 320] could be cultivated in any one year owing to the condition of the soil, it being very thin and over a gravel bed in most places, and if turf is broken owing to the dryness, soil would blow away leaving barren ground only." Despite the thin soil and aridity, Moore said she broke out about twenty or twenty-five acres by actual measurement, but, she complained, "I paid man to break out 40 acres [and] thought said amount was broken."[36]

Moore's efforts hardly paid off. When asked by the land-office agent to describe the number of acres and kind of crops Moore planted, Erastus Herron wrote:

1916: A little crop of something, ten acres, don't think she raised anything

1917: Too dry did not plant anything

1918: Planted quite a bit about twenty-two acres, maize, kaffir corn, sorgum, peas, did not make anything on account of drought

1919: Planted corn, kaffir, maize, and sorgum, peas and several things 40 acres, good crop of all

It was hard for Moore to survive in farming when she only made one year's crop out of four. And in 1919, her "good" year, she harvested only $150 worth of crops.

So Moore, like other homesteaders, kept her off-farm job. She reopened her establishment on South Virginia Avenue for business and luckily found vigorous demand for its services. GLO's residency rule required her to not be absent from her claim for more than six months at a time, so every year she stayed in town only from July to September and December to March. She stated her work there was necessary "for the purpose of earning money to live on."[37]

Moore's absences and her failure to break more acres persuaded Ancil G. Foster, a nearby farmer, to contest her filing. In November 1917 he alleged that she was breaking the rules and in consequence her claim was faulty. Moore beat back the challenge, however, and Foster withdrew it a month later.

When she tried to prove up in 1919, however, the GLO rejected her application for patent. The GLO said, "You do not show cultivation in the amount of one eighth of the area [i.e., 40 acres] during the third year . . . have not maintained sufficient residence . . . gave notice [of proving up] in name of Mittie Moore when it should have been Mittie Wilson [her married name] . . . and failed to appear with two witnesses on the date advertised." Moore's application was indeed filled with minor errors, such as contradictorily declaring in separate documents that she had initiated her residence on the land in November 1915, January 1916, and February 1916. But GLO's inflexible regulations about how much land had to be cultivated, well calibrated to more humid central Nebraska and Kansas, did not fit New Mexico's dry fields. Cultivating a larger portion of a claim often just resulted in its topsoil being blown away. Moore appealed the GLO's rejection and won her patent in 1920.

By 1920 tougher times caused Blackdom to begin to empty out. Residents sold their frame houses, either to be moved elsewhere or for lumber, and the population declined. Bessie Malone, the last postmaster, closed the Blackdom post office in 1919. She had carefully recorded all her office's transactions in an account book, which now rests in the archives of the National Postal Museum in Washington, DC. As Roosevelt Boyer Jr. noted, "the demise of Blackdom was gradual and by the mid-1920s it was practically deserted."[38]

The tougher times were caused, as usual, by drier weather. Rainfall was always highly variable, but farmers got less precipitation entering the 1920s. Particularly disastrous were 1917 (with just 6.27 inches, measured at Roswell), 1918 (9.18 inches), 1922 (6.57 inches), 1924 (5.77 inches), and 1927 (just 4.83 inches). These were devastatingly small amounts of moisture, producing short crops and intense strain on families. Even though wetter years were interspersed with them, the dry years made survival by farming almost impossible. Moreover, artesian water that had been so abundant in Chaves County early in the century began to dry up. By 1920 heavy draws for irrigation dropped the water table significantly. In response, the county prohibited the drilling of new wells, thereby closing off the possibility of compensating for low rainfall by increased irrigation. Farming in the desert prairie proved extremely difficult and unrewarding.

In June 1922 the *Albuquerque Journal*, calling Blackdom "one of the most interesting experiments in negro colonization that has occurred," declared it largely abandoned. The cause? Lack of capital resulting in lack of water. After building the community, the *Journal* noted, "the colored inhabitants soon realized that their capital was not sufficient to drill for water for irrigation purposes."[39]

Only a few vacant houses and the church remained in 1922. Monroe Collins, the deacon who had helped build Second Baptist Church, offered it for sale. He received a few bids and sold the structure to the Cottonwood Methodist Church. Its congregation moved the building thirty miles south to Artesia. The Methodists held services in the building until the 1960s, when they sold it to a man who rehabbed it for use as a storage shed (and may thereby have saved the structure). Eventually someone renovated it as a residence, and today a family lives in it.[40]

Frank and Ella Boyer left Blackdom and moved southwest to the Rio Grande valley. They started over, founding the all-Black town of Vado, New Mexico. With seventy-seven children and grandchildren, Frank claimed to be head of the largest Black family in New Mexico.[41]

There was, however, one final and positive fillip left in the Blackdom homesteaders' story, as discovered by Timothy Nelson: Oil! The Roswell Basin is underlain geologically by the much bigger Permian Basin, stretching from central Texas to eastern New Mexico, 250 miles or more across. Roswell and Blackdom sit on its far western edge. Starting in the 1910s, wildcatters began actively exploring the Permian.

In 1921 drillers in Mitchell County, Texas, on the far eastern side of the basin, brought in the first Permian oil well of commercial value. That well was far from Blackdom, but oil companies, would-be oil companies, leasing agents, speculators, wildcatters, and other get-rich-quick hopefuls nonetheless descended on Roswell. They hoped to snap up oil leases cheaply, ahead of the competition and before the locals caught on to their value. They eagerly incorporated new oil development companies—Lincoln Oil Company, Roswell Oil Development Company—and just as quickly sold out to bigger national firms. One report in the *Roswell Daily Record* claimed that the National Exploration Company of New York City had bought up five hundred thousand acres of leases in the area. Six Los Angeles investors completed another transaction worth $300,000. A Bakersfield, California, group announced plans to drill a deep test well, because, as the *Carlsbad Current-Argus* reported, operators believed that Blackdom was high on the Permian Basin structure and thus a promising target for deep test drilling.[42]

Blackdom's hard-pressed landowners sought to cash in on the frenzy. To make their land more attractive to major lease buyers and strengthen their bargaining power, they pooled their lease rights to form the Blackdom Oil Company. By the end of 1919, they brought lease rights to perhaps ten thousand acres under the company's control. By March 1920 it was reported to have entered into a contract for 4,200 acres with the National Exploration Company in a deal worth $70,000 (worth slightly more than one million dollars in 2022). Rumors abounded about National Exploration's plans to sink deep wells, a similar plan by a California syndicate, the expected imminent arrival of derricks and drilling equipment, and most exciting of all, anticipated big payouts. While we don't know if Mittie Moore or the Boyers joined the Blackdom Oil consortium, they must have seen their land become much more valuable.[43]

As it turned out, the lands between Roswell and Artesia, including Blackdom, did not pan out. Driller O. J. Wortman's rig in Blackdom reached 1,600 feet without finding oil, at which point he ran out of money.[44] Drillers found their most commercially viable producing fields northeast of Roswell and further south of Artesia. And by the onset of the Great Depression, the oil men had mostly abandoned activity in the Roswell Basin anyway. For Mittie Moore, oil leases may have provided income, but drought and the stock market crash left her unable to pay her taxes, and she lost her land. She died in a car crash in Flagstaff, Arizona, in 1936.

Did other poor and hard-pressed Blackdom homesteaders receive substantial payouts through their shares in the Blackdom Oil Company? Unfortunately, the company's contracts, payouts, and other relevant records have been lost. The only information available is from newspaper articles, and given the inflated reports that frenzied speculators and hustlers put about, they must be considered highly unreliable. One report suggests that former Blackdom residents, now scattered across the country, leased their land to giant Gulf Oil Company. Historian Nelson speculates that Blackdom residents did receive substantial payouts and that the money allowed them to move away from Blackdom to more promising or profitable locations. In this interpretation, Blackdom's final chapter was a big financial success, as Blackdom homesteaders went from owning mostly worthless farming land to becoming oil *rentiers*.[45]

If the Blackdom Oil Company did receive $70,000 for leases and that revenue was shared among the sixty-four individuals who proved up homestead claims—both assumptions are uncertain—then each homesteader would have received $1,094. That payment would be worth nearly $16,000 in 2022. But the lease covered only four thousand of the company's ten thousand acres, so if all its land was leased, homesteaders might have received $2,735 each (worth nearly $40,000 in 2022). Absent more records, however, both Nelson's scenario and our interpretation remain speculative.

What we do know is that the Black homesteader community enjoyed at least moderate success over a dozen or more years. Residents built farms, a school, a church, a social life, and a strong sense of having their own "place." If Blackdom failed to survive in the face of repeated droughts, the 1920s farm price collapse, and the Great Depression, its ending would constitute only one measure, and perhaps not the most important one, of its residents' achievements. For a time in Blackdom, to use Nelson's phrase, "Black people were the town elders and controllers of daily life."[46] And they educated the community's children, for which descendants remain permanently grateful.

Today Blackdom is designated only by a roadside marker. No buildings remain. The Methodists removed the church, and residents sold the other structures or they were scavenged. Local scholars and officials, including individuals at the Historic Preservation Division of New Mexico's Office of Cultural Affairs, and geographers at New Mexico State University's Earth Data Analysis Center, have worked to record Blackdom's history. The most energetic and persistent promoter of remembering Blackdom, however, is Dr. Timothy Nelson, who in addition to his pioneering scholarship has organized or partnered with others to create various multimedia presentations about Blackdom.

Blackdom, like Sully County and Dearfield, reflected the power and the limits of strong leadership. These colonies would likely not have come into existence without commitment by Frank Boyer, Ben Blair, and O. T. Jackson. They created new spaces within which African Americans could find freedom and opportunity. They devoted years of their lives to that vision. Dr. Andrew Wall, the late longtime director of Black Studies at New Mexico State University, said about Blackdom, "Here is Francis Boyer motivating people to say, 'Yes, we can establish a whole township as passable people, we can name the town, we can name the streets, we can have our own schools, we can have our own post office, we have these skills, that's the knapsack of experiences we brought from our period of slavery. Let's do it!'"[47]

Ultimately, the colonies' strong leaders couldn't overcome all the external challenges they faced, the droughts, grasshoppers, depressed prices, lack of dryland farming experience, limited access to capital and water, and the national calamity of the Great Depression. In

Blackdom's case, they were further hindered by white prejudice. But their great dreams produced for a time prosperity and places of their own in which they educated their children and passed along their values of high aspirations, hard work, and personal worth. Their descendants continue to benefit from that inheritance.

As Francis Boyer and the other Blackdom leaders struggled to create their new promised land in the Pecos Valley, others worked toward the same goal in Nicodemus, DeWitty, Dearfield and other colonies across the Great Plains, and still others like Henry Burden and Oscar Micheaux followed the path of homesteading alone. One great question millions of Black people remaining in the South had to ask themselves was, should we stay or leave? And if they resolved to leave, where should they go, west or north? Black homesteaders offered their experience to help light the way for the Great Migration.

14

Black Homesteaders and
the Great Migration

Scatter out as did the Jews in England . . . [scatter] out all over this
vast country, each one doing the very best his circumstances allow.
Don't stop at one State, but rather take in the entire country

—ABRAM HALL, *Colored Citizen*, 1879

Black homesteaders heralded the Great Migration. They went west
instead of north, but they served as vanguard to the later millions
of migrants. Both homesteaders and people of the Great Migration
took flight to escape southern whites' intimidation and violence and
the crushing of Black aspirations. Both sought a place where they
could rise by their own talents and toil. Both sought to breathe air
where they could be free and fully equal citizens, enjoying all the
rights they were promised and deserved. They risked and suffered
the pains, psychological as well as physical, caused by migrating
long distances and living so far from home. The homesteaders,
no less than the people in the Great Migration, were searching for
freedom and the chance to better their lives.

Whether Black people should even leave the South was itself
controversial. Frederick Douglass among others urged them after
emancipation to remain in the South. Benjamin "Pap" Singleton
and Robert Knox called on Black southerners to leave the South. But
the biggest and most fraught debate, the argument that revealed
wildly different priorities for how Black people could make progress

in a racist nation, saw W. E. B. Du Bois face off against Booker T. Washington.

Washington counseled Black southerners to remain in the region to which their ancestors had been brought in chains and which was now their home. After Douglass died in 1895, Washington became the most prominent leader of the country's ten million African Americans. He was the first teacher and longtime principal of the Tuskegee Institute. He was celebrated and known across the nation. In 1898 President William McKinley and most of his cabinet came to visit him at Tuskegee. In 1901 President Theodore Roosevelt invited him to dinner at the White House. He had a commanding presence and was a powerful orator. And at the 1895 Cotton States and International Symposium, Washington delivered a famous speech, sometimes disparaged as the "Atlanta Compromise," in which he laid out his views. It caused a sensation.

Washington said Black southerners should focus on raising their own living conditions, and the way they could do that best was by their own hard, persistent, and humble work. He evangelized for the dignity of labor done with one's own hands. "Our greatest danger," he said, "is that in the great leap from slavery to freedom we may overlook the fact that the masses of us are to live by the productions of our hands, and fail to keep in mind that we shall prosper in proportion as we learn to dignify and glorify common labor, and put brains and skill into the common occupations of life." He warned, "No race can prosper till it learns that there is as much dignity in tilling a field as in writing a poem . . . It is at the bottom of life we must begin, and not at the top."[1]

To equip his people for such work, Washington promoted industrial training for large numbers rather than higher education for the few. He made practical education the basis of Tuskegee's curriculum. He advised Black people to stay in the South: "When it comes to business, pure and simple, it is in the South that the Negro is given a man's chance in the commercial world."[2]

Newspapers across the nation, especially white newspapers, reprinted Washington's speech, and editors and politicians praised it for its optimism about relations between southern Blacks and whites. (The white papers may also have liked that he discouraged agitation for Black rights.) Black people throughout the country welcomed Washington's call for an ethic of self-help. Even Du Bois commended him for preaching "Thrift, Patience, and Industrial Training for the masses" and said that it was "a great truth . . . that the Negro must strive and strive mightily to help himself."[3]

But Du Bois and other influential leaders vehemently objected to other aspects of Washington's philosophy. Washington advised that Blacks would best attain equality by proving themselves to be productive members of society, deferring demands for equal rights until later. He suggested that for the present they might need to suffer the unfairness of discrimination and segregation. He cautioned against agitation, saying "Nor should we permit our grievances to overshadow our opportunities." He chose not to make protesting against the suppression of Black voting a main theme of his advocacy. Critics were appalled by these parts of Washington's thinking.

Du Bois encouraged Black people to leave the South. "It has long been the custom of colored leaders to advise the colored people to stay in the South. This has been supplemented by the startling information on the part of southern whites that they are the 'best friends of the colored people', etc." Du Bois rejected that logic: "We might as well face the facts squarely: If there is any colored man in the South who wishes to have his children educated and who wishes to be in close touch with civilization and who has any chance or ghost of a chance of making a living in the North it is his business to get out of the South as soon as possible. He need not seek reasons for so doing."[4]

Du Bois, the first African American to earn a PhD at Harvard and afterward a professor at Atlanta University, was the nation's leading Black intellectual and one of the founders of the NAACP. Du Bois disliked that "Mr. Washington's programme naturally [took] an economic cast, becoming a gospel of Work and Money to such an extent as apparently almost completely to overshadow the higher aims of life." Even worse, he noted, "Mr. Washington's program practically accepts the alleged inferiority of the Negro races."

Du Bois railed against Washington's overall program: "Mr. Washington apologizes for injustice . . . does not rightly value the privilege and duty of voting, belittles the emasculating effects of cast distinction, and opposes the higher training and ambition of our brighter minds." It was simply "a policy of submission." These errors were so serious that "we must unceasingly and firmly oppose them. By every civilized and peaceful method."[5]

Du Bois's own program was quite different. He declared that Black people were "bound to ask of this nation three things: 1. The right to vote. 2. Civic equality. 3. The education of youth according to ability." Du Bois did not fail to imagine a more comprehensive sweeping away of race hatred and discrimination, the pulling down of the "Veil" behind which Black people led lives distorted by prejudice. Rather, he saw these three items as the nonnegotiable minimum of rights that Blacks must expect of their nation. He intended his program to be an alternative to what he saw as Booker T. Washington's policy of submission.[6]

Du Bois's demands for the right to vote and the education of youth according to ability—that is, creating educational opportunities beyond industrial training for those capable of higher learning—are straightforward. His demand for civic equality is less clear. He was writing in 1903, and his thinking was undoubtedly shaped by the terrifying and dispiriting events southern Black people had just passed through. In 1896 whites went on a murderous rampage in

89. Booker T. Washington and W. E. B. Du Bois. Tuskegee University, 2008; National Portrait Gallery, Smithsonian Institution.

Atlanta, killing twenty-five Black people. In 1898 whites in Wilmington, North Carolina, staged a coup and massacred at least sixty Black people and destroyed Black political power. Southern legislatures introduced Black Codes throughout the South, and in 1896 the Supreme Court in *Plessey v. Ferguson* declared that the U.S. Constitution made no objection to the "separate but equal" laws passed by states. As Du Bois put it, these developments amounted to "the legal creation of a distinct status of civil inferiority for the Negro."[7]

Du Bois gave a clue to what he meant by civic equality when he noted that white southern capitalists had for Black people "a simple program: Industry and disenfranchisement; the separation of the masses of the Negroes from all participation in government."[8] If we interpret "civic equality" as distinct and more limited than the broader concept of "social equality," then perhaps we can understand civic equality to mean equality in all of the ordinary intercourse between citizens and their government, including fair enforcement of the law, equal access to courts and justice, fair governmental policy fairly administered, and equal treatment in all the other ways in which government and citizens, including Black people, interacted.

He insisted that to achieve these rights, Black people needed to engage in political action, taking any peaceful measures they could to secure them. He endorsed voting but also a whole range of actions and agitations, including pursuing legal actions, conducting scientific studies, publicizing their oppression and demands in newspapers and journals, organizing Black political groups, and vigorously participating in elections from the county level to the state legislature to Congress. He advocated voting tactically, sometimes even collectively withholding votes, but being actively engaged. He wanted action in all these channels.

Washington and Du Bois thus disagreed along a whole line of points. Washington's ideas of self-reliance and economic self-betterment made sense to leaders like Abram Hall and Frank Boyer. He directly inspired O. T. Jackson, Oscar Micheaux, Ben Blair, and others, who tried to live up to Washington's call to rise economically. There were no more enthusiastic true believers of the self-help philosophy than Black homesteaders—it motivated all their hard work.

On the question of whether Black southerners should stay in the South or leave, however, homesteaders showed their agreement with Du Bois by migrating. They connected owning land to freedom, and they saw their best chance to own land was to take up the government's offer of free homesteads in the Great Plains. And in their new freedom, they expected to exercise all the rights Du Bois demanded. They migrated west, looking to find a place where they could be full and equal citizens.

Having arrived in the West, how fully did Black homesteaders realize their aspirations? They tended to fashion their own goals, sometimes consciously inspired by Washington or Du Bois, but more often working out their own programs for progress as their experiences required. They adopted elements from both Washington's and Du Bois's seemingly contradictory philosophies—Dearfield named its two most central streets Washington Avenue and Du Bois Avenue. By their actions on the ground, homesteaders imparted a reality to the theories advanced by the Black leaders. They sought to achieve for themselves, in a more personal, less cerebral way, what Black leaders articulated for the race.

They had come, either directly or after intermediate stops, from all over the South. A few came with skills, education, and resources, as did some Kentucky and Tennessee migrants moving to Nicodemus and the settlers of Empire. Others came poor and illiterate, as most famously did the Exodusters arriving from Mississippi, Louisiana, and Texas. Other lesser-known migrants, individuals not part of organized migrations such as Moses Speese from North Carolina, Henry Burden from Virginia, and James Monroe Thomas from Alabama, fled slavery or its successor, debt peonage, to find more opportunity. All wanted to leave behind the miseries of the South, where they were, in Isabel Wilkerson's phrase, "stuck in a caste system as hard and unyielding as the red Georgia clay."[9] They sought personal security, escape from the daily humiliations of Jim Crow, and opportunity, all of which were denied them in the South.

Certainly one of their central goals was bettering their material circumstances, as Washington had urged. For the many who left poverty and trampled hopes for improvement in the South, their homesteads, once established, proved a clear step up in living standards. Descendant Teresa Switzer, reflecting on her ancestors' migration from Kentucky and life in Nicodemus, said bluntly, "Whatever they had here was better than what they had back there."[10]

A few homesteaders, like Robert Anderson and the Speese Brothers, got rich, but most Black homesteaders led more ordinary lives, working hard and worrying about the weather, as most farmers did. For a generation or so, some for longer and some shorter, Black homesteaders created secure spaces where they could earn their livelihoods and reap the rewards of their own sweat. That meant that their hard work sometimes paid off in prosperity, as Nicodemus settlers experienced in the 1880s and the Blair family did during the opening two decades of the twentieth century. And at other times, no matter how hard they worked and persevered, they couldn't overcome drought and rock-bottom crop prices, fates nearly all farmers suffered in the late 1920s and the 1930s.

It is not surprising that the most long-lived colony was the first, at Nicodemus. It enjoyed the most favorable location, with deeper soils and more abundant rainfall. Later colonies, along with later white land seekers, were pushed into more marginal lands with more capricious precipitation. When the farmers' hard times of the 1920s turned into catastrophe in the 1930s, Nicodemus held on by a thread, but the others disappeared.

The homesteaders were never able to create the enduring economic communities that Booker T. Washington might have hoped for. Nicodemus and Dearfield and the other colonies never became Black centers of great economic weight. On that basis, some might consign Black homesteaders to history's dustbin, labeling them misguided agrarian migrants who fled unspeakable conditions in the South only to wind up in an unsustainable and unrewarding region for farming. After a generation or so of trying, this view says, the migrants came up dry. Failures.

But neither Black homesteaders nor their descendants saw it that way. Homesteaders like Henry Burden, William P. Walker, Peryle Woodson, Benjamin Blair, and James Monroe Thomas owned their own farms and saw their crops, livestock, and families grow. They must have felt an immense surge of pride in that accomplishment. If we could join Ben Blair in June as he walked his thousand acres of wheat, heads already heavy and bending over the stalks, and gaze over at the equally rich fields of his Black neighbors, we would know his deep sense of achievement. If we could spend a lazy half hour with O. T. Jackson in his Lunch Room, a community center and gathering place as much as an eatery, we would share the camaraderie and pride that Dearfield homesteaders felt deep in their bones. They had taken control of their own destinies. And if we could join the Blackdom Baptist Church choir, as they toured the Pecos Valley singing and clapping and swaying to raise money for their church—vibrant concerts surely overflowing with rich voices and movement and joy—we could begin to understand the enormity of the homesteaders' accomplishments.

So if we, from the often-disdainful perspective of a vastly richer urban culture, cannot appreciate their achievements, they surely did.

Over time, the homesteaders came to see their farms as *transitional* spaces, places where they could escape and recover from the trauma of the South, earn livelihoods for themselves and their families, *and* educate their descendants for successful lives likely to be led elsewhere. Joyceann Gray, a DeWitty descendant, noted that the community "was not built to last." Gray maintained that "the driving force behind every plow, every nail driven, every sod wall built was with one purpose in mind. Not to build a las[t]ing farming town but to be the stepping stone for their children."[11]

Gray is not alone in her view of what the homesteaders hoped would be the "success" of their great venture. Catherine Meehan Blount, another descendant, echoed Gray's assessment, adding, "it was meant to educate their children. DeWitty provided a better life for their children." Denise Scales, a DeWitty descendant of William P. Walker, said simply, "success for William P. was seeing his kids educated."[12]

This puts the homesteader communities' eventual demise in a new light. If their material goal, after securing a place of peace and opportunity for themselves, was to equip descendants for successful lives led elsewhere, persistence on the land is the wrong measure of the colonies' success. Henry Burden's eight children provide a better yardstick: all "bright children, educated and respected" who were "well brought up and are so bright and well-behaved" that "all are good citizens." Dearfield descendant Terri Gentry credited the values passed down, especially "the stuff that's passed down from our ancestors like owning your home and bettering your life by getting an education and making better choices for your lives and all of the stuff that's been passed down generationally to us."[13]

Descendants of homesteaders thus provide a powerful rebuff to seeing the colonies as failures. Yes, the generations following the homesteaders mostly chose lives in which they gave up the land to pursue other careers and other passions. In this they were like so many descendants of white homesteaders, most of whom also left the land but revere their homesteading ancestors. Black descendants did not leave unequipped for success in life. They carried off the land their educations, their work habits, their sustaining values, and their deep sense of self-worth. Virtually to a person, they are in awe of their homesteading ancestors' courage, struggle, and achievements. And they are profoundly grateful for the rich family endowments, in the form of education, work habits, and values, that their ancestors bestowed on them. Descendants see these inheritances as the ancestors' real accomplishments.

But material betterment was never the homesteaders' only goal: they also wanted to be free. Historian Quintard Taylor observed that Black Americans at the end of the nineteenth century "had come to believe that the only way they could have true freedom was to have ownership over a piece of land."[14] Owning land was the key. Jeannettee Parton, a descendant of Sully County Black homesteaders, remembered, "My family sacrificed everything for their land. Success was born and found in the land. Everything we had came from the land." Forrest Stith, writing about his grandparents at DeWitty, simply noted, "Ownership of land was a true symbol of freedom to the former slaves and their offspring."[15] In these expressions and others that run consistently through family oral histories, descendants link land ownership not (only) to improved living standards but also to freedom and self-worth.

Wayne Brown, a lawyer and sixth-generation descendant of DeWitty, said his ancestors desired "the opportunity to own some land." He says, "You know, there's something special that goes to the heart of every African American, it's that promise of 40 acres and a mule and having the opportunity to be an owner in America. . . . Owning a piece of America as the descendants of former slaves, that is the highest form of freedom, to own property in America. It's still the highest form of freedom."[16]

This almost mystical link between land and freedom, an echo (though an ironic one) of the Jeffersonian ideal, continues down to the present. In 2021 John Boyd Jr., a Virginia farmer and president of the National Black Farmers Union, observed, "The ability to own land is the first step to freedom, is what my grandfather, Thomas Boyd, taught me as a nine-year-old boy. If you want to be free, you need to own some land. Land is the most powerful element you can possess."[17] Ashley Scott, vice president and cofounder of the Freedom Georgia Initiative, agreed. Her group is seeking to build a Black town called "Freedom" near Macon. "It is about generational wealth for us," she said. "To have a sense of security as a people, our best investment is the land . . . Anyone who understands anything about wealth generation understands that it starts with land."[18]

Freedom to the homesteaders was multifaceted, not easily captured in "the freedom to do this" or "the freedom to do that." In the South their unfree status stunted almost all aspects of their work and their social interactions and their dreams. Relief from those constraints would have to be similarly all-encompassing, as capacious as the Great Plains sky. But out of this multilayered and pervasive sense of what it would mean to be free, some very specific freedoms stood out.

The homesteaders sought *economic* freedoms, an aspect of freedom so brutally denied them in slavery and debt peonage. Robert Knox had articulated this dream as a place "where there may be enjoyed . . . the earnings of [one's] daily toil." One economic right was for the homesteaders to simply keep the fruits of their own labor. A second was the right to make voluntary contracts and do business with whomever they chose and not to be forced into contracts they did not want. For the most part, Black homesteaders in the Great Plains gained these basic economic rights. They were able to buy supplies, farm materials, and other goods from whomever they wished and sell their corn, wheat, eggs, milk, heifers, mules, and other farm produce to whomever they chose.

Importantly, unlike in debt peonage, they themselves decided what crops or livestock to raise, when to plant and harvest, and how to do their work. Lulu Craig, longtime Nicodemus resident, was asked if the homesteaders were better off in Kansas than they had been in the South. Her immediate response was yes, "they could rest if they felt like it" and "they learned how to find a way of making a living, which had all been planned for them before. They knew when they got up just exactly what they had to do. Now, when they came to Nicodemus and got up, they didn't know what they were going to do. They had to find out for themselves. That helped them"[19]

Their economic freedom in the Great Plains was not complete, because in the pervasively segregated society around them, when they traveled beyond their home communities, they found that many businesses refused their trade. Russel Taylor, the dignified and highly educated leader of Empire, regularly protested that the hotels and restaurants in nearby Torrington were closed to Blacks. When Robert Anderson traveled to Omaha with two white ranchers, he found that most hotels and eateries welcomed the two white men but not him. So in economic rights as in other aspects of freedom, Black homesteaders found expanded rights in the Great Plains as compared to the post-Reconstruction South, but it was still less than fully realized freedom.

Black homesteaders also expected to exercise their *political* rights as fully free and equal citizens. This started with voting, the most basic political right. In their new communities, the homesteaders voted and vigorously participated in political life. Although this has not been well studied, Black homesteaders found few barriers preventing them from voting in the Great Plains. In 1866 Congress rejected Nebraska's first attempt to achieve statehood because it proposed a state constitution that restricted voting to whites. Congress admitted Nebraska only after it dropped the restriction a year later. In 1867 Colorado's new state constitution stipulated that no "distinction or classification of people be made on account of color." In 1868 Dakota Territory eliminated its whites-only limitation on the franchise.[20]

At Nicodemus, Black voters were a key constituency—though on the losing side—in the election to determine the Graham County seat. At DeWitty, Black residents participated fully in the elections organizing school districts and determining district boundaries. In the letters and other documents of Black homesteaders we examined, we have found no complaints that Black people were denied the right to vote, which would have been mentioned if significant informal barriers to voting existed. Oklahoma (discussed in the appendix) was different, following the southern model of suppressing Black voters. Elsewhere in the Great Plains, Black homesteaders appear to have realized Du Bois's first demand.

Homesteaders also saw as a political right the opportunity to hold public office. After Reconstruction, southern whites drove many Black officials, including some six hundred in state legislatures and sixteen in Congress, out of office, and many were killed. Black codes and Jim Crow prevented their return for the next hundred years. In the Great Plains, by contrast, Black people gained public office, though the small Black populations resulted in few Black officials being elected. At Sully County, Benjamin Blair was several times elected to the Fairbank school district, and he served as its chairman for ten years. At Nicodemus, Abram Hall served as Graham County's first census-taker, and E. P. McCabe was initially appointed, then elected, as Graham County clerk. He won two state-wide elections as state auditor. O. T. Jackson for many years held the influential position of the governor's official messenger. Blackdom's Wesley Williams was appointed U.S. Commissioner.

So too, Black homesteaders sought *civic equality*, Du Bois's ambiguous but crucial category of interactions between Black citizens and government. Here also the great risks that Black homesteaders took paid off, though never completely. In most of the Black colonies, residents controlled their local schools. When their students went to high school and beyond, students entered white-dominated systems, some of which encouraged talents like those of the children of Henry Burden and Zachary Fletcher and Rosetta Speese to flourish, while others undoubtedly did not.

Homesteaders also expected fair treatment by courts and law enforcement. After Reconstruction, state judges and officers in the South denied access to courts, and state agencies became instruments of Black suppression and denial of rights. In the Great Plains, Black homesteaders regularly accessed the courts, and they found judges' and agency decisions to be largely unbiased, though not without exceptions. John Wesley Speese complained of bias by the Torrington justice of the peace. In the cases of Charles Sellers, a Black man lynched at Cody, Nebraska, and Erasmus Kirtley, a Black man shot and wounded near Nicodemus, the courts responded quickly to punish the white attackers. In Sellers's case, a white prosecutor charged and a white judge speedily convicted the killers. In

Kirtley's case, the white community sided with the Black victim and reinforced African Americans' belief that in Kansas it was possible to obtain justice.[21]

By contrast, the murder of Baseman Taylor while in the custody of Goshen County sheriff's deputies in Wyoming showed the system at its worst. Deputies tortured and then killed their captive, and prosecutors never brought them to justice. The deputies' wrongdoing had mortal consequences for Baseman, crippled Russel Taylor's leadership, and destabilized the entire community of Empire.

Black homesteaders enjoyed (so far as we can tell) fair treatment in the administration of federal land laws. No homesteaders we studied complained about bias by GLO administrators, although some, like Charles Speese at DeWitty and Mittie Moore in Blackdom, sometimes strongly disagreed with specific decisions.

In these diverse ways, Black homesteaders achieved a measure of civic equality. But civic equality did not reach the vast injuries and injustice of social inequality—the humiliation that Robert Anderson suffered when he returned to Hemingford with his new wife, and the head waiter refused them admission to the hotel dining room. Or the hurt and anger that Russel Taylor felt when Miss Hutchinson, Empire's young teacher wanting to attend an education conference, could find no lodging in Torrington. Or the insult and inconvenience when towns encouraged an informal enforcement of "sundown" laws. Still, as a Black pastor in Philadelphia explained why Black people left the South, "They're treated more like men up here in the North, that's the secret of it. There's prejudice here, too, but the color line isn't drawn in their faces at every turn as it is in the South."[22]

Throughout the four decades during which Black homesteaders filed claims and worked their land, in good times and bad, they determined their own course. Terri Gentry, the Dearfield descendant, mused, "There was so much evolution with who you are and your own ideologies and your belief systems and who you become in the process of the journey from the other side of the Mississippi River to this location, there's so much more to who you are and what you become as part of that journey." Angela Bates, the Nicodemus descendant and preservation hero, summed up the migrants' new home concisely; it was, she said, "A place they could experience real freedom."[23]

Even with all the caveats and exceptions, all the ways in which the search for equality produced only partial victories, we should not lose sight of the fact that Black homesteaders had taken a big risk for freedom, and they had been rewarded for their courage. Terri Gentry concluded, "I'm just honored to be the descendant of the people that I come from. I stand on really broad shoulders. I do. I stand on broad shoulders."[24]

So, if Black homesteaders were the vanguard of the Great Migration, why did later migrants not follow them? Why did the masses of southern Black people go north to cities and industrial jobs rather than west to homesteads?

Black homesteaders certainly invited, urged, and pleaded for other African Americans to come west and join them. Abram Hall advertised the possibilities in articles and letters in the *Colored Citizen* and other newspapers in the 1880s. Ben Blair in 1906 traveled and wrote articles for the Northwest Homestead Movement, hoping to attract Black settlers to South Dakota. Oscar Micheaux in 1910 and 1911 wrote two long, scorching front-page articles for the *Chicago Defender* publicizing the availability of prime land and emphasizing how quickly Black people would see the opportunity slip away. He understood the urgency. "It's to be hoped our race will realize [the rich homesteading opportunities] before it is too late," he wrote, "for the west, if not class, is at least fast . . . the time is at hand."[25] His books and movies likewise dramatically portrayed homesteading opportunities.

Blackdom advertised in the Indianapolis paper *The Freeman* in 1912, seeking five hundred families to migrate. Lucy Henderson published her long letter in the *Chicago Defender*, extolling the opportunities in New Mexico. Abram Hall, James Suggs, Robert Anderson, Russel Taylor, Oscar Micheaux, and others traveled throughout the South and Midwest, spreading the word of the new opportunities, the chance for Washington's call to self-help to pay real rewards. And these were just the public solicitations. Homesteaders wrote back home to kin and friends, describing the possibilities. Yet by 1915 or so, the Black people stopped migrating to the Great Plains to homestead.

There were likely many reasons. The Great Plains' harsh, cold climate, so different from what most southerners knew, deterred migrants. Frederick Douglass had warned them against the "pursuit of homes in a cold and uncongenial climate."[26] Detroit and Chicago could be cold too, but industrial workers mostly labored inside. Northern factories were notoriously hot in summer and cold in winter, but even so, migrants deemed them less uncomfortable than farm chores done under a blistering sun or in bone-chilling blizzards.

Then too, the declining quantity and especially quality of land still open for homesteading may have discouraged new migrants. The center part of the country was filling up, and to claim land, migrants had to enter ever-drier, more marginal, and less attractive ground. Still another reason was that migrants faced higher costs to set up a paying farm. American agriculture was moving to larger scale, and farming success required bigger farm implements, more horses or even tractors, more fencing, bigger barns, and other expanded facilities. All raised the newcomers' cost of entry.

But surely the main reason later migrants went north instead of west was that they came to see cities, not the countryside, as the land of opportunity. Owning actual land, especially farmland, was very important to Black homesteaders, and "free" land was a dream. But for succeeding generations, owning land was less important; they sought wage jobs and the attractions and freedoms of city life. As Du Bois noted in the first of his two 1907 Bull Lectures, "The reason for [Black migration] is clear: the oppression and serfdom of the country, the opportunities of the city. . . . It was natural that the Negro should rush cityward toward freedom, education, and decent wages."[27]

Northern cities were alluring to Black migrants in part because they promised jobs. Starting during World War I, Blacks discovered that employers offered them jobs in northern industrial plants, in stockyards, in construction, and in other sectors. The war cut off immigrant labor from Europe just when foreign governments began placing enormous orders for war materiel. Employers desperately needed workers in order to cash in on the tantalizing war profits. Bosses began hiring Black workers, not in the best jobs and mostly with poor wages and working conditions, but they were nonetheless offering jobs. In World War II, war-production plants in West Coast cities attracted large numbers of Black migrants. Black people increasingly saw northern and western cities—that is, cities outside the Jim Crow South—as offering the best prospects for their own economic betterment.

Equally important, Black migrants began to see cities as more exciting and fulfilling places to lead their lives. As Black communities in Chicago, Detroit, Cleveland, New York, Philadelphia, and Milwaukee grew, migrants found supportive neighborhoods filled with kin and friends. Many northern schools were segregated, if not by law then by informal restrictions, but they still were better than the miserable schools back home. As Isabel Wilkerson observed, "They could send their children to northern schools that were superior to anything back south, acquire a northern accent, save up for suits to replace the overalls and croker sack dresses of the field."[28]

Migrants found solace and community in the growing Black churches in their new northern neighborhoods. They enjoyed the cities' expanding array of services and entertainments oriented to them—Black-run cafes, nightclubs, newspapers, barbershops, dance halls, jazz clubs, even speakeasies and brothels. Cities introduced mechanized public transport systems—the "El" in Chicago, the subway in New York, street railways in Detroit—which made accessible venues like Coney Island in New York and Navy Pier, then called Municipal Pier, in Chicago. All of these services made city life more exciting, more promising, more alluring than country life.

Black people's move to cities paralleled the choices other Americans were making. Whites and others moved from the countryside to the cities, too, responding to the appeal of jobs and city life. America became an increasingly urbanized society—1920 was the first time the census categorized a majority of Americans as urban dwellers.

As we now know, African Americans did not find life in northern cities to be their promised land of milk and honey, or rather of freedom and full acceptance. Just as Black homesteaders found the rural Great Plains was not free of intolerance and racism, so too, migrants to the cities faced new forms of discrimination, including redlining, school segregation, and racist policing.

Yet the migrants who switched their destination from west to north continued what the homesteaders started—the search for freedom and opportunity. Black homesteaders had gone west because that's where they saw the opportunity to reap the rewards of their talent and toil. They left behind all the familiar things they knew, kin and friends and church and community. They risked their lives and accepted an indefinite future of sweat and grind and worry. All was sacrificed to create better lives for themselves and especially for their children and grandchildren. Black people who left the South in the Great Migration continued this search for opportunity, suffering dislocation and loss of everything familiar to find better futures for themselves and their children. Only the direction of their journey was different.

When time and circumstances changed, and people saw greater opportunities in the North (and later the Pacific Coast) instead of the Great Plains, they understandably altered their destinations. Both homesteaders and people of the Great Migration showed Black people's enormous determination to achieve full equality.

For nearly forty years, however, from the time when the Lexington migrants departed for Nicodemus until the tide of Black migration shifted north during World War I, Black homesteaders were the vanguard for Black people determined to remove themselves from the South. Isabel Wilkerson, in her magnificent study, dates the beginning of the Great Migration to 1915. Before then, there were the homesteaders. True, other Black people filtered out of the South. Some went to northern cities, others went west to Texas and Oklahoma to join the all-Black towns movement. Some joined the Buffalo Soldiers and were stationed in the West. Some became cowboys, making up perhaps as many as a quarter of western trail hands.[29]

The Black homesteaders were different. The scale of their vision—they operated in all the Great Plains states—was vast. They had a clear plan for how they would obtain ownership of the most needed and valuable asset, land, on which they would build an economy to support themselves. They intended to turn their vast reservoir of agricultural skills, built up under their decades of oppression, to their own benefit.

They turned a deaf ear to Douglass and Washington, who counseled them to stay in the South. Instead, they wanted land because owning land would lead them, they believed, to freedom. So they listened instead to Robert Knox, O. T. Jackson, and Abram Hall. Hall urged southern Blacks to "Scatter out as did the Jews in England. . . . [scatter] out, all over this vast country, each one doing the very best his circumstances allows. . . . Don't stop at one State, but rather take in the entire country."[30] They lacked money to buy land in the already-settled regions of the North, so they turned instead to the free land that homesteading offered in the West.

Grover I. Pettes Sr., a descendant of Black homesteaders in Las Cruces, NM, noted, "It took a lot of courage, took a lot of vision to realize that [homesteading] was something that's worthwhile. And the only thing they could say is, 'Hey, look, this is 640 acres of land here [and] there's no way that I could go and buy it with money.' Money was out of the question. But homesteading made [the land] available, and they went for it."[31] Many, like O. T. Jackson and Oscar Micheaux, wanted to put into practice Washington's message of self-help, thrift, perseverance, and the dignity of manual work.

They were the vanguard of African Americans seeking a place that could be their own, a place where "they could experience real freedom." Their explorations succeeded for themselves but did not prove to be the right destination for the millions still in the South within whom the pressure to migrate was building.

The homesteaders did prove one very important point, however, a point they demonstrated with their courage, audacity, and grit: Black southerners could leave their home regions and construct rich and fulfilling lives for themselves elsewhere. A subtext of the 1880 Vorhees Committee Senate hearings had been, Could African Americans survive and prosper outside the South? The committee skeptically asked, as Charlotte Hinger phrased it, "Were blacks smart enough, strong enough, or determined enough to endure without the guidance of whites?"[32] What was important was not that they answered this question to the satisfaction of racist white politicians but rather that they answered it for themselves and modeled their answer for any Black people hesitant to move.

And the homesteaders' answer to all such questions was a ringing "Yes!" They could make lives in which they exercised control over the daily decisions of their work and school and community life.

Indeed, Lulu Craig, the Nicodemus resident, said the homesteaders were better off than they had been in the South *because* they were forced to make all these decisions for themselves.

For a Black population dispirited and disheartened by the most horrible and demeaning treatment, people who not only in slavery but in debt peonage and Jim Crow were prevented from making decisions about basic aspects of their own lives, such an example must have been liberating. Even for those future migrants who didn't adopt the homesteaders' destination, the homesteaders' story may have emboldened them to join the Great Migration and dream as big as the homesteaders did.

The homesteaders' greatest dreams lay with their descendants—their children and grandchildren, in whom they invested such hopes and for whom they sacrificed so much. That would be their legacy.

15

Gen H's Legacy

It was like a Superman moment, when you realize,
this is my purpose, my path.

—ASHLEY ADAMS, Nicodemus descendant

The generation of Black homesteaders—let's call them Gen H—gradually changed their goals and developed a new sense of the legacy they were creating. They never fully abandoned the idea that owning land was the key to their being fully free and equal citizens. Some people, including John Boyd Jr., the president of the National Black Farmers Union, continue to express that belief today. But increasingly Gen H came to realize that their legacy would live in later generations, their children and grandchildren, and for them, education, not land, would be the key.

Even the earliest Black migrants had valued education highly. Their commitment came from a profound and deeply personal understanding that reading and writing, denied them in slavery, was a life-affirming competence. So they sacrificed and invested to ensure that their descendants would never have to sign official documents with an X. The cost of Gen H's commitment was not small, because they poured their energies, time, emotions, talents, and money—yes, money that struggling farmers always found so hard to come by—into the schools. They constructed school buildings, paid teachers (many from their own communities), purchased books, lobbied county school boards for resources, served on local school boards, ordered library books, and read to and with their children in the evenings. Gen H knew how far their toil and struggle had taken them, and they expected even greater achievements from their children.

As homesteaders progressed deeper into the twentieth century, they began to rebalance their priorities between owning land and education. Historian Andrew Wall observed about Blackdom, "Emphasis was being placed on preparing their children for not only the twentieth century but the twenty-first century. And at the heart of the society was education."[1] DeWitty homesteaders, like the Nicodemus and Blackdom folks, were motivated to own land, that's why they left their settled life in Overton and sought new lives in the Sandhills. But while DeWitty homesteaders saw land as the answer for themselves, they also saw the growing urgency of education for their children and grandchildren. They wanted to provide their children and grandchildren the education they would need to succeed in the emerging society of America.

And that required not just literacy but higher levels of education as well. They pressed the next generations to aim high. Abram Hall had expressed this point eloquently in his 1879 paper, "Our Needs." Gen H parents like Charles and Rose Speese and John and Ellen McGruder set firm expectations that motivated their children to graduate from high school when that was not yet the norm and to attend normal schools, nurses training, college and university, even law and medical schools.

Blackdom descendant Rodney Bowe remembered the moment when he discovered "that [his] relative [Loney K. Wagoner] affiliated with Blackdom was the so-called educator there." Bowe recalled, "When I first found that out, on the homestead papers, I cried. I cried and then I looked at his signature, and it's just very eloquent, his signature, and it looks like it comes from somebody who is educated and refined." For Bowe, expectations were clear: "My mother was a Headstart teacher, and very, very adamant about us attaining our edu-

90. Loney K. Wagoner and his class at Blackdom, ca. 1920. From *Roswell
(Images of America: New Mexico)* by John LeMay (Arcadia, 2008), 57.
Used with permission of Historical Society of Southeast New Mexico.

cation. And then going on to college, that was the first choice. And I
know that was instilled in her, from her parents and from their parents [in Gen H], that we go to college. And if you don't go to college,
then you will go into the military, which was the second choice."[2]

Just as farm families nearly everywhere learn, Gen H also discovered that children and grandchildren who achieve higher levels
of education rarely want to come back home and work the family
farm. Gen H's descendants became qualified as nurses, teachers,
businesspeople, police officers, artists, pharmacists, postal clerks,
Army officers, a college physics professor, a judge, journalists, and
bankers. So over time, Gen H changed their understanding of their
legacy: Their great enterprise was not about creating multigener-

ational family farms, it was instead about gaining the resources to permit them to educate their descendants to lead successful, productive, and fulfilling lives. Most descendants would live those lives elsewhere than on the land for which Gen H had risked so much and struggled so mightily.

Not all Black homesteaders reconciled themselves to the change. O. T. Jackson, who was himself childless, fought to the end of his life trying to save or revive Dearfield. Frank Boyer abandoned Blackdom but tried to capture a second chance by founding Vado. And one may be permitted to wonder what thoughts passed through Henry Burden's mind, as he lay dying, knowing that none of his children was likely to take stewardship of his beautiful farm, with its lovingly constructed house, its valuable orchards, and its productive fields.

But most Black homesteaders understood the change and redefined their farms as transitional spaces for their families. The success or failure of Gen H's great struggle would ultimately be seen in the lives that their descendants lived and live.

How many descendants of Black homesteaders are there? Trina Williams Shanks, in an ingenious study, calculated the number of current American adults who are descendants of homesteaders (of any race). Shanks, a demographer and now professor at the University of Michigan, employed historical vital statistics including the number of homesteads patented, fertility rates of different generations, the marriage rates for women of child-bearing age, and the number of generations since homestead patents were granted. We used Shanks' model combined with our own estimates of Black homesteaders in the Great Plains to generate estimates of the number of Gen H's descendants.[3]

We project that there are between 97,390 and 239,496 descendants. These estimates only offer rough indicators of magnitude and are not intended as precise counts. There are probably between some 100,000 and 225,000 people alive today who are descendants of Black Great Plains homesteaders.

And how did these descendants fare? We have no general survey to paint a social profile, but we do have lots of individual stories that display the range of talent unleashed by Gen H's flight to freedom. Here are a few.

Delbert Overton DeWitty is the great-grandson of Bryson DeWitty and great-grand-nephew of Miles DeWitty, the DeWitty settlement's first postmaster. Delbert DeWitty descends from two families, the DeWittys, originally freemen from Barbados who found their way to Texas, and the Overtons, slaves from Tennessee. He graduated from Tulsa's Booker T. Washington High School in 1968 and then enrolled at the University of Oklahoma, where he was one of just 348 Black students among the tens of thousands of white students. He graduated in 1972 with a degree in management from OU's Business School. He was hired by Southwestern Bell Telephone, which assigned him to its operations in Topeka, Kansas. He worked more than forty years in the telephonic and computer technology industry.

DeWitty's mother, Dorothy Moses DeWitty, studied at Langston University, Oklahoma's historically Black university (HBCU). In 1946 she was chosen to represent Langston on a forum to discuss integrating the University of Oklahoma.[4] However, when she traveled to Norman to take part in the panel, no hotel would rent her a room—echoes of Empire teacher Miss Wilkinson's experience in Torrington—so instead she stayed with a white family who agreed to put her up for the night. She would later become Tulsa's first Black female school principal and first Black female city counselor.

Delbert DeWitty followed in his mother's footsteps, not only as a student but also as a maker of, to borrow John Lewis's phrase, "good trouble." While at OU he served two years as president of the Zeta Zeta chapter and two years as regional vice president of Alpha Phi

91. Delbert DeWitty, great-grand-nephew of Miles DeWitty, holding a photo of the Dewitty general store and post office. Dewitty, 2016. Permission of Delbert DeWitty.

Alpha Fraternity, the national Black fraternity founded at Cornell University in 1906. The OU chapter began in 1967. DeWitty later discovered that the Norman Police Department had maintained a "Watch List," and it listed Delbert and his brother Michael as Numbers 1 and 2. (Michael was president of the Black Student Union.)

In Saint Louis, in addition to being District Manager, DeWitty served as president of the Black Employee Interest Group. Some white employees expressed concern that because of affirmative action, the company was hiring unqualified minorities. Delbert responded in an article for the company newsletter by pointing out that the company currently had unqualified white males at nearly every level. Mr. DeWitty retired from Southwestern Bell and is now a banquet speaker and participates in dramatic reenactments of the DeWitty settler days.

Ashley Adams, a Nicodemus descendant, teaches public policy at Mills College/Northeastern University in Oakland, California, and at the University of California at Berkeley. She grew up in Kansas City, Kansas. She heard about Nicodemus from her grandmother and regularly attended its annual Homecoming celebrations. She graduated from the University of Kansas in 2003. One of her regrets is that while she was a student at KU, she didn't know about KU's Spencer Library, which has an extensive collection of historical materials about Nicodemus.

Adams then worked in several nonprofit organizations, helping youth in foster care prepare for college. She got a master's degree and moved to California. She studied for a PhD in Public Policy at Walden University.

At that point two events collided that changed her life. She faced a looming deadline to submit her dissertation topic, but she really hadn't thought of an idea that excited her. And she helped organize a big family reunion in Denver, to which she invited Angela Bates to be the guest speaker. After her talk, Angela, in her usual friendly but sometimes disconcertingly direct manner, asked Ashley, "What are you doing with your life?" Ashley mentioned her dissertation dilemma. Angela said, "Have you thought about writing it on how we got Nicodemus designated as a National Historic Site?" Ashley almost dismissed the idea, thinking, "How could I possibly connect Nicodemus to Public Policy?"

When she thought about it more, "It was like a Superman moment, when you realize, this is my purpose, my path. Just as Angela was called to do what she does, this is what I was called to do." She started working on it, and "kept going, and it got deeper . . . way deeper!" In fact, it not only helped her complete her doctorate; it gave meaning to the rest of her life.

Adams is now an inspirational teacher and an expert on how to conserve historically important sites and their histories. She focuses on improving preservation practices for Black history sites, both to enhance public knowledge and to increase empathy for the Black experience. And though she lives and works in California, she serves as the board secretary for the Nicodemus Historical Society.

Adams descends from early Nicodemus settlers John and LeAnna Samuels and Andrew Alexander Sr. Reflecting on how they affected her life, she said, "It's a point of motivation that gives me a sense of pride and determination. When I look at my life and see things that I'm not necessarily happy with, it puts things in perspective for me. I think, 'If they could do this, then I can to that!' I feel empowered by it. Their sacrifices are why we are where we are today!"

Adams recently made another discovery. Through 23andMe DNA testing, she learned that she has ancestral roots reaching to the Tulsa Massacre. Her great-great grandfather, great-great-grandmother, and their two children survived the massacre. However, one son, Ashley's great-grandfather, was fourteen at the time and suffered burns over 70 percent of his body. She had known nothing of this history. "This [discovery] was very shocking." It became part of a flood of family history that rushed at her from all directions. Through it all, she remains determinedly optimistic and forward-looking, helping young people find their callings. "This [work] can be generationally healing. That's why I do it."

Veryl Switzer was the great-grandson of Zachary and Jenny Fletcher, that homesteader couple at the heart of Nicodemus's early history. Veryl was born in 1932 in Nicodemus and grew up there. He was a standout football and track star at Bogue High School, near Nicodemus.

Kansas State University recruited Switzer to be a running back at a time when college teams from the South refused to play opponents with Black players, and even northern teams had few Black players. He had a blockbuster football career at K-State. His best year was 1953, when he led his team in rushing with 558 yards, in receiving with eight catches for 211 yards, in scoring with eight touchdowns and forty-nine points, in punt returns with a 31.0-yard average, and in kick returns with a 22.3-yard average. And he was a "two-way" player, playing defense as well as offense. It seems the only thing he didn't do was lead the marching band.

Seventy years after his last Wildcat game, Switzer still ranks first at KSU in punt return yardage for a season, with his 1953 average of 31 yards. That year the team voted him its most inspirational player, and national sportswriters made him a consensus All-American.

Switzer graduated in 1954 with a degree in physical education. He earned his master's in education from KSU in 1974. He is a charter member of the K-State Sports Hall of Fame and was enshrined in the Kansas High School Hall of Fame and the Kansas Sports Hall of Fame. (Another descendant of Nicodemus homesteaders, whose parents moved to Omaha where he grew up, wasn't too shabby at football either: Gayle Sayers.)

The Green Bay Packers selected Switzer in 1954 with the fourth overall pick in the draft, still KSU's highest-ever NFL draft pick. He played in all twenty-four games for the Packers over two twelve-game seasons, again playing offense, defense, and special teams. In his rookie season, he topped the NFL in punt returns with a thirteen-yard average. But his football career was interrupted when, like Elvis Presley, he faced the military draft. He served as a first lieutenant in the United States Air Force from 1956 to 1958. When Switzer returned to resume his career with the Packers, he was not as successful as before his military service (some would say, also like Elvis Presley), and the Packers released him. He went to the Canadian Football League, where he played for three years.

Switzer then began his second career. Football opened opportunities to showcase his talents other than physical acumen. He became an educational administrator, working for the Chicago Board of Education for a decade. He returned to Kansas State, where he held several positions in both academic and athletic departments, including being associate athletic director for academics.

Switzer maintained his ties to Nicodemus. In 1961 he bought a nearby farm, which he worked after retiring. He became interested in recovering and preserving Nicodemus's history. He started the Back to History Camp, now called the Veryl Switzer/KSU Agricultural Camp, which offers adolescents the opportunity to spend a week visiting K-State and Nicodemus. Veryl Switzer died in 2022.

Elizabeth Burden is the great-granddaughter of Henry and Mary Burden, homesteaders in Saline County, Nebraska. She is the daughter of Franklin Harrison Burden Jr. and Essie Shelton Burden and is a mother and grandmother.

Burden has traversed many paths in her life. She earned degrees in journalism, art, and geographic information science (GIS) technology. She worked for both profit and nonprofit organizations. She was managing editor of a community newspaper, director of education and training of a statewide AIDS project, and executive director of a community center. Currently, she is a senior advisor with the National Council of Mental Wellbeing.

Midlife, Burden created a new chapter for herself as an artist. Her work is multidisciplinary, using painting, video, mapping, and other processes to reflect on social issues. In her series "Carceral Archipelagos," Burden examines the relationships between the elements of the criminal legal system, based on the premise that it is not "broken" but rather works as designed. "Cartographies: Indictments and Impunities" reflects on the lives and deaths of individuals killed by police and on police killed while on duty. Given that her father, Franklin Burden Jr. was a decorated police officer in Lincoln (1935–56), she has a distinct perspective on these issues.

And her art is visually stunning. In "Carceral Archipelagos: Box Stack 1," she uses screen prints on cardboard boxes to create the tension of both burden and instability. The boxes are stacked haphazardly, almost as a tower of blocks a mother repeatedly builds for her child to push over. Yet these are not children's blocks but systemic burdens, challenging the viewer.

One ongoing series, "Palimpsests," focuses on her Nebraska roots and the multicultural history of the West. She says, "I view that homestead land as a geographical palimpsest, where histories were written in blood and sweat, and whose early traces call out to be retrieved."

Could Henry Burden, who used his pocketknife to embellish the window trim on his house, see the torrent of creative talent his quest for freedom would unleash? Perhaps—he was a smart and most far-seeing man.

Norma Speese-Owens. In the photo, Norma Speese-Owens is surrounded by international students come to the United States to be trained as nurses. Not just any nurses, but nurses specializing in oncology, the care of cancer patients. It's the late-1970s, and New York University is hosting a gala. Speese-Owens and her students are dressed in evening gowns, flashing their jewelry, corsages, and smiles. The elegant dress is appropriate for the happy occasion— Speese-Owens is receiving yet another award in her eminent career.

Speese-Owens learned discipline and educational commitment from her mother, Rosetta Speese, who at sixteen drove a team and wagon three hundred miles from Westerville in central Nebraska to Empire, Wyoming, then rushed back to get married, and from her father, Charles Speese, who sustained his family through all the highs and lows of their adventurous lives. They moved from Westerville to Empire to DeWitty to Sully County, always with the determination to find good schools for their children. Norma was educated in the Sully County schools. After high school, she set her sights on being a nurse. She began by studying nursing at the Perth Amboy General Hospital School of Nursing in New Jersey, where she received her RN degree. She then moved across the country to earn her bachelor's degree in nursing from the San Francisco State Teachers College. Not yet done, she returned to the east coast to earn master's and doctorate of education degrees in nursing at New York University.

Professor Speese-Owens served for twenty-nine years on the faculty of the New York University College of Nursing. Her students, especially international students who traveled long distances to study with her, greatly admired her and found her to be an excellent teacher. Norma conducted research as part of a team at the world-famous Memorial Sloan Kettering Cancer Center. Her book, *Nursing Care of the Cancer Patient*, written with her colleague Rosemary Bouchard-Kurtz, became a standard textbook in her field. Untold numbers of nurses and more importantly, their patients, benefited. She wrote on such topics as "Psychological Components of Cancer Nursing," "Nursing Care of the Patient with Cancer of the Gastrointestinal System," and "Nursing Care of a Patient with Terminal Cancer." The book was so successful it went through four editions and was published in England, Japan, Poland and the Philippines.

Dr. Speese-Owens earned many honors during her long career. She received the New York University Alumni Meritorious Service Award, the Estelle Osborne Award, the American Cancer Society Outstanding Service Award, the Three Women of Achievement award, the Distinguished Alumnus Award, and the Lambda Kappa Nu National Citation for Journalism, among others.

These honors simply testified to her outstanding accomplishments in shaping modern cancer nursing. As anyone who has had life-threatening cancer knows, patients rely on competent and caring nurses to give them hope, comfort them, administer their medications accurately, discern the meaning in their pains, calm their fears, understand their prognoses, and be the overall monitor for their care. One who indirectly benefitted from Speese-Owens's work to raise the quality of cancer nursing is a grateful author of this book. Speese-Owens died in 1996.

92. Ashley Adams and Angela Bates at the Spencer Library, University
of Kansas. Permission of Ashley Adams and Angela Bates.

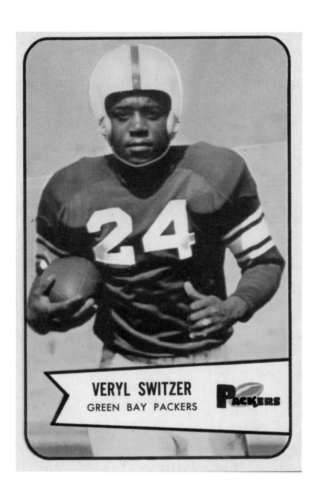

93. Veryl Switzer's 1954 Green Bay Packers player
card. Permission of Topps Inc.

94. *Carceral Archipelagos: Box Stack 1* by Elizabeth Burden.
Permission of Elizabeth Burden.

95. Dr. Norma Speese-Owens at New York University College of Nursing award gala, ca. 1980. Permission of Sylva Speese Gaines.

Nursing care of THE CANCER PATIENT

Rosemary Bouchard-Kurtz
Norma Speese-Owens

FOURTH EDITION

96. Cover of textbook for cancer nurse training, coauthored by Norma Speese-Owens. C. V. Mosby Company.

Are Delbert DeWitty, Ashley Adams, Veryl Switzer, Elizabeth Burden, and Norma Speese-Owens typical of the descendants of Black homesteaders? We do not know, pending more far-reaching surveys of descendants. We do know that others named in this book and still others we have met in the course of our research lead remarkable lives filled with talent and accomplishment—talent given running room to achieve its potential by the courage and grit of their homesteading ancestors.

Black homesteading was not just a curious historical phenomenon, over and now done with, but rather an historical process that continues to have impact and importance. The achievements of Gen H live today in the lives of its descendants. Some descendants inherited land or other material assets, handed down through the generations. Many more received their inheritance in the form of education, a gift borne of Gen H's generosity and sacrifice.

Descendants tell us Gen H's greatest gift to them, however, took the form of habits of the mind, values, and their enduring sense of self-worth. They trace their own strong work ethic, resilience, reverence for family, and commitment to giving back to community to their daring ancestors. Most importantly, descendants draw their sense of self-worth from knowing that they come from strong, courageous, self-sacrificing high achievers.

At Nicodemus, hundreds of descendants return each year to celebrate Emancipation Homecoming Day. They demonstrate a bewildering variety of occupations and pursuits. They carry forward the achievements of their ancestors in the vigor of their own successful careers and in the joyful families who accompany them.

Black homesteaders have been neglected by historians because they were relatively few in number. But as the eminent historian David Hackett Fischer, writing in a different context, reminds us, "size is not a measure of significance."[5] The Tuskegee Airmen were few in number compared to the many white pilots of the Army Air

Force, yet they taught us new lessons about determination and courage. So too, to vary the examples, the Pilgrims, the women who gathered at Seneca Falls, the sit-down strikers of the 1930s, the Freedom Riders and sit-in protesters of the 1960s, the six hundred marchers at the Pettus bridge in Selma—all were few in number yet large in our national narrative. That Black homesteaders in the Great Plains probably numbered no more than about three or four thousand successful filers and perhaps twenty thousand people in all, including family members, does not by itself justify neglecting their story.

Isabel Wilkerson, writing about a migrant to Chicago, might as well have been describing Willianna Hickman or Fernnella Walker Hayes or even Mittie Moore when she observed, "Many years later, people would forget about the quiet successes of everyday people like Ida Mae. . . . Few experts trained their sights on the unseen masses of migrants like her, who worked from the moment they arrived, didn't end up on welfare, stayed married because that's what God-fearing people of their generation did whether they were happy or not, and managed not to get strung out on drugs or whiskey or a cast of nameless, no-count men."[6]

We have a duty to educate all our children, grandchildren, and generations to come about the Black homesteaders' story. Historian Kathleen Harris, referring to white female homesteaders in Colorado, noted that "neither homesteading nor people deserve judgments based [only] on final outcomes. Homesteading, like life, dealt a complex and sometimes subtle mix of successes and failures."[7] Her dictum applies equally to Black homesteaders: they should not be neglected because their descendants left the land, nor should their communities be judged unimportant because they disappeared. Some, like the McGruders in Sully County and the Bateses in Nicodemus, remain; most do not. Nonetheless, for a generation, Black homesteaders pursued their dreams with uncommon courage and pluck. During those years, they created homes, farms, a place, and a society that was all their own. They raised their children, educated them, and saw them move on to fulfilling and accomplished lives elsewhere. The homesteaders experienced that mixture of joys, hardships, disappointments, and triumphs that is the common fate of most of us.

Epilogue

Where Are the Black Farmers?

Today, there are few African American farmers. The years since the demise of the Black homesteader colonies around 1930 have not been kind to Black farmers.

In 1930 the Census Bureau counted 882,852 Black farmers in the United States. They included 392,897, or 45 percent, who were share-croppers. In 2017, the latest year for which data are available, the Census of Agriculture found just 45,508 remaining Black farmers, a 95 percent decline. For every twenty Black farmers in 1930, only one remained on the farm by 2017.[1] With the decline in Black farmers came a corresponding decline in Black ownership of farmland.

The number of non-Black (mainly white) farmers declined as well during these eighty-seven years. They dropped from roughly 5.4 million to 2.0 million, registering a decline of 63 percent. For every twenty non-Black farmers in 1930, about seven survived to farm in 2017. The non-Black farmers' decline would ordinarily be considered a precipitous drop, except when set next to the disastrous demise of Black farmers.

What caused so many Black farmers to leave farming? The first thing we notice is that this decline was almost entirely a *southern* process. In 1930, 98.7 percent of Black farmers—870,936 out of 882,852—farmed in the South. By 2017 the number of southern Black farmers dropped to 42,061. The nation lost 837,344 Black farmers between 1930 and 2017, and 828,875 of them left south-

367

ern farms. *That is, 99 percent of the loss of Black farmers occurred in the South.*

The dynamics of southern agriculture are beyond the scope of this book, but other scholars have documented with increasing force what caused so many southern Black farmers to abandon their farms. In part, the decline was caused by national trends unfavorable to all small farmers, especially the collapse of the national economy in the 1930s. Federal policy also hurried the decline. Early New Dealers put in place programs designed to fix other problems that turned out to disadvantage southern Black farmers. FDR's Agriculture Adjustment Act aimed to raise cotton prices by restricting acreage that could be planted and hence reduce supply, but it resulted in what even the U.S. Department of Agriculture (USDA) admitted was "a bad deal for blacks."[2] More recent policies, such as federal agricultural research that is heavily biased toward large producers, hurt all small farmers, including Black farmers.

In part, developments more specific to the South caused the decline. The volatility of cotton prices hurt small farmers, who had great difficulty surviving periods of low prices. Changes in technology—the two most important being the vastly increased use of chemicals and the invention of mechanical cotton-pickers—devastated Black farmers because they made southern farming much more capital-intensive. International Harvester developed the first commercially successful spindle-type cotton picker in 1941, and landowners subsequently mechanized cotton production from land preparation through harvesting. Average farm size in the South nearly tripled from 86 acres in 1940 to 235 acres by 1974.

Large landowners benefited; small farmers did not, especially in the years between 1950 and 1980. The changes hurt sharecroppers and tenant farmers the most because landowners no longer needed their labor, and anyway they wanted to farm bigger fields. Southern

Black farmers were expelled from the land, declining from 559, 980 in 1950 to just 79,669 in 1978.[3]

These developments hurt, but increasingly scholars have pointed to another cause: USDA's decades-long, vicious, and continuing anti-Black discriminatory practices.[4] Since 1862, when Abraham Lincoln signed into law the predecessor to the USDA, the government has recognized two realities: farmers face peculiar risks of weather, crop cycles, volatile prices, financing needs, soil exhaustion, insects, and plant diseases; and society benefits when public programs help farmers survive these challenges. But as detailed in numerous studies, the USDA denied southern Black farmers loans, critical information and advice, crop insurance, and many other support services that the department showered on white farmers.

The USDA's delivery of services is highly decentralized, building on local extension agents, county ag service centers, and other local and state officials. In the Jim Crow South, these facilities were staffed almost exclusively by white—and judging by their actions, highly racist—individuals. Even after most Jim Crow laws were dismantled, USDA officials continued to discriminate against Black farmers. So too, the USDA's Washington-based leaders and staff have been at least tolerant of bias, and all too often they directly supported the bigotry of local and state operatives.

In 1982 the U.S. Civil Rights Commission published a report called "The Decline of Black Farming in America." It detailed the many ways in which the USDA, especially its local and state operatives in the South, ignored or actively discriminated against Black farmers. The USDA's generous financing programs made loans almost exclusively to white farmers, with Blacks' applications rarely being approved and even then, for drastically less money.

Among its many shocking findings, the commission documented the southern purge of the few Black people who served on local

USDA boards and commissions, precisely the groups supposedly overseeing fair distribution of loans and other benefits. Alabama dismissed 49 percent of its Black committee members, Mississippi, 56 percent, Georgia 61 percent, and Tennessee purged nearly all, 93 percent. The continuing virulent racism inside the USDA helped create unsustainable economic conditions and intolerable social conditions for Black farmers. The Department's discrimination inflicted incalculable harm on southern Black farmers, making its recent boast that "USDA is an equal opportunity provider, employer and lender" a bitter lie.[5]

Black farmers outside the South also saw their numbers decline, although the totals were substantially smaller and rate of decline less. From 1930 to 2017, Black farmers outside of the South declined from 11,916 to 3,447, a drop of 71 percent, compared to the decline of 95 percent for Black farmers in the South. Outside the South, Black farmers' decline (71 percent) was modestly more than white farmers' decline (63 percent).[6] Still, nearly three out of four Black farmers outside the South left farming during this period.

Black farmers in the North and West undoubtedly suffered many of the same adversities that caused so many of their white neighbors to leave farming. But Black farmers faced additional problems as well. For one thing, the USDA's racial bias, although most intense and damaging in the South, was likely not confined to the South. Black farmers in the North, like their southern counterparts, had difficulty getting USDA loans, and the loans they did receive were smaller than those extended to whites.

Bernard Bates was one of those denied USDA help. He was Angela Bates's cousin and a Nicodemus farmer. He described how during the 1980s, like other farmers, he suffered "bugs, hail, wind and rain, freeze, and everything for three, four years in a row." And like many others, he fell behind on his mortgage payments. But he said, while white farmers went to the USDA and got loans to tide them over during the tough times, his applications were denied. The result was that he lost the land that had been in his family since homesteader days. He watched, brokenhearted, and even photographed the dismantling of his farm in foreclosure. JohnElla Holmes, a Nicodemus resident and director of the Kansas Black Farmers Association, lamented in 2021 that if he could have gotten aid, "Bernard would still be farming, because that's what he love[d] and that's what he wanted to do." Bernard Bates died at age eighty-five in 2022.[7]

When we trace more specifically what happened to land that Gen H homesteaded, some descendants continue to own land, but most of it was sold off. The McGruder family still owns land in Sully County, and various Bates and other Nicodemus descendants own land in Graham County. However, all the land around DeWitty, most of the land around the other colonies, and (so far as we know) land homesteaded by Robert Anderson, Oscar Micheaux, and others is no longer owned by their descendants.

We have seen that there were many reasons why the Black homesteaders did not pass their land on to descendants. Henry Burden's children did not want to farm, and son George Hastings Burden sued his siblings to force an auction sale of Henry's farm. The DeWitty homesteaders valued education highly and sacrificed to educate their children, who became professionals or qualified for other occupations, resulting in their not being interested in farming. At Dearfield, O. T. Jackson held on, even as other Dearfield farmers abandoned their farms during the tough 1920s and calamitous 1930s. Blackdom farmers, who earlier had experienced wetter years, found persisting on the land during the drier 1920s and 1930s was impossible. There were thus many individual or local reasons why most Black homesteaders did not establish multigenerational family farms and pass on ownership of their land. Some reflect choice, and others were driven by external conditions.

We'll never know how many Black homesteaders' descendants might have stayed on the land if USDA loans and other support services had been administered fairly. Could some of those Dearfield and Blackdom farmers have survived the dry times if they had been given fairer access to loans to install irrigation equipment or to insure their crops or to make the transition from farming to ranching? Even *with* USDA support, three out of five non-Black farmers left agriculture between 1930 and 2017. There's no reason to think a similar percentage of Black farmers might not have failed even if the USDA had provided them with the same support it gave white farmers.

But that still leaves a very large gap. If during this period Black farmers left farming at the same rate (63 percent) as non-Black farmers, there would have been 326,655—not 45,508—left in farming in 2017. That calculation suggests that 281,147 Black farmers—326,655 minus 45,508—were lost due to racist USDA discrimination and related causes. More than a quarter-million lost Black farms is a heavy debt.

What we do know is that for a time Black people came to the Great Plains to claim and own land and to find freedom, and they succeeded in doing so. They constructed homes, farms, communities, and places of their own. And on the basis of that achievement, they equipped their children and grandchildren and generations beyond with the education, life skills, and values to be successful in their own lives. Those descendants have more than lived up to Gen H's high expectations for them.

Appendix

Black Homesteaders and White Racism

We have intentionally focused this book on the Black homesteaders' struggles and achievements, not on the whites who surrounded them locally and nationally. But Black people lived in a world sharply limited by racial prejudice. The national climate during the homesteading years was one of great and growing racial repression. Southern whites used violence and intimidation to reassert white supremacy. They denied Black people the right to vote, established the network of Jim Crow laws, "redeemed" the myth of the Lost Cause, set up monuments to Confederate heroes all across the South, tightened the fetters of sharecropping and debt peonage, enacted laws segregating schools and all public accommodations, and debased Black roles in the U.S. military. During the twenty years from 1905 to 1924, whites, mostly in the South, went on a lynching frenzy, producing the "strange fruit" hanging from southern live oaks. They lynched fifty-six African Americans on average *every year*.[1]

This explosion of southern racial suppression had its echo, its effect, in the North as well. It started in the nation's capital. Before the Civil War, Washington functioned as a southern city. Enslaved people worked in all the major public buildings, slave markets flourished, and residents created the ambiance of a southern city. Nine of the first fifteen presidents were major slaveowners themselves, most of the others highly sympathetic to the South. Southerners dominated Congress. Southern ladies set the cultural styles and hosted the most important social events. During and after the Civil War, this changed. Northern Republicans dominated the national government and Black people gained new freedoms. But starting with the election of 1876, southern Democrats and their northern allies returned to the ascendency. The election of Woodrow Wilson in 1912 delivered a sharp setback to racial progress. Many Black people were squeezed out of federal jobs, and southern dominance of the city's culture and institutions, as well as of national politics, returned.

More broadly across the North, racial integration faltered in the decades after 1877. Even before the Great Migration, small Black populations began to gather in New York, Chicago, Cincinnati, Philadelphia, and other cities. Black people typically clustered in separate neighborhoods, with segregated schools, churches, and civic spaces. They lived the practical reality of segregation, even when it was not formally enforced by Jim Crow laws. No law excluded Black doctors from the American Medical Association or Black nurses from the American Nurses Association, but excluded they were. Despite individual breakthroughs—W. E. B. Du Bois earning his PhD at Harvard, Edward Johnson becoming the first Black person elected to the New York legislature—the *presumption* of separation underlay everyday life.

This larger racial environment impinged on Black homesteaders in the Great Plains as well. When Nicodemus homesteaders traveled to nearby Stockton to buy supplies, they were required to be out of town by sundown. When Blackdom residents sought employment in Roswell, they were restricted to a range of low-paying, mostly out-of-sight jobs. When Miss Hutchinson, the Empire teacher, tried to find lodging in Torrington, the hotels refused her a room. When Robert Anderson sought a mortgage, he felt he was charged a higher interest rate than white borrowers. When Russel Taylor sought accountability for his brother's murder, he found the doors of justice closed to him. When Lena Speese and her siblings attended the Brownlee church one Sunday, the white parishioners made certain they felt unwelcome. When Rose Speese took her children to enroll in the Seneca schools, they were told the schools were full. When Oscar Micheaux's one great love in life was a neighboring white woman, he knew they could not be together. In all these ways and more, ways that outrage our sense of both justice and simple humanity, Black homesteaders found their lives hemmed in by racist institutions and prejudiced people.

Even Black people's white friends did not escape the racial presumptions. When white newspaper editors and writers sought to praise Henry Burden, whom they greatly admired and respected and effusively said so in print, they fell into racial tropes. The *Nebraska State Journal*, in a long article in 1902 praising Burden for his sagacity, persistence, and excellent character (and also extolling the Republican Party), noted, "Under the black wool that covered his cranium there was some good white gray matter." It quoted him, again very favorably, but gratuitously rendered his quote with "dats" and "deys" and "deirs" in an exaggerated minstrelsy rhetoric. We don't know how Burden spoke, but this man who had seen and experienced more of the country than most white editors, learned Czech, and was elected treasurer and board member of a white church, was far from the ignorant caricature. *The Dorchester Star*, concluding a lengthy and sincere encomium when he died, declared that Henry Burden "gained . . . the reputation which extended far beyond the boundaries of Saline county, of being the whitest black man that ever lived."[2]

Nor was the Great Plains free of anti-Black violence. In 1911 near Cody, Nebraska, about eighty miles northwest of DeWitty, four white men lynched a Black ranch hand, Charles P. Sellers, supposedly because he was wooing a white woman, Eunice Murphy. In 1919 in Omaha, a white mob numbering thousands lynched Will Brown, a Black man accused of assaulting a white woman. In 1921, in the half-southern, half-western state of Oklahoma, a white invasion force—it was too organized, with too much official connivance, to be called a "mob"—killed hundreds of Black people and destroyed "Black Wall Street" in the terrible Tulsa Massacre. In 1929 a white mob in North Platte, Nebraska, became enraged after a Black petty criminal shot and killed a law officer (who also happened to be Black). The mob turned on all Black people in town, and while none were killed, the mob completely cleared North Platte of its two hundred Black residents. People escaped with only the goods on their backs.[3]

Yet our outrage at these terrible wrongs shouldn't blind us to important differences in racial regimes. The Great Plains was not the South. One difference was simple personal security. Black people in the South, including would-be homesteaders, regularly suffered beatings, intimidation, and murder. That was extremely rare in the Great Plains. White southerners lynched 3,240 Black people between 1888 and 1968. In the same span in the Great Plains (not including Oklahoma), whites lynched 40 Black people. Southerners committed 94 percent, 3,240 out of 3,446, of lynchings nationally. Forty lynchings over eighty years is still a shameful barbarity, but it is on a completely different scale from the atrocities in the South. (Oklahoma, reflecting its half-southern, half-plains composition, was a middling case: whites lynched 40 Black people and more than twice that many whites—82. But these figures do not include the hundreds of Black people killed in the Tulsa Massacre, a by-other-means mass lynching.) Whites in the Great Plains were ten times more likely—419 to 40—to lynch other whites than Black people.[4]

Ida B. Wells, the great antilynching crusader, proposed that America had two quite different lynching circumstances, or what she called "lynching laws." In a 1909 speech to the conference that launched the NAACP, she argued, "[W]hile frontier lynch law existed, [lynchings] showed a majority of white victims. Later, however, as law courts and authorized judiciary extended into the far West, lynch law rapidly abated and its white victims became few and far between."

But as the western lynchings wound down, a new type of lynching started in the South. "This was wholly political, its [initial] purpose being to suppress the colored vote by intimidation and murder." But, she said, "In a few years, the purpose was accomplished and the black vote suppressed. But mob murder continued."

The mob movement in the South focused entirely on Black people (or occasionally their white friends), and lynchers worked alongside or were often assisted by sheriffs and other local lawmen. Wells termed this "color-line murder," and more than just murder, it frequently involved castration and other mutilation, burning, torture, burning at the stake, shooting the mutilated body, and other humiliations. Modern social scientists, drawing on extensive data sets, have largely confirmed Wells's idea: they speak of two lynching "regimes," western and southern, and they add a third "minor" regime along the Texas-Mexico border which victimized Mexicans.[5]

The case of Charles Sellers's murder illustrates some of the differences between the Great Plains and the South. In most southern lynchings, local authorities could never seem to identify any of the perpetrators, despite usually having clear photographic and other evidence. In those cases no one was punished for the killing. The Sellers case had a different outcome.

Sellers worked as a ranch hand in Cody, Nebraska. He supposedly made sexual advances to a young white woman, Eunice Murphy, who likely encouraged Sellers in his attentions and had accepted numerous presents from him. On June 20, 1911, Murphy's brother and three other white men showed up at Sellerses' door with revolvers. They dragged him out and hanged Sellers from a telephone pole.

The sheriff arrested the four men and Murphy the next day, detained them in the Valentine jail, and charged them with murder. The defendants asked for a bench trial rather than a jury trial, and Judge Westover scheduled them for quick adjudication. The culprits initially sought to defend themselves by calling on the classic racist imagery of a Black man sexually assaulting a white woman. They claimed that Murphy had rejected Sellers's romantic advances, and this caused Sellers to become so angry he threatened to wipe out her whole family.

The county attorney, however, was having none of it. His version was that the lynchers were actually seeking to profit from a $7,000 life insurance policy they believed Sellers held. The judge accepted the prosecution's argument, at which point the men pleaded guilty. Judge Westover convicted them and sentenced all four to life in prison. (Murphy was released.) Within weeks, authorities had convicted the killers, sentenced them, and transported them to cells in the state prison in Lincoln.

Lynchings were both individual tragedies and acts of terrorism. They wreaked horrific brutality upon their specific victims. But they were also intended to intimidate Black populations by showing them that Black people could be killed with impunity and that the white perpetrators would suffer no consequence. The Sellers case, too, was a heinous crime against an individual, but its wider effect was different. The perpetrators were quickly forced to face harsh punishment. This was not a convincing advertisement for intimidation and white impunity. Rather, it showed that whites could be prosecuted for crimes against Black people. (By contrast, the lynchers in Omaha and the killers in Tulsa were never identified or punished.)

Property damage was a second difference between the South and the Great Plains. It too can be an act of terrorism and intimidation. Unlike the devastation and burnings inflicted by night riders in the South, Great Plains homesteaders suffered no malicious damage to their fields, barns, or livestock.

Moreover, most Black settlers homesteaded at a time when ranchers, most of whom were white, opposed any homesteaders. For two or three decades, the ranchers had grazed their cattle on the open range, and they sometimes reacted violently to the loss of it. Kansas ranchers sought for a time to hassle homesteaders, including Nicodemus settlers in Graham County. The homesteaders organized biracial self-protection groups. In Wyoming, actual armed conflict broke out in the murderous "Johnson County War." Big ranchers hired twenty-three Texas gunman to intimidate and stamp out an armed association of small ranchers and homesteaders, by killing them if necessary. Only the U.S. Army, including a detachment of Buffalo Soldiers, stopped the mayhem.

In Nebraska, too, ranchers sought to bully the federal government into granting them grazing leases, or if not, to ignore the ranchers' land grab. In 1906 the powerful Spade Ranch tried to simply flout federal law entirely when it aggressively occupied the range. But the Roosevelt Administration rejected ranchers' proposals and insisted on enforcing the federal Van Wyck Law against fencing public land. The owners of the Spade Ranch went to jail. The ranchers' final defeat was passage of the Kinkaid Act (1904) and the Enlarged Homestead Act (1909), which opened the way for the arrival of the homesteaders in the drier parts of the West.

So ranchers were not inclined to look favorably on any new arrivals, yet in DeWitty there was no violence. In the only recorded confrontation, a rancher and some cowboys challenged DeWitty homesteader William P. Walker, but the conflict was quickly defused in Walker's favor. This confrontation, like the standoff in Kansas when cowboys drove some Nicodemus cows from watering at a stream, had more to do with grazing access and competition for sparse grass than it did racial differences. Disputes seem to have been settled peacefully, sometimes in court.

Voting was another difference between the South and the Great Plains. *The Colored Citizen* of Wichita reported on February 21, 1903, that in the South the government "failed in the practical application of the thirteenth fourteenth and fifteenth amendments of the constitution. . . . The truth is that under these amendments and in spite of them the Negro vote in the South is largely suppressed, that the Negro is, in fact, disenfranchised." As if further proof were needed, it later reported that voter registration books in Richmond had been closed to Black people under the headline, "TAKE VOTE FROM NEGROES. Five-Sixths of Colored Population in Virginia Disenfranchised."[6]

By contrast, that same spring, The Colored Citizen urged Black people to vote in the Wichita mayoral election. It noted, "The negro holds the key to the [election]. He is the balance of power in the cities and United States and it is up to us to say whether we elect the Republican ticket." Perhaps wanting to defend itself from anticipated criticism from readers unhappy with the party, the newspaper quickly assured readers, "Where the Republicans failed to give our people representation [The Colored] Citizen made a strong fight against them. The result was that the Republicans gave us all we asked for and we have no fight coming."[7]

In Kansas, although a minority, Black men constituted an important voting bloc. (Women of neither race were eligible to vote in state elections until 1912.) As the Millbrook Herald argued, "There are more than 30,000 colored Republicans [men] in Kansas, and the party ought to recognize them."[8] Black Republicans actively participated in the local and state party conventions, and Black men voted in mayoral and council elections in Wichita and Leavenworth.

Nicodemus leaders held office and vigorously participated in running Graham County and even occasionally, as in E. P. McCabe's case, the Kansas state government, too. Charlotte Hinger noted about the Nicodemus homesteaders that they "exert[ed] remarkable control over local, county, and state affairs from the beginning of settlement. It would have been impossible for ex-slaves to achieve this degree of influence and authority in the South. The magnitude of their success [was due to] their substantial land ownership, made possible through the Homestead Act, coupled with [their] capable leadership."[9]

Of the Great Plains states, only Oklahoma restricted Black voters. (Texas also did, but we do not include it as part of the Great Plains, because it was a Confederate state and its culture, racial regime, and laws made it part of the South, even though half of the state is within the Great Plains ecological boundary.) Black men in Oklahoma voted from the first Territorial election in 1890 until 1910. Then the legislature passed its infamous "grandfather clause" to exclude them. In 1915 the U.S. Supreme Court declared the grandfather clause unconstitutional, so the legislature passed a "temporary" registration law, giving Black men only nine days to register or forever be disenfranchised. It took until 1939 before the Supreme Court declared it unconstitutional, though in the meantime apparently many Blacks did vote.[10] But these measures reflected Oklahoma's southern race relations and were not prevalent elsewhere in the region. Black homesteaders regularly exercised their franchise in other Great Plains states.

Anti-Black prejudice in the Great Plains, unfair and wrong as it was, simply didn't translate into the massive violence and repression witnessed in the South. The Exodusters fled to Kansas because they knew its reputation as a "free" state and its importance in the Underground Railroad. The Walker family and the families associated with them returned to the United States, leaving Buxton for Overton, because they expected their rights to be respected. Moses Speese escaped North Carolina to get to Nebraska because he knew the difference, and we shouldn't second-guess his judgment.

The Great Plains was certainly far from perfect as a promised land for Black people, but it had a racial regime different from that in the South. The Black journalist Kate D. Chapman described her hometown, Yankton, SD, in 1889, as a place where "The schools, churches, and hotels are thrown open to all regardless to color, the feeling that exists between the two races is friendly in the extreme."[11] Charlotte Hinger noted that "white Kansans were much more likely than whites in the South to give immigrants of all ethnic origins a chance to prove themselves based on character. . . . To Kansans, the determining factor for assessing the quality of newcomers to the Great Plains was whether they could prevail against the environmental odds."[12] Most residents in other Great Plains states, especially those in rural areas, measured people by the same standard.

And Black people felt the difference. Lulu Craig was a child when her parents homesteaded in Nicodemus. Late in life she was asked if the homesteaders were better off in Kansas, despite all its climate and other challenges, than they had been in the South. Without hesitation, she said yes. Original Nicodemus homesteader Thomas Johnson stated that "by coming to the state [from Kentucky] he had decidedly bettered his condition in life." Anderson Boles, another Nicodemus homesteader, declared he would "never return to old Kentucky."[13] Most others agreed.

Not all whites in the Great Plains shared the same racial views. Whites in the cities—Omaha, Denver, Tulsa—seemed to hold more prejudiced attitudes than rural folks. As historian James Bish, in his detailed study of "The Black Experience in Nebraska," wrote: "It appears that in many areas of the state, especially rural ones, blacks and whites worked and lived together harmoniously."[14] Cities varied in their prevailing racial attitudes: the kind of harmony Chapman described in Yankton seemed completely missing when Russel Taylor visited Torrington. Even rural villages varied: Pleasant Hill neighbors accepted Henry Burden with admiration in a way that contrasted sharply with the Saint Paul (Nebraska) audience's racist taunting of the Speese Jubilee Singers, despite the villages being only a hundred miles apart.

The system was far from perfect. The Baseman Taylor and Will Brown killings proved that. John Wesley Speese served as the family's attorney for most Empire suits (as long as one branch of the family wasn't suing another). He complained that Justice of the

Peace James Jackson's court in Torrington was prejudiced against African Americans.

Despite their imperfections, courts in the Great Plains proved much more accessible and fairer to Black people than the courts they had known in the South. When William Sheppard, a white man, shot Erasmus Kirtley, a Black man, outside of Nicodemus, Sheppard was arrested and the nearby white community sided with Kirtley. Charlotte Hinger concluded that this episode reinforced the belief in the African American community that in Kansas it was possible to obtain justice.[15] When John Niles likely committed fraud, using nonexistent bushels of corn as his collateral for a bank loan, he was tried in Stockton before a presumably all-white jury. His eloquent defense resulted in a hung jury in his first trial and acquittal in his retrial. The Speese Brothers won a twenty-three-hundred-dollar judgment against their white tormentor, Yorick Nichols. Reverend James Suggs, falsely identified and accused of murder, spent two nights in the Osborne County jail, but he was released as soon as he appeared before a magistrate. The white man who falsely accused Suggs spent some weeks in jail. Mittie Moore was repeatedly found guilty by the Roswell town court but given very small fines which she could easily afford to pay.

We do not know what effect, if any, the Sellers lynching had on Black homesteaders. DeWitty and Empire were the closest colonies to Cody, the site of the crime. No letter writers or interviewees that we know of mention the lynching, and it does not come up in any of the descendants' accounts we examined. So we have no evidence to suggest that DeWitty or Empire residents knew of it or that they feared similar violence might strike them. That said, any extralegal hanging of a Black man surely caused shudders.

Baseman Taylor's killing, by contrast, shocked and disheartened the Empire community, and news of it certainly would have reached DeWitty residents and must have shocked and enraged them as well. Baseman was the widower of Nebraska-born Maggie Shores, and both Baseman and Maggie had multiple relatives at DeWitty.

But most Black homesteaders' daily lives were more mundane, not filled with such dramatic or tragic events. How did they get along day by day with their white neighbors? The colonies and unaffiliated Black homesteaders met with differing welcomes from nearby whites. In Empire, Black homesteaders lived among chronically hostile whites. In Blackdom, Black-white relations started well but got worse over time. As Roosevelt Boyer Sr. observed, relations soured when an influx of white migrants from the South changed the area's culture. In both locations, whites not only failed to offer support, cooperation, or friendship, they intentionally made Black peoples' lives more difficult.

Still, as antagonistic as the Wyoming and New Mexico neighbors were, they (excluding the Goshen County deputies) did not inflict violence on Black homesteaders. The whites around Empire and Blackdom mostly left the Black settlers alone. Colony residents, Russel Taylor in particular, were not happy with this unhelpful, un-Christian neglect. He railed against it in his *Goshen County Journal* columns and in frequent letters to editors. In the worst intervention, the Baseman Taylor killing, Russel Taylor himself had called in the sheriff. But the relative lack of violence and being largely left to themselves was a big advance for those who, in Joyceann Gray's words, came in search of "most of all, peace. The peace to make a living, peace to educate their children, peace to sit out on their porches and look over their land, with confidence that it was truly theirs, knowing that no one was coming over the next knoll to take and destroy!"[16]

At Nicodemus and Dearfield, some nearby whites were friendly and helpful, and most others were simply distant and indifferent, neither hostile nor intrusive. As Charlotte Hinger noted, "By spring of 1878, many of the [Nicodemus] settlers had established congenial relationships with the white community." E. P. McCabe and Abram Hall worked cooperatively with leaders of the majority-white population in the county to administer its business. Then in the 1880s, Nicodemus went through a period when white businessmen were active participants in town business and in its cultural life. In the countryside, whites claimed land among the more numerous Black homesteaders, creating a checkerboard pattern, and Black and white farmers lived peacefully with each other.[17]

At DeWitty and Sully County, and for unaffiliated Black homesteaders Henry Burden, Robert Anderson, George Washington Carver, and Oscar Micheaux, white neighbors were welcoming and helpful. There is much evidence of interracial cooperation, positive intermingling, and mutual benefit. Burden, Anderson, Carver, and Micheaux all had white friends with whom they socialized, traded labor, conducted business, depended on and helped out. They called white witnesses at proving-up. Their white friends were clearly important to them, as they were important to the whites.

Many DeWitty residents worked on the nearby ranches to earn extra cash, apparently without any unusual discord or strife. Blacks and whites played baseball together, occasionally volunteered together on community tasks like building a church, celebrated the big Fourth of July together, shared festival meals together, and socialized together. As DeWitty descendant Denise Scales said, "The most important thing was survival. So as far as color, there was no color line. It was all about mutual understanding, sharing, and getting along. [Black and white homesteaders] had picnics together every year in August, where they celebrated together. They traded together. It was all about survival, not about color at that time."[18]

Joyceann Gray, the DeWitty descendant, listened to the stories her family passed down orally about their pioneer ancestors. She used them to write a novelized version, called *Our DeWitty: And Now We Speak*. She puts these words in the mouth of Charlotte Walker,

William P. Walker's second wife: "One really nice thing about living in this part of the country were those white folks living in and around Overton, Seneca and Brownlee. They came to help us get settled without having been asked. We went to school together at times and shared in games on Sunday afternoons. We had the best baseball team and played the best music and we always shared our meals after the games." Gray, speaking through the fictionalized Charlotte Walker, acknowledges, "We did have white dances and Black dances though." Walker concludes, "I will forever be thankful for our part of the world because we felt safe and secure and our white neighbors supported that comradery. The racism if you want to call it that was subtle. Never causing either group a lot of concern. Both groups made adjustment when and where necessary."[19]

So as best we can tell, Black homesteaders in the Great Plains, except for Baseman Taylor and Erasmus Kirtley, did not themselves experience racial violence.[20] They were not subjected to racial assaults, destruction of property, or other major crimes or acts of intimidation or racial hatred. We have found no suggestion of violent acts or attempted intimidation being perpetrated against Great Plains Black homesteaders in any of the interviews, diaries, letters, books, or other written or oral sources we have examined. Aside from Baseman Taylor and Erasmus Kirtley, we could find no Black homesteader who was killed or assaulted, no barns burned or cattle mutilated, no attempts to drive Blacks out or to intimidate them into abandoning their homesteads.

The good will, or sometimes simply the lack of bad will, that most Black colonies and unaffiliated Black homesteaders experienced occasionally lasted longer than the colony itself. DeWitty and Brownlee residents and neighboring ranchers maintained good relations well beyond DeWitty's abandonment in the 1930s. Ava Speese Day's return in the 1960s to visit with the ranching Hanna family renewed bonds of friendship. And when descendants and ranchers in 2016 celebrated the dedication of DeWitty's historical marker, their great goodwill and mutual respect was evident.

What role, then, did race and racism play in the fates of the Black homesteaders? In the larger scheme of society, racist hatred limited Black people's opportunities and stunted their lives. Residents of the Black homesteader colonies could not escape national racism's crippling grasp. In their day-to-day lives, however, colony residents, except for those in Empire and to a lesser extent Blackdom, were able to go about their lives largely untroubled. They found the space to construct lives filled with joy and meaning as well as hardship and struggle. They made that opportunity themselves. They chose great risks and mustered great courage to overcome the challenges they faced. They toiled and struggled and suffered to wrest livelihoods from the difficult and unforgiving plains climate. But in the end, they persevered and showed great creativity, and for a time, they made places that were all their own.

Notes

1. Land!

1. *Louisville Courier-Journal*, September 7, 1877, 4; *Kentucky Advocate*, September 14, 1877, 3.
2. Craig manuscript, folder 2, 27.
3. Craig manuscript, folder 2, 27.
4. Baton and Walt, "A History of Blackdom," 6.
5. Wall interview.
6. Mikal Brotnov Eckstrom interview of Rodney Bowe, unpublished video conference conducted for this project, August 27, 2021; Suggs, *Shadow and Sunshine*, 16.
7. Painter, *Exodusters*, 6; Baton and Walt, "A History of Blackdom," 6.
8. Hamilton, "Settlement of Nicodemus," 6.
9. Hamilton, "Settlement of Nicodemus," 8–9; Noble L. Prentis, "Through Northern Kansas: Nicodemus," *Atchison Daily Champion*, July 16, 1881, 2.
10. O. C. Gibbs, "The Negro Exodus," *Chicago Tribune*, April 25, 1879, 9.
11. Prentis, "Through Northern Kansas," July 16, 1881, 2.
12. *Omaha Daily Bee*, April 29, 1907, 1. Papers carrying the Blackdom founding included the *Spokesman-Review* (Spokane WA), the *Southern Watchman* (Mobile AL), *The Republic* (Columbus IN), the *Marshfield (Wisconsin) News*, the *Times-Democrat* (New Orleans), the *St. Louis Post-Dispatch*, the *North Adams (Massachusetts) Transcript*, the *Semi-Weekly Messenger* (Wilmington NC), the *Montpelier (Vermont) Evening Argus*, the *Louisville Courier-Journal*, and nearly a hundred others, including the German-language *Amerika* (Saint Louis).
13. Baton and Walt, "A History of Blackdom," 8.
14. Quintard Taylor, the eloquent historian of the Black experience in the West, observed that many African Americans in the late nineteenth cen-

tury "had come to believe that the only way they could have true freedom was to have ownership over a piece of land." Quintard Taylor, quoted in Karaim, "Discover the Kansas Town."

2. Push and Pull

1. Baker, *Following the Color Line*, 131, 133.
2. Quoted in Lanza, *Agrarianism and Reconstruction Politics*, 21; Edwards, "African Americans."
3. Painter, *Exodusters*, 6; Edwards, "African Americans."
4. Wharton, *Negro in Mississippi*, 50, 217.
5. Wharton, *Negro in Mississippi*, 190–91.
6. Wharton, *Negro in Mississippi*, 190–91; Foner, *Reconstruction*, 428.
7. Wharton, *Negro in Mississippi*, 190–91, including internal quote.
8. Aptheker, *Negro in the South*, 107–8; Battle-Baptiste and Rusert, *W. E. B. Du Bois's Data Portraits*; Wilcox, "1900 Census," table 6; U.S. Census Bureau, "1900 Census." Total area of the eleven formerly Confederate states amounts to 494,075,440 acres.
9. U.S. Senate, "Report and Testimony," 6, 10, 13.
10. Hoffnagle "The Southern Homestead Act," 612, 617–28; Lanza, "'One of the Most Appreciated,'" 72–86.
11. Zinn Education Project; Seguin and Rigby, "National Crimes"; Wells, *Crusade for Justice*, chap. 6.
12. Wells quote in Ball, "Memphis and the Lynching."
13. Lynching Sites Project of Memphis; Wells, "Southern Horrors," 52; *Memphis Commercial*, December 15, 1892, 49–73.
14. G. W. Jones, *Memphis Watchman*, reprinted in *Western Cyclone*, May 19, 1887, 2.
15. Ball, "Memphis and the Lynching."
16. Arrington, "Free Homes for Free Men"; Merritt, *Masterless Men*; Waite, *West of Slavery*.
17. Act of May 20, 1862 (Homestead Act), Public Law 37–64 (12 STAT 392). These requirements changed slightly over the decades during which the act was operative. For example, later laws reduced the residency period to three years and increased the allowable claim to 320 or 640 acres.
18. Hanner, "Government Response to the Buffalo Hide Trade," 239–71.

19. Fen, *Encounters*; Wishart, *An Unspeakable Sadness*, 80–81.
20. Hansen, *Encounter on the Great Plains*; Edwards, Friefeld, and Wingo, *Homesteading the Plains*, chap. 5.
21. Edwards, Friefeld, and Eckstrom, "Canaan on the Prairie."
22. Bordewich, *Congress at War*; Edwards, "Homestead Act."
23. *Congressional Globe*, Thirty-Seventh Congress, 2nd sess., 2231.

3. New Start at Nicodemus

 1. Zachary Fletcher to the Pension Office, November 12, 1918, in Davis, "Exodus to Kansas."
 2. Fraser, "Nicodemus," 41–42.
 3. Hamilton, "Settlement of Nicodemus," 6; Painter, *Exodusters*, 148.
 4. Hamilton, "Settlement of Nicodemus," 7–8; O'Brien, "With One Mighty Pull," 119; Schwendemann, "Nicodemus," 11–12. Note that there are varying estimates of how many settlers arrived from each departure point; Hamilton states that Hill recruited "over 300 people in two groups [who] moved to Nicodemus from the Georgetown area." Claims of "300" or "200" or "75" migrants are clearly rounded estimates.
 5. Willianna Hickman, in Sterling, *We Are Your Sisters*, 375–76.
 6. Willianna Hickman, in Sterling, *We Are Your Sisters*, 375–76.
 7. Abram Hall to Mrs. Kathryne Henri, September 6, 1937, in Belleau, "Nicodemus Colony of Graham County"; Angela Bates, "Ellis Trail a Living History Tour to Nicodemus," *Hays Daily News*, April 29, 2015.
 8. Hamilton, "Settlement of Nicodemus," 7–8.
 9. Willianna Hickman, in Sterling, *We Are Your Sisters*, 375–76.
10. Prescott, *Geology and Ground-Water*. See also Don Burden et al., "Historic Resources Study"; quote in Hinger, *Nicodemus*, 32.
11. Craig manuscript, folder 2, 27.
12. Frederick Douglass, *Colored Citizen* (Fort Hall), May 24, 1879, quoted in Hinger, *Nicodemus*, 100; quote in Athearn, *In Search of Canaan*, 233.
13. U.S. Senate, "Report and Testimony," 13.
14. Ashley Adams phone interview of Alice McDonald, n.p., January 27, 2016; used with permission.
15. *Saline County Journal*, March 28, 1878, 3.
16. Craig manuscript, folder 1, 7.

17. Hinger, *Nicodemus*, 50; *Hays City Sentinel*, April 6, 1878, 1.

18. Hamilton, "Settlement of Nicodemus," 7–8.

19. *Saline County Journal*, March 28, 1878, 3; Root, "Biographical Sketch," 5.

20. *Saline County Journal*, March 28, 1878, 3; Root, "Biographical Sketch," 5; Hinger, *Nicodemus*, 48–49.

21. *Woodstock (Illinois) Sentinel*, July 22, 1880, 5; *Inter Ocean* (Chicago), October 8, 1879, 4; Hamilton, "Settlement of Nicodemus," 8–9.

22. *Saline County Journal*, March 28, 1878, 3.

23. *Saline County Journal*, March 28, 1878, 3.

24. Craig manuscript, folder 2, 27.

25. Hamilton, "Settlement of Nicodemus," 8, 27n54.

26. Lockard, *History of Early Settlement*; Hinger, *Nicodemus*, 50–52.

27. Hinger, *Nicodemus*, 60; *Kirwin Chief*, July 23, 1879, 3.

28. Hinger, *Nicodemus*, 60.

29. Quoted in Hinger, *Nicodemus*, 112–14; Painter, *Exodusters*, 231–32.

30. For more on political and class differences regarding Exodusters arriving in Nicodemus, see Athearn, *In Search of Canaan*; and Hamilton, "Settlement of Nicodemus," 9.

31. O'Brien, "With One Mighty Pull," 119–21; *Colored Citizen*, May 10, 1878. 1, emphasis in original.

32. Willianna Hickman, 375–76; Craig manuscript, folder 2, 27.

4. Nicodemus Flourishes

1. Fraser, "Nicodemus," 41–42; O'Brien, "With One Mighty Pull," 119–26.

2. Schwendemann, "Nicodemus," 26.

3. Belleau, "Nicodemus Colony of Graham County," 20.

4. *Millbrook (Kansas) Herald*, August 8, 1882, 2.

5. *Beloit (Kansas) Gazette*, November 18, 1882, 2; *Kansas Weekly Herald* (Hiawatha ks), September 8, 1882, 2; *Leavenworth Standard*, November 19, 1882, 1; Hinger, *Nicodemus*, 170–95, 137.

6. *Topeka Daily Capital*, November 29, 1884, 6; *Wichita Beacon*, December 19, 1884, 2.

7. Quoted in Hinger, *Nicodemus*, 62–63.

8. *Atchison Weekly Champion*, July 23, 1881, 1.

9. *Millbrook Herald*, June 27, 1882, 3; *Atchison Weekly Champion*, July 23, 1881, 1; Hamilton, "Settlement of Nicodemus," 8.
10. *Millbrook Times*, August 20, 1880, 2, and June 27, 1882, 3.
11. Abram Hall, "Our Needs: A Paper Read by A. T. Hall, Jr., Before the St. John's Literary Society, Topeka, Kans, Jan. 21st, 1879," *Colored Citizen* (Ft. Scott KS), February 1, 1979, 1, emphasis in original.
12. Hall, "Our Needs," 1.
13. Adams interview of Alice McDonald.
14. *Western Cyclone*, July 8, 1886, 3.
15. *Western Cyclone*, July 8, 1886, 3, and August 12, 1886, 2; Hamilton, "Settlement of Nicodemus," 15; McDaniel, "A History of Nicodemus," 71; O'Brien, "With One Mighty Pull," 125–26.
16. Hamilton, "Settlement of Nicodemus," 16–17.
17. Hamilton, "Settlement of Nicodemus," 18; Fraser, "Nicodemus," 48.
18. Hamilton, "Settlement of Nicodemus," 18; O'Brien, "With One Mighty Pull," 126.
19. *Millbrook Times*, August 5, 1887, 4; Hinger, *Nicodemus*, 155–56; Hamilton, "Settlement of Nicodemus," 18; O'Brien, "With One Mighty Pull," 126.
20. Hamilton, "Settlement of Nicodemus," 15–18; O'Brien, "With One Mighty Pull," 119–26.
21. Hamilton, "Settlement of Nicodemus," 17.
22. This process is well described in Hinger, *Nicodemus*, 128–46, 173–78.
23. *Millbrook Times*, May 14, 1880, 2.
24. Blackmar, *Kansas*, 767.
25. Hamilton, "Settlement of Nicodemus," 21–23.
26. Hamilton, "Settlement of Nicodemus," 23–24; Fraser, "Nicodemus," 51.
27. Hamilton, "Settlement of Nicodemus," 21.
28. USDA National Agricultural Statistics Service, "Kansas Wheat History," press release, October 2019.
29. Thompson and Clarke, "Ghost Town," 277–78.
30. Thompson and Clarke, "Ghost Town," 277–78.
31. Thompson and Clarke, "Ghost Town," 278.
32. Kenneth Hamilton unearthed this episode and reports it in Hamilton, "Settlement of Nicodemus," 15.
33. *Western Kansas World* (WaKeeney), September 24, 1887, 2.

34. O'Brien, "With One Mighty Pull," 117–18.
35. Hamilton, "Settlement of Nicodemus," 14.
36. Angela Bates, quoted on a Center for Great Plains Studies poster created by Katie Nieland, "Learn about Black Homesteaders," July 20, 2021.

5. Burdens' Flight to Freedom

1. The Burlington and Missouri River Railroad was an Iowa corporation operating in Nebraska when Henry Burden filed. It was purchased in 1872 by the Chicago, Burlington, & Quincy Railroad and continued operation as a subsidiary of that line. After many corporate mergers and buyouts, it became part of the BNSF Railway. "Introducing the Chicago Burlington and Quincy Railroad," Burlington Route Historical Society, accessed September 24, 2022, https://web.archive.org/web/20140308194515/https://www.burlingtonroute.com/cbq.html; see also, "Burlington and Missouri River Railroad," Wikipedia, accessed June 18, 2021, https://en.wikipedia.org/wiki/Burlington_and_Missouri_River_Railroad; Henry Baumer, General Land Office Land Patent, Township 7N, Range 3E, Section 28, March 20, 1872, accessed September 18, 2021, https://glorecords.blm.gov/details/patent/default.aspx?accession=0309-115&docClass=ags&sid=u35vtawg.b5q.
2. Burden's discharge papers listed his age as eighteen in 1866; this was likely incorrect. Henry Burden, Homestead Records: Nebraska, Lincoln Land Office, Township 7N, Range 3E, Section 22, Fold3 Digital Archive, accessed September 24, 2022, https://www.fold3.com/image/245867825.
3. National Park Service, National Underground Railroad Network to Freedom Program nomination form for the Henry Burden house in Saline County, Nebraska.
4. National Park Service, National Underground Railroad Network to Freedom Program nomination form for the Henry Burden house in Saline County, Nebraska.
5. Dorchester-Pleasant Hill Centennial History Committee, *History*, 177–80.
6. Henry Burden, Homestead Records: Nebraska City/Lincoln Land Office, Township 7N, Range 3E, Section 22, Fold3 Digital Archive, accessed September 23, 2022, https://www.fold3.com/image/245867821; the file contains an affidavit by F. [Ferdinand] Sukraw and William Elert.

7. *Nebraska State Journal*, July 24, 1873, 4.

8. U.S. General Land Office, "Circular," August 23, 1870, 6–7, reproduced by the Library of Congress, accessed September 24, 2022, https://www .loc.gov/resource/dcmsiabooks.circularfromgene00unit_0/?sp=8&r=0 .291,0.949,0.678,0.328,0. The circular explains the change authorized by section 25 of the act of July 15, 1870.

9. Lockwood, *Locust*, 7–8, 12.

10. Nebraska State Historical Society, "Saline County Historic Resource Survey," 19.

11. Dorchester-Pleasant Hill Centennial History Committee, *History*, 178.

12. *History of the Dorchester-Pleasant Hill Communities*, 177–80.

13. *Dorchester Leader* (Dorchester Nebraska), April 5, 1940, 1; July 5, 1940, 5; and August 30, 1940, 8.

14. *Crete (Nebraska) News*, October 16, 1913, 1.

15. *Nebraska State Journal*, August 23, 1902, 4.

16. *Crete (Nebraska) Democrat*, October 15, 1913, 3.

17. *Dorchester (Nebraska) Star*, October 16, 1913, 2.

18. *Crete (Nebraska) Democrat*, October 15, 1913, 3.

19. Henry Burden, at Find a Grave, accessed October 20, 2019, https://www .findagrave.com/memorial/108446149/henry-burden; originally printed in the *Wilber (Nebraska) Republican*, October 17, 1913, 3.

20. *Nebraska State Journal*, August 23, 1902, 4.

21. *Crete (Nebraska) Democrat*, October 15, 1913, 3.

6. Homesteading Alone

1. Suggs, *Shadow and Sunshine*, 14.

2. James Suggs, Civil War Service Record, 55th USCT, folder 3, accessed December 10, 2021, https://www.fold3.com/image/268890844; James Suggs, Civil War Service Record, 59th USCT, folder 3 accessed December 10, 2021, https://www.fold3.com/image/302273277.

3. Suggs, *Shadow and Sunshine*, 29.

4. *Lawrence (Kansas) Tribune*, December 26, 1878, 6; *Beloit (Kansas) Courier*, March 6, 1884, 3.

5. Suggs, *Shadow and Sunshine*, 19–20, 23; James Suggs, Homestead Records: Gregory Land Office, Township 5s, Range 19w, Section 12,

National Archives, Washington DC (RG49.B 1174.F.9455.8); U.S. Census Bureau, Phillips County, Kansas, 1880.

6. *Phillips County Freeman* (Logan KS), June 18, 1885, 2.

7. *Gaylord (Kansas) Herald*, July 2, 1885, 4; *Phillipsburg (Kansas) Herald*, June 20, 1885, 1.

8. *Phillips County Freeman* (Logan KS), July 23, 1885, 3.

9. *Phillips County Freeman* (Logan KS), June 9, 1887, 4; *Neosho Rapids (Kansas) Pilot*, May 29, 1889, 1.

10. Vella, *George Washington Carver*, 16, 9; Kremer, *George Washington Carver*, 10–12.

11. Vella, *George Washington Carver*, 25.

12. Vella, *George Washington Carver*, 1–3, 19–21, 21–22; Kremer, *George Washington Carver*, 19–20.

13. Vella, *George Washington Carver*, 34–35.

14. Vella, *George Washington Carver*, 32–33.

15. *Ness City (Kansas) Times*, August 11, 1887, 8; December 15, 1887, 1; February 16, 1888, 4; March 1, 1888, 4; September 13, 1888, 4.

16. *Ness City (Kansas) Times*, April 7, 1887, 8; December 22, 1887, 1; April 16, 1887, 5; *Ness City (Kansas) Sentinel*, August 21, 1886, 5.

17. Vella, *George Washington Carver*, 37. Vella discusses Carver's possible sexual orientation in a chapter called "Passion Pure and Simple," 210–34.

18. Vella, *George Washington Carver*, 36–39; "George Washington Carver Homestead Site," Kansas Travel, accessed June 26, 2021, http://kansas travel.org/gwcarverbeeler.htm.

19. Anderson, *From Slavery to Affluence*, 1–3. Daisy Anderson's own reflections, titled "Have You No Shame?," was appended to Robert's story and reprinted in multiple editions; one edition was published by *Steamboat Pilot* (Steamboat Springs CO), 1967. Pagination of Robert's part remained the same in the several editions.

20. We identified 642 specific successful Black homesteaders for whom we have confirmed names and specific claim locations in our database. A "cluster" was defined as any county with at least five Black homesteaders. We mapped Black homesteaders by county and defined "unaffiliated" homesteaders as those not locating within a cluster. In Holt and Wheeler counties, Nebraska, the Bliss community sat on the Holt-Wheeler county-

line; we treated it as a single community cluster. There were 185 (28.8 percent) homesteaders not in clusters. Elsewhere we estimate there to be a total of 3,405 Black homesteaders in the eight states we studied plus Oklahoma, allowing us to estimate that 981 [3,405 X .288] of them were unaffiliated Black homesteaders.

21. Anderson, *From Slavery to Affluence*, 1–3.

22. Anderson, *From Slavery to Affluence*, 1–11.

23. Anderson, *From Slavery to Affluence*, 42–44.

24. Anderson, *From Slavery to Affluence*, 48.

25. Anderson, *From Slavery to Affluence*, 48; Wax, "Robert Ball Anderson," 164.

26. Anderson, *From Slavery to Affluence*, 48–51.

27. Edwards, Friefeld, and Wingo, *Homesteading*, chap. 7.

28. Anderson, *From Slavery to Affluence*, 53.

29. Anderson, *From Slavery to Affluence*, 55–56.

30. Wax, "Robert Ball Anderson," 169–70.

31. Wax, "Robert Ball Anderson," 170; Anderson, *From Slavery to Affluence*, 55–56.

32. Wax, "Robert Ball Anderson," 177.

33. *Hemingford (Nebraska) Journal*, April 10, 1913, 8; November 21, 1912, 4; March 18, 1915, 1; September 18, 1913, 1; September 30, 1909, 8; August 1, 1912, 5; May 16, 1912, 4; April 15, 1914, 1; August 5, 1909, 6.

34. Anderson, *From Slavery to Affluence*, 51; *Hemingford (Nebraska) Journal*, May 13, 1914, 1.

35. Wax, "Robert Ball Anderson," 180–81; Brown, "Rough Forms," 159–218.

36. Wax, "Robert Ball Anderson," 185.

37. Anderson, *From Slavery to Affluence*, 58.

7. DeWitty and the Sandhills

1. U.S. Census Bureau, "Following the Frontier Line."

2. Descendants of DeWitty, video.

3. Roper and Scales, "Realm of Descendant History," 48–55.

4. Stith, *Sunrises and Sunsets for Freedom*, 26; *Alfalfa Herald* (Overton NE), May 1, 1903, 1; 1900 U.S. Census Bureau, Nebraska, Dawson County, Overton, District 0093, accessed September 13, 2021, https://www.ancestry

.com/imageviewer/collections/7602/images/4119884_00145?treeid=&
personid=&rc=&usePUB=true&_phsrc=fan24&_phstart=successSource
&pId=76641203.

5. *Alfalfa Herald* (Overton NE), November 20, 1903, 1; October 4, 1902, 1;
July 8, 1904, 1; August 1, 1903, 1; April 7, 1903, 8; October 9, 1903, 1;
August 14, 1903, 1; May 22, 1903, 8.

6. Day, "Ave Speese Day Story," 261.

7. Gray, *Our DeWitty*, 30.

8. *Omaha Daily Bee*, April 29, 1907, 1.

9. *Omaha Daily Bee*, April 29, 1907, 1; Richards and Myers, "Man," 317–39.

10. *Omaha Daily Bee*, April 29, 1907, 1.

11. Blount, "Those Audacious Meehans."

12. McIntosh, *The Nebraska Sandhills*, 230; Wolters, "As Migrants and as
Immigrants," 333–55; *Omaha Daily Bee*, April 29, 1907, 1.

13. Gray, *Our DeWitty*, 73.

14. Farrar, "Black Homesteaders Settle," 40; McIntosh, *The Nebraska Sandhills*, 230; McIntosh Papers, "Notes for DeWitty Paper #2."

15. *Omaha Daily Bee*, April 29, 1907, 1; Burckhardt, "The History of the
Negro Settlement"; McIntosh Papers, "Overton Blacks"; "Letter to Mrs.
Walker from Ava Speese Day," March 28, 1964.

16. Calloway and Smith, *Visions of Freedom on the Great Plains*, 30–32. Also
see U.S. Census, Year: 1910; Census Place: Kennedy, Cherry, Nebraska;
Roll: T624_840; Enumeration District: 0051; FHL microfilm: 1374853;
Year: 1910; Census Place: Loup, Cherry, Nebraska; Roll: T624_840; Enu-
meration District: 0057; FHL microfilm: 1374853.; Year: 1930; Census
Place: Loup, Cherry, Nebraska; Roll: 1268; Enumeration District: 0026;
FHL microfilm: 2341003; 1930; Census Place: Kennedy, Cherry, Nebraska;
Roll: 1268; Enumeration District: 0021; FHL microfilm: 2341003.

17. *Omaha Daily Bee*, April 29, 1907, 1.

18. McIntosh Papers, "Newspaper Articles, Black Homesteaders"; Stith,
Sunrises and Sunsets, 31; Farrar, "Black Homesteaders Settle," 42.

19. McIntosh Papers, "Notes for DeWitty Paper #2,"; Kay et al., "Nebraska
Historic Buildings Survey," 18.

20. Day, "Ava Speese Day Story," 261.

21. McIntosh Papers, "Ava Speese Day Correspondence" and "Interview Notes, Riley, Miles, and Walker"; Farrar, "Black Homesteaders Living," 16, 18.

22. Stith, *Sunrises and Sunsets for Freedom*, 31–32; McIntosh Papers, "Letter to Mrs. Walker," Ava Speese Day Correspondence.

23. Farrar, "Black Homesteaders Living," 45; "Negro Homesteading in Nebraska" in Alberts, *Sod House Memories*, 267; Day, "Ava Speese Day Story," 268.

24. McIntosh Papers, "Interview Notes, Riley, Miles, and Walker," 267–68; McIntosh Papers, "Cherry County Historical Society Notes," n.d.; McIntosh Papers, "Letter to Mrs. Walker," Ava Speese Day Correspondence; Farrar, "Black Homesteaders," 19. This is consistent with evidence for white homesteaders. See, for example, Edwards, Friefeld, and Wingo, *Homesteading the Plains*, table 6.3; and "Negro Homesteading in Nebraska" in Alberts, *Sod House Memories*.

25. McIntosh Papers, Ava Speese Day to William Schmidt, May 23, 1964, Ava Speese Day Correspondence; McIntosh Papers, "Interview Notes, Riley, Miles, and Walker," 1972; McIntosh Papers, "Newspaper Articles, Black Homesteaders," 1907–1992; "Negro Homesteading in Nebraska" in Alberts, *Sod House Memories*, 267.

26. McIntosh Papers, Ava Speese Day to William Schmidt, May 23,1964, Ava Speese Day Corrspondence.

27. McIntosh Papers, "Interview Notes, Riley, Miles, and Walker" and "Cherry County Historical Society Notes"; Stith, *Sunrises and Sunsets*, 32.

28. Ransom and Sutch, *One Kind of Freedom*.

29. Gray, *Our DeWitty*, 40.

30. Fraser, *African American Midwifery*; Sandoz, "Marlizzie," 60; Mikal Eckstron interview of Wayne Brown, Omaha, Nebraska, October 30, 2020; Day, "Ava Speese Day Story," 270–71.

31. Day, "Ava Speese Day Story," 265–66.

32. Katannah Day interview of Lena Day, November 1995, https://thoseaudaciousmeehans.com/lenas-memories.

33. McIntosh Papers, "Interview Notes, Riley, Miles, and Walker," and "Newspaper Articles, Black Homesteaders"; Stith, *Sunrises and Sunsets*, 33.

34. Lena Day interview; McIntosh Papers, "Interview Notes, Riley, Miles, and Walker."

35. Gray, *Our DeWitty*, 41.

36. Calloway and Smith, *Visions*, 31; McIntosh Papers, "Letter to Mrs. Walker from Ava Speese Day," Ava Speese Day Correspondence; Decker, "Lost Pioneers," 63–66; Burckhardt, "The History of the Negro Settlement"; Magnuson, *Last American Highway*, 32; Farrar, "Black Homesteaders," 41. Also see Cherry County Centennial Committee, *A Sandhill Century, Book 1, The Land*, 150.

37. Farrar, "Black Homesteaders," 39–43; Meehan, *Portrait of a Janitor*, 25.

38. Day, "Ava Speese Day Story," 267–68.

39. *Lincoln Journal Star*, March 22, 1980, 9.

40. Lena Day interview; McIntosh Papers, "Notes for DeWitty Paper #2" and "Interview Notes, Riley, Miles, and Walker."

41. "Segregated Healthcare Left Kansas City," *The Voice*, accessed August 29, 2021, https://www.communityvoiceks.com/news/featured_stories /segregated-healthcare-left-kansas-city-blacks-lacking-until-the-opening-of -new-general-hospital-no/article_04dc3eb8-d9ad-11e5-a0e8-c38538ecff6e .html.

42. Wayne Brown interview.

43. McIntosh Papers, "Notes for DeWitty Paper #2."

44. Lena Day interview.

45. Day, "St. James RMC Church and Cemetery," 247; McIntosh Papers, "Letter to Mrs. Walker from Ava Speese Day," Ava Speese Day Correspondence; "Negro Homesteading in Nebraska" in Alberts, *Sod House Memories*, 260; McIntosh Papers, "Cherry County Historical Society Notes."

46. McIntosh Papers, "Letter to Mrs. Walker from Ava Speese Day," Ava Speese Day Correspondence; Stith, *Sunrises and Sunsets*, 35; Farrar, "Black Homesteaders: Remembering," 432; McIntosh Papers, "Cherry County Historical Society Notes."

47. Wayne Brown interview.

48. Don Hanna Jr., "DeWitty Community, the Negro Settlement," in Cherry County Centennial Committee, *A Sandhill Century, Book 1, The Land*, 261; "Negro Homesteading in Nebraska" in Alberts, *Sod House Memories*, 271.

49. Descendants of DeWitty, video.

50. Meehan, *Portrait of a Janitor*, 27; Wayne Brown interview.

51. "Receive Life Sentence," *Valentine Democrat*, October 19, 1911, http://nebnewspapers.unl.edu/lccn/sn95069780/1911-10-19/ed-1/seq-1/. For further contextualization of violence on the Great Plains see, McKanna, "Black Enclaves of Violence," 147–60.

52. The law also prohibited marriage between whites and "Mongolians." In 1913 it was amended to add Japanese. Pascoe, *What Comes Naturally*, 21, 91, 195; Karthikeyan and Chin, "Preserving Racial Identity," 1–40.

53. Stith, *Sunrises and Sunsets*, 34.

54. Day, "Ava Speese Day Story," 274–75.

55. McIntosh Papers, "Letter to Mrs. Walker from Ava Speese Day," Ava Speese Day Correspondence; Sully County Centennial History Book Committee, *100 Years of Proud People*, 289; Mikal Eckstrom unpublished personal interviews conducted for this project with celebration participants, May 15, 2016.

56. Drozd and Deichert, "Nebraska Historical Population Report," table 6.

57. "Negro Homesteading in Nebraska" in Alberts, *Sod House Memories*, 259–60; McIntosh Papers, "Interview Notes, Riley, Miles, and Walker"; Aeschbacher, "Development of the Sandhill Lake Country," 221.

58. Jacob K. Friefeld telephone interview of Joyceann Gray, July 10, 2019.

59. McIntosh Papers, Ava Speese Day to William Schmidt, May 23, 1964; McIntosh Papers, "Letter to Mrs. Walker from Ava Speese Day," Ava Speese Day Correspondence; McIntosh Papers, "Newspaper Articles, Black Homesteaders"; Wayne Brown interview.

60. Day, "Meehan and Speese Families," in *A Sandhill Century, Book 2*, 259. Also see Sully County Centennial Book Committee, *100 Years of Proud People 1883–1983*, 289; Stith, *Sunrises and Sunsets*, 37; McIntosh Papers, "Letter to Mrs. Walker from Ava Speese Day," Ava Speese Day Corresondence; Hanna, "DeWitty Community," 246; Farrar, "Black Homesteaders," 43.

8. Speese Family Odyssey

1. *Lincoln Star*, May 8, 1908, 4.

2. "A Brief History of the Westerville Church," *Custer County Chief*, December 16, 1930, 1.

3. Carter, *Solomon D. Butcher*, 55.

4. Guenther, "Empire Builders," 180.

5. Carter, *Solomon D. Butcher*, 43. See also figure 53 of the Moses Speese family on homestead, Custer County, 1888; "U.S. Wind Engine & Pump Company," Batavia Historical Society, accessed June 6, 2021, http://www .bataviahistoricalsociety.org/exhibits-collections/companies-overview/u -s-wind-engine-pump-company/; and personal email communication from Issiaih Yott, Kregel Windmill Factory Museum executive director, June 6 and 8, 2021.

6. Edwards, "To Commute or Not Commute."

7. Carter, *Solomon D. Butcher*, 26.

8. *Custer County (Nebraska) Chief*, September 17, 1936, 11.

9. *Nebraska State Journal* (Lincoln), February 2, 1899, 7; *Custer County (Nebraska) Chief*, August 7, 1903, 8; July 10, 1908, 6; and *Brewster (Nebraska) News*, December 27, 1907, 5.

10. *Custer County (Nebraska) Republican*, May 3, 1900, 8.

11. *Custer County (Nebraska) Republican*, May 3, 1900, 8, and December 5, 1907, 5.

12. Quoted in Guenther, "Empire Builders," 182; *Sherman County Times* (Loup City NE), January 3, 1896, 2, and January 10, 1896, 3; *Alliance (Nebraska) Times-Herald*, January 31, 1896, 1; and *Fullerton (Nebraska) News*, February 21, 1896, 5.

13. *Alliance (Nebraska) Times-Herald*, January 31, 1896, 1; and *Fullerton (Nebraska) News*, February 21, 1896, 5.

14. *Morrill Mail*, July 19, 1923, 1; *Casper (Wyoming) Star-Tribune*, January 15, 1954, 10; and *Henry Dispatch*, July 27, 1921, 8.

15. *Alliance (Nebraska) Times-Herald*, "Land Sales," February 15, 1910, 5; *Sandhills Brewster News*, February 27, 1903, 5; and *Brewster (Nebraska) News*, October 18, 1907, 4.

16. *Custer County Chief*, February 28, 1908, 7; Carter, *Historical Statistics of the United States*, table Ba4282.

17. *Morrill (Nebraska) Mail*, July 1, 1908, 5; *Mitchell (Nebraska) Index*, February 7, 1908, 4; and *Brewster (Nebraska) News*, June 19, 1908, 5.

18. *Custer County Chief*, July 27, 1906, 1; *Lincoln (Nebraska) Star*, May 8, 1908, 4, and May 13, 1908, 13; Guenther, "Empire Builders," 184–85; "Heirs

of Speese vs. Estate of Shores," in Nebraska Supreme Court, *Reports of Cases*, 81:593.

19. *Natrona County Tribune*, February 15, 1911, 2.
20. Charles Speese Homestead Record, Record Group 49, NARA, file 350496.

9. Opportunity in Sully County

1. Blair, *For the People!* 8.
2. Blair, *For the People!* cover, 3.
3. Sully County Centennial History Book Committee, *100 Years of Proud People*, 282–83; Saxman, "To Better Oneself," 319–29. See also Rohr, "Norvel Blair."
4. "Fairbank Township" and "Little Bend Township" maps, from *Sully County 1916*; and Benjamin Blair Homestead Record, Record Group 49, NARA, file 669.
5. Hotaling, *Great Black Jockeys*, 208–37; Andrews, "Freedom in Sully County."
6. *Pierre (South Dakota) Weekly Free Press*, August 11, 1893, 5; June 30, 1904, 5; June 13, 1907, 5; August 1, 1907, 5; December 17, 1908, 5.
7. Pengra, "Sully County Colored Colony"; Andrews, "Freedom in Sully County."
8. *Pierre (South Dakota) Weekly Free Press*, August 24, 1905, 5; *Des Moines Register*, August 17, 1905, 10.
9. *Pierre (South Dakota) Weekly Free Press*, October 12, 1905, 3.
10. Vanepps-Taylor, *Forgotten Lives*, 10.
11. Gatewood, "Kate D. Chapman Reports," 32–35.
12. Vanepps-Taylor, *Forgotten Lives*, 97–98.
13. *Pierre (South Dakota) Weekly Free Press*, November 8, 1906, 3, and April 18, 1907, 5.
14. Andrews, "Freedom in Sully County," 2; Thompson, *75 Years of Sully County*, 261; Vanepps-Taylor, *Forgotten, Lives*, 97–99. Most of the $35,000 likely wasn't paid in cash; it may have been paid in stock, because the Warranty Deed shows McGruder paid for the land with one dollar in cash and "other valuable considerations." Sully County Recorder of Deeds, Warranty Deed: Grantors Thomas and Capitola Lytle to Grantee John McGruder, 23 March 1908.

15. Reprinted in *Pierre (South Dakota) Weekly Free Press*, April 13, 1911, 5.
16. This narrative is different from that given in Vanepps-Taylor, *Forgotten Lives*, 100–101; Vanepps-Taylor claims that the McGruder family kept ownership of the original Lytle ranch property, which passed to John's son William and that William and his descendants stayed on the land. Vanepps-Taylor's account does not appear accurate.
17. Sully County Centennial History Book Committee, *100 Years of Proud People*, 283. Andrews, "Freedom in Sully County," 2; Thompson, *75 Years of Sully County*, 261; Vanepps-Taylor, *Forgotten Lives*, 98; and Rogge, "Early History of Sully County," 33. The McGruders may have lost John's original property shortly after his death. On his deathbed it appears John took out a $28,600 mortgage on his property—likely to provide for Ellen after his death. Soon afterwards Ellen claimed her homestead and then defaulted on paying back the bank, so they lost the land. Sully County Recorder of Deeds, Warranty Deed: Grantors John and Ellen McGruder to Grantee Title Insurance and Trust Company, September 10, 1913; and Sheriff's Deed: Foreclosure by Action, 25 February 1916.
18. Jacob K. Friefeld interview of Cecil Leo McGruder, Pierre, South Dakota, December 11, 2018.
19. Jacob K. Friefeld interview of Jeanettee Parton, Lonoke, Arkansas, September 29, 2019; McGruder interview.
20. Parton interview; Thompson, *75 Years of Sully County*, 261.
21. Parton interview.

10. Tragedy and Failure at Empire
1. Gregg, "Imagining Opportunity," 257–79.
2. Guenther, "Empire Builders," 197; and Galbreath, "Making a Home."
3. Guenther, "Empire Builders," 182.
4. Charles Speese Homestead Record, Record Group 49, NARA, file 350496.
5. Guenther, "Empire Builders," 187; and Galbreath, "Making a Home," 2–3. Otis and Sarah's bistate house must not have been located on their homestead, because Otis's claim did not straddle the state line.
6. Galbreath, "Empire, Wyoming"; and Friefeld, Eckstrom, and Edwards, "African American Homesteader 'Colonies,'" 11–37.
7. Charles Speese Homestead Record, Record Group 49, NARA, file 350496.

8. Galbreath, "Empire, Wyoming;" Guenther, "Empire Builders," 190.

9. *Goshen County Journal*, October 8, 1914, 1.

10. Stewart, *Letters of a Woman Homesteader*; and Smith, "Single Women Homesteaders," 163–83.

11. *Nebraska State Journal* (Lincoln), December 1, 1912, 23; and *Lincoln (Nebraska) Star*, January 19, 1913, 13.

12. Guenther, "Empire Builders," 189, 198n30.

13. *Natrona County Tribune*, February 15, 1911, 2; Galbreath, "Making a Home," 5; Guenther, "Empire Builders," 182, 186, 192, 198n30; and *Mitchell (Nebraska) Index*, October 27, 1911, 6, and February 14, 1913, 1.

14. *Goshen County Journal*, November 19, 1914, 1, December 3, 1914, 8, and December 17, 1914, 1.

15. Carter et al., *Historical Statistics of the United States*, table Bc524.

16. Guenther, "Empire Builders," 188–89. Guenther states that there was only one attempt to segregate, in Cheyenne, and it failed. Galbreath, "Empire, Wyoming."

17. *Goshen County Journal*, August 6, 1914, 8.

18. *Goshen County Journal*, August 13, 1914, 8.

19. Guenther, "Empire Builders," 187, 191–92; and Galbreath, "Making a Home," 5–6.

20. Guenther, "Empire Builders," 190–91.

21. *Torrington Telegraph*, April 1, 1920, 12.

22. *Omaha Daily News*, October 30, 1924, 10; November 5, 1924, 10; *Omaha Daily News*, September 1, 1925, 6; *Omaha Daily Bee*, November 30, 1925, 7; and *Omaha Evening Bee-News*, March 17, 1928, 6.

11. Oscar Micheaux, "The Homesteader"

1. Micheaux, *The Conquest*, 35–36.

2. VanEpps-Taylor, *Oscar Micheaux*, 1–10, 144; Moos, *Outside America*, 53.

3. Micheaux, *The Homesteader*, 7. Micheaux biographers assume his fictional work, especially his first novels, are accurate accounts of his actual life. He was somewhat secretive about personal matters and may also have been cautioned by lawyers that to avoid lawsuits, he needed to fictionalize his accounts. Biographer Betti VanEpps-Taylor noted that scholars and family members "accepted [*The Conquest*] as fairly accurate autobiogra-

phy." Janis Hebert observed that Micheaux "recorded his South Dakota experiences in two novels, *The Conquest: The Story of a Negro Pioneer* published in 1913 and *The Homesteader* published in 1917." Scholar J. Ronald Green agreed that Micheaux's fiction is "fundamentally trustworthy as autobiography and history." Patrick McGilligan, author of the most extensive Micheaux biography, found that "again and again . . . available documents and accounts corroborate the details and the chronology of Micheaux's early life as recorded in his fiction." The various accounts, nonfiction letters, and records, as well as his several fictional retellings of his life, create minor discrepancies in details which we do not attempt to resolve here; in the main, however, the accounts are highly consistent. VanEpps-Taylor, *Oscar Micheaux*, 9; Hebert, "Oscar Micheaux," 62; and McGilligan, *Oscar Micheaux*, 15.

4. Micheaux, *The Conquest*, 2.

5. Micheaux, *The Conquest*, 75, 84; McGilligan, *Oscar Micheaux*, 4, 6–11; and VanEpps-Taylor, *Oscar Micheaux*, chapter 2.

6. McGilligan, *Oscar Micheaux*, 12.

7. Calculated from statistics in Carter et al., *Historical Statistics of the United States*, table Bc, 258–64; Snyder, *120 Years*, 31; "Metropolis," *Massac Journal-Republican*, August 10, 1916, accessed October 11, 2021, http://genealogytrails.com/ill/massac/history_towns.html; and McGilligan, *Oscar Micheaux*, 10–11, 30–34.

8. W. E. B. Du Bois lamented that the influence of Black preachers and teachers was being eroded by "farmers and gardeners, the well-paid porters and artisans, the business-men." Du Bois, *Souls of Black Folk*, 55.

9. Du Bois, *Souls of Black Folk*, 55; VanEpps-Taylor, *Oscar Micheaux*, 23.

10. Micheaux, *The Conquest*, 22.

11. For a vivid participant account of the openings, see Kohl, *Land of the Burnt Thigh*.

12. McGilligan, *Oscar Micheaux*, 30–34; Carter et al., *Historical Statistics of the United States*, table Ba 4314–4319; Greene and Woodson, *Negro Wage Earner*, 103.

13. McGilligan, *Oscar Micheaux*, 28–29, 38.

14. Micheaux, *The Conquest*, 42–43.

15. Don Coonen to John R. Milton, December 1970, as quoted in Hebert, "Oscar Micheaux," 62.

16. Oscar Micheaux, Homestead Records, Record Group 49, National Archives and Record Administration (file: 1267210); and McGilligan, *Oscar Micheaux*, 60.

17. Oscar Micheaux, Homestead Records, National Archives.

18. Don Coonen to John R. Milton, December 1970, as quoted in Hebert, "Oscar Micheaux," 62; and VanEpps-Taylor, *Oscar Micheaux*, 46.

19. Micheaux, *The Conquest*, 93.

20. Micheaux, *The Conquest*, 103.

21. Micheaux, *The Conquest*, 120.

22. Micheaux, *The Conquest*, 119–20.

23. Du Bois, *Souls of Black Folk*, 58; and Micheaux, *The Conquest*, 120.

24. Micheaux, *The Conquest*, 152–55.

25. Micheaux, *The Homesteader*, 2, 73; and VanEpps-Taylor, *Oscar Micheaux*, 63.

26. *Chicago Defender*, March 19, 1910, 1.

27. *Chicago Defender*, October 28, 1911, 1.

28. McGilligan, *Oscar Micheaux*, 93–94.

29. Micheaux, *The Exile*.

30. Musser, "The Films of Oscar Micheaux"; Phillip Lopate, "The Independent," *New York Times*, August 5, 2007; Susan King, "Focus on Black Pioneers," *Los Angeles Times*, September 11, 2009; and Tambay Obenson, "Why Has Hollywood Still Not Given Pioneering Black Filmmaker Oscar Micheaux His Due?," *IndieWire*, accessed September 19, 2021, https://www.indiewire.com/2021/05/oscar-micheaux-pioneering-black-filmmaker-1234636108/.

31. *Chicago Defender*, August 2, 1913, 1.

12. Sand and Success at Dearfield

1. Junne et al., "Dearfield, Colorado," 106; and *Greeley (Colorado) Daily Tribune*, February 29, 1932, 1.

2. *Greeley (Colorado) Daily Tribune*, June 3, 1930, 8; February 29, 1932, 1; October 4, 1937, 12.

3. U.S. Census Bureau, "1910 Abstract, Supplement for Colorado"; Carter et al., *Historical Statistics*, table Aa2603–2665.

4. Brunswig et al., "Dearfield Dream Project," 2.

5. "Colorado Negro Colony," *Breckenridge (Colorado) Bulletin*, June 27, 1908; and "Negro Town for Colorado," *Colorado Transcript*, August 5, 1909, 2.

6. Bob Jackson, "Black Pioneers of Colorado Helped Build the State," *Rocky Mountain News*, May 15, 2005, 8.

7. Homestead National Historic Park, "James Thomas," U.S. National Park Service, accessed May 5, 2022, https://www.nps.gov/people/james -monroe-thomas.htm.

8. *Denver Star*, February 23, 1918, 5.

9. *Denver Star*, February 23, 1918, 5.

10. *Greeley (Colorado) Daily Tribune*, December 23, 1929, 10.

11. Mikal Brotnov Eckstrom video interview of Terri Gentry, August 6, 2021.

12. Norris, *Dearfield, Colorado*, 31; Junne Jr. et al., "Dearfield, Colorado" 108–9; and *Colorado Encyclopedia*, s.v. "Dearfield," accessed December 2, 2017, https://coloradoencyclopedia.org/article/dearfield.

13. Norris, *Dearfield, Colorado*, 139, 142.

14. *Greeley (Colorado) Daily Tribune*, October 25, 1917, 8.

15. *Greeley (Colorado) Daily Tribune*, October 25, 1917, 8.

16. *Colorado Encyclopedia*, "Dearfield"; Norris, *Dearfield, Colorado*, 139, 142; and Bureau of Land Management, General Land Office Records.

17. *Modern Farmer* (Nashville and Chicago), January 15, 1930, 1. Reported in *Greeley (Colorado) Daily Tribune*, February 13, 1930, 4.

18. Gentry interview; *Colorado Encyclopedia*, "Dearfield"; Norris, *Dearfield, Colorado*, 139, 142; and Bureau of Land Management, General Land Office Records.

19. Cech, "1969 Water Rights."

20. *Denver Star*, July 4, 1914, 2.

21. *Denver Star*, December 27, 1913, 13.

22. *Denver Sun*, December 13, 1913, 1.

23. *Denver Star*, January 27, 1917, 7.

24. *Greeley (Colorado) Daily Tribune*, October 25, 1917, 8.

25. Norris, *Dearfield, Colorado*, 158; and Junne et al., "Dearfield, Colorado" 117n48.

26. *Greeley (Colorado) Daily Tribune*, October 25, 1917, 8.

27. *Greeley (Colorado) Daily Tribune* February 2, 1920, 4.

28. *Fort Collins (Colorado) Coloradoan*, November 23, 1920, 5.

29. *Greeley (Colorado) Daily Tribune*, November 6, 1929, 8.

30. Betts, *Dearfield*.

31. Junne et al., "Dearfield," 101; and Betts, *Dearfield*.

32. Quoted in Norris, *Dearfield*, 145, 164.

33. "Negro Colony in Dearfield is Big Success," *Denver Post*, October 17, 1917, 13; "Weld County's Negro Colony," *Weld County News*, November, 1921 (Harvest edition), 60; and Junne et al., "Dearfield," 110.

34. "Klu Klux Klan Leaders," History Colorado, accessed July 12, 2021, https:// www.historycolorado.org/kkkledgers; *Denver Post*, April 23, 2021, 1, and June 6, 2021, 1.

35. Colorado Board of Immigration and Eunice Norris quoted in Junne et al., "Dearfield," 111–12.

36. Junne et al., "Dearfield," 110.

37. USDA, Bureau of Agricultural Economics, "Wheat Situation," 1.

38. USDA, "The Wheat Situation," 1; and Norris, *Dearfield*, 171.

39. Norris, *Dearfield*, 158; and Junne et al., "Dearfield" 117n8.

40. "Last Woman in Town," *Ebony Magazine*, December 1955, 31–34; and *Greeley (Colorado) Daily Tribune*, October 4, 1937, 12.

41. Raboteau, "Black Cowboys"; see also the Black Cowboy Museum in Rosenberg, Texas, at http://www.blackcowboymuseum.org/ and the Black American West Museum in Denver, at www.denver.org/listing /black-american-west-museum/4467/.

42. *Windsor (Colorado) Beacon*, September 15, 1927, 5, and September 4, 1930, 8; *Greeley (Colorado) Daily Tribune*, August 22, 1930, 12; and *Fort Collins (Colorado) Coloradoan*, September 4, 1927, 5.

43. *Chicago Defender* (national ed.), May 16, 1931, 3.

44. *Greeley (Colorado) Daily Tribune*, July 27, 1931, 1, 9; July 29, 1931, 16.

45. *Greeley (Colorado) Daily Tribune*, July 29, 1931, 16.

46. Junne et al., "Dearfield," 112–15.

47. Gentry interview.

13. Struggles at Blackdom

1. Baton and Walt, "History of Blackdom," 3–7; *Las Cruces (New Mexico) Sun-News*, March 30, 1947, 9; and Miller, "Blackdom," 1–4.

2. Family oral histories and descendant stories present somewhat varying details of Boyer's trip.

3. *Roswell (New Mexico) Daily Record*, September 14, 1903, 3.

4. *Roswell (New Mexico) Daily Record*, October 8, 1903, 2.

5. Crowe, "The Dual Rainfall Regime"; Bean, "Geology," 1–2, 5–7; and Earth Data Analysis Center, University of New Mexico, "Blackdom."

6. Nelson, "Significance of the Afro-Frontier," chap. 2.

7. *New Mexican* (Santa Fe), December 30, 1911, 1.

8. John Boyer Homestead Record, Record Group 49, NARA, file 1384.

9. U.S. Geological Survey, "Artesian Water"; Miller, "Blackdom: Interpreting," 70–76; and Miller, "Blackdom: Revisiting," 77–100.

10. Nelson, "Significance of the Afro-Frontier," 47–49, 67.

11. Nelson, "Significance of the Afro-Frontier," 19.

12. Baton and Walt, "History of Blackdom," 7.

13. Mikal Brotnov Eckstrom interview of Rodney Bowe, August 27, 2021.

14. *Roswell (New Mexico) Daily Record*, October 8, 1903, 2; Nelson, "Significance of the Afro-Frontier," 17; and David Kammer, "Roswell," New Mexico History, accessed February 14, 2018, http://newmexicohistory .org/places/roswell.

15. U.S. GLO homestead files; Earth Data Analysis Center, "Blackdom,"; U.S. census data; and Nelson, "Significance of the Afro-Frontier," 90.

16. Timothy Nelson unearthed and recounts the colorful story of Mattie Moore (aka Mittie Moore Wilson) in "Significance of the Afro-Frontier," 85, 108–36, also 21, 83; and Earth Data Analysis Center, "Blackdom, Women landowners."

17. May, "'Government' Moral Crusade," 4–5.

18. Mittie Wilson (aka Mattie Mittie Moore) Homestead Record, Record Group 49, NARA, file 765165.

19. Nelson gives a similar estimate. Nelson, "Significance of the Afro-Frontier," 153.

20. Baton and Walt, "History of Blackdom," 8.

21. *New Mexican* (Santa Fe NM), January 2, 1912, 1 [Williams is misidentified as Leslie T. Williams]; *Western Liberal* (Lordsburg NM), January 19, 1912, 1; *Cimarron (New Mexico) News and Cimarron Citizen*, September 24,

1914, 3; Lindquist, "Origin and Development," 1–2; and *New Mexican* (Santa Fe NM), August 9, 1916, 3.

22. *Albuquerque (New Mexico) Morning Journal*, January 25, 1914, 4; *New Mexican* (Santa Fe NM), August 9, 1916, 3; and January 20, 2020, A1, A4.

23. *New Mexican* (Santa Fe NM), April 28, 1985, 20; Daniel Gibson, "Blackdom," *New Mexico Magazine*, February 1986, reprinted in Weigle et al., *Telling New Mexico*, 50.

24. *The Freeman* (Indianapolis IN,), December 14, 1912, 7; and *Chicago Defender*, December 21, 1912, 3.

25. Miller, "Blackdom: Interpreting," 8; Binkovitz, "Welcome to Blackdom"; Baton and Walt, "History of Blackdom," appendix, 1; and Nelson, "Significance of the Afro-Frontier," 98–99.

26. Nelson, "Significance of the Afro-Frontier," 50.

27. Nelson, "Significance of the Afro-Frontier," 50, 54, 66–67, 80–81.

28. *Albuquerque Journal*, October 14, 1910, 5; Baton and Walt, "History of Blackdom," 9, 10–12; and Nelson, "Significance of the Afro-Frontier," 80, 170.

29. Gibson, "Blackdom," 50.

30. Quoted in Earth Data Analysis Center, "Blackdom"; and Miller, "Blackdom: Interpreting," 26.

31. Gibson, "Blackdom," 47; *New Mexico Magazine*, February 1986, 47; and Baton and Walt, "History of Blackdom," 12.

32. Gibson, "Blackdom," 51.

33. Gibson, "Blackdom," 50; and Miller, "Blackdom: Interpreting," 40–41.

34. Baton and Walt, "History of Blackdom," 12.

35. *New Mexico Magazine*, February 1986, 47.

36. Mittie Wilson (aka Mattie Mittie Moore) Homestead Record, Record Group 49, NARA, file 765165.

37. Mittie Wilson, (aka Mattie Mittie Moore) Homestead Record, Record Group 49, NARA, file 765165, including affidavit by Erastus Herron.

38. Baton and Walt, "History of Blackdom," 13.

39. *Albuquerque (New Mexico) Journal*, June 8, 1922, 2.

40. *Albuquerque (New Mexico) Journal*, June 8, 1922, 2; *Carlsbad (New Mexico) Current-Argus*, July 30, 2000, 17.

41. *Las Cruces (New Mexico) Sun-News*, March 30, 1947, 9; "Blacks in a Border Country," *Frontera (New Mexico) NorteSur*, New Mexico State University, September 22, 2001.

42. *Carlsbad (New Mexico) Current-Argus*, July 29, 1926, 8.

43. Timothy Nelson deserves full credit for discovering the genesis and role of the Blackdom Oil Company and its relation to Blackdom's final years, and our treatment relies heavily on his research. Nelson, "Significance of the Afro-Frontier," 153–59.

44. *Roswell (New Mexico) Daily Record*, August 30, 1930, 8.

45. *Las Cruces (New Mexico) Sun-News*, March 30, 1947, 9; Vertrees, "Permian Basin"; *Roswell Daily Record*, August 8, 1919.

46. Nelson, "Significance of the Afro-Frontier," 20.

47. Wall interview.

14. Homesteaders and Great Migration

1. Hamilton, *Booker T. Washington*, 2, 167–71; and Washington, "Speech at the Cotton States."

2. Frederick Douglass, *Colored Citizen* (Fort Hall), May 24, 1879, quoted in Hinger, *Nicodemus*, 100; and Washington, "Speech at the Cotton States."

3. Du Bois, *Souls of Black Folk*, 40.

4. "Editorial," *The Crisis: A Record of the Darker Races*, October 1916, 267–74.

5. Du Bois, *Souls of Black Folk*, 40, 35.

6. Du Bois, *Souls of Black Folks*, 37, 35.

7. Du Bois, *Souls of Black Folk*, 37, 34–35.

8. Aptheker, *Negro in the South*, 109.

9. Wilkerson, *Warmth of Other Suns*, 8.

10. McInroy, *Nicodemus*.

11. Gray, *Our DeWitty*, 149.

12. Gray, *Our DeWitty*, 149; Mikal Brotnov Eckstrom interview of Catherine Meehan Blount and Joyceann Gray, May 15, 2016; Mikal Brotnov Eckstrom interview of Denise Scales, August 6, 2021.

13. *Nebraska State Journal*, August 23, 1902, 4; Gentry interview.

14. Wilkerson, *Warmth of Other Suns*, 8; U.S. Senate, "Report and Testimony"; and Quintard Taylor, quoted in Karaim, "Discover the Kansas Town."

15. Parton interview; Vossberg, *Hector's Bliss*, 3; and Stith, *Sunrises and Sunsets*, 26.

16. Brown interview.

17. Peter O'Dowd and Allison Hagan, "Black Farmers Disappointed in Biden's Pick for Secretary of Agriculture," *Here and Now*, WBUR, January 5, 2021.

18. Nedra Rhone, "In Decades after Civil War, Promise of West Lured Black Homesteaders," *Atlanta Journal Constitution*, February 16, 2021.

19. Kaplan, "Happy Birthday Mrs. Craig."

20. Berenson and Eggers, "Black People," 242–43; and Archer et al., *Atlas of Nebraska*, 51–61.

21. Hinger, *Nicodemus*, 60.

22. Baker, *Following the Color Line*, 133.

23. Gentry interview; and Angela Bates quoted on a Center for Great Plains Studies poster created by Katie Nieland, "Learn about Black Homesteaders," July 20, 2021.

24. *Nebraska State Journal*, August 23, 1902, 4; and Gentry interview.

25. Oscar Micheaux, "Where the Negro Fails," *Chicago Defender*, March 19, 1910, 1.

26. Douglass, *Colored Citizen* (Fort Hall), May 24, 1879, 1.

27. Washington, *Negro in the South*, 102–3.

28. Wilkerson, *Warmth of Other Suns*, 416.

29. Katz, *Black West*, 148–49, 200–231; Raboteau, "Black Cowboys"; Kesha Morse, "The Federation of Black Cowboys" series, *Village Voice*, 2016.

30. Abram Hall, *Colored Citizen*, July 26, 1879, 1.

31. Mikal Brotnov Eckstrom interview of Grover I. Pettes, September 17, 2021.

32. Hinger, *Nicodemus*, 96.

15. Gen H's Legacy

1. Wall interview.

2. Mikal Brotnov Eckstrom interview of Rodney Bowe, August 27, 2021.

3. Shanks, "Homestead Act," chapter 2; and Edwards, Friefeld, and Eckstrom, "Canaan on the Prairie."

4. Hubbell, "Desegregation," 370–84.

5. Fischer, *Washington's Crossing*, 5.

6. Wilkerson, *Warmth of Other Suns*, 415.

7. Harris, *Long Vistas*, x.

Epilogue

1. All data taken or calculated from U.S. Census, "1930 Census," table 1, 12; U.S. Census, "2017 Census of Agriculture," table 64, "Selected Principal Producer Characteristics by Race: 2017"; USDA, "Black Farmers and Their Farms." Notes: (i) The years in which the Census of Agriculture was conducted changed from decennial census years to every four or five years in off-decennials. (ii) Census definitions changed frequently, making long-time series susceptible to errors. (iii) The Census defines the South as the eleven Confederate states plus Kentucky, West Virginia, and Oklahoma. (iv) The Census differentiates "Black farmers" or "Black producers," who are Black adults primarily engaged in agriculture, from "Black farm operators," defined as one person per farm; there are fewer Black farm operators than Black farmers.

2. USDA, "Black Farmers in America," 8.

3. U.S. Census Bureau, "1950 Census of Agriculture"; USDA Historical Archive, "1978 Census of Agriculture." The latter figure includes Blacks and other races.

4. Daniel, *Dispossession*; and Newkirk, "Great Land Robbery."

5. U.S. Civil Rights Commission, "Decline of Black Farming," 93–94; U.S. Census Bureau, 2017 Census of Agriculture Data Now Available.

6. The figure given is for all non-South farmers; however, given the extremely small number of non-South Black and other farmers relative to non-South white farmers, the figure is a close proxy for white farmers.

7. Lazaro and Lancaster, "Historically Denied 'Pivotal' Loans."

Appendix

1. University of Missouri Kansas City Law School, "Lynchings by Date and Race, 1882–1968," accessed June 11, 2021, http://law2.umkc.edu/faculty /projects/ftrials/shipp/lynchingsstate.html. The "South" here includes the eleven Confederate states plus the non-Confederate slave states of Kentucky and Missouri.

2. *Nebraska State Journal* (Lincoln), August 23, 1902, 4; and *Dorchester (Nebraska) Star*, October 16, 1913, 2.

3. On Sellers case, see E. C. Rodgers, "Young Nebraska Girl Charged with Inciting Jealous Lovers to Deed so that She Might Get Fiance's Money," *Pittsburgh Press*, September 26, 1911; and "Crimes and Murders," Cherry County Genealogy Trails, accessed September 26, 2022, http://genealogytrails.com/neb/cherry/crimesandmurders.htm. On North Platte, see *Casper (Wyoming) Tribune-Herald*, July 14, 1929, 10; and *Grand Island (Nebraska) Daily Independent*, July 15, 1929, 2.

4. University of Missouri Kansas City Law School, "Lynchings by Date and Race,1882–1968," accessed June 11, 2021, http://law2.umkc.edu/faculty /projects/ftrials/shipp/lynchingsstate.html.

5. Wells, "Lynching"; Seguin and Rigby, "National Crimes."

6. *Colored Citizen* (Wichita ks), October 10, 1903, 2.

7. *Colored Citizen* (Wichita ks), February 21, 1903, 2, April 4, 1903, 1, and October 10, 1903, 2.

8. *Millbrook (Kansas) Herald*, August 8, 1882, 2.

9. Hinger, *Nicodemus*, 39.

10. Darcy, "Did Oklahoma?"

11. Gatewood, "Kate D. Chapman," 32–35.

12. Hinger, *Nicodemus*, 43.

13. Quoted in Hinger, *Nicodemus*, 203–4.

14. Bish, "Black Experience," 178.

15. Hinger, *Nicodemus*, 60.

16. Gray, *Our DeWitty*, 19.

17. Fly, "Into the Twentieth Century," 65–84.

18. Hinger, *Nicodemus*, 60; Baton and Walt, "A History of Blackdom," 7; Mikal Eckstrom interview of Denise Scales, August 6, 2021.

19. Gray, *Our DeWitty*, 77–78.

20. We know of one other case, not confirmed, of a Black man being beaten. Sam Hood was one of two Black barbers in Brownlee. In a poker game with five white cowboys, Hood was caught cheating by using the barber's wall mirrors to see the other players' cards. He was beaten severely and permanently injured.

Bibliography

Aeschbacher, W. D. "Development of the Sandhill Lake Country." *Nebraska History* 28 (1947): 205–21.

Alberts, Frances J., ed. *Sod House Memories*. 2 vols. Sod House Society of Nebraska, 1963–67.

Anderson, Daisy. *From Slavery to Affluence: Memoirs of Robert Anderson, Ex-Slave*. Hemingford NE: Hemingford Ledger, 1927.

Andrews, John. "Freedom in Sully County." *South Dakota Magazine*, February 4, 2014. https://www.southdakotamagazine.com/sully-county-colored-colony.

Archer, J. Clark, et al. *Atlas of Nebraska*. Lincoln: University of Nebraska Press, 2017.

Arrington, Benjamin Todd. "'Free Homes for Free Men': A Political History of the Homestead Act, 1774–1863." PhD diss., University of Nebraska, 2012.

Athearn, Robert G. *In Search of Canaan: Black Migration to Kansas, 1879–80*. Lawrence: Regents Press of Kansas, 1976.

Baker, Ray Stannard. *Following the Color Line*. New York: Doubleday, Page, 1908.

Ball, Nathaniel C. "Memphis and the Lynching at the Curve." Benjamin L. Hooks Institute for Social Change at the University of Memphis. Accessed January 22, 2022. https://blogs.memphis.edu/benhooksinstitute/2015/09/30/memphis-and-the-lynching-at-the-curve/.

Baton, Maisha, and Henry J. Walt. "A History of Blackdom, N.M., in the Context of the African American Post Civil War Colonization Movement." Report to the Office of Cultural Affairs, Historic Preservation Division. State of New Mexico Project No. 35-95-10009.09. Santa Fe: Historic Preservation Division, Office of Cultural Affairs, 1996.

Battle-Baptiste, Whitney, and Britt Rusert, eds. *W. E. B. Du Bois's Data Portraits: Visualizing Black America*. New York: Princeton Architectural Press, 2018.

Bean, Robert G. "Geology of the Roswell Artesian Basin, New Mexico, and Its Relation to the Hondo Reservoir." Technical Report 9. Santa Fe: State Engineer Office, State of New Mexico, 1949.

Belleau, William J. "The Nicodemus Colony of Graham County, Kansas." Master's thesis, Fort Hays State College, 1943.

Berenson, Sara L., and Robert J. Eggers. "Black People in South Dakota History." *South Dakota History* 7, no. 3 (June 1977): 241–70.

Betts, Donnie L. *Dearfield: The Road Less Traveled* (film). Denver: No Credit Productions. www.nocredits.com.

Binkovitz, Leah. "Welcome to Blackdom: The Ghost Town That Was New Mexico's First Black Settlement." *Smithsonian Magazine*, February 4, 2013, 21–28. www.smithsonianmag.com/smithsonian-institution/welcome-to -blackdom-the-ghost-town-that-was-new-mexicos-first-black-settlement -10750177/.

Bish, James D. "The Black Experience in Selected Nebraska Counties, 1854– 1920." Master's thesis, University of Nebraska at Omaha, 1989.

Blackmar, Frank. *Kansas: A Cyclopedia of State History, Embracing Events, Institutions, Industries, Counties, Cities, Towns, Prominent Persons, Etc.* Chicago: Standard, 1912.

Blair, Norvel. *For the People! To Be Read by All Voters, with Thrilling Events of the Life of Norvel Blair, of Grundy County, State of Illinois*. Joliet IL: Joliet Daily Record Steam Print, 1880.

Blount, Catherine Meehan. "Those Audacious Meehans" (website and blog). https://thoseaudaciousmeehans.com/?blogcategory=Genealogy.

Bordewich, Fergus. *Congress at War: How Republican Reformers Fought the Civil War, Defied Lincoln, Ended Slavery, and Remade America*. New York: Penguin Random House, 2020.

Brown, Rachel Linnea. "Rough Forms: Autobiographical Interventions in the U.S. West, 1835–1935." PhD diss., University of Kansas, 2019.

Brunswig, Robert, George Junne, Gillian Bowser, and Erin Renfrew. "Dearfield Dream Project: Developing an Interdisciplinary Historical/Cultural Research Network." *Social Sciences* 2, no. 3 (August 16, 2013): 169–79.

Burckhardt, O. J. "The History of the Negro Settlement in Cherry Co. Near Brownlee." Manuscript Collections, Nebraska State Historical Society, Record Group: 3248.AM.

Calloway, Bertha W., and Alonzo N. Smith. *Visions of Freedom on the Great Plains: An Illustrated History of African Americans in Nebraska.* Virginia Beach VA: Donning, 1998.

Carter, John E. *Solomon D. Butcher: Photographing the American Dream.* Lincoln: University of Nebraska Press, 1985.

Carter, Susan, Scott Sigmund Gartner, Michael R. Haines, Alan L. Olmstead, Richard Sutch, and Gavin Wright, eds. *Historical Statistics of the United States, Millennial Edition.* Cambridge: Cambridge University Press, 2006.

Cech, Tom. "The 1969 Water Rights Determination and Administration Act and the 2006 Well Shutdown along the South Platte River of Colorado: Background and Perspective, Part 3, Development of the Colorado Water Law System." *University of Denver Water Law Review*, March 10, 2020. http://duwaterlawreview.com/the-1969-water-rights-determination-and -administration-act-and-the-2006-well-shutdown-along-the-south-platte -river-of-colorado-background-perspective/.

Cherry County Centennial Committee. "A Sandhill Century." Valentine NE: Cherry County Centennial Committee, 1985.

Crowe, P. R. "The Dual Rainfall Regime of Roswell, New Mexico." *Monthly Weather Review* (February 1941): 1–2.

Craig, Lulu. Manuscript and papers. Nicodemus Historical Society, Nicodemus, Kansas.

Daniel, Pete. *Dispossession: Discrimination against African American Farmers in the Age of Civil Rights.* Chapel Hill: University of North Carolina Press, 2013.

Darcy, R. "Did Oklahoma African Americans Vote between 1910 and 1943?" *Chronicles of Oklahoma* 93 Number 1 (Spring 2015): 72–98.

Davis, Damani. "Exodus to Kansas." *Prologue Magazine* 40 no. 2 (Summer 2008).

Day, Ava Speese. "Ave Speese Day Story." In *Sod House Memories*, edited by Frances Jacobs Alberts, 261–75. Lincoln NE: Sod House Society, 1972.

———. "St. James RMC Church and Cemetery." In *A Sandhill Century, Book 1, The Land* and *Book 2.* Valentine NE: Cherry County Centennial Committee, 1985.

Decker, Beryl. "The Lost Pioneers: Negro Homesteaders in Nebraska." *Negro Digest* 12 (May 1963): 63–66. At National Archives and Records Administration (NARA). https://www.archives.gov/publications/prologue/2008/summer/exodus.html.

Descendants of DeWitty [Organization focused on educating the public about DeWitty]. Documentary video. Accessed August 18, 2021. http://descendantsofdewitty.org/index.php/activities/documentary.

Dorchester-Pleasant Hill Centennial History Committee. *History of the Dorchester-Pleasant Hill Communities, Saline County, Nebraska: 1881–1981 Centennial Celebration.* Dorchester NE: Dorchester-Pleasant Hill Centennial History Committee, 1981.

Drozd, David J., and Jerry Deichert. "Nebraska Historical Population Report." University of Nebraska at Omaha, Center for Public Affairs Research, Paper 37. 2007.

Du Bois, W. E. B. *The Souls of Black Folks.* Chicago: A. C. McClurg, 1903.

Earth Data Analysis Center, University of New Mexico. "Blackdom: The First All-Black Settlement in New Mexico" (interactive map). https://rgis.unm.edu/blackdom/.

Eckstrom, Mikal Brotnov, and Richard Edwards. "Staking Their Claim: DeWitty and Black Homesteaders in Nebraska." *Great Plains Quarterly* 38 (Summer 2018): 295–317.

Edwards, Richard. "African Americans and the Southern Homestead Act." *Great Plains Quarterly* 39, no. 2 (Spring 2019): 103–20.

———. "The Homestead Act and the Struggle for African American Rights." *Great Plains Quarterly* 41, no. 3–4 (Summer-Fall 2021): 175–94.

———. "The New Learning about Homesteading." *Great Plains Quarterly* 37 (Winter 2018): 1–24.

———. "To Commute or Not Commute, the Homesteader's Dilemma." *Great Plains Quarterly* 38, no. 2 (Spring 2018): 129–50.

Edwards, Richard, Jacob Friefeld, and Mikal Eckstrom. "Canaan on the Prairie: New Evidence on the Number of African American Homesteaders in the Great Plains." *Great Plains Quarterly* 39, no. 3 (Summer 2019): 223–41.

Edwards, Richard, Jacob Friefeld, and Rebecca Wingo. *Homesteading the Plains: Toward a New History.* Lincoln: University of Nebraska Press, 2017.

Farrar, John. "Black Homesteaders Living Off the Land." *Nebraskaland* 6, no. 7 (August-September 1988).

————. "Black Homesteaders: Remembering the Good Times." *Nebraskaland* 6, no. 9 (November 1998).

————. "Black Homesteaders: Scratching Out a Living." *Nebraskaland* 6 no. 8 (October 1988): 38–41.

————. "Black Homesteaders Settling the North Loup Valley." *Nebraskaland* 6, no. 6 (July 1998): 40–49.

Fen, Elizabeth. *Encounters at the Heart of the World: A History of the Mandan People*. New York: Hill and Wang, 2014.

Fischer, David Hackett. *Washington's Crossing*. Oxford: Oxford University Press, 2004.

Fly, La Barbara W. "Into the Twentieth Century." In *Promised Land on the Solomon: Black Settlement at Nicodemus, Kansas*, edited by the U.S. National Park Service, 65–83. Washington DC: Government Printing Office, 1986.

Foner, Eric. *Reconstruction: America's Unfinished Revolution, 1863–1877*. New York: Harper and Row, 1988.

Fraser, Clayton. "Nicodemus: The Architectural Development and Decline of an American Town." In *Promised Land on the Solomon: Black Settlement at Nicodemus, Kansas*, edited by the U.S. National Park Service, 35–63. Washington DC Government Printing Office, 1986.

Fraser, Gertrude Jacinta. *African American Midwifery in the South: Dialogues of Birth, Race, and Memory*. Cambridge MA: Harvard University Press, 2009.

Friefeld, Jacob K., Mikal Brotnov Eckstrom, and Richard Edwards. "African American Homesteader 'Colonies' in the Settling of the Great Plains." *Great Plains Quarterly* 39, no. 1 (Winter 2019): 11–37.

Galbreath, Robert. "Empire, Wyoming." Alliance for Historic Wyoming (website). Accessed August 10, 2016. https://www.historicwyoming.org/profiles/empire-wyoming.

————. "Making a Home in Empire, Wyo." WyoHistory/Wyoming State Historical Society. https://www.wyohistory.org/encyclopedia/making-home-empire-wyo.

Gatewood, Willard B., Jr. "Kate D. Chapman Reports on 'The Yankton Colored People,' 1889." *South Dakota History* 7 (Winter 1976): 32–35.

Gray, Joyceann. *Our DeWitty: And Now We Speak*. Self-published, 2018.

Greene, Lorenzo J., and Carter G. Woodson. *The Negro Wage Earner*. Association for the Study of Negro Life and History, 1930.

Gregg, Sara M. "Imagining Opportunity: The 1909 Enlarged Homestead Act and the Promise of the Public Domain." *Western Historical Quarterly* 50 (Autumn 2019): 257–79.

Guenther, Todd. "The Empire Builders: An African American Odyssey in Nebraska and Wyoming." *Nebraska History* 86 (Winter 2008): 176–200.

Hamilton, Kenneth. *Booker T. Washington in American Memory*. Champaign: University of Illinois Press, 2017.

———. "The Settlement of Nicodemus: Its Origins and Early Promotion." In *Promised Land on the Solomon: Black Settlement at Nicodemus, Kansas*, edited by the U.S. National Park Service, 1–32. Washington DC: Government Printing Office, 1986. Revising and extending "The Origins and Early Promotion of Nicodemus: A Pre-Exodus, All-Black Town." *Kansas History* 5, no. 4 (Winter 1982 [1983]).

Hanna, Don, Jr. "DeWitty Community, the Negro Settlement." In "A Sandhill Century, book 1, The Land," edited by Marianne Brinda Beel, Ruth Johnson Harms, and the Cherry County Centennial Committee. Valentine NE: Cherry County Centennial Committee, 1985.

Hanner, John. "Government Response to the Buffalo Hide Trade, 1871–1883." *Journal of Law and Economics* 24, no. 2 (October 1981): 239–71.

Hansen, Karen V. *Encounter on the Great Plains: Scandinavian Settlers and the Dispossession of Dakota Indians, 1890–1930*. Oxford: Oxford University Press, 2014.

Harris, Kathleen. *Long Vistas: Women and Families in Colorado Homesteads*. Niwot: University of Colorado Press, 1993.

Hebert, Janis. "Oscar Micheaux: A Black Pioneer." *South Dakota Review* (Winter 1973–74).

Hinger, Charlotte. *Nicodemus: Post-Reconstruction Politics and Racial Justice in Western Kansas*. Norman: University of Oklahoma Press, 2016.

Hoffnagle, Warren. "The Southern Homestead Act: Its Origins and Operation." *Historian* 32, no. 4 (August 1970): 611–28.

Honebrink, Jennifer K., Chris Jensen, and Alley Poyner Macchietto Architecture Inc. *Reconnaissance Level Survey For: Saline County Historic Resource Survey and Inventory, 2015*. Lincoln: Nebraska State Historical Society, 2015.

Hotaling, Edward. *The Great Black Jockeys: The Lives and Times of the Men Who Dominated America's First Sport*. New York: Three Rivers, 1999.

Hubbell, John T. "The Desegregation of the University of Oklahoma, 1946–1950." *Journal of Negro History* 57, no. 4 (October 1972): 370–84.

Junne, George H., Jr., et al. "Dearfield, Colorado: Black Farming Success in the Jim Crow Era." In *Enduring Legacies: Ethnic Histories and Cultures of Colorado*, edited by Arturo Aldama, 101–18. Boulder: University Press of Colorado, 2011.

Kaplan, Richard. "Happy Birthday Mrs. Craig" (documentary). Paley Center, 1971.

Karaim, Reed. "Discover the Kansas Town Settled by Black Homesteaders in the 1870s." *Preservation Magazine*, Spring 2020. https://savingplaces.org/stories/discover-the-kansas-town-settled-by-black-homesteaders-in-the-1870s#.X6RMPlBlBPY.

Karthikeyan, Hrishi, and Gabriel J. Chin. "Preserving Racial Identity: Population Patterns and the Application of Anti-Miscegenation Statutes to Asian Americans, 1910–1950." *Asian American Law Journal* 9, no. 1 (2002): 1–40.

Katz, William Loren. *The Black West*. Rev. ed. Wheat Ridge CO: Fulcrum, 2019.

Kay, John, David Anthone, Robert Kay, and Chris Hugly. "Nebraska Historic Buildings Survey: Reconnaissance Survey Final Report of Cherry County, Nebraska." Nebraska State Historical Society, May 15, 1989.

Kohl, Edith Eudora. *Land of the Burnt Thigh*. New York: Funk and Wagnalls, 1938.

Kremer, Gary R. *George Washington Carver: A Biography*. Westport CT: Greenwood, 2011.

Lanza, Michael L. *Agrarianism and Reconstruction Politics: The Southern Homestead Act*. Baton Rouge: Louisiana State University Press, 1990.

———. "'One of the Most Appreciated Labors of the Bureau': The Freedmen's Bureau and the Southern Homestead Act." In *The Freedmen's Bureau and Reconstruction: Reconsiderations*, edited by Paul M. Cimbala and Randall M. Miller, 72–86. New York: Fordham University Press, 1999.

Lazaro, Fred de Sam, and Simeon Lancaster. "Historically Denied 'Pivotal' Loans, Black Farmers Still Struggle to Get Support." *PBS Newshour*. December 7, 2021. https://www.pbs.org/newshour/tag/black-farmers.

Libecap, Gary D., and Zeynep Kocabiyik Hansen. "'Rain Follows the Plow' and Dryfarming Doctrine: The Climate Information Problem and Homestead Failure in the Upper Great Plains, 1890–1925." *Journal of Economic History* 62, no. 1 (2002–3): 86–120.

Lindquist, Charles A. "The Origin and Development of the United States Commissioner System." *American Journal of Legal History* 14, no. 1 (January 1970): 1–16.

Lockard, F. M. *The History of Early Settlement of Norton County, Kansas.* Norton KS: Norton Champion, 1894.

Lockwood, Jeffrey A. *Locust: The Devastating Rise and Mysterious Disappearance of the Insect that Shaped the American Frontier.* New York: Basic, 2004.

Lynching Sites Project of Memphis. "Sites." Accessed January 22, 2022. https://lynchingsitesmem.org/lynching/sites.

Magnuson, Stew. *The Last American Highway.* CreateSpace, 2015.

May, Zachary. "The Government's Moral Crusade: America's Campaign against Venereal Diseases at Home during World War I." *Bound Away: The Liberty Journal of History* 1, no. 1 (2015), article 6. https://digitalcommons.liberty.edu/ljh/vol1/iss1/6.

McDaniel, Orval L. "A History of Nicodemus, Graham County, Kansas." Master's thesis, Fort Hays State College, 1950.

McGilligan, Patrick. *Oscar Micheaux: The Great and Only: The Life of America's First Black Filmmaker.* New York: Harper Collins, 2007.

McInroy, Patricia. "Nicodemus." YouTube video, 11:45, accessed April 30, 2022. https://www.youtube.com/watch?v=8xHHMNRm8Sw.

McIntosh, Charles Barron. *The Nebraska Sandhills* Lincoln: University of Nebraska Press, 1996.

McIntosh, Charles Barron. Papers. Ava Speese Day Correspondence for 1960, 1964, 1980–1981. Nebraska State Historical Society, Lincoln NE. RG5410.AM. S1 SS1, file 1.

———. "Cherry County Historical Society Notes." Nebraska State Historical Society, Lincoln NE. RG5410.AM. S1 SS1, file 5.

———. "Interview Notes, Riley, Miles, and Walker," 1972. Nebraska State Historical Society, Lincoln NE. RG5410.AM. S1 SS1, file 5.

———. "Newspaper Articles, Black Homesteaders," 1907–1992. Nebraska State Historical Society, Lincoln NE. 9RG5410.AM. S1 SS1, file 10.

————. "Notes for DeWitty Paper #2." 1907, 1974, 1978, 1980–1981. Nebraska State Historical Society, Lincoln NE. G5410.AM. S1 SS1, file 13.

————. "Overton Blacks." Nebraska State Historical Society, Lincoln NE. RG5410.AM. S1 SS1 file 11.

McKanna, Clare V., Jr. "Black Enclaves of Violence: Race and Homicide in Great Plains Cities, 1890–1920." *Great Plains Quarterly* 23, no. 3 (Summer 2003): 147–60.

Meehan, William H. *Portrait of a Janitor: A Poetic Autobiography.* Self-published with Catherine E. Meehan Blount, 2016.

Merritt, Keri Leigh. *Masterless Men: Poor Whites and Slavery in the Antebellum South.* Cambridge: Cambridge University Press, 2017.

Micheaux, Oscar. *The Conquest: The Story of a Negro Pioneer.* Lincoln NE: Woodruff, 1913.

————. *The Exile.* Film. National Museum of African American History and Culture. Accessed April 25, 2022. https://nmaahc.si.edu/object/nmaahc_2012.79.1.30.1abc.

————. *The Homesteader.* Sioux City IA: Western Book Supply, 1917.

Miller, Austin Joseph. "Blackdom: Interpreting the Hidden History of New Mexico's Black Town." Master's thesis, University of New Mexico, May 2018.

————. "Blackdom: Revisiting Race in New Mexico's Black Town." *Panhandle-Plains Historical Review* 90 (2019): 74–98.

Moos, Dan. *Outside America: Race, Ethnicity, and the Role of the American West in National Belonging.* Lebanon: University Press of New England, 2005.

Musser, Charles. *The Films of Oscar Micheaux.* Criterion video, 8:52, accessed April 25, 2022. https://www.criterionchannel.com/videos/the-films-of-oscar-micheaux?utm_source=criterion.com&utm_medium=referral&utm_campaign=search-redirect&utm_content=results.

National Archives and Records Administration (NARA). "Exodus to Kansas." Accessed April 4, 2022. https://www.archives.gov/publications/prologue/2008/summer/exodus.html.

National Park Service. "Dearfield Agricultural Colony." *Historic American Landscapes Survey* No. CO-7.

Nebraska Supreme Court. *Reports of Cases in the Supreme Court of Nebraska.* Vol. 81, 593.

Nelson, Timothy E. "The Significance of the Afro-Frontier in American History: Blackdom, Barratry, and Bawdyhouses in the Borderlands, 1900–1930." PhD diss., University of Texas at El Paso, 2015.

Newkirk, Vann R., II. "The Great Land Robbery." *The Atlantic*, September 2019.

Norris, Melvin Edward. *Dearfield, Colorado—the Evolution of a Rural Black Settlement: An Historical Geography of Black Colonization on the Great Plains.* Boulder: University Press of Colorado, 1980.

Nucholls, Charles. *Remnants of a Dream: The Story of Dearfield, Colorado* (film). Vimeo, 2019. https://vimeo.com/318819103.

O'Brien, Claire. "'With One Mighty Pull': Interracial Town Boosting in Nicodemus, Kansas." *Great Plains Quarterly* 16 (Spring 1996): 117–30.

Painter, Nell Irvin. *Exodusters: Black Migration to Kansas after Reconstruction.* New York: W. W. Norton, 1986.

Pascoe, Peggy. *What Comes Naturally: Miscegenation Law and the Making of Race in America.* Oxford: Oxford University Press, 2009.

Pengra, Lilah. "Sully County Colored Colony." The Black Past (website). Accessed April 30, 2022. http://www.blackpast.org/aaw/blair-norvel-1825-1916/.

Prescott, Glenn C., Jr. *Geology and Ground-Water Resources of Graham County, Kansas.* Kansas Geological Survey, Bulleting 110, 1955. Accessed December 18, 2017. http://www.kgs.ku.edu/General/Geology/Graham/index.

Raboteau, Emily. "Black Cowboys: Busting One of America's Defining Myths." *New Yorker*, January 22, 2017. https://www.newyorker.com/culture/photo-booth/black-cowboys-busting-one-of-americas-defining-myths.

Ransom, Roger, and Richard Sutch. *One Kind of Freedom.* Cambridge: Cambridge University Press, 1977.

Richards, Susan L., and Rex C. Myers. "'Man + Opportunity = Success' D. Clem Deaver Sells Himself." *Great Plains Quarterly* 34, no. 4 (Fall, 2014): 317–39.

Rogge, Charles H. "Early History of Sully County." Master's thesis, Nebraska Wesleyan University, 1924.

Rohr, Nicolette. "Norvel Blair and The Sully County Colored Colony: A Family Story of Freedom and Migration." Paper presented at the Western History Association meeting, St. Paul, Minnesota, October 20–23, 2016.

Roper, Avis, and Denise Scales. "A Realm of Descendant History: African American Families Homesteading the Great Plains." *Black History Bulletin* 83, no. 2 (Fall 2020): 48–55.

Sandoz, Mari. "Marlizzie." In *Hostiles and Friendlies: Selected Short Writings of Mari Sandoz*, edited by Virginia Faulkner, 59–66. Lincoln: University of Nebraska Press, 1959.

Saxman, Michelle C. "To Better Oneself: Sully County's African American 'Colony.'" *South Dakota History* 34, no. 4 (Winter 2004): 319–29.

Schwendemann, Glen. "Nicodemus: Negro Haven on the Solomon." *Kansas Historical Quarterly* 34, no. 1 (Spring 1968): 10–31.

"Segregated Healthcare Left Kansas City." *The Voice.* Accessed August 29, 2021. https://www.communityvoiceks.com/news/featured_stories /segregated-healthcare-left-kansas-city-blacks-lacking-until-the-opening-of -new-general-hospital-no/article_04dc3eb8-d9ad-11e5-a0e8-c38538ecff6e .html.

Seguin, Charles, and David Rigby. "National Crimes: A New National Data Set of Lynchings in the United States, 1883 to 1941." *Socius: Sociological Research for a Dynamic World* 5 (January–December 2019). https://journals .sagepub.com/doi/10.1177/2378023119841780.

Shanks, Trina Williams. "The Homestead Act: A Major Asset-Building Policy in American History." In *Inclusion in the American Dream: Assets, Poverty, and Public Policy*, edited by Michael Sherraden, chap. 2. Oxford: Oxford University Press, 2005.

Smith, Sherry L. "Single Women Homesteaders: The Perplexing Case of Elinore Pruitt Stewart." *Western Historical Quarterly* 22, no. 2 (May 1991): 163–83.

Snyder, Thomas D., ed. *120 Years of American Education: A Statistical Portrait.* National Center for Education Statistics, US Department of Education, 1993.

Sterling, Dorothy, ed. *We Are Your Sisters: Black Women in the Nineteenth Century.* New York: W. W. Norton, 1984.

Stewart, Elinore Pruitt. *Letters of a Woman Homesteader.* New York: Houghton Mifflin, 1914.

Stith, Forrest. *Sunrises and Sunsets for Freedom.* New York: Vantage, 1973.

Suggs, Eliza. *Shadow and Sunshine.* Self-published, 1906.

Sully County (South Dakota) Centennial History Book Committee. *100 Years of Proud People, 1883–1983: A History of Sully County.* Onida SD: State, 1983.

"*Sully County 1916, South Dakota.*" *Standard atlas of Sully County, South Dakota.* Chicago: George A. Ogle, 1916.

Thompson, E. L., ed. "75 Years of Sully County." *Onida Watchman* [1958?].

Thompon, Isabel M., and Louise T. Clarke. "Ghost Town—Almost: The Depression Hits a Negro Town." *Opportunity: Journal of Negro Life* 13 (September 1935): 277–78.

U.S. Census Bureau. "1900 Census: Volume 1: Population." Part 1, table 1. U.S. Census Bureau, 1901. https://www.census.gov/library/publications /1901/dec/vol-01-population.html.

———. "1910 Abstract, Supplement for Colorado." Accessed September 25, 2022. https://www2.census.gov/library/publications/decennial/1910 /abstract/supplement-co.pdf.

———. "1930 Census: Agriculture Volume 3, State Tables." U.S. Census Bureau, 1932. https://www.census.gov/library/publications/1932/dec /1930d-vol-03-agriculture.html.

———. "1950 Census of Agriculture Preliminary Area Reports: Farms, Farm Characteristics, Farm Products, Volume 1, Farms, Farm Characteristics, and Farm Products—United States." Farms by Color and Tenure of Operator. U.S. Census Bureau, 1950. https://www.census.gov/library /publications/1951/dec/ac50-1.html.

———. "2017 Census of Agriculture, United States Summary and State Data, Volume 1, Table 64. Selected Principal Producer Characteristics by Race: 2017." U.S. Census Bureau, 2017. https://www.nass.usda.gov /Publications/AgCensus/2017/Full_Report/Volume_1,_Chapter_1_US.

———. "Following the Frontier Line." Data Visualization of information mined from the decennial censuses, 1790–1890. 2012. Accessed August 14, 2021. https://www.census.gov/dataviz/visualizations/001/.

U.S. Civil Rights Commission. "The Decline of Black Farming in America." Washington DC, February 1982. https://eric.ed.gov/?id=ED222604.

U.S. Department of Agriculture (USDA). Bureau of Agricultural Economics. "Black Farmers and Their Farms." Vera J. Banks, Economic Research Service, Rural Development Research Report No. 59, 1986.

———. "Black Farmers in America, 1865–2000: The Pursuit of Independent Farming and the Role of Cooperatives." Rural Business–Cooperative Service RBS Research Report No. 194, 2002.

———"Historical Archive, 1978 Census of Agriculture, Table 29. Summary by Tenure of Operator: 1978, Race and Tenure of Operator." https:// agcensus.library.cornell.edu/census_parts/1978-united-states/.

———. "The Wheat Situation." WSP 61, November 1944.

U.S. Geological Survey. "Artesian Water and Artesian Water Wells." Accessed March 22, 2022. www.usgs.gov/special-topics/water-science-school /science/artesian-water-and-artesian-wells.

U.S. Senate. "Report and Testimony of the Select Committee of the United States Senate to Investigate the Causes of the Removal of the Negroes from the Southern States to the Northern States." 46nd Congress, 2nd sess., Report 693. Washington: GPO, 1880.

VanEpps-Taylor, Betti. *Forgotten Lives: African Americans in South Dakota.* Pierre: South Dakota State Historical Society Press, 2008.

———. *Oscar Micheaux: Dakota Homesteader, Author, Pioneer Film Maker.* Rapid City SD: Dakota West, 1999.

Vella, Christina. *George Washington Carver: A Life.* Baton Rouge: Louisiana State University Press, 2015.

Vertrees, Charles D. "Permian Basin." Texas State Historical Society. https:// tshaonline.org/handbook/online/articles/ryp02.

Vossberg, Dennis. *Hector's Bliss: Black Homesteaders at Goose Lake, Nebraska.* Kearney NE: Morris, 2006.

Waite, Kevin. *West of Slavery: The Southern Dream of a Transcontinental Empire.* Chapel Hill: University of North Carolina Press, 2021.

Wall, Andrew. Interview in *Blackdom* (video). *¡Colores!* New Mexico PBS (KNME-TV), 1997.

Washington, Booker T. "Speech at the Cotton States and International Exposition in Atlanta." (1895). In *History Matters: The U.S. Survey Course on the Web.* Accessed October 21, 2021. http://historymatters.gmu.edu/d/39/.

Washington, Booker T., and W. E. B. Du Bois. *The Negro in the South.* Introduction by Herbert Aptheker. Reprint of 1907 William Levi Bull Lectures. New York: University Books, 1989.

Watchman, Onida. *100 Years of Proud People 1883–1983: A History of Sully County*. Onida SD Watchman, 1983.

Wax, Donald D. "The Odyssey of an Ex-Slave: Robert Ball Anderson's Pursuit of the American Dream." *Phylon* 45, no. 1 (1984): 67–79.

———. "Robert Ball Anderson, Ex-Slave, A Pioneer in Western Nebraska, 1884–1930." *Nebraska History* 64 (1983): 162–92.

Weigle, Marta, et al., eds. *Telling New Mexico: New History*. Santa Fe: Museum of New Mexico Press, 2009.

Wells, Ida B. *Crusade for Justice: The Autobiography of Ida B. Wells*. 2nd ed. Edited by Alfreda M. Duster. Chicago: University of Chicago Press, 2020.

———. "Lynching Our National Crime." Speech delivered at the National Negro Conference, June 1, 1909, New York Proceedings of the National Negro Conference. New York, May 31 and June 1, 1909.

———. "Southern Horrors: Lynch Law in All Its Phases." New York Age Print, 1892. Reprinted in *Southern Horrors and Other Writings*, edited by Jacqueline Jones Royster, 49–73. New York: Bedford St. Martin's, 1997.

Wharton, Vernon Lane. *The Negro in Mississippi, 1865–1890*. Chapel Hill: University of North Carolina Press, 1947.

Wilcox, Walter F. "1900 Census: The Negro Population." Washington DC: U.S. Census Bureau, 1901. https://www2.census.gov/prod2/decennial/documents/03322287no8ch1.pdf.

Wilkerson, Isabel. *The Warmth of Other Suns: The Epic Story of America's Great Migration*. New York: Vintage, 2010.

Wishart, David J. *An Unspeakable Sadness: The Dispossession of the Nebraska Indians*. Lincoln: University of Nebraska Press, 1994.

Wolters, Rachel. "As Migrants and as Immigrants: African Americans Search for Land and Liberty in the Great Plains, 1890–1912." *Great Plains Quarterly* 35, no. 4 (Fall 2015): 333–55.

Zinn Education Project. Rethinking Schools and Thinking for Change. Accessed January 20, 2022. https://www.zinnedproject.org/news/tdih/peoples-grocery-lynchings/This Day in History 9.

Index

Illustrations are indicated by italicized page numbers or by page numbers with F.

Burden, Mary Barbour, 109, *109*, *111*, 112; children of, 108; death of, 110, 114; marriage of, 108

Burden, William, 108

Burden family: Nerud family and, *109*, 110, *111*, *113*

Bureau of Refugees, Freedmen, and Abandoned Lands, 22

Burlington and Missouri River Railroad, 100, 394n1

Burlington Railroad, 15, 136, 138, 151, 194

Butcher, Solomon, 189, 192, 197

Butler County KS, 133, 134, 136, 137

Buxton, Ontario SD, 147, 148, 166, 381

C&NW. *See* Chicago and Northwestern Railroad (C&NW)

Cache la Poudre River, 287

Camp Amache, 299

"Carceral Archipelagos" (Burden), 360–61

Carceral Archipelagos (Burden), F94

Carlsbad Current-Argus, 325

Carlson, George, 294

Carver, George Washington, 124, 125, *126*, 142, 385; farming and, 127–28, 129; homesteading by, 100, 130; sexual orientation of, 129, 396n17

Carver, Jim, Moses, Sarah, and Susan, 124

Castle Rock, 128

Cather, Willa, 271

Cayton, H. R., 96

census data, 69, 72, 84, 90, 101, 110, 155, 180, 205, 216, 245, 247; school, 237; taking, 237–38

Census of Agriculture, 367, 414n1

Chambers, W. L., 96

Chapelton CO, 291, 292

Chapelton Presbyterian Church, 294

Chaplin, Charlie, 273

Chapman, Kate D., 213, 381, 382

Chautauqua Dining Hall, 277

Chaves County NM, 302, 306, 310, 323

Cherry County NE, 147, 153, 161, 176; designation for, 145; population of, 180; racial mixing in, 170; racial violence in, 177; social life in, 172

Cherry County Historical Society, 145

Cheyenne warriors, 36, 52

Chicago IL, 211, 245, 251, 262, 265, 266, 267, 268, 286; Black population of, 374; public transport in, 347

Chicago and Northwestern Railroad (C&NW), 209, 256, 258, 261, 262

Chicago Board of Education, 359

Chicago Board of Trade, 90–91

Chicago, Burlington, and Quincy Railroad, 394n1

Chicago Conservator, 49, 74, 75

Chicago Defender, 247, 315, 344, 345; Micheaux and, 269, 270, 273–74; "Rev. McCracken Sued for $10, 000," 274

Chicago Tribune, 13–14, *14*

Cincinnati OH, 230, 374

Cincinnati Southern railroad, 1

"A Citizen" (*Beloit Courier*), 121

citizenship, 18, 38, 40, 341

City Auditorium (Omaha), 245

civil rights, 331, 332

Civil Rights Act (1866), 40

Currens, Reverend, 243
Curtis, A. P.: work for, 161
Curtis, Chester, 154
Curtis, Sarah V., 154
Custer County NE, 188, 189, 192, 194, 198, 225
Custer County Chief, 185, 192, 194, 195, 197, 199, 200
Custer County Republican, 194
Czech neighbors, relations with, 109–10

Dakota Central Railway, 209
Dakota Territory, 207, 209, 341
Dallas SD, 257, 260, 261, 262; homestead in, 267–68; promoting, 258
Daniel, Miss, 237
Daughters of Zion, 82
Davenport, Ira, 31
Davis, Patsy, 187
Davis, William, 204–5, 211, 214–15
Dawes Act, 254
Day, Ava Speese, F42, 149, 155, 158, 161, 163, 167, 169, 170, 175, 179–80, 183, 205, 217, 386; quote of, 145; Sluggers and, 174; on sod house, 159
Day, Lee, 179–80, 205
Day, William, 204–5, 215
Day family, 211, 220
Dearfield CO, 10, 13, 18, 277, 285, 289, 316, 327, 328, 337, 371, 384; celebrations in, 298; decline of, 296–97; economic wealth of, 336; homesteading in, 284, 295; investors and, 290; land at, 288, 292; naming of, 281; as National Historic

Site, 300; photo of, 283; population of, 291, 297; saving/reviving, 354; school at, 293; settlers for, 281–82; street names for, 335; success for, 293–95, 296; water at, 287, 288
Dearfield Agency, boosterism and, 290
"Dearfield Colorado Township and Settlement" (brochure), 295
Dearfield, The Road Less Traveled (Betts), 299
Deaver, D. Clem, 15, 151, 152, 153, 156
debt peonage, 186, 340, 350, 373
Declaration of Independence, 73, 74
"The Decline of Black Farming in America" (U.S. Civil Rights Commission), 369
Dee, Ruby, 98
Democrats, 32, 60, 71, 278
Denver CO, 86, 177, 277, 281, 282, 284, 289; African Americans in, 279; colonization and, 280; Dearfield and, 290
Denver Post, 294
Denver Star, 288, 290
Denver Sun, 290
DePrad, John, 45, 69, 70, 93
Desert Land Act (1877), 225, 227, 281
Desert Land Homestead Act (1916), 228
Des Moines Register, Blair and, 212
Devereaux, Oscar, 249
De Witt Times Union, 114
"DeWitty" (*Valentine Democrat*), 156
DeWitty NE, F47, F48, 10, 17, 18, 143, 153, 156, 203, 204, 205, 206, 217, 239, 246, 316, 328, 337, 338–39; community life in, 155–56, 179–80;

Furrow, Uncle Johnny, 55
"The Future of Kansas" (Garland), 82

Gandy, Henry, 59, 60
gardens, 54, 58, 65, 68, 107, 127, 136–37, 191, 230, 254, 286, 288, 305, 314, 321
Garland, Samuel, 82
Gaugh, Belle, 249
Gee, Bird, 127, 128
Gen H, 351, 353–54; achievements of, 352, 371, 372; descendants of, 354–55, 363
General Land Office (GLO), 36, 40, 133, 135, 136, 227, 228, 229, 232, 311, 322, 323, 343; circular from, 105; lottery by, 256; proving up and, 33; letter to, 204, 228
general stores, F20, F22, 68, 82, 87, 155, 157, 165, 166; photo of, 88, 356
Gentry, Terri, 300, 338, 343, 344
Gering NE: trial in, 234
Gettysburg KS, 70, 85
Gettysburg Township KS, 70, 85
"Ghost Town—Almost" (Thompson and Clarke), 92
Gibson, Thomas and Eliza, 127
Gields, Leroy, 147, 154
Glick, George Washington, 71
Goff, Louisa, 260
Goodwin, Reverend, 44
Goose Creek School District, 170
Gorham, Ed, 215
Goshen County WY, 197, 223, 231, 240, 343, 384; African Americans in, 245
Goshen County Journal, 231, 234, 235, 238, 241, 384

Gough, Louisa, 264, 266, 268
Grace AME Radio Choir, 197
Grace Presbyterian Church, 232, 242, 243
Graham County KS, xiv, 30, 54, 64, 70, 71, 72, 77, 83, 96, 371, 379, 380; Black farmers in, 45; census for, 84, 342; county seat for, 84, 85, 93; Nicodemus and, 46; politics in, 67; public school in, 68, 78; railroad and, 86; voting in, 341
Grand Army of the Republic, 113, 139
Grand Benevolent Society, 82
Grandview Township SD, 215, 216, 217
Grant, Ulysses S., 119, 132
grasshoppers, 17, 65, 106, 107, 127, 134, 157, 259, 297, 327
Gray, Joyceann, 145, 146, 149, 166, 181, 182, 337, 384, 385, 386
grazing, 4, 59, 179, 210, 227, 245, 305, 379
Great Depression, 183, 220, 325, 326–27
Great Emancipation, 2
Great Migration, 8, 18, 96, 219, 275, 328, 329, 347, 348, 350, 374; drama of, 12; vanguard of, 344
Great Plains, xv, 8, 9, 17, 18, 21, 40, 89, 90, 99–100, 128, 130, 136, 139; environment of, 15, 16; opportunity in, 11, 348; racism and, 11, 347, 374, 382; settlement of, xiv, 12, 36, 37; South and, 379–80
Greeley, Horace, 235
Greeley CO, 281, 285, 293, 296, 298
Greeley Daily Tribune, 292, 297, 299
Green, J. Ronald, 406n3
Green, William, 67, 68

Greenfield school district: Blackdom and, 317
Gregg-Steely ranch, 127
Gregory SD, 36, 260, 261, 262, 267, 268
Gregory County SD, 247, 248, 257, 267
Griffith, Bert, 292
Griffith, James, 182
Griffiths, D. W., 272, 273
Groves, Junius, 264
Guenther, Todd, 200, 225, 405n16
Gulf Oil Company, 326

Hall, Abram, 45, 46, 51, 61, 64, 65, 67, 69, 70, 93, 172, 329, 345, 348, 385; advertising by, 344; appointment of, 72, 84; census by, 84, 342; county seat and, 84; departure of, 89; economic self-betterment and, 334; education and, 94, 352; Graham County and, 84; homesteaders and, 57, 344; Niles and, 75; paper by, 74, 76–77; Roscoe and, 85; writing of, 49, 74, 76–77
Hall, Abram, Jr., 72, 73
Hamilton, Kenneth, 75, 96, 391n4
Hamilton County Ledger, 303
Hanback, Lewis, 94
Hanna, Don, Jr., 170, 180
Hanna, Don, III (Sonny), 146, 173, 174, 179, 183
Hanna, Francis, 170
Hanna family, employment with, 17, 161–162
Hannahs, Edward, 154, 159, 160
Hannahs, Herbert (Herbie), 166, 170, 173

Hannahs, Robert H., F50, 166, 173
Hannahs, Rosetta, 166
Hannahs family, F50, 160, 179
Harris, Bill: store of, 87
Harris, Grant, 45
Harris, Kathleen, 364
Hastings, George, 107, 112, 114, 207
Hastings, Robert R., 114
Hauser, Mary, 187
Hawkins, H. C., 82–83
Hawkins, J. R., 93
Haycraft, Reverend, 242–43
Hayes, Arnetta, 154
Hayes, Fernnella Walker, 364
Hayes, Goldie Walker, 146, 167, 168, 171, 172
Hays City Sentinel, 54, 74
Hazell, J. A. Thomas, 294
Heartland (film), 232
Heavenrich family, 153
Hebert, Janis, 406n3
Hemingford NE, 137, 139, 343
Hemingford Hotel, 140, 258
Hemingford Journal, 138–39
Henderson, Lucy H., 315, 345
Henrie, H. S., 83
Henry Dispatch, 197
Herron, Erastus, 321, 322
Herron, Ester, 318
Herron family, 309
Hickman, Daniel, 1, 3, 33, 44, 47, 93; departure of, 2–3; homesteading and, 31; Nicodemus and, 45; patent of, 34
Hickman, Willianna, 47, 65–66, 364
Hicks, Mme., F76

Jackson, Oliver Toussaint (*cont.*)
  influence of, 342; investors and,
  289–90; Lunch Room and, 294,
  298, 337; on Matlock, 282; political
  ties of, 277–78, 279; self-help and,
  349; Washington and, 334
Jackson, Peter, 53
Japanese Americans, 299, 401n52
Jefferson, Thomas, 31
Jefferson Barracks MO, 132–33
Jessen, George, 139
Jessen, Mrs., 139
Jews, 12, 329
Jim Crow, 22, 278, 306, 315, 342;
  challenging, 167; impact of, xv, 18,
  350; laws, 369, 373, 374; tightening,
  xiii, xv, 307
Johnson, Andrew, 22–23, 32, 40
Johnson, Artes, 146
Johnson, Edward, 374
Johnson, Henry, 69, 73
Johnson, Thomas, 69, 382
Johnson County War, 178, 379
Joiner, John, 215
Joiner, William, 211
Jones, George Washington, 30, 69,
  87, 93
Jones, Isaac, 304, 317
Jones, Squier, 234
Jones, W. A., F76, F77, 288, 289
Joseph, J., 81
Juneteenth, 319, 320
Junne, George, Jr., 296, 299

Kansas Black Farmers Association, 371
Kansas Colored State Immigration
  Bureau, 63

"Kansas Fever Exodus," 62
Kansas Freedmen's Relief Associa-
  tion, 63
Kansas-Nebraska Act (1854), 31
Kansas State University, 358, 359
Kansas Wesleyan University, 236
Kearney State Normal School, 171
Keillor, Garrison, 128
Kemp, John, 25
Kent, Deputy, 73
Kentucky Advocate, 3, 18
Kentucky Derby, 210
Keteral, Mary, 207
Keys, Daniel, 302
Kidderville District, 167
King Real Estate Company, 214
Kinkaid, Moses, 147, 148, 224
Kinkaid Act (1904), 147, 149, 151, 153,
  155, 173, 178, 181, 204, 227, 228,
  379
Kirtley, Erasmus, 60–61, 65, 78, 95,
  383; racial violence and, 342–43, 386
Kirtley, William, 76
Kirwin Chief, 61
Klemke, Constantine, 137, 138
Knox, Robert H., 27, 340, 348; on
  Black homesteaders, 94; migration
  and, 50, 329
Krivohlavek, Ray, 110
Ku Klux Klan, 24, 295
Kupka, Frank, 117

Ladies of Brownlee, 146
Lakotas, 35, 36
Lambda Kappa Nu National Citation
  for Journalism, 362
Lancaster County NE, 133, 134, 136

Murphy, Eunice, 375, 377, 378
Murphy, W. H., 154
Muse, Mme., F76
music, 169, 173, 195–97
Musser, Charles, 273
Myers House, 67

NAACP, 282, 332, 376
Nash, William, 215
National Black Farmers Union, 339, 351
National Exploration Company, 325
National Federation of Colored Farmers, 286
National Park Service (NPS), 41, 98, 299–300
National Postal Museum, 323
National Registry of Historic Places, 42
National Trust for Historic Preservation, 220, 246
Native Americans, 39, 52, 301; land from, 33, 35; removal of, 36
Natrona County Tribune, 203
Navajos, 301
"Nebraska" (Meehan), 168
"Nebraska Room," 233
Nebraska State Hospital for the Insane, 240
Nebraska State Journal, 102, 111, 375
Nebraska Supreme Court, slave marriages and, 200, 201
Negro Baptist Churches, 297
"Negro Colony at Dearfield is Big Success" (Denver Post), 294
"The Negro Exodus" (Chicago Tribune), 14
Negro Townsite and Land Company, 281

Neguse, Joe, 300
Nelson, Jacob, 133
Nelson, Timothy, 310; Blackdom and, 324, 326, 327, 410n16, 412n43; on racial tension/Chaves County, 306
Neosho School for Colored Children, 125
Nerud, Albert, 110
Nerud, Bert, 113, 113
Nerud family: Burden family and, 110
Ness City Sentinel, 128
Ness City Times, 128
Ness County KS, 126, 129
New Mexico Military Institute, 306
New Mexico Office of Cultural Affairs, 327
New Mexico State University, 11, 327
Newth, C. H., 67, 68, 82, 83, 94
New York City, 346, 347, 374
New York Times, 273
New York University (NYU), 185, 273, 361, 362
NHM. See Northwestern Homestead Movement (NHM)
Nichols, Yorick, 233–34, 383
Nicodemus KS, F15, F19; appeal of, 13, 49; arrival in, 4, 5–6, 17, 21, 41, 47, 61, 70, 88, 384–85; as biracial community, 82; building, 10, 40, 89; businesses in, 87; county seat decision and, 85, 89; decline of, 89, 90; described, 41, 44, 46, 48, 49; drought in, 17; economic weight of, 336; founding of, xiii, xv, 6, 15, 52–53, 152; future in, 1415; golden years of, 67; hostility for, 83; migration to, 8, 10, 335, 348; naming, 42–43; as

Thomas, James Madison, 289
Thomas, James Monroe, F78, 282, 283, 284, 286, 335, 336; wood shanty by, 283
Thompson, E. L., 126
Thompson, Isabel M., 92
Timber Culture Act (1873), 65, 136; claims, 93, 148, 194, 210
Topeka KS, 18, 44, 54, 55, 63, 76, 355
Topeka Opera House, 63
Torn, Rip, 232
Torrington WY, 23, 197, 202, 203, 224, 231, 234, 239, 240, 242, 342, 355, 374, 383; segregation in, 235, 236, 340, 343
Torrington Hotel, 240
Torrington Telegram, 226, 234
Torrington Telegraph, 237, 241
Townsend, W. B., 64
tractors, 16, 215–16, 244, 345
Triple-L ranch, 162
Tripp County SD, 260, 262, 268, 271; opening of, 264, 270
Tulsa OK, 175, 295, 355, 378, 382
Tulsa Massacre, 176, 295, 358, 376
Turkey Creek, 106
Tuskegee Airmen, 363–64
Tuskegee Institute, 129, 330
Twenty-fourth U.S. Infantry Regiment, 301
Tyler, Warren, 24–25

Underground Railroad, 133, 236, 381
Union Army, 52, 102, 132
Union Colony, 287. *See also* Greeley CO
Union House, 67
Union Pacific Railroad, 86, 88, 289

Union Presbyterian Mission Church, 294
United Brethren Church, Burden and, 108–9
University of Kansas, 357
University of Nebraska, 171, 289
University of Nebraska at Kearney, 171
University of Northern Colorado, 285, 299
U.S. Air Force, 359
U.S. Army, 7, 115, 379
U.S. Army Air Force, 363–64
U.S. Census Bureau, 145, 367
U.S. Civil Rights Commission, report by, 369
U.S. Colored Troops, 102, 120
U.S. Constitution, 333
U.S. Department of Agriculture (USDA), 289, 369–70, 372
U.S. Department of Justice, 150
U.S. House of Representatives, 224
U.S. Land Commission, 94, 97
U.S. Post Office, F81, 157, 291
U.S. Senate, 23, 26
U.S. Supreme Court, 333, 381
U.S. Wind Engine and Pump Company, 191
Utterback, W. E., 320

Vado NM, 324, 354
Valentine NE, 145, 154, 171, 204, 377; segregation in, 177; traveling to, 156
Valentine Democrat, 156
Vandenbon, Cora, 318
VanEpps-Taylor, Betti, 216, 252, 267, 404n16, 405n3; on vote/education, 212–13